The Underground
Railroad in the
Adirondack Region

The Underground Railroad in the Adirondack Region

Tom Calarco

McFarland & Company, Inc., Publishers
Jefferson, North Carolina, and London

The author wishes to thank Furthermore: A
Program of the J.M. Kaplan Fund, for its support
in helping to make this book possible.

LIBRARY OF CONGRESS CATALOGUING-IN-PUBLICATION DATA

Calarco, Tom, 1947–
    The Underground Railroad in the Adirondack region / Tom
Calarco.
      p.   cm.
    Includes bibliographical references and index.

    ISBN 0-7864-1627-0 (illustrated case binding : 50# alkaline paper)

    1. Underground railroad—New York (State)—Adirondack
Mountains Region.   2. Antislavery movements—New York
(State)—Adirondack Mountains Region—History—19th century.
3. Adirondack Mountains Region (N.Y.)—History—19th century.
I. Title.
F127.A2C25   2004
973.7'115—dc22   2003022087

British Library cataloguing data are available

On the cover: C.W. Jefferys' illustration of fugitive
slaves stopping at a Quaker station (from Jesse Macy,
The Anti-Slavery Crusade, Yale University Press, 1919)

Manufactured in the United States of America

McFarland & Company, Inc., Publishers
  Box 611, Jefferson, North Carolina 28640
  www.mcfarlandpub.com

This book is dedicated to my father, Babe Calarco,
who passed away while I was writing it, and who would
be pleased to know that I finally finished it.

And to my good friend, Sylvia Jimison,
who had to deal with me on a daily basis
as I brought the work to a finished product.
Thank you for your patience with me.

ACKNOWLEDGMENTS

There are so many people to thank for their assistance that I know I will forget some. Please forgive me if I make a few oversights.

I'll begin where I started with Helen Brownell of the Easton Library, Sally Brillon and John Mead of the Washington County Historical Society, and Helen Hoag and Ernest Tilford, local historians of Washington County. Another very helpful individual during the early stages of my research was Christopher Densmore, now the curator of the Friends Historical Library of Swarthmore College, who directed me to the Blassingame bibliography of abolitionist newspapers. I also shouldn't forget Benj White of Hubbard Hall in Cambridge, New York, and Joan Davidson of Furthermore in Hudson, New York, who helped me get my first grants.

Others who were most helpful were local historians: Addie Shields, Clinton County historian, who gave of her time and information and laid out the Underground Railroad in Clinton County; Marilyn Van Dyke, president of the Warren County Historical Society, who worked diligently with me in locating sites in her county; and Joe Cutshall-King, Washington County historian, with whom I had many useful conversations. I want to thank Mark Frost, editor-in-chief of *The Chronicle* in Glens Falls, who gave my project exposure by publishing a series of my columns devoted to the Underground Railroad, and Paul Loding, Kingsbury town historian, who provided information on the Stone Chair. Thanks also to Rachel Clothier and Mrs. Francis Reed of Corinth, who helped me find the remnants of Mr. Fitch's cabin, and Martin Fish and Art Perryman of Weavertown, who revealed the legend of Mr. Cutler and showed me the remnants of his cabin. Others who were generous of their time and information were Robert F. Jones, history chair at Fordham University, who read an early draft; Cathy Barber, the Greenwich Town historian, who supplied the Diantha Gunn letters; David Patrick of the Clinton County Historical Association, who provided additional information about his ancestor, Noadiah Moore; Dona Robinson of Edinburgh, who showed me the hiding place in the old John Barker building; Wayne Miller of the Fineberg Library at SUNY Plattsburgh, who helped me find sources at his library; Paul and Mary Liz Stewart, who worked with me on developing information on the Underground Railroad in Albany, New York; and Jane Meader-Nye of Quaker Springs, New York, who helped with Quaker genealogy and showed me the rich, untapped source of information it can yield for the study of the Underground Railroad.

Last but not least, thank you to the staff of the New York State Library, where I spent many hours making new discoveries.

CONTENTS

Part II: The Underground Railroad Stops in Eastern New York from New York City to Canada

PREFACE

I have taken the liberty of making changes to quoted materials with regards to punctuation, tense, and archaic or incorrect usage. This was done to facilitate reading, especially considering that many of the quoted passages date from 1850 or earlier. In addition, the word "black" has been used to connote persons of color rather than the current, more politically correct term "African American." This was done in an effort to use a more inclusive term, which was brought to my attention by persons of color who do not consider themselves African in any way. Interestingly, the desire of blacks in America to dissociate themselves from Africa goes back to the first protests against the colonization movement during the early part of the 19th century. It is hoped that persons of color who prefer the term "African American" will not be offended by the use of the term "black."

In Part II, I have created maps that show possible locations and routes in various sections of northeastern New York. These are not definitive and are based on information with varying degrees of reliability. In other words, some of the stops shown were almost definitely stations, while others verge on hearsay. They represent, however, the best information that I have been able to obtain. Along with the appendices that in some cases provide exact street addresses of the participants, they will serve as a guide to future researchers who wish to map out the Underground Railroad with greater certitude.

PART I

The Underground Railroad in Northern New York and Its Role in the Abolition of Slavery

The legend of the Underground Railroad in northern New York has lingered long in the memory of its people despite its omission from the history books. This lack of readily available information coupled with the neglect of the region by Wilbur Siebert, who in 1898 wrote the seminal work on the topic, *The Underground Railroad: From Slavery to Freedom*, has resulted in little study of its participation. For instance, the recent Freedom Trail Survey had little to report about the region, and none of it had any relation to the Underground Railroad north of Albany.

Transforming legend into history required searching local archives, talking to local historians, collecting unpublished documents and stories, and combining the information with published accounts from that time. A clear picture emerged of abolition as a hotly contested, combustible issue here from the middle of the 1830s. It caused mob violence, attracted slave catchers, and drew many prominent white and black abolitionists to frequent and enthusiastic anti-slavery conventions. A number of factors made the area receptive to abolition: the strong attachment of the communities to their churches and the influence of "Burned-Over District" revivalism; the significant number of Quakers, including three abolitionist Quaker communities—Peru in Clinton County, Easton in Washington County, and Quaker Springs in Saratoga County, who formed their own anti-slavery societies; the connection to abolitionists in nearby Vermont; and finally, the remoteness of the area and its proximity to Canada, coupled with a direct and accessible water route to the "Promised Land." This made northern New York a destination for fugitive slaves.

Estimating the number of fugitive slaves who passed through the Adirondack region is virtually impossible, but intelligent guesses can be made about where they stopped. By identifying those who participated in anti-slavery societies and belonged to churches that took strong stands against slavery, and then locating their homes, we can begin to map out the tracks.

But the study of the Underground Railroad is much more than simply locating the stops and routes used by fugitive slaves. It is a story of the heroic struggle of blacks and whites working together for freedom and dignity, and of the American quest for human rights and respect for the individual. Perhaps even more important is the lesson it teaches about the devastating effects of racial prejudice.

It is hoped this book will be a useful tool for researchers who wish to unravel the mysteries of the Underground Railroad. To assist this process, appendices with lists of abolitionists by county, with background information on the most important, are provided. The roster of those who participated on the second day of the organizational meeting of the New York State Anti-Slavery Society in 1835 also is included.

Chapter 1

THE LEGEND

All the tracks of the Underground Railroad have vanished. All the fugitive slaves are gone. All the abolitionists have rejoiced with their maker, and all the slaveholders have turned to dust. Yet their story lives on. In northern New York, so many stories have survived that it might make one wonder if any are true. As many historians have said over the years—even if the Underground Railroad did happen here, it can't be proven because it was all kept secret. But if we take the position that a kernel of truth dwells within every legend, we can begin to discover the true history of the Underground Railroad in northern New York.

C.W. Jefferys' painting of fugitive slaves stopping at a Quaker Station. (From Jesse Macy, *The Anti-Slavery Crusade*, Yale University Press, 1919.)

While organized efforts to aid fugitive slaves existed as early as the time of the American Revolution, most historians agree that they were sporadic and that the Underground Railroad, as legend has portrayed it, did not begin except in a few isolated areas until after 1830. The traditional view developed mainly by the work of Siebert is that because of its illegal nature, it left few written records and never became a formal organization. Nevertheless, it became a far reaching enterprise that adopted terminology from the railroad, the technological wonder of the age. Thus, places of shelter came to be known as *stations*; persons who helped runaways, *agents*; and local supervisors, *conductors* or *stationmasters*. Another interesting term probably coined by fugitive slaves was the "hideyhole," the hideaways behind fireplaces, beneath trapdoors, or in attic crawl spaces often equipped with beds and other comforts. A system of passwords also was used. For example, communications of approaching fugitives came to be known as "the grapevine telegraph," which was cloaked in figurative language such as "you will receive two volumes of the Irrepressible Conflict" (Siebert 56–57). Other terms include "terminals," used by historians to describe major centers of the Underground, and "trunks" or "lines" used to describe the various routes.

Fugitives usually started their journey on foot at night guided by the North Star, and traveled along rivers and canals. Their obstacles were formidable. Plantation owners had developed a rigid system to prevent slaves from running away. All slaves were required to carry a pass when off the plantation, and nightly patrols watched for runaways or signs of insurrection. Solomon Northup, the free black man from Washington County who wrote a popular book about his kidnapping that forced him into twelve years of slavery, described the patrol used in Bayou Beouf, Louisiana: "They ride on horseback, headed by a captain, armed, and accompanied by dogs. They have the right, either by law, or by general consent, to inflict discretionary chastisement upon a black man caught beyond the boundaries of his master's estate without a pass, and even to shoot him, if he attempts to escape" (Northup 181).

Fugitive slaves were prey to starvation, swamps infested by snakes and alligators, and trained bloodhounds, which were used in packs to hunt and sometimes kill them. If they were lucky to reach a Northern state, there was no guarantee they would find the Underground Railroad, as many had little knowledge of geography. Some did not even know that Canada existed (Gara 36) and others had been told preposterous stories about abolitionists being cannibals who used the skin of blacks to make shoes. As Frederick Douglass, himself a former fugitive slave, wrote: "The railroad ... was under regulations so stringent, that even free colored travelers were almost excluded. They must have free papers; they must be measured and carefully examined.... The steamboats were under regulations equally stringent. [And] all the great turnpikes leading northward, were beset with kidnappers ... who watched the newspapers for advertisements for runaway slaves..." (Douglass 189).

If slaves found the Underground Railroad, agents sometimes delivered them to the next station, concealing them in hay wagons or specially constructed carriages. The next station often was determined by the circumstances. "An Underground Railroad conductor had almost always a choice between two or more routes," Siebert wrote. "The underground path ... formed an intricate network, and it was in no small measure because this great system converged and branched again at so many stations that it was almost impossible for slave hunters to trace their Negroes" (Siebert 62).

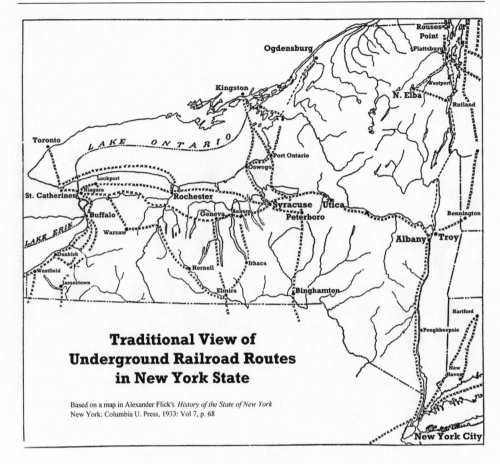

**Traditional View of
Underground Railroad Routes
in New York State**

Based on a map in Alexander Flick's *History of the State of New York*
New York: Columbia U. Press, 1933: Vol 7, p. 68

Map by the author.

Various sources have traced three main routes running through New York State. The traditional view has been that the earliest started in New York City and went up the Hudson River to Albany, from where fugitive slaves could travel either west to Syracuse and Lake Ontario, or east to Vermont and north to Canada. A second route led up through western New York by way of Fredonia and Niagara Falls to Canada. A third route led through the central part of the state from Elmira and branched off either northwest through the Finger Lakes region to Rochester, or slightly northeast through Auburn and Syracuse to the port of Oswego on Lake Ontario. Frederick Douglass identified some of the most important conductors along these routes. They included David Ruggles and Isaac T. Hopper in New York City; Stephen Myers, and Lydia and Abigail Mott in Albany; the Rev. Samuel May and the Rev. J.W. Loguen in Syracuse; and Douglass and J.P. Morris in Rochester (Douglass 272). Western New York's trunk line is given credence by conductor Eber Pettit's 1879 autobiography (Pettit). A little-used route that led from John Brown's North Elba home through Clinton County is the only trunk attributed by traditional sources to northern New York (Flick 68).

Though neglected in most history books, the identity of many of the individuals in northern New York who aided fugitive slaves can be found in the region's local his-

Job and Esther Wilbur farmhouse, Easton, New York. (Photograph by the author).

tory archives, most of it until now unpublished. As we move north of Albany up the Hudson River, we discover the memoirs of Oren B. Wilbur who recorded the deeds of his Quaker grandfather and step grandmother in the farming town of Easton.

One of Wilbur's stories concerned a fugitive slave who had been tracked down by slavecatchers to Job and Esther Wilbur's farmhouse, which still sits along Route 40 in an area much like it was 150 years ago. The runaway had been at the house only a short time, when two men, probably on horseback, came down the dirt road that led to the Wilbur house. Seeing his pursuers, the runaway panicked and grabbed a carving knife on the dining room table. The Wilburs objected, but he insisted he would not be taken alive. The runaway hurried up a ladder to a trapdoor that concealed a small garret. Then came a knock at the door. The visitors likely were disarmed at first by the small, frail Esther who greeted them at the door. Nevertheless, a handsome reward awaited them and they were determined. They asked the Wilburs if they had seen a certain runaway slave, but when the Wilburs pleaded ignorance, they demanded that the Wilburs release him. The Wilburs insisted they knew nothing and said the slavecatchers could search their house if they wished. After failing to find the runaway, they noticed the ladder leading to the garret. The Wilburs, who were pacifists, were not about to interfere, and one of the slavecatchers climbed up and stuck his head through the trapdoor. The runaway stood there, brandishing the long knife. He warned the slavecatcher not to come any closer, or he would kill him. The slavecatcher tried to reason with the runaway, saying that if he didn't surrender now, he would be captured later. Instead, the runaway thrust the knife at the slavecatcher, who jumped down the ladder. Deciding they would need more help, the slavecatchers left.

As soon as the men were out of sight, Job hitched up the carriage, and Esther dressed up the runaway in her Quaker dress and bonnet with the thick veil. Job cracked the whip and his horses raced to Union Village, about five miles north, to the home of Dr. Hiram Corliss, the area's stationmaster. Legend claims Corliss had a small windowless room in his cellar from which a tunnel led to the banks of the Battenkill River behind his house (Wilbur; George Corliss Papers).

All the locals know that Union Village, now known as Greenwich, was a "hotbed" of antislavery. For years, the daughters of Leonard Gibbs, one of the leading agents and agitators, entertained the Willard's Mountain chapter of the Daughters of the American Revolution with stories about their father's deeds. Both died in 1918, but none of their stories seem to have been written down (Bacon 38).

Two artifacts along Vaughn Corners Road in the Washington County town of Kingsbury bordering Warren County have been source of conjecture and fascination since anyone can remember.

Guideboard sign, Kingsbury, Washington County, New York. (Photograph by the author.)

The first is an extraordinary sign at the intersection with Bentley Road that depicts a caricature of a black man with a cane and top hat, dressed in his Sunday best, pointing north to: "4½ Miles to Fort Ann." The sign is supposed to have been painted by Collins Doubleday, but the current sign is actually the third such sign. It was put up in the 1960s and replaced a sign that was created in the 1930s. The second sign is supposed to have replaced the original sign dating from the antebellum period (Calarco "Did Sign...").

An even more intriguing artifact is the stone chair inscribed with the date 1841 about a half mile southeast of the Guideboard sign. This relic had other markings now mostly worn away by time and formerly rested on small legs. Many believed it served as a map for fugitive slaves traveling the Underground Railroad. A drawing of the chair as it looked in the 1930s made by George LaMere has been preserved by his nephew, Kingsbury historian Paul Loding, who believes he can decipher the markings. Loding suggests that what looks like a fort with a flag represents the village of Fort Ann and its Underground Railroad stations of legend, the Goodman farm and Old Stone Library; the triangular shape, Putnam Mountain; the smokestack above it, the Mt. Hope Blast Furnace that was north of the mountain; and the sailboat in the top right corner, the boats waiting in South Bay, the inlet to Lake Champlain (Loding).

Drawing showing detail visible on the Stone Chair, circa 1930. (Courtesy of Paul Loding, Kingsbury town historian.)

The Rev. George Brown has been thought by many to be the creator of the stone chair. (See page 65 for further discussion.) A free black man, he came to Kingsbury in 1827, and not long after experienced a religious conversion. He became a minister for the Methodist Church and developed a reputation as an inspirational preacher. He also had a reputation as an excellent stonemason. Not only did he build many stone walls on farms in the towns of Kingsbury and Queensbury, but also a stone house on the corner of Geer and Underwood, a short distance from the stone chair, which some have also associated with the Underground Railroad (McIlvaine B1).

In Glens Falls in Warren County, a couple of incidents from the Underground Railroad were recorded by Samuel Boyd, who was a boy at the time. One involved the protection of a fugitive slave, which will be covered later; the other involved Boyd's father, Rufus. One winter morning while feeding their cow in the barn, Samuel heard someone snoring and saw a pair of shoes sticking out from a pile of hay. He ran out and told his father, who told him to calm down, then set him in a chair. "Now you are not to say a word about this to anyone," his father ordered. Twice that day, he saw his father take out food in a pail to the barn. When darkness fell, his father loaded their sleigh and hitched up the horses, then drove it into the barn before leaving on a three-day trip. During that time, his mother explained everything to him. His father was taking two runaway slaves to Swanton, Vermont, where they would be conveyed across the border to Canada. What was most impressed on him was that this was to be kept secret, and Boyd wrote that he never told anyone about it until after the Civil War (Boyd 7).

Another 25 miles or so northwest of Glens Falls, the hamlet of Johnsburg was the beginning of a route north with several stops. In 1855, a Wesleyan Methodist minister, the Rev. Enos Putnam, settled on a farm along Garnet Lake Road and four years later built a church a short distance from his farm. One night Putnam's stepdaughter, Lucia Newell Oliver, then about six years old, accidentally discovered fugitive slaves in their house. She later wrote about it in her diary: "I came down the stairs in my nightgown. Father was just opening the cellar door. He had a lighted candle in one hand and a plate of food in the other. He did not see me and I followed him part way down the cellar stairs. He set the plate of food on a box and unlocked the door of a room in the cellar where mother kept her preserves. I could see from my perch, two or three steps down that there was a kind of bed in the room and a young man, very black, sat on it. I was frightened for I had never seen a black man before and I hurried to go back to bed" ("Rev. Enos Putnam Sleeps in Churchyard at Johnsburg" 3).

Family legend adds that the fugitives would arrive at Putnam's at night, hidden in

Enos Putnam. (From Jeanne Roberts Foster, *Adirondacks Portraits*, Noel Riedinger-Johnson, ed., Syracuse University Press, 1986; courtesy of the Adirondack Research Library of the Association for the Protection of the Adirondacks, Inc.)

Darrowsville Wesleyan-Methodist Church, Warren County, New York. (Photograph by the author.)

a wagonload of hay. They would stay at Putnam's until the next moonless night and then move on. Adding weight to this, Putnam's granddaughter, the Adirondack poet Jeanne Roberts Foster, confirmed "he kept an Underground Railroad station in his home" (Jeanne Roberts Foster).

Ten miles northwest of Johnsburg, we find two more possible locations on the Underground Railroad, one of which involved another Wesleyan-Methodist preacher.

The Rev. Thomas Baker, the second pastor of the Darrowsville Wesleyan-Methodist Church, is believed to have hidden fugitive slaves at the church parsonage, which was located next to the church (Parrott). Former Clinton County historian Emily McMasters claimed that Baker then took them through Schroon Lake to the old Bradford House in New Russia near Elizabethtown, where the MacDougall family brought them to Keene, Wilmington, or John Brown in North Elba (Shields Item 14).

Just a couple miles north of Baker lived the Quaker Joseph Leggett. Family legend insists his house still resting off Route 9 south of Chestertown was a stop. The legend was passed down from Leggett's son, Benjamin, who remembered seeing fugitive slaves at their house late at night ("History of the Chestertown Leggett Homestead").

Continuing north, perhaps another 50 miles, we reach the revered resting place of northern New York's greatest legend, John Brown, who first came to the region in 1849. His involvement in the Underground Railroad is accepted as fact, though there are no specific stories to relate. In any case, the events at Harpers Ferry overshadowed any aid he may have provided fugitive slaves. More substantial information exists for

Old photograph of the Leggett House. (Courtesy of Craig Leggett.)

two stops testified to in an 1887 interview with Quaker Stephen Keese Smith, of Peru, in Clinton County.

"There were stations at Albany, Glens Falls and then here in Peru," Smith said. "The Negroes would come through the woods and be nearly famished" (Everest 57).

The stationmaster was Samuel Keese, and his agents were John Keese, his son; Stephen Keese Smith, his nephew; and Wendell Lansing, who was publisher of *The Essex County Republican* and later *The Northern Standard* at Keeseville. Smith said they hid and fed the runaways, then sent them to Noadiah Moore in Champlain, who lived only five miles from Canada and helped them find jobs there.

Jabez Parkhurst, who lived in Fort Covington, Franklin County, lived only a half mile from the Canadian border. His involvement is reported in Frederick Seaver's *His-*

Stephen Keese Smith, Peru, Clinton County, New York. (From Duane Hamilton, *History of Clinton and Franklin Counties* [1880], Plattsburgh, NY: Clinton County Bicentennial American Revolution Commission, 1978.)

torical Sketches of Franklin County published in 1918, which cites three sources that insist Parkhurst's home was a stop. "Mr. Parkhurst was an ardent abolitionist, and many a runaway was harbored and fed at his home," a letter from Marshall Conant stated. David Streeter, who lived on the same street as Covington as a boy said that "wagons often rumbled past ... late at night," which people said was "a train on the move on the Underground Railroad." The third source, a letter from a Mr. Cheney, claimed that Parkhurst, Daniel Noble, and Cheney's father were the three principal abolitionists in Fort Covington (Seaver 645–646).

A common element in the legends about the runaways is the use of disguises to conceal their identity. For example, the Wilburs dressed up the runaway they assisted in women's clothing. Fugitive slaves also devised their own disguises. Frederick Douglass used a false ID that identified him as a free sailor. But the most creative of all ruses was that of the famed Henry "Box" Brown, who had himself sent through the mail in a box. Though it did not involve northern New York, the seldom heard description of his passage to freedom merits repeating:

Jabez Parkhurst House, Fort Covington, Franklin County, New York. (Photograph by the author.)

> The box which I had procured was three feet one inch wide, two feet six inches high, and two feet wide, and on the morning of the 29th day of March, 1849, I went into the box—having previously bored three gimlet holes opposite my face for air, and provided myself with a bladder of water, both for the purpose of quenching my thirst and for wetting my face, should I feel getting faint [Brown 53].

Brown was conveyed from a wagon to a train and then loaded on a boat. Much of this time he spent upside down.

> In this dreadful position [I] had to remain nearly an hour and a half, which, from the sufferings I had thus to endure, seemed like an age to me, but I was forgetting the battle of liberty, and I was resolved to conquer or die. I felt my eyes swelling as if they would burst from their sockets; and the veins on my temples were dreadfully distended with pressure of blood upon my head. In this position I attempted to lift my hand to my face but I had no power to move it; I felt a cold sweat coming over me that seemed to be a warning that death was about to terminate my earthly miseries. But as I feared even that, less than slavery, I resolved to submit to the will of God... [54].

Fortunately, his box was put right side up before he fainted and his misery was relieved. After being thrown around several times, Brown finally was on his way by railroad to his destination of Philadelphia, and right side up. After 27 hours in the box, the individual arrived, to whom Brown had been sent.

> I heard a person inquire for such a box as that in which I was. I was then placed on a wagon and conveyed to the house where my friend in Richmond had arranged I should be received. A number of persons soon collected round the box after it was taken into the house, but as I did not know what was going on I kept myself quiet. I heard a man say, "let us rap upon the box and see if he is alive;" immediately a rap ensued and a voice said, tremblingly, "Is all right within?" to which I replied—"all right." The joy of the friends was very great;

Henry "Box" Brown gaining his freedom through the mail. (From William Still, *The Underground Railroad*, Philadelphia: Porter & Coates, 1872 [rev. 1886]; reprinted, Arno Press, 1968.)

when they heard that I was alive, they soon managed to break open the box, and then came my resurrection from the grave of slavery. I rose a freeman, but I was too weak, by reason of long confinement ... to be able to stand, so I immediately swooned away. After my recovery ... the first thing that arrested my attention was the presence of a number of friends, every one seeming more anxious than another, to have an opportunity of rendering me their assistance, and of bidding me a hearty welcome to the possession of my natural rights. I had risen, as it were, from the dead [56–57].

These are some of the legends; there are more. Our goal is to verify, document, and, where possible, provide the rest of the story. Northern New York certainly had its share of fugitive slave traffic. Documented reports with the numbers who passed through Albany and Troy during several time periods, and the continual presence of slave hunters locally, especially in Saratoga Springs, bear witness.

Chapter 2

ROOTS

Since the publication of Larry Gara's *Liberty Line* in 1961, historians have been less open to claims about the Underground Railroad. Gara contended that the Underground Railroad's role was exaggerated and that most runaways gained their freedom without it (Gara 42–69). Other revisionists feel that the role of the Underground Railroad has been exaggerated because much of the information collected by Wilbur Siebert, which was the foundation for its history, was based on recollections that had become distorted over time. The debate continues, but both sides can agree that thousands of good Samaritans aided fugitive slaves during the antebellum period.

Rear view of Hiram Corliss' Underground Railroad stop in Greenwich, New York—the house no longer remains. (Courtesy of Edward C. Robinson.)

Aid to fugitive slaves can be traced at least to the time of the American Revolution. Two letters written by George Washington in 1786 refer to the Society for the Relief of Free Negroes unlawfully held in Bondage, in Philadelphia (Turner 26). He speaks of a runaway owned by a certain Mr. Dalby of Alexandria, who escaped to Philadelphia and "whom a society of Quakers in the city ... have attempted to liberate" (McGowan 6). Washington also warns that "if the practice ... is not [stopped]," slaveholders will not come to Philadelphia (Boller 84).

Slaveholders had good reason to worry because it was common for slaves to run away, and they often advertised descriptions of their missing slaves with rewards for their return. One study found 7,846 such advertisements in newspapers from 1732 to 1790 (Windley 107). The Underground Railroad of legend was still years in the making at this time. However, two unrelated events in 1793 led to its eventual organization: the first Fugitive Slave Law, and Eli Whitney's cotton gin, which efficiently removed the cotton seeds and enabled a slave to clean 50 times more cotton in a day (White 15).

The Fugitive Slave Law of 1793 imposed a fine of $500—equal to $5,000 today (Friedman)—on those convicted of helping runaway slaves. Among its provisions was the suspension of the alleged fugitive slave's right to a jury trial. Testimony of a slave owner or his representative before any legally appointed judge was enough to commit the alleged fugitive to slavery. However, it did not work well for slave owners. The American judiciary was in its infancy and it was not always easy to locate a judge. In addition, the travel and time needed to apprehend slaves was expensive. As a result, slave owners became dependent on slavecatchers. At the same time, the provisions of the law facilitated the kidnapping of free blacks and selling them into slavery, a practice which even before its passage was not uncommon.* By 1796, the annual number of such kidnappings was reported to be in the hundreds (Wilson 90), and though laws were passed in both the North and the South against the practice, the kidnapping of free blacks continued until the Civil War.†

In northern New York, runaway slaves were not a major problem. Few residents owned slaves.‡ Among those early settlers whose descendents played a significant role in the Underground Railroad were Captain John Corliss, a Revolutionary War veteran, and Lydia Haynes Corliss, who had moved from Haverhill, Massachusetts, to the farming community of Easton in Washington County, New York, not far from the Vermont border. They had thirteen children; Hiram, the twelfth, was born that fateful year of 1793, in a house that remains today along Route 40. A future surgeon, Hiram became one of the region's leading abolitionists and Underground Railroad conductors (Corliss-Sheldon...).

The move toward eventual emancipation already had begun in the North. All

---

*As early as 1785, the New York Society for Manumission was formed to protect free blacks from kidnapping, and in 1789 an anti-slavery society in Maryland was formed for the same purpose (Hendricks 5; Adams 134).

†The term slave catcher and kidnapper were used interchangeably by abolitionists, because they viewed the Fugitive Slave Law to be immoral and that the legally sanctioned practice of apprehending a fugitive slave as kidnapping. At the same time, there were many illegal acts of kidnapping free blacks for sale in the domestic slave trade.

‡In 1790, there were about 400 slaves in the entire Adirondack region, with more than 90 percent of them concentrated in towns that now occupy Saratoga and Washington counties. This number remained fairly stable through 1820 (U.S. Census).

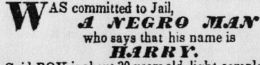

$100 REWARD.—Ranaway from, &c. a negro man named WILEY, about 37 or 38 years of age—one of his fore-fingers has been injured. It is possible that he will make his way to Tennessee, where *he says he has a wife.*   J. C. CABINESS.
[Alabama State Intelligencer, Tuscaloosa, Oct. 16, 1837.

Or thus:

WAS committed to Jail,
A NEGRO MAN
who says that his name is
HARRY.
Said BOY is about 30 years old, light complexion and bald head; has a scar on his left knee; also, one on his forehead, and one on his right hand; he is VERY MUCH MARKED WITH THE WHIP.
The owner, &c.   B. W. HATCH, Jailor.
[Port Gibson (Mi.) Correspondent, Sept. 16, 1837.

Two advertisements for runaways from two different southern newspapers in 1837. (From Nathaniel Southard, *Why Work for the Slave?* New York: American Anti-Slavery Society, 1838.)

of the New England states and Pennsylvania had either freed their slaves or started the process, and New York and New Jersey were soon to follow.* General Simon Deridder, whose grandfather had settled in Washington County, New York during the 1730s, less than ten miles from the Corlisses, decided to free his slaves in 1812. That same year he had been chosen Deacon and Elder of the newly formed Dutch Reformed Church in Whipple City, the same church to which the Corlisses belonged.

One evening the General met with all 13 of his slaves in their living room. A two-story building with nine bedrooms that still stands across the Hudson River from Schuylerville, the house had been divided to make separate quarters for his family of 12 and his slaves. They had no idea that they were about to be freed.

"You are free to go where you like and do as you like," he said. "Whatever you have now is yours. The older ones may stay as long as they like, but the younger ones must go" (Britten 337).

Three stayed and the rest found homes in the nearby towns of Jackson and Greenwich. Once a year thereafter the slaves, who took the surnames of Deridder and Weeks, and their families gathered at the Deridder household. Among the good times they recalled was Christmas, when Master Deridder declared a holiday for as long as the backlog that they would drag to their master's huge fireplace burned. Naturally, they searched the forest for the largest log they could find and usually came up with one that burned for many days.

Legend claims the house was a station on the Underground Railroad in later years, which is credible because descendents of the Deridder slaves, Priscilla and Susan

*On May 29, 1799, New York State decreed that all slaves born after July 4, 1799, were bound as slaves to their mother's master until the age of 25 if women, and 28 if men. However, the master was allowed to release them before they reached the age of one year, and thereafter those children were required to be supported by the overseers of the poor.

Weeks, married Washington County's most sought-after fugitive slave, John Salter, and his fugitive slave brother Charles, sometime around 1850 (Jones Interview). Ironically, it was not uncommon in the region for a slaveholder's home to become a refuge for fugitive slaves. Numerous legends connect the homes of former slaveholders with the Underground Railroad. Though there were displays of cruelty by northern slaveholders, they generally had a more benevolent attitude toward their slaves than southern slaveholders (Adams 10–13).

A vivid picture of the harshness of slavery in the South was revealed by Austin Steward, a former slave who became a prosperous Rochester grocer. Steward had fled from slavery after his family's master had moved his entire plantation from Virginia to upstate New York. In 1857, he wrote his autobiography. In the following excerpt, he describes the conditions endured by slaves working in the fields:

> Capt. H. employed an overseer, whose business it was to look after each slave in the field, and see that he performed his task. The overseer always went around with a whip, about nine feet long, made of the toughest kind of cowhide, the butt-end of which was loaded with lead, and about four or five inches in circumference, running to a point at the opposite extremity. This made a dreadful instrument of torture, and, when in the hands of a cruel overseer ... was truly fearful. With it, the skin of an ox or a horse could be cut through. Hence, it was no uncommon thing to see the poor slaves with their backs mangled in a most horrible manner. Our overseer, thus armed with his cowhide, and with a large bulldog behind him, followed the slaves all day; if one of them fell in the rear from any cause, this cruel weapon was plied with terrible force. He would strike the dog one blow and the slave another, in order to keep the former from tearing the delinquent slave in pieces—such was the ferocity of his canine attendant....
>
> The usual mode of punishing the poor slaves was to make them take off their clothes to the bare back, and then tie their hands before them with a rope, pass the end of the rope over a beam, and draw them up till they stood on the tips of their toes. Sometimes they tied their legs together and placed a rail between.... Thirty-nine was the number of lashes ordinarily inflicted for the most trifling offence.... Who could remain unmoved, to see a fellow-creature thus tied, unable to move or to raise a hand in his own defense; scourged on his bare back, with a cowhide, until the blood flows in streams from his quivering flesh? ... The overseer would continue to wield the bloody lash on the broken flesh of the poor, pleading slave, until his arm grew weary, or until the slave sank down, utterly exhausted, on the very spot where already stand the pools of blood....
>
> [Afterwards, the slave] was untied, and left to crawl away as best he could; sometimes on his hands and knees, to his lonely and dilapidated cabin, where, stretched upon the cold earth, he lay weak and bleeding and often faint from the loss of blood ... groaning in the agony of his crushed spirit. In his cabin, which was not as good as many of our stables at the North, he might lie for weeks before recovering sufficient strength to resume the labor imposed upon him, and all this time without a bed or bed clothing, or any of the necessaries considered so essential to the sick [Steward 14–19].

Not all Southerners sanctioned such cruelty. In fact, the call for emancipation originated in the South. Before the movement radicalized behind William Lloyd Garrison, who called for immediate emancipation, there were more than 100 anti-slavery societies in the U.S. with two-thirds of them in the slave states (Adams 116–118). They advocated gradual emancipation and a period of adjustment that included education for the slaves.

Most of the pioneers in northern New York had little knowledge of the conditions of slavery in the South in the days before Garrison's Liberator. Their tiny hamlets were striving to become villages with lumber and gristmills, carriage and harness shops, blacksmiths, tailors, carpenters, shoemakers, grocers, lawyers, and physicians. Less than ten miles from the Deridder and Corliss homestead, an enterprising Quaker from Rhode Island, Job Whipple, stumbled upon two dwellings and a gristmill along one of the several falls in the vicinity which would power the community's industries (Tefft 3). Whipple went back to Rhode Island but returned in 1781 and purchased the land surrounding the gristmill and moved his family there, building his own saw, grist, and wool carding mills. He called the hamlet Whipple City.

Whipple's good nature, the waterpower of the Battenkill and its bounty of shad, as well as the large fields of flax, which was used for homespun clothing, attracted other settlers. In 1800, he visited Rhode Island and brought back 22-year-old William Mowry, a budding entrepreneur. Four years later, Mowry, Joseph Anthony, father of future activist Susan B. Anthony, and John McClean established the nation's second cotton spinning factory and the first in New York. In 1807, Mowry married Whipple's daughter, Lydia, and became the sole proprietor of the factory. In 1809, Whipple City changed its name to Union Village—so-called, one legend stated "on account of the harmony and goodwill that prevailed among the inhabitants" (Morhous 1–3). In 1816, Mowry went to England, where he pilfered some of their cotton manufacturing techniques, and upon returning built the nation's "first double speeder" for yarn making ("Hearsay and History" 20), which fueled the prosperity of his little village. At its zenith, Mowry's factory operated 80 looms and 2,500 spindles (Morhous 2; Thurston 47). It was ironic that Union Village, whose prosperity derived from the toil of slave labor, became northern New York's most abolitionized community.

About the time Mowry moved from Rhode Island, a female Quaker minister from Vermont founded another of the region's future abolitionist communities. With her infant on her back, Huldah Hoag rode nine miles on horseback, crossed Lake Champlain during a thunderstorm, then walked five miles to her destination in Peru, Clinton County, where she founded the Union. (Meader 42). Several of the descendants of her husband, Joseph, would move there and become abolitionists, bringing with them his personal mission to end slavery, the legacy of his vision of 1803 (see *Journal of the Life of Joseph Hoag*).

Alone in a Vermont field that year, Hoag had heard a voice speak to him from out of a dark patch of clouds. It foretold of a "dividing spirit" that would affect the nation and its churches because of the iniquity of slavery. This divisiveness, the voice foretold, would culminate "many days in the future" in a civil war and the end of slavery (Meader 115).

Such visions were not unusual during this time of the Second Great Awakening. When the people weren't working, they often were in church. Social life centered around the churches and enthusiasm for revivals of spiritual uplift had become popular. Taking place during the first three decades of the 19th century, the Awakening brought a period of unprecedented religious growth in America. The 18th century

Calvinist doctrine of predestination taught by the Presbyterians was an outdated legacy of aristocratic Europe and offered salvation only to the elite, whose high station in life indicated they had been chosen by God. A nation whose political system was guided by the wishes of all the people needed a religion that met everyone's needs. In the first decade of the century, revival camp meetings in Kentucky were drawing crowds of up to 25,000 (Weisberger 35), and the born-again spirit of the revival spread throughout the nation.

In 1818, for example, a religious editor from Albany published a report of the awakenings the previous two years. He cited letters of 47 ministers of different denominations and drew on the records of numerous synods, presbyteries, conventions, and associations. What he found was that continuous awakenings were occurring in villages throughout New York State (Weisberger 81–82).

Religious fervor was likely instilled in such future abolitionists as Hiram Corliss, Gerrit Smith, Theodore Weld, Fayette Shipherd, and John and Abel Brown. All grew up in rural areas during the Awakening period. But it also was a time when slavery still existed in the North, so they saw its inequity first hand. John Brown's compassion for blacks is said to have begun when he became attached as a boy to a slave his age and empathized with his condition; Weld's originated out of an experience in school when he was six years old.

How Corliss, who exemplified the northern New York conductor, reacted to slavery as a boy is not known. But a desire to help people developed in him at an early age, for he already was teaching school by age 16 and apprenticing with local doctors Nathan Thompson and Jonathan Mosher. In 1816, after a year studying at the New York (City) Hospital, he received his medical certificate and began to practice in Easton.

Corliss was typical of those who emerged as leading abolitionists and Underground Railroad conductors. Sons and granddaughters of Revolutionary War veterans, mid-level professionals, devout church-goers, men and women with unflinching ideals, they reached their maturity during a period of "increasing spirit of inquiry in respect to Christian ethics and the bearing of religious principles upon the social relations and political duties of man" (Goodell 388). Their dream was to purge the world of evil and rededicate America to the great ideal that all men are created equal and entitled to life, liberty, and the pursuit of happiness.

Chapter 3

THE HIGHER LAW

The story of the Underground Railroad is part of a larger story of the struggle by blacks in America for civil rights. It shows that while freedom for blacks in the North was preferable to slavery in the South, it was hardly the end to their problems brought on due to their race. As Gara wrote: "Fugitive slaves who succeeded in making their way to the free states quickly learned that they were not yet in the Promised Land. Work was hard to come by.... Wages were 'unusually low and uncertain'.... [and] Northerners kept a greater distance from the Negroes and insulted them more about their color ... There is no reason to believe that at that time prejudice [against blacks] was stronger in the South than in the North" (Gara 62–63).

To combat this prejudice, blacks in the North took steps to elevate their status as the process of manumission unfolded. They organized their own churches and schools and began to establish improvement societies. However, there was little of what we would describe today as ethnic pride. In fact, some blacks who became successful separated themselves from those of their race and tried to blend into white society. One of the most successful free blacks during this period, the Rev. Lemuel Haynes, who lived in northern New York, followed such a pattern on the road to international renown as a Congregational minister and theologian.

Born of a white servant and black slave in colonial Massachusetts, Haynes had little contact with black society, marrying a white woman and ministering to white congregations in Massachusetts, Vermont, and northern New York. He seldom spoke about race but did address the issue during a July 4, 1801, sermon in Rutland, Vermont. "The poor Africans, among us," he said, "What has reduced them to their present pitiful abject state? Is it any distinction that the God of nature hath made in their formation? Nay—but being subjected to slavery, by the cruel hands of oppressors, they have been taught to view themselves as a rank of being far below others, which has suppressed, in a degree, every principle of manhood, and so they became

23

despised, ignorant, and licentious. This shows the effects of despotism, and should fill us with the utmost detestation against every attack on the rights of men..." (Mitchell B41).

Haynes's reference to Africans in the third person is peculiar but understandable. As the number of free blacks grew during this period of manumission, so did the efforts of whites to restrict them. In Ohio, a "free" state, a series of "black laws" beginning in 1804 were put into effect. These included fees for certificates of residence and bonds to ensure good behavior; prohibitions against them testifying in court against whites; and exclusions from public schools, poor houses, and asylums. Throughout the nation, blacks generally were confined to separate pews in churches and separate areas in public places; they were barred from various apprenticeships and excluded from most professions; their right of suffrage was gradually rescinded in most states.* Despite their efforts at self-improvement, the American dream of life, liberty, and the pursuit of happiness was not available for them because white society considered them an inferior race and vehemently opposed giving them the opportunities for equality.

In 1816, the same year Hiram Corliss began his apprenticeship in the medical profession, an organization was formed to deal with the problem of blacks in American society. The American Colonization Society desired to send both free and enslaved blacks to Africa to form their own nation. There they would have the freedom to form a life on their own terms without the legacy of slavery hindering them. Portraying itself as an anti-slavery organization, its founders included some of the most illustrious figures of our nation: Thomas Jefferson, James Madison, James Monroe, Chief Justice John Marshall, Senator Henry Clay, and Francis Scott Key (Pendleton 45).

It seemed like a good plan. However, the society ignored the wishes of the people it claimed to be helping. Most free blacks in the U.S. considered America, not Africa, their homeland. As early as 1817, an assembly of blacks met in Philadelphia to consider the idea (Adams 199). One of the participants was a black barber from Schenectady, New York, Richard P.G. Wright, who squeezed into the Bethel Church among 3,000 others to hear three prominent black ministers speak in the colonization society's favor, including the respected Bishop Richard Allen, founder of the American Methodist Episcopal Zion Church. When meeting organizer James Forten called for a show of approval, however, not a single voice was heard; when he asked how many were opposed, a resounding "no" resonated through the church ("Forte letter to Cuffe"). Black leaders later charged that the colonization society's propaganda served to increase racial discrimination because it stressed that the poverty and ignorance of free blacks in America was the result of their natural inferiority. Those opposed to colonization also believed that the removal of free blacks from America would help slavery endure rather than bring its end, and they pledged themselves never to abandon their brothers in slavery.

The true motive of colonization later was exposed as racism and its actual goal to be the removal of blacks from the U.S. For example, Thomas Jefferson, had writ-

*In New York State, a law was adopted in 1821 allowing suffrage only to blacks with three years citizenship in the state and owning property worth at least $250; prior to this, there had been no such requirement.

ten that the "amalgamation [of blacks] with other colors produces a degradation to which no lover of this country, no lover of excellence in human character, can innocently consent" ("The Underlying Factors of the Civil War"). Fear undoubtedly was another factor. A number of slave insurrections, including the revolt planned in 1800 by Gabriel Prosser, whose conspiracy involved thousands of slaves in Virginia, had put the South on guard. For this reason they not only were reluctant to free the slaves, but they looked for a plan of emigration.

This was not readily apparent to whites in the North because of the professed benevolence of the colonization society and the support it received from religious institutions. In fact, many who later embraced immediate emancipation were advocates of colonization. The reason it gained so many adherents, however, was because of the separation between the races, which prevented whites from knowing the true wishes of blacks. North country native Jehudi Ashmun of Champlain, New York, in Clinton County, was among the most zealous.

At age 25, Ashmun moved to Washington, D.C., and became editor of *The Theological Repository*, an Episcopal publication. He also wrote the *Memoirs of Rev. Samuel Bacon* about a colonization agent who had died in Africa in 1820 while attempting to establish a colony for black Americans in Liberia. This inspired him to follow in Bacon's footsteps, and in 1822 he left Baltimore with his wife to assume direction of the small colony then struggling for existence ("Noted Men..." 1).

Ashmun found 130 settlers, mainly women and children, who had to contend with primitive conditions, local diseases, and hostile natives. Less than three months after their arrival, his wife succumbed to illness, and two months later Ashmun and his small band had to fight off the attacks of 600 natives. Such hardships make it easy to understand why free black Americans had little desire to be sent to Africa.

Ashmun remained in Liberia for six years as a virtual dictator, and Nigerian historians today suggest that the Nigerian Civil War of the 1980s was rooted in this early despotism. They also claim that the land on which Liberia was settled was taken by force from the natives. Nevertheless, Ashmun stabilized the colony, which had grown to 1,200 by 1828. Whatever he had sown, however, did not sustain him, for on his way back to America, he became ill and died fifteen days after arriving, failing to see either his native Champlain or any of his family again (Ibid.; "The Underlying Factors of the Civil War").

The malevolent intentions of the

The Rev. Jehudi Ashmun. (From Ralph Randolph Gurley, *Life of Jehudi Ashmun, Late Colonial Agent in Liberia*, Washington, DC: J.C. Dunn, 1835.)

colonizationists never were fully understood by most whites, and they would have adherents in northern New York throughout the antebellum period. But the thought of being "deported" to another foreign land galvanized free blacks and they continued to hold anti-colonization meetings throughout the North. It was largely through these efforts that whites took notice of the capabilities of blacks and began to realize that their inferior status had nothing to do with their innate ability (Goodman 56–57).

Most historians contend that the movement for immediate emancipation began with Garrison and the publication of *The Liberator* in 1831, but both the Massachusetts General Colored Association in 1826 and *Freedom's Journal*, the first black newspaper debuted by John Russworm and Samuel Cornish in New York City in 1827, already had called for immediate emancipation.

On July 4 of that year, full emancipation was granted in New York State. The Rev. Nathaniel Paul, pastor of the first African Baptist Society in Albany, gave an eloquent sermon that day and looked into the future: "The progress of emancipation, though slow, is nevertheless certain: ...I therefore have no hesitation in declaring from this sacred place, that not only throughout the states of America, but throughout every part of the habitable world where slavery exists, it will be abolished..." (Paul 15).

Paul never would have imagined how slow progress would be. While a big step forward had been taken by blacks with the abolition of slavery in the Northern states, the atrophy of their civil rights continued. In 1829, after more than 20 years of overlooking Ohio's black laws, the city of Cincinnati decided to enforce them. Its free black population had grown to more than 3,000, and this had made whites uncomfortable. However, blacks in Cincinnati refused to comply with the laws, and mobs of whites went on a rampage against them. More than 1,000 blacks fled the city, and many headed for Canada, where a plot of land had been obtained to start a colony. The affair troubled free blacks throughout the nation and set in motion the organization of the first National Negro Convention in Philadelphia in 1830.

A circular was issued announcing the convention "to meet on the 20th day of September, 1830, to devise plans and the means of establishment of a colony in upper Canada, under the patronage of the General convention" (Foner and Walker xi). Forty delegates from seven states met; among them was Austin Steward, who for a time would move his family to the Canadian colony, for which he would coin the name Wilberforce, and of which he was elected president. The high measure of respect accorded him at the convention was indicated by his election as vice president, but such respect was not accorded by white society, as this excerpt from his autobiography shows:

> Pursuant to a call given in the summer of 1830, by the colored residents of Philadelphia, for a National Convention ... I started in company with a friend to attend it; having previously engaged seats inside Mr. Coe's stage-coach as far as Utica, N. Y., to which place we had paid our fare the same as other passengers. We rode on to Auburn very pleasantly, but when at that place, we with others moved to resume our seats; we were met by a stern rebuke for presuming to seat ourselves on the inside, and were ordered to ride on the outside of the coach. In vain ... we reminded the driver of the agreement, and of our having paid for an inside seat; [but] we were told to take the outside of the coach or remain behind [Steward 164–165].

At the convention, delegates took a strong stand against colonization, not only because of the vilification of blacks in America by exaggerating their crime, poverty, and inferiority, but also because "we who have been born and nurtured on this soil; we, whose habits, manners, are the same in common with other Americans, can never consent to take our lives in our hands, and be the bearers of the redress offered by that Society to that much afflicted country" (Gross 436). The convention also urged blacks to unite and cooperate in efforts at mutual aid and moral improvement, as one means to combat racial prejudice. Efforts at moral and educational improvement continued in Northern black communities throughout the decade, and by 1838 there were 110 black improvement societies in the U.S. (Goodman 23). However, it did little to dispel the plague of racial prejudice that had hardened in the nation.

Similar efforts at moral improvement were occurring in white communities, especially in the Northern rural communities as enthusiasm for revivalism peaked (Cross 11–12). The American Home Missionary Society, for example, which formed out of many separate religious societies in 1826, reported sending out 169 preachers that year, 120 of them in New York State alone (Cross 21). These circuit riders believed they had a divine mission to save the world from sin. Settlers in rural areas were usually less educated, prone to superstition, and more susceptible to the emotional appeals of the circuit rider. As a result the revivals were often the scene of visions, premonitions, and visitations by God, or what might be described today as the "Born Again" experience. At times, those converted were physically overwhelmed with throbbings of their bodies, and they would moan and shriek as the Lord took possession of their souls (Weisberger 28). Such revivals, like the one in Lake George, Warren County, New York, in 1831, at which 14 converts were made by the black circuit rider the Rev. Charles Bowles, were commonplace (Johnson 452). In areas with larger populations, the numbers of course were much larger (Weisberger 104).

Supporting the circuit riders were the religious publications. By 1827, the American Tract Society in New York City alone had printed forty-four million pages of religious literature, the bulk of which were circulated in New York State. In the next ten years it published thirty million tracts, nearly a million Christian Almanacs, and over two million miscellaneous magazines, books, and pamphlets. More than three-quarters of these were circulated in New York State. This is in addition to the output of the Baptist General Tract Society, which formed in 1824 and also operated predominately in New York (Cross 24).

In northern New York, many of the earliest and most prevalent denominations were Baptist and Quaker. The Baptists had a strong tradition of ministering to the poor and needy, and many of their ministers became active in the anti-slavery movement. The Quakers were the first group to publicly condemn slavery, in 1688, the first to organize anti-slavery societies, and the first to disown fellow church members who owned slaves. They maintained close-knit networks among the various Meetings and strongly discouraged marrying out of one's meeting. Among the largest Quaker Meetings in the region were those in Quaker Springs, Saratoga County; Easton, Washington County; Glens Falls, Warren County; and Peru, Clinton County.

Historians generally date the climax of the Second Great Awakening around 1830, when the age's greatest evangelist, Charles Finney, reached the pinnacle of his career.

"Now the great business of the Church is to reform the world, to put away every kind of sin," he preached,... "until every form of iniquity be driven from the earth!" (Finney).

This was not only Finney's message, but that of the entire evangelical movement. The fact that those in rural areas were more receptive to evangelism is an important distinction for understanding the development of the Underground Railroad in northern New York. It was why many churches in the rural areas broke away from their denominations and formed their own churches based on anti-slavery principles (for a detailed discussion, see Cross 216–226).

Finney, who for a time was based in Rensselaer County, was a mesmerizing figure. Six-foot-two with long arms that whirled about when he was preaching, hypnotic eyes that seemed to burn into the gaze of his audience, and a dramatic voice that sometimes slipped into mad groaning, Finney made his listeners cry, laugh, and writhe in violent agonies called the "jerks" until they fainted. He crushed his listeners with the threat of damnation lest they repent and ask Christ's forgiveness. Within a short time, he had a national reputation (Weisberger 93–95) and by 1830 had taken up the cause of Temperance. At the beginning of 1833, when there were only three anti-slavery societies in the North, there were 1,400 Temperance societies, with 700 in New York State alone. Campaigns also were being waged against gambling, theaters, fashion, Sabbath breaking, and the mistreatment of Native Americans. Finney also espoused abolitionism, and one historian points out that a Finney revival in central New York that coincided with the debut of *The Liberator* may have had a role in the newspaper's early success (Cross 217). As William Goodell concluded, this "period of unwonted if not unprecedented moral and political inquiry" led to the movement for abolition (Goodell 389).

Temperance continued as an important issue among northern New Yorkers throughout the antebellum period; however, it soon took a backseat to abolition. The reason for this is self-evident; the issue of slavery struck deeper into the nation's conscience, questioning the fundamental principles upon which America was founded. At the same time, most abolitionists continued as Temperance advocates, and vice versa.

Temperance societies were commonplace in northeastern New York. The city of Albany, for instance, had a string of Temperance taverns and houses, almost all of them operated by those active in the abolition movement. In fact, the frequent meetings of peripatetic abolitionists like Abel Brown, who is said to have aided as many as 1,000 fugitive slaves (Brown 225), and Gerrit Smith, New York State's most influential abolitionist, as well as ads placed by Temperance houses in anti-slavery and black periodicals, suggest that they may have been meeting places for the Underground Railroad. Most of the region's important black leaders in the Underground Railroad also were leading Temperance advocates. Among them were Albany conductor Stephen Myers, who actually had a Temperance Society named after him in Lee, Massachusetts. The stated mission of his newspaper, *The Northern Star and Freemen's Advocate*, published in Albany from 1842 to 1849, was "the cause of temperance and reform and the equal rights of man" ("List of the Colored...").

Ending slavery was only half the battle for blacks. As soon as they became free, they found their freedom limited by law and custom. Little did they realize that their struggle for civil rights in America was just beginning. The early black leaders believed that moral improvement was the means to achieve this end. Unfortunately, the moral improvement of the rest of the nation left much to be desired, and more than 150 years later, the equality of blacks continues to be hindered by the legacy of slavery. Nevertheless, the holy spirit fostered by the era of moral improvement moved many white abolitionists to break the law of man in favor of the higher law of God and sanctioned their participation in the Underground Railroad.

Chapter 4

JEHOVAH HAS DECREED IT!

Most traditional histories have credited whites as the prime movers of the abolitionist movement and downplayed the contributions of blacks. However, much of the impetus for the movement came from blacks protesting their conditions. David Walker's revolutionary *Appeal* was a black message that resonated up until the Civil War.

Born free in North Carolina prior to 1800, Walker moved to Boston during the 1820s after a life of travel and opened a used-clothing shop near the waterfront, where most of his customers were black seamen. He became relatively prosperous, but his pride and intelligence compelled him to protest the inferior conditions of blacks in America. First, he organized meetings and then began submitting articles to *Freedom's Journal* in New York. In 1829, he compiled his thoughts in the *Appeal to the Coloured Citizens of the World*, which he published and distributed through the many contacts he had made.

The extent of the *Appeal*'s influence on the Abolition movement is uncertain, but judging by the events that occurred after its publication, it had a lasting impact. Walker condemned colonization, excoriated Thomas Jefferson and Henry Clay, attacked the hypocrisy of the nation's so-called Christianity, blasted the Southern laws that prohibited slaves from being taught to read, and admonished all blacks whether free or slave for their submissiveness (Walker).

"I write without the fear of man," he declared, addressing words alternately to whites and blacks. "I am writing for my God, and fear none but himself; they may put me to death if they choose...."

Walker stated that the condition in which blacks lived in America made them "the most wretched, degraded and abject set of beings that ever lived since the world began...."

"Look into our freedom and happiness," he wrote, "They are the most servile and abject kind, that ever a people was in possession of!"

Walker also ridiculed his own race, in an effort to exhort them to fight for their freedom.

"The man who would not fight under our Lord and Master Jesus Christ, in the glorious and heavenly cause of freedom and of God ... ought to be kept with all of his children or family, in slavery, or in chains, to be butchered by his cruel enemies."

He anticipated Martin Luther King by nearly 150 years when he advised blacks "that your full glory and happiness, as well as all other coloured people under Heaven, shall never be fully consummated, but with the entire emancipation of your enslaved brethren all over the world."

He pricked the conscience of white America by referring to the Declaration of Independence.

"Now, Americans!" he asked, "was your suffering under Great Britain one hundredth part as cruel and tyrannical as you have rendered ours under you?"

Repent, he warned the white American, or "[You] will ... curse the day that you ever were born...."

Walker's militance was disturbing. Thoughts of using forceful means to end slavery were still years away. Both Benjamin Lundy, then the nation's foremost white abolitionist, and William Lloyd Garrison, as well as most black leaders, condemned Walker's militance, though Garrison applauded his intelligence. In fact, Walker's references in the *Appeal* showed that he was erudite in history, classical literature, and scripture.

Nevertheless, his words probably had more influence on American blacks, especially the slaves in the South, than has been credited. As many as 20 percent of New England seaman during this time were blacks (Bolster 2), and he gave them his pamphlet for distribution, sometimes sewing copies into the lining of their clothing. With their help he was able to get a wide distribution of the pamphlet through the South. It wasn't long before a $3,000 reward was offered for his life and a $10,000 reward for anyone who could bring him to the South alive. Walker's friends urged him to flee to Canada, but he ignored their warning. "Somebody must die in this cause," he said. "I may be doomed to the stake and the fire, or to the scaffold tree, but it is not in me to falter if I can promote the work of emancipation" (*Africans in America: Judgment Day* Part 4).

Two months after the *Appeal*'s formal publication, Walker was found dead in his home. The cause was never determined.

While Walker and other free blacks were making their first appeals for equality, a young New England printer was entering the newspaper business in Bennington, Vermont. William Lloyd Garrison's articles in support of gradual emancipation and colonization attracted Benjamin Lundy, who had been traveling across the nation during the 1820s spreading the message of gradual emancipation and publishing his portable journal, *The Genius of Universal Emancipation*. Living a peripatetic existence while spreading his message, Lundy published his newspaper wherever he might be at the moment and carried with him the necessary tools—the type, heading, the column-rules, and direction-book. He claimed to have traveled 25,000 miles from 1820 to 1830, 5,000 on foot (Macy 30). Lundy visited Garrison and recruited him to work on *The Genius* in Baltimore.

Garrison went to Baltimore in 1829. There he became acquainted with the black community and first heard the arguments against colonization and for immediate emancipation. He also saw firsthand the operation of the domestic slave trade and learned of the involvement of a captain from Newburyport, Massachusetts, Garrison's hometown. Garrison attacked the captain in print and provoked a lawsuit that put him in prison. He spent seven weeks there until his fine was paid by Arthur Tappan of New York City.

Garrison returned to Boston in 1830 and began speaking in favor of immediate emancipation and against colonization. On January 1, 1831, he launched *The Liberator*.

"I do not wish to think or speak or write with moderation," he wrote. "No! No! Tell a man whose house is on fire to give a moderate alarm; tell him to moderately rescue his wife from the hands of the ravisher; tell the mother to gradually extricate her babe from the fire; but urge me not to use moderation in a cause like the present. I am in earnest. I will not equivocate; I will not excuse; I will not retreat an inch; and *I will be heard*" (Pillsbury 15).

In his second issue, however, Garrison made it clear that he did not support David Walker's call for violence and that he believed only in using peaceful means. His call for immediate emancipation was shocking enough. But when Nat Turner's Slave Rebellion in Virginia caused the brutal death of more than 50 Southern whites during the summer of 1831, Garrison and Walker were held equally responsible, though it is unlikely that either of them influenced it.

Turner, a 31-year-old slave, believed he had been chosen by God to lead his people out of bondage. In his confession to Thomas Gray, just before his execution, he said he had believed he was destined to be a prophet since he was three years old, and that after a series of visions, "the Holy Ghost had revealed itself to me and made plain ... the great day of judgment was at hand" ("Turner's Confession"). Joined by perhaps as many as 40 slaves, they rode on horseback, armed with axes and clubs, attacking every house and killing every white man, woman, and child they encountered until they were stopped by the local militia. Turner escaped and went into hiding for two months before he was captured, hanged, and his body skinned (*Africans in America* Part 3).

After the Turner massacre, tighter restrictions were put on slaves in the South. Neighboring Maryland, for example, forbid the sale of liquor or guns to blacks and prohibited them from attending religious services if no whites were present. Laws were passed in some Southern states that went so far as to banish all free blacks, unless a white person testified to their good character. The Southern anti-slavery societies soon ceased to exist (Macy 67).

Meanwhile, the Northern abolitionists forged ahead despite overwhelming opposition. In 1832, the New England Anti-Slavery Society was founded, and a year later the New York City Anti-Slavery Society. A mob of 5,000 gathered to protest and obstruct the latter meeting at its intended location. Secretly, it was moved to the Chatham Street Chapel. Chosen as president was Arthur Tappan, and its board of managers included individuals who became widely known in the movement: Lewis Tappan, Joshua Leavitt, Isaac T. Hopper, and William Goodell. Before long, enough support had grown for a national society, and on December 4, 1833, the American Anti-Slavery Society was formed, based in New York City, with Arthur Tappan as president.

The South's reaction to abolition came as no surprise, but what was more discouraging to free blacks was that most people in the North were far from ready to give them equality. Black leaders attempted to put a bright face on the situation. At the meeting of the fourth annual National Negro Convention in June 1833 at Philadelphia, they reported that progress had been made in the building of churches and schools, and in the establishment of black-owned businesses. However, they continued to express their concern with the racist propaganda of the Colonization Society and stated that "a deep and solemn gloom has settled on that new bright anticipation [of freedom], [as] that monster, *prejudice*, is stalking over the land..." (Gross 21).

They were probably referring to the failure to establish a manual labor college in New Haven, Connecticut, under the Rev. Simon Jocelyn, and the brutal opposition faced by Prudence Crandall in her effort to enroll blacks at her school for girls in Canterbury, Connecticut. Not only was a law passed prohibiting Crandall from enrolling black students, but her house was also burned down, and she was put in jail. The Rev. Samuel May, who had come to her assistance, later wrote of the experience: "Twenty harmless, well-behaved girls, whose only offense against the peace of the community was that they had come together there to obtain the useful knowledge and moral culture, were to be told that they had better go away, because ... the house in which they dwelt, would not be protected by the guardians of the town..." (Pendleton 124).*

In northern New York, the stage may have been smaller but the mood was the same when its first known anti-slavery society formed on November 18, 1834, in Argyle, Washington County. A small number of enthusiastic abolitionists arrived at the Dutch Reformed Church that morning to find "an effigy suspended at the door, representing a Negro, on which was fastened a slip of paper, signed 'Judge Lynch'" with a warning written in rhyme ("Spirit of the Times ..." 3). They also found the doors locked and the windows nailed shut.

Nevertheless, they made their entry through a window. Among them were Doctors Hiram Corliss and Ira Hatch, attorney Erastus Culver, grocer Edwin Andrews, and newspaper publisher Wendell Lansing, all of Union Village; the Rev. A.C. Tuttle and Col. John Straight of Hartford; and Dr. I.S. Bigelow and attorney Martin Marsh. At the church, the group nominated officers and drafted resolutions, then recessed for dinner at a local public house.†

A mob of about 20 drunken individuals greeted the abolitionists when they returned to the church. "[They] had barred the door, bracing iron bars and rails against it; had fastened down the windows, while the church rung with the savage shouts of those within," wrote Erastus Culver, whose report of the meeting first appeared in the *Vermont Tribune* and later in *The Liberator* (Ibid.).

Colonel Straight, who presided over the convention, demanded entry but was threatened with a beating. Being peace-loving men, the abolitionists returned to the public house, where their meeting resumed.

*More tragedy would follow for Crandall, whose brother was arrested the following year in Washington, D.C., and put in prison for possessing abolitionist literature. He was held for eight months and eventually was acquitted but soon after his release died of ailments developed while in prison (Aptheker 104).

†The site of Argyle's former Dutch Reformed Church is now occupied by the home of Argyle Central School principal Larry Patswald; the public house was Rouse's Tavern, whose lot today is occupied by Warren Tire Service (longtime village historian Ernest Tilford provided this information).

Dr. Hiram Corliss. (Courtesy of John Hay Library, Brown University Special Collections.)

Dr. Corliss was elected president. A Temperance man and devout member of the Dutch Reformed Church, he had moved to Union Village in 1825 during a period of booming growth and purchased 50 acres in the center of town along the Battenkill River. There he set up his medical office and residence on 31 Main Street. Just the year before, he had been elected president of the newly-formed county medical society and was establishing an image of himself that was fixed in the minds of locals for years—that of the good doctor atop his horse, dashing off with medical bags stropped onto his saddle (Morhous 26). His skill as a surgeon also became renowned in 1826, when he succeeded in a bold operation that never had been performed in the U.S. ("Hiram Corliss Obituary"). Corliss personally constructed his own surgical instruments for the procedure, and as a result of this success, he became widely known. Medicine was only one of his many occupations. He commanded the village firefighting unit, was a trustee of the village library, sang bass in his church choir, and operated a general store. But his prominence did not deter the rowdy bunch that had moved from occupying the church to the entrance of the public house.

"...[Two] entered the convention ... [who] broke in upon the proceedings. The landlord immediately asked them to civilly go out. They refused, with an oath. He then promptly seized the largest one by the shoulder ... [who] soon found himself some feet in the street ... his face in close contact with the rough ground. He [the disrupter] gathered up and made for the house, at the landlord. Assistance was called for, and he was bound with a rope" (Ibid.).

The mob meanwhile stood by and did nothing. But soon their cause was given support by a "well-dressed, fair looking citizen of Argyle," driving a stylish horse and buggy.

"[He] drove several times through the street with an image representing a large Negro with arms extended and fastened to the hind end of the wagon. Finding that this did not disturb the convention, he soon drove round to the North side of the house, and backed his wagon and image up directly into the window of the room where the convention was sitting, and there remained till the meeting was through, the mob in the streets raising shouts of triumph" (Ibid.).

Culver, the writer of the report, concluded by predicting that slavery would be abolished. "Rest assured," he wrote, "Jehovah has decreed it. The frowning tyrant at the South, his cringing echo at the North, the cowardly minister, the fawning politician and the mob-encouraging press, are preparing for the condemnation that awaits them ... Persevere, then, in your good work."

This unsettling affair marked the official beginning of abolitionism in the Adirondack region. Such chaos continued to follow abolition meetings into the next decade. It did not deter the abolitionists. By the end of 1834, there were 124 anti-slavery societies in the North calling for immediate emancipation, and their number was growing (*Emancipator* 34).

Chapter 5

THE SWORD IS NOW DRAWN

Being an abolitionist during the 1830s could be life threatening. Things became so inflammatory that rewards of up to $10,000 were actually offered in the South for the assassination of Garrison and Arthur Tappan (May 135). Being a free black in the wrong place at the wrong time also could be a provocation. During a riot at an 1834 convention in New York City, abolitionist literature was destroyed, and the homes, businesses, and churches of local abolitionists and blacks were damaged (Henderson 18).* This was only one of hundreds of such riots that were occurring wherever abolitionists scheduled meetings. Well-traveled abolitionist lecturer Henry Stanton, the husband of feminist Elizabeth Cady Stanton, wrote that he was mobbed at least 200 times between 1834 and 1846 (Stanton 48). In northern New York, riots occurred in Plattsburgh and Union Village.

One might think that the anti-slavery societies were advocating some type of violent overthrow of the government; however, their agenda was simply education. Called "moral suasion," it was developed under the guiding influence of Garrison. Its objective was to persuade others through anti-slavery tracts, books, and newspapers like *The Liberator* and *Emancipator*; by dispatching lecturers to spread the abolitionist gospel; and holding meetings and rallies. A notable campaign was a direct mail effort led by the American Anti-Slavery Society targeting the South (Savage 150–184). Southern states quickly undermined it. In South Carolina, for example, a $1,000 fine and a year in prison was the punishment for those caught with "incendiary" literature, and the city of Charleston offered a $1,000 bounty for information leading to the arrest of anyone distributing such literature. For free blacks the punishment was worse—$1,000 for the first offense, 50 lashes for the second, and death for the third (Savage 156).

*Among the targets of the rioters was both the home and store of Arthur Tappan, and St. Philip's African Episcopal Church (Kerber 31–33).

When the abolitionists refused to stop their mail campaign, southern municipalities formed vigilance committees that broke into local post offices and confiscated all the abolitionist mail. The most publicized incident occurred on July 29, 1835, in Charleston. This situation put Southern postmasters in a difficult predicament, as they were required by law to deliver this mail. One postmaster was advised by the Postmaster General to acquiesce to the wishes of the local community: "We owe an obligation to the laws but a higher one to the communities in which we live and if the former be prevented to destroy the latter, it is patriotism to disregard them ... Your justification [in allowing abolitionist mail to be confiscated] must be looked for in the character of the papers detained, and the circumstances by which you are surrounded" (163).

President Andrew Jackson recommended a law to prevent the mailing of "incendiary" literature, but such a law was never passed because it was thought to be unconstitutional. Nevertheless, Southern postmasters continued to acquiesce to the local communities, and the distribution of abolitionist mail to the South was suppressed.

Abolitionist meetings, so often mobbed, were anything but incendiary. In fact, they were a combination of a religious service and business meeting. Many were held in churches and almost always began and ended with a prayer led by clergy. Around 1840 abolitionist songs were added to the meetings. Individuals, groups, or even full choirs performed. Following the prayer and song, the business meeting took place. If it were an annual meeting, the first order of business was to nominate officers and read the annual report. This was followed by a discussion of issues during which members would offer resolutions that were voted on following the discussion. The guest speaker concluded the meeting. Touring lecturers were common during this time, and various large societies like the American Anti-Slavery or the New York Anti-Slavery Societies commissioned many of them. Generally, meetings concluded with collections for various efforts such as expenses for food, clothing, and transportation of fugitive slaves.

Among the early efforts of the societies was the political act of petition. Because immediate abolition was highly unlikely, the abolitionists decided early to work for the abolition of slavery where it was under federal control. Two specific areas were the District of Columbia, and new territories and states. The plan of action was to send petitions to Congress. Though this started slowly, by 1835 the huge number of petitions from anti-slavery societies had upset Southern representatives.

Because abolitionists were gadflies, the public had come to view them as madmen. Ironically, it was not the abolitionists, but the mobs opposing them who acted like madmen. Such a mob occupied the Utica courthouse where the organizational meeting of the New York State Anti-Slavery Society was scheduled on October 21, 1835. An estimated 1,000 delegates arrived that day to organize a state society in order to coordinate the increasing number of anti-slavery societies in the state ("Proceedings..." 48).

On learning of the opposition's plans the night before, the meeting was moved to a local church. Alvan Stewart, a renowned trial lawyer who had turned his talents to abolition and was president of the Utica Anti-Slavery Society, made an inspirational opening speech. Stewart recalled the legacy of the Founding Fathers and urged the delegates to remain steadfast in the face of opposition or see their liberties erode (Henderson 61–62).

After Stewart's speech a constitution was passed, with the primary objectives of the society being the abolition of slavery in the U.S. and the elevation of its people of color. Lewis Tappan was reading a declaration of sentiments to the convention when a committee representing the mob at the courthouse barged in and demanded to speak (63–64). Consent was given and their spokesperson, Judge Chester Hayden, read a series of statements that condemned the society and abolitionists in general. The protesters also demanded an apology from the abolitionists for disrupting their community, but further interruptions from the drunken mob intruding from outside caused an adjournment (May 163–165).

Before the meeting concluded, however, a tall man of distinction arose. Gerrit Smith, who was not a member of an anti-slavery society at the time but had come by invitation, said that though he did not consider himself an abolitionist, he believed that Americans had the right to express their beliefs and was appalled that a mob could prevent this. In order that the abolitionists be allowed to speak freely, he offered the use of his estate in Peterboro and suggested the meeting be reconvened at the Presbyterian Church in Peterboro. His offer was accepted and the convention recessed (Frothingham 165).

As the delegates departed, the angry mob outside hurled obscenities. They did not physically attack the delegates, however, reserving their violence for the Utica *Standard and Democrat*. While its workers were at supper, the mob broke into the newspaper's office and threw the type into the street so it could not publish a report of the day's events (Henderson 65).

In Peterboro, the entire Smith household worked round the clock for the next day, mixing bread, grinding coffee, making pies, baking rolls, and preparing the necessities of hospitality while Smith worked on his speech. It rained the next morning, but 30 guests arrived for breakfast. By afternoon the sun was shining on the 590 delegates who attended the convention at the church in Peterboro and signed their names to the convention roster (Frothingham 165; "Proceedings ..." 44–48).

The proceedings resumed and resolutions were discussed. Among them were recommendations that monthly concerts of prayer be held the last Monday of the month to pray for the slave, that ladies' anti-slavery societies be formed, and that citizens appeal to their congressmen for the abolition of slavery in the District of Columbia. A strong denunciation of the actions of the mob was approved, and pledges were accepted for $1,200, to be paid by the end of the year.

When these items were concluded, Smith addressed the delegates. His speech that day was among the most memorable in his prolific career. Foremost in his thoughts was the sacred right of free speech, which he observed was being threatened by those attempting to suppress the abolitionists throughout the nation.

> If God made me to be one of his instruments for carrying forward the salvation of the world, then is the right of free discussion among my inherent rights: then may I, must I, speak of sin, any sin, every sin, that comes in my way ... which it is my duty to search out and to assail.... This right is, for the most part, defended on the ground, that it is given to us by our political constitutions; and that it was purchased for us by the blood and toil of our fathers. Now, I wish to see its defense placed on its true and infinitely higher ground: on the ground, that God gave it to us; and that he, who violates or betrays it,

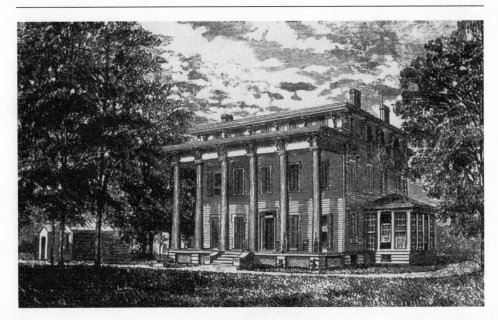

Gerrit Smith's mansion. (From Octavius Books Frothingham, *Gerrit Smith: A Biography*, New York: G.P. Putnam's Sons, 1878.)

> is guilty, not alone of dishonoring the laws of his country and the blood and toil and memory of his fathers; but, that he is guilty also of making war upon God's plan....

Smith stopped short of committing himself to the abolitionist side, but his closing words left little doubt where he stood.

"True permanent peace can never be restored, until slavery, the occasion of the war, has ceased. The sword, which is now drawn, will never be returned to its scabbard, until victory, entire, decisive victory is ours or theirs" ("Freedom of Discussion" 1).

That same weekend a mob in Boston seized William Lloyd Garrison, "tore off his clothes, dragged him through the streets, and would have hanged him, had it not been for the almost superhuman efforts of several gentlemen, assisted by some of the police" (May 157). A third mob in Montpelier, Vermont, broke up an anti-slavery meeting there and caused some abolitionists to wonder if there might be some sort of conspiracy being hatched against them (162). But the conversion of Gerrit Smith, who had been a supporter of the American Colonization Society, was a great victory for the abolitionist cause. He would rival Garrison as its strongest adherent, and he certainly was its most generous benefactor in the years ahead.

During the next year, the American Anti-Slavery Society hired the Rev. Theodore Weld, a disciple of Charles Finney, to oversee their traveling lecturers. Under his direction, these lecturers traveled to every likely village and formed more than 200 new societies in New York State during the next two years. This process was advanced by the launching of a state society weekly, *Friend of Man*, during the summer of 1836. While their cause was progressing on the state level, abolitionists were faced with another setback overall as a result of another assault on their rights. Following an angry debate in Congress, South Carolina Congressman Henry Pinckney offered his infamous resolution that "all petitions, memorials, resolutions, propositions, or papers, relating in any way, or to any extent whatever, to the subject of slavery, or the abolition of slavery, shall, without being either printed or referred, be laid upon the table, and that no further action whatever shall be had thereon" (Ludlum 207). Passed on February 8, 1836, it meant that discussion of slavery was forbidden on the House floor and became known as the Gag Rule. As a result, petitioning, one of the anti-slavery societies' major efforts and a basic right provided in the Constitution, had been suspended.

Another setback for the abolitionists was the unfavorable response of the nation's churches. To their surprise, most churches in the North resisted the call for immediate emancipation: not because they believed slavery moral, but because they were not ready to abolish it. As abolitionist minister Samuel May wrote, "the most serious obstacle to the progress of the antislavery cause was the conduct of the clergy and churches in our country" (May 329).

The reasons for this ironic state of affairs were complex. One factor was the link between the denominations in the North and the South. This relationship fostered a financial dependence on the wealthy slaveholders (Brown 108–110). To disguise this, clerical apologists emphasized that the laws sanctioned slavery and made it a serious crime to aid fugitive slaves. An even weightier argument was made through Scripture. Because Abraham, Isaac, Jacob and other patriarchs of the Old Testament held slaves, clergy suggested, then God must approve of it. Furthermore, they argued that not only had the slaves been rescued from a primitive existence, but that they also had been saved from heathenism.

Though the majority of the nation's churches did not support abolitionism, clergymen or devout church members, sometimes acting in defiance of their own churches, organized many anti-slavery societies in the northern New York. Their outreach methods were patterned after the circuit riders of the Awakening period, and they were cast in the mold of the Rev. Theodore Weld's famous seventy: "he-goat men," as another of the great evangelists of the period, Lyman Beecher, the father of Harriet Beecher Stowe, described them, "butting everything in the line of their march" and "made up of vinegar, aqua fortis, and oil of vitriol, with brimstone, saltpeter and charcoal to explode and scatter the corrosive matter" (Cross 219). Weld, a native of Granville in Washington County, was among those preachers who introduced the abolitionist message to northern New York in 1836. Others included the Rev. Edward C. Pritchett of Utica, who

The Rev. Nathaniel Colver. (From J.A. Smith, *Memoir of Nathaniel Colver, D.D.*, Boston: Durkee and Foxcroft, Publishers, 1873.)

helped organize abolition societies in Essex and Clinton counties; the Rev. Ovid Miner, a native of Middlebury, Vermont, who ministered to churches in Franklin, Clinton and Essex counties; and the Rev. Luther Lee, a native of Schoharie, New York, who did abolition outreach in both Franklin and Clinton counties. Laymen Thomas Canfield of Franklin County and Thomas B. Watson, a lawyer from Keeseville, Clinton County, also made notable contributions, as did Rev. Nathaniel Colver, a native of Champlain, New York, who had begun his ministerial career in neighboring Franklin County before moving to Washington County.

Colver had already begun an abolitionist ministry as the pastor of Union Village's Bottskill Baptist Church. In 1834, en route to Richmond for a pastorate interview before accepting the Bottskill pastorate, he experienced an epiphany that changed his life.

"I saw an old man, with gray hair and tottering limbs, going down Pennsylvania avenue," he wrote, "hobbling upon his crutches as fast as he could, weeping and lamenting, trying to catch a glimpse of his lost child, sold to the soul-drivers, and now bound for the rice-swamps of the South, and saying, 'They promised me he should never be taken from me, but they've sold him, and I shall never see him again!'" (Smith 124).

After his conversion, despite being assaulted by mobs and heckled during his sermons (Thurston 44), Colver was very effective in shaping the abolition sentiment of the region. On his first tour as a representative of the American Anti-Slavery Society in October of 1836, he revisited his former congregations in Franklin County and helped organize a countywide anti-slavery society with little opposition.

"Rev Mr. Colver is laboring as an agent in the region. Has visited Constable and Fort Covington and Chateauguay with good success. A county society has been formed ... not a symptom of violence was seen. All went from the Convention, if we are allowed to judge from expressions which can not well be mistaken, with their souls refreshed and their faith strengthened ..." ("N. York ..." 87). He later assisted the Rev. Ovid Miner in forming a society in Ticonderoga, New York, signing up 204 members ("Rev. N. Colver" 182).

It was a different story for Weld at Union Village. He had assisted in the formation of the Fort Ann Anti-Slavery Society the year before (Henderson 396), but it did not deter the protesters who used stones, eggs, and even cannons!*

Nevertheless, at the anniversary meeting of the Union Village Anti-Slavery Society on July 4, 1836, Weld "commanded the closest attention of the large audience for the space of three hours" as he "leveled ... mountain after mountain of anti-abolition sophistry..." ("Anti-Slavery Movements" 18). With Weld's help, the society added 118 new members to its rolls, bringing its total to 283. He also spoke at Fort Ann, West Granville, Hartford, and Adamsville, where new societies were formed (Ibid.).

Pritchett visited the towns of Moriah in Essex County and Champlain in Clinton County, which borders Canada, in October 1836 and formed societies, reporting the people in Champlain to be "favorable to abolition" ("Champlain, NY" 78). This was surprising to Pritchett because Champlain was the home of Ashmun, the colonizationist.

---

*In the spring of 1837, during an anti-slavery lecture in Massachusetts by the Rev. Colver, a mob fired a cannon into the church and blew off the hand of a young man ("Rev. Nathaniel Colver" 174).

Watson lectured during the spring of 1837 in the villages of Keene, Wilmington, AuSable Forks, Lewis, and Jay, where a society had already formed ("J.B. Watson..." 186). Four months later, he and Pritchett organized the Essex County Anti-Slavery Society on July 11, 1837, at the Baptist Meeting House in Westport. Representatives included those from Jay, Moriah, Willsboro, Elizabethtown, Lewis, Keene, Westport, Chesterfield, and Ticonderoga. Among their resolutions were that "the Legislature of New York should be urgently requested to repeal every law which oppresses the colored American and to grant a trial by jury to all persons claimed as fugitive slaves" ("Essex County Anti-Slavery Convention").

There is no mention of violence at the Essex County organizational convention, but hostility erupted at the formation of the Clinton County Anti-Slavery Society on April 25, 1837, also organized by Watson and Pritchett. It came as no surprise, for a petition of protest had been signed by 114 residents and had been circulated the day after the announcement of the convention ("Clinton County Convention" 23).

Nevertheless, "...delegations [from the town societies at Champlain, Beekmantown, Schuyler Falls, and Peru] were to meet in the courthouse in Plattsburgh and organize a county anti-slavery society," Underground Railroad conductor Stephen Keese Smith said in an 1887 interview. "When our procession ... came into Plattsburgh, we were egged and hooted and otherwise mobbed. Elder Andrew Witherspoon of the Methodists, [my uncle] Samuel Keese and my grandfather, Stephen Keese rode together at the head of the procession" (Everest Recollections 59).

The mob threatened the elder Keese by shouting, "Your gray hairs shall be no protection to you," and a petticoat was held out of a window on Margaret Street to ridicule the abolitionists' manhood.

"We drove around to the Cumberland House," Smith continued, "but were not allowed to hold our meeting in the court house. Samuel Chatterton, an officer in the army, I think, was president of this meeting [a meeting of those who were not abolitionists]. St. John, B. L. Skinner and others ... spoke nobly. The speaking was from the Cumberland House steps. Skinner begged ... the mob to desist and the meeting [adjourned] to Beekmantown.... The meeting was held the rest of that day and the next. The county society afterward continued to hold meetings in different towns" (60).

At the meeting Watson, Pritchett, and Samuel Keese of the Union were appointed a committee to prepare a constitution and preamble. Elected as president was Noadiah Moore of Champlain, and as corresponding secretary, Orson B. Ashmun, brother of the late colonizationist ("Clinton County Convention" 23).

That month also saw the formation of the St. Lawrence Anti-Slavery Society in Potsdam. Among its attendees were Franklin County residents Jabez Parkhurst, a Fort Covington lawyer, and Thomas Canfield, who had helped form several societies in Franklin County in 1836 and had been doing abolition outreach in St. Lawrence County along with the Rev. Pritchett. Presiding over the convention were Alvan Stewart, the state society's executive committee chairman, and William L. Chaplin, its secretary ("St. Lawrence Anti-Slavery Convention" 63). At the same time, the Methodist Episcopal Church was holding a conference in Potsdam "to reconcile anti-slavery men to slaveholding in the Church as it existed in the South." (Lee 135). The Rev. Luther Lee was among the participants, and Bishop Hedding of Troy presided. Hedding used the occasion to justify the church's association with its members in the South who were slaveholders. He based the church's position on the Golden Rule: "The right to hold a slave is founded upon this rule," he said. "'All things whatsoever ye would that men should do to you, do you even so to them; for this is the law and the prophets'" (136). In other words, Hedding claimed Northerners did not have the right to tell their Southern brethren to give up their slaves if the law sanctioned it. No opposition was expressed at the convention, but Lee remarked in his autobiography that the "storm seemed to be gathering" (137), and the following year he accepted a position as an anti-slavery lecturer.

Division over the question of slavery among churches and church members was not uncommon in northern New York. A number of churches joined together and formed synods or associations in which they took an official stand in opposition to slavery. This often severed their relations with their denomination or parent church. Some of those will be discussed later when we examine their connections with the Underground Railroad.

By 1837, there were at least 274 anti-slavery societies in New York State, and by this author's count, 45 in northern New York by the end of 1839 (Henderson 389–406),* including three female societies, one in Albany and two in Clinton County. These societies were auxiliaries to the state society, which coordinated their activities. It was from this network that the Underground Railroad in New York State developed.

---

*The author's count includes societies in the northeast region of the state, including St. Lawrence County. The list is derived from Henderson and adds four societies that Henderson has not listed.

Chapter 6

ON ACCOUNT OF COLOR

"I have just returned from Pattison's Eating House, where I have just been refused a cup of tea, on the account of my color—it is the first time in my life I have been so treated in this city," wrote Samuel Cornish to the *Emancipator* in 1837 ("My friends please notice" 63).

A native of Philadelphia, where he was educated in free African schools, Cornish came to New York City in 1821 when he was 26 and organized the first Black Presbyterian Church. In 1827, he founded, with John Russworm, the nation's first African-American newspaper, *Freedom's Journal* (Wesley 82–83), and the year he wrote of his personal encounter with prejudice, he had founded his second black newspaper, *The Colored American*. Cornish was a respected leader in the black community, and yet his stature meant nothing to the average white person.

The problem of racial discrimination in the North was among the major topics of the annual meeting of the New York State Anti-Slavery Society that year. The Rev. Theodore Wright, the first black graduate of Princeton University and pastor of the Shiloh Presbyterian Church in New York City, riveted the audience with the story of his wife, who had died from complications following an illness she developed after a night spent on the open deck of a steamboat because blacks were not allowed indoors on boats. He also talked about employment problems, the exclusion from apprenticeships in trades, the refusal of service in restaurants, and the exclusion from public schools (Henderson 145–146).

Both Wright and Cornish were leaders in New York City's Phoenix Society, organized in 1833 to provide self-improvement in the hope those restrictions excluding blacks from public and educational facilities would be removed. Wright himself had been refused entry to the Alumni of Nassau Hall literary meeting. The Phoenix Society was open to all who paid a small fee and who were judged by the board of directors as of good moral character. Its programs included the establishment of a colored high school for black youth; a lecture series; a registry that catalogued the reading, writing, and job skills of those in the black community, and assisted with job placement; and the offering of courses for adults. Above all, it stressed high standards of moral conduct (Porter 565–566).

Such efforts to gain acceptance were common. The "Union Society of Albany, Troy and vicinity, for the improvement of the colored people in Morals, Education, and the Mechanical Arts" formed in 1837. Elected president was Albany minister the Rev. Nathaniel Paul, who had been an agent for the Wilberforce Colony and had spent two years in England raising money and promoting its cause.* Other leaders included William Rich of Troy, Benjamin Lattimore of Albany, Fresly Way of Lansingburgh, and Richard P.G. Wright of Schenectady ("Union Meeting..."). What is especially interesting is that all of these individuals were or would be members of vigilance committees, which assisted fugitive slaves with food, clothing, lodging, medical care, legal help, travel funds, and letters of introduction to help them find new homes and jobs.

Though there were earlier such organizations, and other important vigilance committees like those in Boston and Philadelphia, serious discussion about the origins of the Underground Railroad as a far-reaching network must begin with the New York Committee of Vigilance. It was organized in 1835 because of the frequency with which free blacks were being arrested as fugitive slaves or kidnapped into slavery ("First Annual Report..." 3). Its leaders included David Ruggles, secretary and general agent during its formative years; the Rev. Wright, who was its president for many years; Charles Ray and William P. Johnson, who for a time shared a residence, the former being the Committee's prime mover during its later years (The *New York City Directory* 1843); William Johnston, who succeeded Ruggles as the Committee's secretary; Cornish; and Dr. James McCune Smith, attending physician at the New York Colored Orphan Asylum.

Foremost among its efforts was to provide aid to blacks who had come from the South. These could have been fugitive slaves, many who arrived aboard ships in New York Harbor and which some sources claimed to number as many as 5,000 in the city (*Emancipator* 104); slaves who had been brought into the state for longer than nine months and who by law were free; and free blacks, who had left the South to escape the persecution begun since the call for immediate emancipation.

An example of the latter was a resolution adopted in Somerset County, Maryland: "...all free Negroes who shall not leave the said District on or before the first day of September next, shall be considered ... insurgents, and ... opposed to the good order and well being of the white citizens..." ("First Annual Report..." 17).

Other concerns were illegal slave ships that would secretly dock in the port,[†] and slave catchers. The latter had organized in New York City under the leadership of Tobias Boudinot, a police constable; D.D. Nash, a Virginia slave catcher; and F.H.

Paul, whose eloquence and leadership abilities are unquestioned, is strongly criticized in Austin Stewart's autobiography. Paul raised a substantial sum in England for the Wilberforce Colony but returned not one cent of it to the colony. Instead, he spent it all, living extravagantly and courting an English bride, as well as extending a loan to William Lloyd Garrison to pay for his passage on a boat back to the U.S.

†Though the international slave trade had been outlawed in 1808, the South continued its involvement in the trade and slave ships were reported in New York Harbor right up through the Civil War. A notable example was the Amistad, on which the captive Africans mutinied and took over the ship in 1839.

Pettis, an attorney from Virginia who had moved to New York in order to assist the rendition of fugitive slaves ("First Annual Report..." 53). However, while they had legal authority to seize fugitive slaves, they also were in the business of kidnapping. On at least one occasion in 1836, Boudinot and Nash attempted to kidnap David Ruggles (Hodges 11) and sell him into slavery. This occurred after Ruggles had a Portuguese ship captain arrested for slave trading and kidnapping upon learning he had enslaved five blacks for the purpose of taking them to the South and selling them.

The Committee also attempted to free blacks being detained illegally in the South and provided legal assistance. This was handled by white attorney Horace Dresser, who for a time shared his location with David Ruggles' bookstore at 36 Lispenard Street, which also was listed as the Committee's headquarters during its early years (*Mirror of Liberty* 7).

As the NYCV developed, it turned New York City into perhaps the nation's most important terminal of the Underground Railroad. The number of fugitive slaves it aided easily numbered in the thousands (*Mirror of Liberty* 7; Quarles 154; Campbell 6; Ray 33). In its early years the Committee was a predominately black organization. However, because of the aid they had given to fugitive slaves, white abolitionists Gerrit Smith and Alvan Stewart, another central New Yorker, were invited to speak at the Committee's annual meeting in May 1837. Among Stewart's declarations at that meeting was, "I do say, and I care not who hears me, the man who delivers a slave from his pursuers, does an act upon which Heaven will smile" (Henderson 144). White abolitionist Arthur Tappan also attended its meetings during this time and said that it was from the Committee that he "learned the ropes of working in the Underground Railroad" (Tappan 182).

The Committee's most celebrated runaway was Frederick Douglass, who came to Ruggles for assistance in 1838. The drama that unfolded during his daring escape and arrival in New York merits repeating not only because of its inherent interest, but also because of the picture it provides of a fugitive slave. Douglass, who assumed the identity of a free sailor, managed with the help of a friend who worked for the railroad to get a ticket and sneak aboard a train leaving Baltimore. He did this to avoid going through the ticket office and the scrutiny that might reveal his true identity, for he didn't have papers that identified him as a free man but only a sailor's ID, which described a person who did not look like him. The scene begins in the "Negro" car when the conductor is taking Douglass's ticket and examining his identification.

"He was somewhat harsh in tone," Douglass wrote, "and peremptory in manner until he reached me, when, strangely enough, and to my surprise and relief, his whole manner changed. Seeing that I did not readily produce my free papers, as the other colored persons in the car had done, he said to me in a friendly contrast with that observed towards the others.

"'I suppose you have your free papers?'"

"To which I answered: 'No, sir; I never carry my free papers to sea with me.'"

"'But you have something to show that you are a free man, have you not?'"

"'Yes, sir,' I answered; 'I have a paper with the American eagle on it, and that will carry me round the world.'"

"With this I drew from my deep sailor's pocket my seaman's protection, as before described. The merest glance at the paper satisfied him, and he took my fare and went on about his business ... This moment of time was one of the most anxious I ever experienced ... though much relieved, I realized that I was still in great danger: I was still in Maryland, and subject to arrest at any moment. I saw on the train several persons who would have known me in any other clothes, and I feared they might recognize me, even in my sailor 'rig,' and report me to the conductor..." (Douglass *Life and Times* 199).

Frederick Douglass. (From Frederick Douglass, *My Bondage and My Freedom*, New York: Miller, Orton & Mulligan, 1855.)

"After Maryland I was to pass through Delaware—another slave State, where slave catchers generally awaited their prey, for it was not in the interior of the State, but on its borders, that these human hounds were most vigilant and active. The borderlines between slavery and freedom were the dangerous ones, for the fugitives. The heart of no fox or deer, with hungry hounds on his trail, in full chase, could have beaten more anxiously or noisily than did mine, from the time I left Baltimore till I reached Philadelphia."

Douglass successfully completed the first train ride. The next obstacle was a ferryboat ride across the Susquehanna River. During this short trip, he encountered several colored acquaintances whom he feared might unintentionally betray him. He managed to evade this, but when he got off the boat, he saw a white man whom he had worked under just a few days before. Luckily, the man didn't notice him. Yet another threat materialized on the next train to Wilmington and the Delaware border, where a white man who knew him saw him. Again fate looked kindly upon him, for the man paid him no attention. The last leg of his flight into the North was a steamboat from Wilmington to Philadelphia. All went without a hitch, and from Philadelphia, he took another train to New York (200–201). In New York, Douglass found himself overwhelmed by the experience of freedom.

"In less than a week after leaving Baltimore, I was walking amid the hurrying throng, and gazing upon the dazzling wonders of Broadway," he wrote. "A free state around me, and a free earth under my feet ... A whole year was pressed into a single day. A new world burst upon my agitated vision. I have often been asked, by kind friends to whom I have told my story, how I felt when first I found myself beyond the limits of slavery; and I must say here ... It was a moment of joyous excitement ... sensations too intense and rapid for words. Anguish and grief, like darkness and rain, may be described, but joy and gladness, like the rainbow of promise, defy alike the pen and pencil..." (336).

Soon, however, Douglass began to feel the loneliness and insecurity of being in a new and strange place.

I had been but a few hours in New York, before I was met in the streets by a fugitive slave, well known to me, and the information I got from him respecting New York, did nothing to lessen my apprehension....

Jake told me all about his circumstances, and how narrowly he escaped being taken back to slavery [by his master]; that the city was now full of southerners, returning from the springs; that the black people in New York were not to be trusted; that there were hired men on the lookout for fugitives from slavery, and who, for a few dollars, would betray me into the hands of the slave-catchers; that I must trust no man with my secret ... worse still, this same Jake told me it was not in his power to help me. He seemed, even while cautioning me, to be fearing [that] I might be a party to a second attempt to recapture him ...I was much troubled ... I was without home, without friends, without work, without money, and without any definite knowledge of which way to go ...Some apology can easily be made for the few slaves who have, after making good their escape, turned back to slavery, preferring the actual rule of their masters, to the life of loneliness, apprehension, hunger, and anxiety, which meets them on their first arrival in a free state....

At last [I] was forced to go in search of an honest man—a man sufficiently human not to betray me into the hands of slave-catchers. I found my man in the person of one who said his name was Stewart. He was a sailor, warm hearted and generous, and he listened to my story with a brother's interest....

He took me to his house, and went in search of the late David Ruggles, who was then the secretary of the New York Vigilance Committee, and a very active man in all anti-slavery works. Once in the hands of Mr. Ruggles, I was comparatively safe. I was hidden with Mr. Ruggles several days. In the meantime, my intended wife, Anna, came on from Baltimore—to whom I had written, informing her of my safe arrival at New York—and, in the presence of Mrs. Mitchell and Mr. Ruggles, we were married, by the Rev. James W. C. Pennington.

Mr. Ruggles was the first officer on the under-ground railroad with whom I met after reaching the north, and, indeed, the first of whom I ever heard anything. Learning that I was a caulker by trade, he promptly decided that New Bedford was the proper place to send me. "Many ships," said he, "are there fitted out for the whaling business, and you may there find work at your trade, and make a good living." Thus, in one fortnight after my flight from Maryland, I was safe in New Bedford, regularly entered upon the exercise of the rights, responsibilities, and duties of a freeman [337–341].*

Ray described the typical iteneraries of runaways forwarded by the committee.

New York was a kind of receiving depot, whence we forwarded to Albany, Troy, sometimes to New Bedford and Boston, and occasionally ... Long Island.... When we had parties to forward from here, we would alternate in sending between Albany and Troy, and when we had a large party we would divide between the two cities. We had on one occasion, a party of twenty-eight persons of all ages.... We destined them for Canada. I secured passage for them in a barge, and Mr. Wright and myself spent the day in providing food, and personally saw them off on the barge. I then took the regular passenger boat.... Arriving in the morning, I reported to the Committee at Albany, and then

*New Bedford with its large Quaker population and prosperous whaling and shipping industry was an ideal location for blacks in America during this time. Not only was it one of the nation's wealthiest communities with plenty of jobs for blacks (Allen 82), but it was a community in which racial tolerance was part of the religion practiced by most of its residents.

returned to Troy and gave Brother Garnet notice, and he and I spent the day in visiting friends of the cause there, to raise money to help the party through to Toronto, Canada, via Oswego. We succeeded ... to send them all the way from here with safety" [Ray 35].*

The New York Committee of Vigilance also worked with the tireless conductor the Rev. Abel Brown when he lived in Albany and Troy. An 1887 letter written by Catherine Brown revealed the collaboration of Brown and Charles Ray and mentioned Lake Champlain as a forwarding destination:

An extremely interesting case occurred, concerning a fugitive forwarded by Mr. Ray to Albany, care of Mr. Abel Brown. He arrived one morning during the absence of Mr. Brown, and was sheltered and cared

The Rev. Charles Ray. (From Florence T. Ray, *Sketch of the Life of Rev. Charles B. Ray,* New York: Press of J.J. Little & Co., 1887.)

for by his companion in labors three days, constantly in dread of being taken by his pursuers! The account of himself as a slave and of his journey on his way to a land of freedom was so *peculiar,* that Mrs. B. wished to retain him. Mr. Brown, in the meantime, had found a place near Lake Champlain for this class of human beings, to which the fugitive was immediately conveyed [Ray 66].

Brown's work with the NYCV is also reported in his biography, also authored by Catherine Brown. In discussing papers that Brown left after his death, she wrote the following: "A member of the Vigilance Committee of New York, (Mr. Johnson) writing to the Rev. Mr. Garnet, says, 'The bearer is traveling northward, in quest of his wife (who obtained her freedom by operation of natural assumption,) and he is also endeavoring to secure to himself the same advantage. I am under the impression, that she did not go to Troy, but was directed to Mr. Abel Brown, of Albany, to whom I have directed some forty or fifty, within a short time'" (Brown 127).

The large number of runaways indicated makes it apparent that Underground Railroad conductors in New York and Albany worked together regularly. Another collaboration between upstate abolitionists and the Committee is revealed in a somewhat cryptic note in the 1843 annual report of the Eastern New York Anti-Slavery Society of which Abel Brown was the secretary and general agent. The note also included the names of three fugitive slaves: "They [ran] away because they were going

---

Brother Garnet was Henry Highland Garnet, who was born a slave and escaped to freedom with his family as a child. He grew up in New York City, where he came under the tutelage of Mr. Wright [the Rev. Theodore Wright]. In 1840, Garnet moved to Troy, where he became pastor of the Liberty Street Church from 1841 to 1848.

to sell them. Heard of the abolitionists, but did not know whether they were his friends or not. Johnston gave him $3, paid their passage—sent on same day. Gave him $2, and gave letter to Emp. Wright and Ellis Clizbe" (*Annual Report of the Committee 3*).* Of particular interest is "Emp. Wright," who was probably Richard P.G. Wright, the Schenectady barber, who was the Rev. Theodore Wright's father and who is known to have participated on occasion at NYCV meetings (*Emancipator* 22 Nov. 1838).

As racial prejudice increased, the efforts by free blacks to protect and improve themselves grew. Their self-help organizations also were in the forefront in providing humanitarian aid to their brothers and sisters fleeing from slavery. The evidence is clear and undeniable that the nation's foremost organization devoted to this effort, in New York City, worked closely with those in Albany and Troy, who sometimes forwarded runaway slaves to northern New York at least as early as 1837.

---

*Wright and Clizbe were members of the Eastern New York Anti-Slavery Society, which aided hundreds of fugitive slaves from 1842 to 1846.

Chapter 7

THE BYWAY TO FREEDOM

Contrary to popular belief, the Adirondack region of northern New York was quite accessible by 1830. Numerous turnpikes of dirt, planks and corduroy (log roads) skirted the valleys and the hills. A look at an 1836 map shows three overland routes leading north that could take a traveler to Canada—one that began in Saratoga County and led from Edinburgh all the way to Ogdensburg; another that began in that county, passed through Warren County and to Chestertown, where it allowed the traveler a choice of a route either to Ogdensburg or through Essex and Clinton counties; and a third through Washington County between Lake George and Lake Champlain that passed through Essex and Clinton counties (Burr).

Many lakes, rivers, kills, and canals also were available for transport. Such waterways were the most important thoroughfares for the Underground Railroad. Not only did they help direct the fugitive traveler, but they also were a good source for food. The most notable system that led fugitive slaves to the North Country and into Canada linked the Hudson River with the Champlain Canal to Lake Champlain and its fleet of steamers based in Whitehall. This was a direct water route from the port of New York City.

The Hudson River route from New York to Albany was perhaps the most important route taken by fugitive slaves in the entire state. Sand Lake, New York historian Judith Rowe, who has been researching the Underground Railroad for 30 years, believes the route was in use as early as 1811 when the city of Cohoes opened its cotton mills. Rowe contends that slaves in the South loaded the cotton on the ships that took it to the port of New York, and often hid among the bales to escape (Calarco 13).

When the connection between agents in Albany and New York was made is uncertain. Fugitives sent to Albany could have continued north, east, or west. North took them through the Adirondack region in New York or the Green Mountain region in Vermont; west to Syracuse and Lake Ontario; and east through the Berkshires.

51

A major factor in the development of the Underground Railroad in northern New York was the Champlain Canal. Completed in 1823, it linked the Hudson River ports of Albany and Troy with Lake Champlain and was used mainly to transport the Adirondack's rich supply of lumber, iron, coal and grain. Union Village's prosperous cotton factory also made use of the canal, and, if Rowe's contention is correct, there may have been some fugitive slave traffic in connection with it, especially considering that the son of its owner devoted his life to abolition and the Underground Railroad. The canal's packet boats also were a major conveyance from Washington County to Troy and Albany throughout the antebellum period and, during the early years of the canal, were the only public transportation in that vicinity to Albany and Troy (Meader Nye 3). The end point of the canal was Whitehall, the southernmost port of Lake Champlain, where travelers could board a steamboat directly to Canada.

How early did fugitive slaves begin coming to northern New York? We know that fugitive slaves had begun fleeing to Canada more than a decade before the British Emancipation of 1833 (Winks 142). Considering the date of the Champlain Canal's completion, it is possible that fugitive slaves may have passed through before 1830. However, the earliest documented report of a fugitive slave using the canal was in 1837. It appeared in a letter from Alvan Stewart first printed in the *New York Evangelist* and later in the *National Enquirer and Constitutional Advocate of Universal Liberty*: "A slave of middle age, of noble size, six feet high had made his escape from the southern States, and passed up the Champlain canal, and from Clinton county, passed through Franklin county, into the north part of St. Lawrence county, with intent to go to Ogdensburg, and cross over into Canada" ("Story of..." 8).

The report continued with the conclusion of the fugitive slave's journey and the assistance he received in getting across the St. Lawrence River into Canada. It also mentioned that the fugitive slave took this circuitous route because of his ignorance of geography. Apparently, he did not receive help from the Underground Railroad; otherwise, he probably would have entered Canada through a more direct route.

That account concurs with the statement of William Wells Brown, a prominent black author and speaker of the time who escaped to freedom in 1834. Brown received little help from the Underground Railroad. Traveling at night, he slept in vacant barns, and stole corn and food from fields along his way (Gara 45).

The first documented evidence of a fugitive slave seeking aid from the Underground Railroad in northern New York occurred in 1837.

"Not 36 hours since, the writer of this note was called on by a colored man who had with him testimonials of the highest character, from several clergymen, and gentlemen known to the writer, showing him to have recently been a slave in _____ [space left blank], and now on his way to Canada, a land of freedom" ("A Fugitive Slave" 94).

So began an anonymous letter from Union Village in the October 12, 1837 issue of the *Emancipator*. The writer explained that he had asked the runaway various questions to test his truthfulness, and all were answered satisfactorily. The letter probably was written by the Rev. Colver, who had colleagues in the South, and is an indication of growing ferment in Union Village.

Earlier that year, a new church formed on the basis of anti-slavery principles had formed out of a schism in the Dutch Reformed Church. It involved only 13 members in the beginning, but these included Dr. Corliss and William H. Mowry, the son of wealthy village forefather William, who were its organizers. Officially named the Orthodox Congregational Church, but called the "Free Church," its *Manual* stated that it was formed because the "practical love of mankind" was being abandoned in much of the Christian world by the "tolerance and even endorsement with ... huge evils like intemperance, slavery, and war" (*Manual* 9–10).

In addition to Corliss and Mowry, the *Manual* shows that Ann Caroline and Mary Mowry, the sisters of William, joined during its first year. Ann was the wife of banker Henry Holmes, who became a Free Church trustee in 1839, and Mary later married the entrepreneur John T. Masters, who also became a trustee. This gave the church enormous influence. Other prominent villagers who became church members were William M. Holmes, son of Henry and Ann; Edwin Wilmarth, who occupied various town government posts during this time; Luke Prentiss, blacksmith, pound master, fire warden; Abel Wilder, blacksmith; Charles Gunn, grocer; and Charles H. Holmes, dairy farmer (Corey 10–12). Prior to the building of its own church, it held services in Dr. Corliss's house or at the Bottskill Church. By the end of 1837, it had more than 50 members (*Manual* 25–26).

One of the church's first major meetings was held in conjunction with the Bottskill Church to express outrage at the murder of Elijah Lovejoy, the editor of a religious newspaper in Alton, Illinois. The meeting was one of many that occurred throughout the North.

Lovejoy, who was white and a native of Maine, had moved to St. Louis, Missouri, a slave state, where he started his newspaper. He was not an abolitionist, but on April 28, 1836, a black man named McIntosh, who had assaulted a police officer, was seized by a mob in St. Louis. The Alton *Telegraph* described what happened thereafter: "All was silent as death while the executioners were piling the wood around the victim. He said not a word till he felt that the flames had seized him. He then uttered an awful howl, attempting to sing and pray, then hung his head and suffered in silence. After the flames had surrounded their prey—his eyes burned out of his head, and his mouth apparently parched to a cinder—someone in the crowd ... proposed to end his misery by shooting him. But it was replied that he was already out of his pain.

"No, no," cried the [victim], "I am suffering as much as ever. Shoot me! Shoot me!"

"No," exclaimed one of the fiends, "no, he shall not be shot. I would sooner slack the fire if that would increase his misery!" (Pillsbury 63).

Lovejoy's problems began after he wrote an editorial condemning the atrocity. A mob broke into his office and destroyed his printing press. This forced Lovejoy to move 20 miles north to the city of Alton in the free state of Illinois. He resumed his publication and his attacks on the mob. But after only two issues, the mob again descended upon his office and destroyed his press. Lovejoy remained undaunted. He announced that he would resume publication once again as soon as his new press arrived. By this time, he had drawn support from the city's mayor and many others. When the new press arrived on the night of November 6, 1837, it was placed in the store of a man named Gilman, where a number of armed men were stationed to protect it.

Word spread of the press's arrival, and the following night a mob surrounded the store. Gilman attempted to reason with them and warned that anyone who tried to enter his store would be shot. Suddenly, there came a hail of stones and other objects, followed by bullets. Gilman and the other men, who included Lovejoy, returned the fire, killing one of the mob. This caused a retreat, but only a brief one as they returned with a ladder and a torch to set fire to the store. As they mounted the ladder, the Rev. Lovejoy stormed outside. He began firing wildly at the mob but failed to hit anyone. Instead, he made himself an easy target, and the mob riddled him with bullets, killing him (May 221–230).

At the Bottskill Church on December 13, the Lovejoy meeting speakers included the Rev. Colver, Daniel Frost, a trustee of the Free Church who provided a biographical sketch of Lovejoy, and Erastus Culver, then a state assemblyman. Culver resolved that Lovejoy's "untiring zeal in attempting to continue a religious newspaper whose columns were open to free discussion on the great principles of freedom embodied in the Declaration of Independence is what led to his death" ("New York" 168). Lovejoy's martyrdom was probably the most celebrated event of the cause until John Brown seized the arsenal at Harpers Ferry, and his martyrdom sparked a new enthusiasm in the antislavery movement that reinvigorated the Underground Railroad.

An analysis of the Underground Railroad must begin with the consideration of its organization, of the efforts by individuals working together to help fugitive slaves find shelter, sustenance, jobs, and the means to get to the Promised Land, whether it was Canada or a home in the North. Though there is debate about the degree of organization that occurred within the Underground Railroad, there is no question that organization did occur.

An important convention that linked abolitionists in northern and eastern New York met in Albany from February 28 to March 2, 1838, at the Presbyterian Church ("Albany Anti-Slavery Convention" 149–150). Nearly 200 individuals attended, including many who would be linked to the Underground Railroad: Hiram Corliss, who chaired the convention; Gerrit Smith; William Goodell, editor of *Friend of Man*; Beriah Green, president of the Oneida Institute, the state's only institution of higher education that enrolled blacks; Hiram Wilson, an advocate for fugitive slaves in Canada; black leaders Stephen Myers and Nathaniel Paul of Albany; Benjamin Cutler, another black from Albany, whose name would be the subject of an interesting legend 15 years later; Nathaniel Safford, Christopher Hepinstall, William Tweed Dale, and E.P. Freeman, leading white abolitionists of Albany; R.P.G. Wright, the Schenectady barber; the Rev. John D. Lawyer of West Sand Lake; Jabez Parkhurst, the Fort Covington, New York, lawyer; Leonard Gibbs, W.H. Mowry, and Erastus Culver of Union Village; Cornelius Dubois of Saratoga and Thomas C. Green of Saratoga, who donated money to the Canadian mission of Wilson; E.W. Goodwin, future editor of the *Tocsin of Liberty*, a radical anti-slavery newspaper established in Albany in 1841; William L. Chaplin, then secretary of the state society; the Rev. E.C. Pritchett, abolitionist lecturer and future pastor of the Free Church; Charles Van Loon of Dutchess County; Asa Warren from Erie County, George Cuyler from Chenango County, and William C. Bloss from Rochester, New York, all western New York conductors; and Chauncey P. Williams, then from Connecticut, who later would move to Albany and became a member of two local vigilance committees. There also were representatives from New York City, Massachusetts, Vermont, the Finger Lakes region, and Essex County ("Albany Anti-Slavery Convention" 149).*

Thirty-one resolutions were passed by the convention. Among them were number 28, which referred to aiding fugitive slaves, resolving that "we deeply sympathize with our colored brethren on their way from the great prison house of slavery; and also with those who have made good their escape from it and are now located in the province of Canada..."; number 5, which referred to the necessity of using "political power" in addition to "moral suasion" to end slavery; and number 16, which condemned racial prejudice and drew poignant comments from the Rev. Paul (150).

"This is an important resolution in whatever light it is viewed," Paul said in his comments. "No obstacle in the way of abolition is more powerful than prejudice against color. Were I a slaveholder, and you should come to me and ask for the abolition of slavery, I would say to you, go home and do away your wicked prejudice, which prevents colored students from entering your colleges and seminaries, colored children from enjoying the instructions of your infant schools, and pious colored people from sitting at your communion tables, before you preach to me. After you have done that, I will listen; until you do it, I can not hear you" (Ibid.).

This convention was a preview of events to come. Not only was there significant integration—black delegations from Albany and Schenectady attended—but also a large number of delegates (often from disparate locations) that later became associated in the Eastern New York Anti-Slavery Society, which worked closely with the New York Committee of Vigilance.

Another meeting that may have contributed to the region's Underground Railroad followed that summer. The fourth annual convention of the Washington Union Baptist Association consisted of 16 Baptist churches from Washington County, three from Warren County, and two from western Vermont,[†] and took place in the Washington County town of Kingsbury. It issued the following resolution: "Whereas this Association have [sic] for the last two years passed resolutions condemning the abstract sin of slavery ... [and] therefore, wishing to evince our deep abhorrence of the crime of slaveholding, and bear our testimony against the guilt of slaveholders—the time has come when our churches are called upon to proclaim ... that the slaveholder, the man who buys, and sells, and makes merchandize of his fellow beings, who uses his hire without pay, and holds him in bonds of servitude and oppression, should no longer be entitled to our fellowship" (Minutes of ... 6–7). This break with Baptists who did not support abolition preceded by seven years a major schism in the Baptist Church that divided churches in the North and South. Among the participants were anti-slavery society members Erastus Culver and Francis Weldon from the Bottskill Church in Union Village; Hiram Shipman, from the Fort Ann Village Church and

*Cutler and Freeman were members of the Albany Vigilance Committee in 1845 ("Albany Liberty Party Convention"); Corliss, Mowry, Goodwin, Hepinstall, Dale, C.P Williams, and Dubois were officers or members of the vigilance committee of the Eastern New York Anti-Slavery Society in 1842 ("Eastern New York Anti-Slavery Society..." 7); Corliss, Mowry, Van Loon, C.P. Williams, Safford, Chaplin, Pritchett, and Freeman were officers or members of the vigilance committee of the ENYASS in 1845 ("Anti-Slavery Society" 110). Various other sources identify the others.

†The churches: Adamsville, Bottskill, Fort Ann Village, Fort Ann, Hartford, Hartford South, Hebron, Ft. Edward, Kingsbury & Hartford, Kingsbury, Lakeville, Granville, Salem, White Creek, Dresden, and N. Greenwich in Washington County; Queensbury, Glens Falls, and Luzerne in Warren County; Rupert and Pawlet in Vermont.

president of the Fort Ann Anti-Slavery Society; the Rev. William Cormack from the Kingsbury Church; John Carlisle from Hartford; and the Rev. Andrew Wait and the Rev. B. Allen from Vermont.

The Vermont connection is particularly interesting. A look at the roster of convention delegates supports Siebert's claim that an Underground Railroad route was established from New York to Vermont "at the point where the Battenkill River crosses the western boundary of the State" (Siebert 68). The Battenkill River, which passes through the middle of Union Village, navigates gently thereafter through a conveniently situated valley between the Green Mountains into Vermont. Among the Vermont towns that may have harbored fugitive slave along this route were the town of Rupert, just over the border from New York and about ten miles north of the Battenkill. Today only a tiny hamlet without a stop light, Rupert in 1830 was a thriving community of more than 1300, larger than Union Village. Rupert's Baptist Church was a member of the Washington Union Baptist Association (WUBA), and an 1899 history of the town states, "few communities [were] as largely anti-slavery [as Rupert and] several of [their] citizens were familiar with the Underground Railroad (Hibbard 37–38). Another nearby Vermont town that may have been a stop was Pawlet, whose Baptist Church also was a WUBA member. Its pastor, the Rev. Andrew Wait, a participant at the 1838 convention, also was for a time pastor of the Rupert Baptist Church. In addition, the the Rev. B. Allen was a member of the executive committee of the Washington County Anti-Slavery Society in 1836.

The WUBA served more than 3,000 individuals and its abolitionist views undoubtedly had a strong influence in the region (*Minutes of...* 3–5).

As abolitionists organized in northern New York, the state society urged its members to increase its efforts to aid fugitive slaves. In April, 1838, William L. Chaplin, secretary of the state society, called for the organization of vigilance committees in the larger communities in *Friend of Man*. "Cases proper for the action of a vigilance committee are occurring every week in the year in this city [Utica]," he wrote. "And what is true of this city is also true of Albany, Syracuse, Oswego, Rochester, Lockport, Buffalo, and Ogdensburg. Let these committees be organized immediately in all these and perhaps some other places and open a correspondence with the committee in the city of New York" ("Vigilance Committees" *Friend of Man* 170). The next month the American Anti-Slavery Society made a similar request ("Vigilance Committees" *Emancipator* 103).

By the end of 1838, more than 1,300 anti-slavery societies had formed in the North, and the number was still growing (Goodman 122). Nevertheless, racial prejudice, slavecatchers, and mobs were in equal abundance. Despite the opposition, the public calls by the New York State and American Anti-Slavery societies for the formation of vigilance committees and the report by the New York Committee of Vigilance that it had aided 522 fugitive slaves as of August, 1838, made it clear that the Underground Railroad had become a going concern (*The Mirror of Liberty* 4). The struggle was about to begin a new phase of optimism, and during the next seven years or so, northern New York would play its most active role.

Chapter 8

ESTABLISHING OUTPOSTS

By 1838, Washington County had at least seven anti-slavery societies; the major portion of a large association of churches (the WUBA) committed to anti-slavery; the Free Church in Union Village, small but very influential; and two representatives in the state assembly who were outspoken abolitionists.* But the acknowledged leader was Dr. Corliss, president of the county society. Such was the esteem in which Corliss was held statewide, that in the absence of president Gerrit Smith, he was chosen to preside at the state society's annual meeting in 1837.

The growth of anti-slavery in Washington County also owed much to the Rev. Colver. However, Colver was approached to take over a small congregation in Boston, and he was anxious to put his zeal to work on a large stage. In 1838, he decided to resign from the Bottskill Church, after having added 600 members and a monthly abolition service in concert with the Free Church (*Minutes* 10). The church trustees requested that Colver remain another year and he agreed, leaving Union Village for Boston in the fall of 1839 to take over as pastor of the then nascent Tremont Street Church, which under Colver became nationally renowned as a meeting place of abolitionists.

Colver's departure did not affect the cause in Union Village. There were many other devoted abolitionists there and in the rest of the county. Nearby Argyle, for instance, was home to the United Presbyterian Church, an association of three churches that supported abolition. These churches were ministered to by the Rev. Alexander Bullions in Cambridge, the Rev. George Mairs in Argyle village, and the Rev. James P. Miller in South Argyle. Among its prominent abolitionist members was elder and town official Anthony McKallor.

In 1836, Miller spent time establishing missions in the Lower Canada communities of Hemmingford, Hinchinbrook, and Beach Ridge, close to the Clinton and

Erastus Culver and Leonard Gibbs.

Franklin county borders. This association also established a mission in Spencerville, Canada, near Prescott, which was just across the St. Lawrence from Ogdensburg, a terminus of a fugitive slave route (Scouller 69). This is not to say that any evidence of the churches forwarding fugitive slaves over this route exists, but it is interesting that the churches had ties in these locations just across the Canadian border.

In nearby Saratoga County, Quaker Mason Anthony of Greenfield had begun aiding fugitive slaves at least as early as 1838 and was taking them up through Warren County. An August 20 letter that year from conductor Chauncy L. Knapp, the Vermont secretary of state, stated: "[The] lad who is indebted to your and your father's great kindness for a safe arrival at my friend R.T. Robinson's, is now sitting in my office in the State House. He wishes, first of all to return to yourself and your father's family ten thousand thanks for the generous assistance afforded him in his extremity. Providentially, I arrived at friend Robinson's only an hour after your departure; and on Saturday last took the lad (now Charles) and brought him on to Montpelier, a distance of 43 miles" ("Anti-Slavery in Action in 1838..." 7–8). Further evidence of Underground Railroad organization in that county is supported by the presence at anti-slavery meetings in Ballston Spa in September of R.P.G. Wright, and in October 1838 of his son, the Rev. Theodore Wright, and James Canning Fuller, a well-documented conductor from Central New York ("Anti-Slavery Convention"; "Saratoga Anti-Slavery Meeting").

During the summer of 1839, a major regional convention was held in Union Village that attracted Gerrit Smith; Henry Stanton, the state society's president; Joshua Leavitt, editor of *Emancipator*; William L. Chaplin, the state society's secretary; R.G. Williams, the state society's treasurer; and prominent anti-slavery lecturers E.M.K. Glen and the Rev. Luther Lee. The convention was the second of two major conventions called by the state society that month, the first held the week before in Auburn. Stanton covered both of them for the *Pennsylvania Freeman*. In his narrative, which in those days included a kind of travelogue, Stanton refers to an overnight stay at Safford's Temperance House in Albany, "the house where all abolitionists stop." Nathaniel Safford, who was the proprietor, also was mentioned as among the participants in Auburn.

The convention in Union Village was held for two days, in both the Bottskill Church and the new Free Church. It must have been an attractive building, white with pillars like a Greek temple, but apparently made of wood as it was built by carpenter Samuel Randall and his son, Orlando (Morhous 14). It had a turret-like steeple, which after 1850 had a clock, and sat almost directly across the street from Dr. Corliss's house, where he also kept his office. It would host many more anti-slavery events and lecturers, including William Lloyd Garrison, George Thompson, England's greatest anti-slavery orator, and Frederick Douglass.

Strong support for abolition was demonstrated by the pledge of $1,400 to the state society ($22,000 based on the year 2001). Among matters discussed were political action and the advocacy of voting against the Whigs Van Buren and Clay in the upcoming election; the lack of support from the churches; and the duty to aid fugitive slaves. Stanton remarked that the latter was a topic of great interest both here and at the Auburn convention, with Gerrit Smith leading the discussion at both.

"Unless I greatly misread the signs of the times," Stanton wrote, "the day is

Orthodox Congregational "Free" Church, Greenwich, New York. (From Helen Andrews-Hoag, *A Walk in the Village*, Greenwich, NY, 1997.)

rapidly approaching when it will be ... impossible for the despots of the South to carry the panting fugitive back to chains from central and northern New York..." ("Letter from Mr. Stanton" 4).

Such statements were being made throughout the state. For instance, the Dutchess County Anti-Slavery Society, which forged a link in the chain comprising the network between New York City and northern New York, declared in 1840 that, "We will collectively and severally will do all in our power to assist those of our brethren, coming through this county that may have thus far escaped the iron grasp of tyranny, by giving them meat, money, and clothes, to enable them to prosecute their journey to a LAND OF LIBERTY" ("The Second Anniversary..." 35).

We also find a letter that year regarding the forwarding of fugitive slaves from Troy abolitionist the Rev. Fayette Shipherd. The letter is addressed to Garret Van Hoosen, of Hoosick in northern Rensselaer County near the border with Washington County, but is written to Charles Hicks of Bennington County, Vermont. Apparently, Shipherd did not think it wise to send the letter by mail, but had it delivered personally by Van Hoosen. Not only does the letter indicate a route from Troy to Vermont, but also one through Washington County via the Champlain Canal, which was apparently closed at this time because of the onset of winter. The letter is dated November 24:

> As the canal has closed I shall send my Southern friends along your road & patronize your house. We had a fine run of business during the season. C.G. We had 22 in two weeks 13 in the city at one time. Some of them noble looking fellows I assure you. One female so near white & so beautiful that her master had been offered at different times $1,200–1,500 & 2,000 for foulest

ANTI-SLAVERY SOCIETY.
Elected Sept. 1840.

President.—ALVAN STEWART, of Utica.

Vice Presidents.—John Northrup, Lewis, co.; Jesse Campbell, Herkimer co.; Arthur Tappan, N. Y. co,. Jabez Parkhurst, Franklin co.; Horatio Pattingell Otsego co.; Fayette Shipherd, Renssellaer co.; L. P. Noble, Albany co.; James C. Fuller, Onondaga co.: J. Copeland, Chenango do ; John Thomas, Cortland co.; Marcus Smith, Jefferson co.; Samuel Keese, Clinton co.; Henry Sackrider, St. Lawrence co. S. W. Stewart, Oneida co.; John Rankin, Kings co.; Samuel Thompson, Dutchess co.; Zebulon Shepard, Essex, co.; Hiram Corliss, Washington co ; Asa Raymond, Madison co.: James Brown, Oswego co ; Thomas C. Green Saratoga co., Gurdon Judson, Fulton co.; John Fry, Montgomery co.; R. P. G. Wright, Schenectada co ; A G. Hawley, Warren co.; Peter Roe, Orange co.

Executive Committee.—UTICA—James C. Delong, Chairman, Job Parker, Alfred H. Hunt, John B. Owens, Asaph Seymour, Edward Vernon, D. Plumb, Geo. L. Brown.

WHITESBORO—William Goodell, Beriah Green, Reuben Hough, Thomas Beebe.

NEW YORK MILLS—Ira Pettibone, Stephen S. Sheldon.

Treasurer.—Samuel Lightbody, Utica.

Corresponding Secretary.—Edward C. Pritchett, Utica.

List of officers of the New York State Anti-Slavery Society, 1840. (From Friend of Man, 23 September 1840: 200.)

purposes. A Baltimore officer—a man hunter was seen in our city making his observations but left without giving us any trouble. Several slaves were in our city from Baltimore at the time. Our Laws are now a terror to evil doers who live by robbery [Letter from Fayette Shipherd...].

Shipherd was referring in the last sentence to the passage of two laws in May 1840 by the state legislature. The first guaranteed a trial by jury to alleged fugitive slaves, and the second provided protections to free citizens of New York State "from being kidnapped, or reduced to slavery." The latter law gave power to the governor to send a commissioned agent to restore the liberty of any free citizen of the state, of whom the governor believed the evidence warranted that they were wrongly being held in slavery.

How far north the network extended by 1840 is not known, but a possible indicator is the passage of the Habeas Corpus Act in the Province of Lower Canada. This made it illegal to kidnap any "subject of his Majesty that now is or hereafter shall be an inhabitant of this Province" ("Plattsburgh, Jan. 20, 1838" 2). A report of its passage with a verbatim text of the law was published in the Plattsburgh Republican in Clinton County. This indicates that it was a matter of some importance to its readership, some of whom already may have been assisting fugitive slaves.

The Peru Female Anti-Slavery Society confessed as much in their 1841 report: "Shall we withhold this cup of cold water from the toil-worn slave and the panting fugitive ... In the name of humanity, we answer NO! Remember that we are candidates for immortality, and let us perform our part, that at the final review, when there shall be neither servant nor master, the soul-cheering language may be applicable to us, 'inasmuch as ye did it unto none of the least of these my brethren, ye did it unto me'" ("Sixth Annual Report..." 2–3).

Peru, the home of the large Quaker meeting, the Union, was another likely

Underground Railroad terminal. There already were three anti-slavery societies in that community when the county society organized in 1837: the female society, a male counterpart at the Union, and the West Peru society. In all, there were ten anti-slavery societies in the county by 1839—this in a county whose population was half that of Washington County.

The year 1840 was one of growing

{ UNIONVILLE, WASHINGTON CO.,
September 1, 1840.

Dear Bro. Goodell,—While waiting here for the arrival of a fugitive whom we are going to take towards the North Star, I write to let you know we have have had a pretty good meeting at Waterford and here, besides other lectures. The Saratoga folks will let you know about their meeting. Here they passed strong resolutions on ecclesiastical and political action, approving the National and State nominations, and called a county meeting for making county nominations, an Monday, Sept. 14, at Argyle, Yours, &c.,
EDWARD C. PRITCHETT.

Report of a Liberty Party meeting in Union Village, where aid is being provided to a fugitive slave. (From *Friend of Man*, 9 September 1840: 189.)

acceptance of the Underground Railroad. An editorial that year in *Friend of Man* proclaimed: "Look through the whole country. What measure of the abolitionists is regarded with more sympathy and favor than efforts to assist the fugitive?" ("The Progress..." 190). A similar sentiment also was expressed at the annual meeting of the state anti-slavery society three weeks later: "We view with increased interest and approbation the efforts of slaves to escape from the southern Bastille and the efforts of Vigilance Committees and others to 'hide the outcasts, to protect them that wander, and to be a covert to them from the face of the spoiler'" ("State Anti-Slavery Meeting" 201).

Among the list of the officers of the New York State Anti-Slavery Society elected in September 1840 were likely associates in the Underground Railroad. Elected as vice-presidents of counties in northeastern New York were Jabez Parkhurst of Franklin County, Samuel Keese of Clinton County, Zebulon Shipherd of Essex County, Hiram Corliss of Washington County, A.G. Hawley of Warren County, Thomas C. Green of Saratoga County, Fayette Shipherd of Rensselaer County, R.P.G. Wright of Schenectady County, and L.P. Noble of Albany County ("List of the Officers..." 200). What is intriguing about this list is that all but Hawley have legends or associations that link them to the Underground Railroad.

Further testimony supporting the existence of an Underground Railroad organization in the region at this time was a brief item in *Friend of Man* in 1840 by the Rev. Pritchett writing from Union Village and beginning: "While waiting here for the arrival of a fugitive whom we are going to take towards the North Star, I write to you..." ("Communications" 189). Pritchett became pastor of the Free Church the following year, a position he held for five years.

By 1840, abolitionists in New York State had effectively organized the framework of the Underground Railroad that would remain in place until the Civil War. In northern New York, the next five years would be its most extroverted period.

Chapter 9

ANOTHER STRATEGY

The Gag Rule, the suppression of abolitionist mail, the resistance of the nation's churches, and the continued support for colonization led many abolitionists to realize that moral suasion alone could not succeed in ending slavery. For several years, New York State leaders had been discussing the need for political action. However, William Lloyd Garrison, the nation's leading abolitionist, was adamantly opposed to the use of political action to end slavery. For him, it was futile because he believed the Constitution, which allowed slavery, was a pro-slavery document. If abolitionists were unable to persuade the South to give up slavery, according to Garrison's position, the only remedy was disunion. A growing faction of abolitionists, and the majority of those in New York State, took a different view; they believed that based on the Declaration of Independence, slavery was unconstitutional and that the Constitution could be amended to bring its abolition. For them political action was necessary and the next logical step for the abolitionist movement.

To achieve this end, a national convention was held in Albany on April 1, 1840, to form the first anti-slavery political party, to be called the Liberty Party. Chosen president of the convention was Alvan Stewart. Among its vice-presidents was Charles Turner Torrey, a young Congregational minister from Worcester, Massachusetts, who had been an early advocate of the third party movement. Devout and brash, he had already confronted Garrison for his refusal to support political action and had been one of the leaders of the schism of the Massachusetts Anti-Slavery Society over this issue (Brooks 324–327). After two brief pastorates in Providence, Rhode Island, and Salem, Massachusetts, he had begun to focus his energies on writing for abolition publications and wanted to start his own newspaper. In the fall of 1842, he would move to Albany.

No representatives north of Rensselaer County attended the Liberty convention, but Hiram Corliss sent a letter that was read into the minutes. The purpose of the meeting was to select presidential and vice-presidential candidates for the 1840 election. The main resolution began with a reference to a prior convention in Albany that had urged abolitionists to refrain from voting for candidates who did not support immediate abolition. It continued as follows: "And, whereas, in the judgment of this Convention, it becomes the anti-slavery electors of our country to unite their votes upon well qualified candidates, for those high offices at the ensuing election, and, in our estimation, no such candidates are yet nominated, and none are likely to be without an interference:—Therefore, Resolved, That we owe it to the sacred cause of HUMAN RIGHTS, and our desire to advance it by all peaceful and constitutional means, to make such nomination" ("National Anti-Slavery Nominating Convention" 1).

James G. Birney, a former slaveholder and member of the Colonization Society, was selected as the presidential candidate. Birney, a native of Kentucky, had freed his slaves in 1834 and moved to Cincinnati in 1836, where he started an abolitionist newspaper, the *Philanthropist*. Three times his press was destroyed and his life was threatened. Finally, in 1837, he moved to New York City to become secretary of the American Anti-Slavery Society (Macy 33–40). Now he was accepting the nomination of a party that challenged the authority of his society.

One month later, the American Anti-Slavery Society met in New York, and disagreement arose over another issue. This concerned the participation of women on an equal footing in the society. The two sides were at odds and could come to no agreement. Finally, a large though minority group split off and established the American and Foreign Anti-Slavery Society, installing the former president of the American Anti-Slavery Society, Arthur Tappan, as its president (Brooks 327). The new organization supported political action but did not support the full participation of women. It was supported by many abolitionist clergy, who had been alienated by Garrison's growing anti-clericalism. Like the new Liberty Party, which many in the American and Foreign Anti-Slavery Society supported, they believed that the Constitution was fundamentally anti-slavery.

The majority of upstate abolitionists supported the American and Foreign Anti-Slavery Society and Liberty Party. The influences of religion, so important in northern New York, played a strong role. As one historian has remarked, "Ecclesiastical abolitionism, as expressed in ... anti-slavery congregations, and political abolitionism, as expressed in the ... Liberty party, were two manifestations of the same movement" (Strong).

Northern New York's involvement in the Liberty Party, although slow at first, increased gradually. In Washington County, among candidates placed on the 1840 election ballot under the Liberty Party banner were Hiram Corliss for Congress; Hiram Shipman of Fort Ann for Sheriff; and William Mowry of Greenwich for Clerk ("Washington County" 7). In Saratoga County, candidates included Thomas C. Green for Congress and Asa Anthony of Greenfield for Assembly ("Saratoga County" 10). Birney drew only about 7,000 votes nationwide in the 1840 election, with about 2,800 coming from New York State, and little more than 200 votes from the counties north of Albany.* However, the new party soon attracted the majority of the state's abolitionists as evidenced by the large turnout in February 1841 for the state convention of abolitionists in favor of political organization in Albany. Presiding over the con-

*Exact counts of the vote vary among sources.

vention were Alvan Stewart as president with Hiram Corliss and Nathaniel Safford of Albany as vice-presidents.

Many of those associated with the Underground Railroad were on the roster of the convention, though noticeably absent were the names of black abolitionists ("Convention at Albany" 67). This might be explained by the outcome of the first state convention of black Americans that had been held in Albany during the summer of 1840. The lack of progress in the cause of anti-slavery was paralleled by a similar intractability in the movement for equal rights and had caused a similar division among the nation's black leaders. Some saw their best hope to be Canadian colonization, others moral improvement, and others put their faith in political action (Foner and Walker xii).

Black leaders in New York were inclined to agree with their white brethren on the matter of political action, and the focus of the black state convention was the reinstatement of full suffrage for blacks, whose right in New York had been limited by a property qualification in 1821. In all, 140 delegates attended, including New York Committee of Vigilance members the Rev. Wright, Charles Ray, William P. Johnson, and R.P.G. Wright. Chosen president of the convention was Austin Steward, and other participants included William H. Topp, Stephen Myers, and Charles Morton of Albany, Henry Garnet of Troy, and John Wendall of Schenectady. The plan of action chosen was the selection of a committee of correspondence to circulate petitions calling for the reinstatement of full suffrage that would be submitted to the state legislature. A resolution to support the Liberty Party was defeated because it was not thought advisable at this time "for a body of disenfranchised men to adopt a measure which identified them with a voting party," though "the third party ... had in the convention warm friends, and some of its ablest men" (7).

The search for a new strategy for change through political action was an unconscious admission by abolitionists that ending slavery and gaining equal rights was going to take a lot longer than they had anticipated. As they discussed their new strategy in the ongoing battle, right under their very noses, in northern New York, the foes they were battling continued at work. Among them was an unlikely emissary of the colonization society, the Rev. George Brown, a Methodist minister, who also was black.

The son of an elder in the Baptist Church, Brown had left his native Rhode Island in 1821 at the age of 20. For a number of years he traveled about and engaged in drinking and other worthless pursuits before coming to Washington County, where he got a job on the farm of Samuel Cole in Kingsbury in 1827 (Brown 8, 13). An interesting entry from 1828 refers to his meeting with the famed abolitionist preacher Nathaniel Colver for help with his alcohol problem. Brown states directly that he did not like Colver, and though this is before Colver became an abolitionist, it does foreshadow his future relations with abolitionists (Brown 13). Nevertheless, he did find help from others, was born again, joined the Methodist Church, and began preaching.

Brown's first service was held in the little Beach schoolhouse on Vaughn Road. In 1829, he moved in with Goold Sanford in Queensbury, joining the Quarterly Conference of the Methodist Episcopal Church (Graham 5). Two years later, he became a licensed preacher and conducted the Sunday school at Sanford's Ridge. His preaching circuit included Caldwell, Dunham's Bay, Cedar Landing, Tavern House, and Gage Hill. From that point forward, "crowds came to hear him that no building was large enough to hold ... [and] many hundreds were soundly converted" (McIlvaine B1).

In 1835, he became an agent for the colonization society, and his journal that year shows generous support for the society in Warren and Washington counties as he toured the area (Brown 64–65). In 1836, he undertook his first mission to Liberia. By 1840, he had already completed two missions there and was preparing for a third, having received a commission to travel and take up collection for the colonization society.

His journal of September 10, 1840, reads: "I have just returned from a blessed camp meeting in Chester, Warren county. Here I saw probably three hundred of the church with whom I had been acquainted for years. This was a great refreshment to me, because their devotion sounded so much like our devotion to Africa.... I preached a Missionary sermon at this meeting, and raised $120" (180).

His journal also shows appearances that month in Hebron, Washington County, and in Pawlet, West Poultney, and Brandon, Vermont. However, in the latter place, he "was attacked by an abolitionist" (181). Among the places his travels took him thereafter were Troy, Albany, Fort Ann, Schuylerville, Mechanicville, Saratoga, and Schenectady, and most contributed generously to the colonization cause. By the middle of October, he writes: "I am now on my way to Africa. This morning I left all my one thousand friends at Glens Falls, and my two thousand enemies at the north, until we all meet at the Judgment seat of Christ" (181).

It is apparent that while the colonization society still had supporters in northern New York—it is not unreasonable to assume that much of his support was the result of prior friendships and associations—there also was opposition that based on his own description was double that of his support.

Brown indicates in his journal that he reached Africa again on March 2, 1841. This is important in light of the conjecture surrounding the creator of the Stone Chair in Kingsbury, Washington County. On the stone is inscribed the date May 23, 1841. It is not known what it signifies, but some believe it to be the date the markings on the stone were made. If so, this would mean that Brown was not its creator. In any case, it is highly unlikely that Brown, a missionary for the colonization society, was involved in the Underground Railroad. The latter also puts in question the belief that the house he built at the corner of Geer and Underwood Roads in the town of Kingsbury was a station on the Underground Railroad.

The experiences of Brown are important because while they show the colonization of blacks was already being rejected by many in the North by 1840, it still had many adherents. The prejudice it engendered was a great hindrance to the rights of blacks and indirectly contributed to a climate that allowed kidnappers to operate even in northern New York, as shown by the ordeal of Solomon Northup, a free black man who was a native of the same community as the Rev. Brown.

About the time Brown was arriving in Africa, the 33-year-old Northup was taking a morning stroll through the village of Saratoga. Two white strangers approached him. They said they worked for a circus and needed a musician. Northup was known to be a fiddle player and occasionally found work performing. They asked if he would

Close-up photograph of the Stone Chair. (Photograph by the author.)

come to New York and work with them for a few days in the performances they did to advertise the circus. At the time, Northrup's wife was working in Sandy Hill, about 25 miles north, and living there with their children. He figured it was a good opportunity and agreed to join them.

In retrospect, it seems naive of Northup to readily agree to join these men of whom he knew nothing, especially considering the frequency of kidnappings that occurred in New York City. But this was Saratoga, nearly 200 miles north of the city, and in fact, such kidnappings were actually more likely in states like Pennsylvania or Delaware whose borders touched the South. Considering the great distance they were from the South, and the period in which they lived, when such distances were relatively much greater, it is easier to understand his lack of fear.

After performing one night in Albany, they went to New York City where they urged him to continue to Washington to join their circus. They promised more work and good wages. At their suggestion, they visited the Custom House and obtained the necessary papers that certified Northup as free, an important precaution for a free black man entering a slave state, though Northup thought "at the time ... that the papers were scarcely worth the cost of obtaining them—the apprehension of danger to my personal safety never having suggested itself to me in the remotest manner" (Northup 15).

Northup had been totally conned by the strangers whom he viewed as friends. In fact, in his book, he admits that after everything that had happened he still wasn't totally convinced that they were the individuals responsible for his kidnapping. "They were then, as they had been from the time of our first meeting, extremely kind," Northup wrote of their conduct upon their arrival in Washington. "No opportunity was omitted of addressing me in the language of approbation; while, on the other hand, I was certainly much prepossessed in their favor.... Their constant conversation and manner towards me—their foresight in suggesting the idea of free papers and a hundred other little acts, unnecessary to be repeated—all indicated that they were friends indeed" (16).

In Washington, they further ingratiated themselves by paying him a generous sum for his employment. But the following day they took him to a saloon and drugged him. When Northup awoke, he found himself in chains in a slave pen without his papers or money. He protested but was beaten and the following day was taken south, where he was sold into slavery. While en route farther south, Northup was chained to another slave who, like himself, was a kid-

Solomon Northrup.

napped free man. His predicament was similar to Northup's in that he was hired on a job and taken south before being kidnapped into slavery. So began an ordeal that for most free blacks would continue for the rest of their lives. Fortunately, for Northup, it did come to an end, but only after 12 long years.

What is important about the Solomon Northup incident is that it shows kidnappers were at work in northern New York. It shows that they were crafty individuals and not at all the kind of low class people who are often described as involved in such dealings. Indirectly, their presence there also suggests the presence of fugitive slaves, whom it is apparent were now being regularly aided in the region.

Chapter 10

THE FORGOTTEN ABOLITIONIST

In May 1841, a law was passed that granted automatic freedom to any slave brought into New York State by a slaveholder. Previously, Southerners could bring their slaves into the state for a period of up to nine months. This was a big victory for the abolitionists, especially those committed to change through political action, which applied to most of the abolitionists in the state.*

But more significant to the Underground Railroad in northern New York would be the emergence of a young minister of whom we have already spoken—the Rev. Abel Brown. A small man of nervous temperament and all-consuming fervor, "He seemed to think, one ought to be thankful, to be told of his faults ... [that the greatest kindness was] to convince a person [of this], and point him the remedy in Christ (Brown 210). On May 5, 1841, he took over as pastor of the Sand Lake Baptist Church. A thoroughly abolitionized community west of Albany and Troy, Sand Lake was one of the homes of the Franckean Synod, a small group of Lutheran churches that had split from their denomination in 1837 ("Franckean Lutheran Synod"), and which is believed to have played a large role in the region's Underground Railroad (Rowe Personal Interview).

Brown had come from Northampton, Massachusetts, where his support for those who led the schism of the Massachusetts Anti-Slavery Society had put him out of favor with his congregation. Before coming to Massachusetts, he had been an agent for the Western Anti-Slavery Society in Beaver, Pennsylvania, located along the Ohio River. There he lectured tirelessly on anti-slavery, which led to several assaults upon him. When he wasn't speaking for anti-slavery, he was aiding fugitive slaves. On one trip to Baltimore for this purpose, he was arrested but released after no evidence was found (Brown 86–87).

---

*The state society's annual meeting that year resolved "that the Liberty Party has the strongest claims to the sympathy and support of all the friends of freedom; and that all who have access to the ballot box ought to express that sympathy, and give up their support by voting only for abolitionists" (Friend of Man 21 Sept. 1841: 186).

While at Sand Lake, Brown joined the staff of a new anti-slavery paper based in Albany, the *Tocsin of Liberty* ("tocsin" meaning alarm). It debuted on October 15, 1841, with Edwin W. Goodwin, a portrait painter from Auburn, as its editor. From the start, it was fearless in its comments and in its reports of local aid to fugitive slaves. The announcements, boldly contemptuous in tone, were packaged in a series of letters written by Brown. Among them are the following excerpts:

> E. W. GOODWIN, Esq. Dear Sir :—The vigilance committee are up to their elbows in work, and are desirous to have you inform a few of those men who have lately lost *property* ... that we are always on hand, and ready to ship cargoes on the shortest notice, and ensure a safe passage over the 'Great Ontario' [119].

> Mr. Editor: *Certain gentlemen,* who take such a deep interest in the welfare of Miss Leah Brown, lately held in servile bondage by Mrs. McDonald, are hereby informed that Leah ... is beyond the *reach* of those men who have lately offered *one hundred dollars* for her delivery... [120].

> *Please also inform* Robert Gilmore of Baltimore, that he need not give himself further trouble about his very intelligent and noble slaves, Marianna, Polly, Elisabeth Castle, and her fine little girl, for they have got safe over the great Ontario ... Tell him also, that his slave John Weston left here more than a week since, at full speed, in a fine carriage drawn by fleet horses, and report says, there were not less than six well loaded pistols in the hands of John and his associates [120–121].

> Not many weeks since, a licensed exhorter of the Methodist Episcopal Church arrived in this city, and came so well recommended that there could hardly be a doubt but that he was just what he professed to be, a pious Christian man, who had been a slave more than thirty years. He had taken his wife and children, and in the night fled from the land of robbers. The woods and swamps were the abodes of himself and family for weeks. He found at last a friend, who kindly offered to protect his wife and little ones, until he should flee to Canada, and earn sufficient to defray the expense of moving his family to that land of freedom [122].

> There is one Mr. Woodford, living far below Baltimore, whom we wish you to inform ... respecting that woman, Eliza Wilson, whom he pounded with sticks of wood, whom he stripped naked again and again, and whipped with the cat and nine tails, until her body was completely lacerated ... Tell him that ... she is now beyond his reach [123].

> Tell Mrs. Widow Margaret A. Culver, that the reward of $100 which she offered for her slave Levi, put us on the watch, and sure enough, he came [to] us ... We trust she will send us forthwith, $25.00, as a reward for telling her where he may be found. We think he is now about half way over the *Great Ontario* [123].

> One day last week eight noble persons arrived, all panting for liberty. It only cost about twenty-five dollars to colonize them. A certain knave in New-Orleans owned two of them, and another who intended to have come with them, and who laid the plan for their escape, was whipped to death by Joseph Wolcott [123].

Letter of introduction for a fugitive slave from Abel Brown to Charles Hicks. (Courtesy of the Vermont Historical Society.)

Another letter during this period not published but preserved by the Vermont Historical Society has Brown sending a fugitive slave to Charles Hicks of the town of Bennington, Vermont. Dated June 9, 1842, it says in part, "Please receive the Bearer as a friend who needs your aid and direct him on his way if you cannot give him work he come to us well recommended was a slave a few weeks since" (Letter from Abel Brown...).

Brown helped these fugitive slaves through his agency with the Eastern New York Anti-Slavery Society. Its organizational meeting, a two-day session at Albany's City Hall, brought together about 100 delegates, representing 16 northeastern New York counties, as well as supporters from Vermont, Massachusetts, and Rhode Island. Its territory included "all those [counties] bordering the Hudson, those on Long and Staten Islands, together with Delaware, Schoharie, Montgomery, Schenectady, Fulton, Essex, Hamilton, Washington and Warren" (116). Brown became its corresponding secretary and general agent. Vice-presidents from northern New York included Noadiah Moore from Clinton County, Dr. Conant from Franklin County, Oliver Arnold from Warren County, Cornelius Dubois from Saratoga County, Ellis Clizbe from Montgomery

County,* and William H. Mowry from Washington County. Elected president was Hiram Corliss.† Perhaps the most intriguing revelation, in terms of the network forged by the society, is that Arthur Tappan also was a vice-president, representing Kings County ("Eastern New York..." 7).

Joining them was the Rev. Charles T. Torrey, who had moved to Albany after a harrowing experience while reporting a slaveholders' convention in Annapolis, Maryland, for the *New York Evangelist*. Torrey, who had been suspected of aiding fugitive slaves in Washington, D.C., because of his frequent trips to the black community there, found himself before an angry mob who might have murdered him had not police intervened and arrested him. Charged with distributing incendiary literature, he was released after the prosecution was not able to present sufficient evidence (Lovejoy 91–99). Appropriately, it was Torrey who made the motion at the Eastern New York Anti-Slavery Society organizational meeting for the following resolution: "That the Executive Committee be authorized to collect and disburse funds for the purpose of aiding fugitive slaves, at their discretion, accounting for the same to the society, as a part of the general duties of the committee" (Brown 151).

Interestingly, three members of the executive committee attended the 1838 Albany convention, and in all, at least ten of those who were either officers or members of the society's executive committee during its four-year existence had attended that earlier convention ("Eastern New York..." 7). The executive committee also shared members with the Albany Vigilance Committee, which reported in December of that year to have aided 350 fugitive slaves (Brown 151). A report by the Eastern New York Anti-Slavery Society dated September 1843 would state that, "It is impossible to estimate the number of slaves that have passed through this route during the past year. The names and history of a large number have been obtained and are on record, but these were only casually taken, many having been passed without any record being made. The Committee would remark that the whereabouts of the Underground Railroad still remain an impenetrable mystery to the whole herd of man-stealing oppressors. Hundreds are yet annually finding their way to freedom" (Annual Report 2).

In any case, these years of the Underground Railroad were perhaps more active than has generally been acknowledged. According to Canadian fugitive slave missionary Hiram Wilson, who had close ties to the Capital Region, about 1,500 fugitive slaves were entering Canada annually during this period ("Upper Canada" 46).

Torrey not only became one of the committee's most active members, but he also joined the *Tocsin* staff. It was apparently the brash, young Torrey, still only 28, who precipitated a feud between the *Tocsin* and another, less "radical" anti-slavery newspaper in Albany, *The Northern Star and Freemen's Advocate*. Published for the first time on January 20, 1842, by "three colored persons," Stephen Myers, John Stewart, and Charles Morton—all of whom attended the 1838 Albany convention as part of the Thompson Society delegation, an organization of blacks devoted to temperance—*The*

---

*Clizbe is one of the individuals identified in the cryptic note from the Eastern New York Anti-Slavery Society annual report to whom NYCV secretary William Johnston sent letters of introduction regarding three fugitive slaves forwarded in 1843.

†Like the New York Anti-Slavery Society, the Eastern New York Anti-Slavery Society strongly supported the Liberty Party and most of its leading members headed up the party organizations in their respective counties. For example, Moore, Corliss, Mowry, and Arnold were officers in their county party organizations.

THE NORTHERN STAR,
And Freeman's Advocate.

JOHN G. STEWART, Editor.

In consequence of not being able to obtain our
dues, we are obliged to suspend the weekly publication of our paper for the present. It will be issued monthly until May next. Publication day,
first Monday of each month.

TERMS.—$1.50 per year; to which will be
added 50 cents, if not paid within six months from
the time of subscribing. Single copies 12¼ cents.

All Agents abroad are requested to collect their
subscriptions as soon as possible.

All persons wishing to subscribe for this paper,
can have it by forwarding their names to STEPHEN
MYERS, Albany, at the office of the Star.

Letters or communications for the Star must be
post-paid.

AGENTS.

C. Van Husen, Hudson.   J. Houghtail, Lenox, Ms.
F. Leppeus, Utica.   J. W. Duffin, Geneva.
J. Jackson, Clarksville.   M. Cross, Catskill.
Wm. A. Tyson, N. York.   J. Springsteen, Boston.
A. White, Ballston Spa   S. Smith, Lee, Mass.
N. Boston, Po'keepsie.   D. S. Thomas, Pittsfield.
R. Johnson, Sandlake.   J.C. Morel, Newark, N.J.
W. W. Brown, Buffalo.   J. W. Logan, Syracuse.
C. S. Remond, Salem.   F. Dana, Schenectady.
Wm. Rich, Troy.   J. Van Pelt, Saratoga.
J. W. Lewis, Concord, N. H.

STEPHEN MYERS, General Agent.
THOMAS HIGGINS, Travelling Agent.
J. W. LOGAN, Travelling Agent for Western
New-York.

Masthead of Northern Star and Freeman's Advocate. (From Northern Star
and Freeman's Advocate, 8 December
1842: 1.)

Northern Star advocated temperance, abolition, and the moral and educational improvement of blacks. It had a wide distribution, likely made through the contacts the publishers had made at the state and national Negro conventions, with agents stretching from Buffalo to Salem, Massachusetts, and Concord, New Hampshire, and from New York City to Saratoga.

References to the feud between the Tocsin and The Northern Star can be found in the latter paper, and it can be inferred that the criticisms had been directed at Stephen Myers ("We have been much amused..." 30).* The dispute apparently dealt with the moderate political view of The Northern Star. However, the feud continued throughout the year and later references mention The Northern Star's incorrect grammar ("The Tocsin...").

In one response to the attack by the Tocsin, Myers penned a lengthy rebuttal, which in part stated:

We supposed that while they advocated the rights of man and the cause of suffering humanity, that they would have been foremost in opening every avenue, and destroying every barrier in their power that was closed against us, or that retarded our progression.... They profess to be opposed to slavery, but with the greater portion of them we believe that it is that slavery only which exists at the south [italics added].

Myers continued with words that echoed those of Nathaniel Paul five years earlier at the Albany convention:

Now we ask if the prejudice which exists at the north is not akin to the slavery of the south? We firmly believe it to be so, and if the prejudice of the northern abolitionists will not permit them to take as apprentices colored boys, or if their regard for the prejudices of others will not allow them to do so, we also believe that the influence of their example is more injurious to colored people at large, than the disinclination of the slave holder to release the victims of his avarice. And until abolitionists eradicate prejudice from their own hearts, they never can receive the unwavering confidence of the people of color (italics added). We

*Unfortunately, because only few extant issues of the Tocsin have survived, the author has been unable to view those in which the attacks on The Northern Star appear.

do not ask for money, neither do we wish them to educate our children; these we will endeavor to provide for by the sweat of our brow, but we do ask that their workshops may be opened to our youth, and that those of us who are already in business may be patronized. These things (if there be any meaning in their language) we think we have a right to ask ... and if they will grant what we actually want ... we shall the more readily believe them sincere in their professions ["For several years..."].

In retrospect, the criticisms of the *Tocsin* appear to be the result of their lack of sensitivity to the position of black leaders at this time. The latter's more moderate position had developed because of the greater likelihood that unpopular and radical views expressed by blacks would provoke retaliation. For example, the decision not to officially endorse the Liberty Party at the 1840 black state convention was made in order not to alienate any of their fellow abolitionists, and so a middle-ground position was taken.

Stephen Myers. (From William Henry Johnson, *Autobiography of Dr. William Henry Johnson*, Albany: Argus Company Printers, 1900.)

An issue that has not been studied is whether disagreements like this and the national schism over the use of political action affected the operation of the Underground Railroad. *The Northern Star and Freeman's Advocate*, which represented Albany's black community, claimed that locals had been aiding fugitive slaves since 1831 (Editorial).* In its December 8, 1842, issue, Stephen Myers wrote, "I will say a few words in relation to slaves who have passed through this city. There was one sent to our office by Mr. Morrell of Newark. We put him on board of a canal boat, paid his passage to Oswego, and furnished him with money to go into Canada.... We assisted two slaves that were sent to our office by William Garner of Elizabethtown [N.J.]; we furnished them with money for Canada by way of Lake Champlain" ("To the Public" 2). In the following decade, a group led by Myers claimed to be helping hundreds of fugitive slaves, so this admission and the reference to 1831 show that by Meyers's aid to

---

*An illustration of the early concern with anti-slavery by Albany's black community was the formation of a black female Lundy Society there in 1833.

fugitive slaves probably was ongoing throughout the antebellum period. The question is whether they worked separately from or in tandem during the time the Eastern New York Anti-Slavery Society group of Brown and Torrey was active. In any case, so far as we can tell, Abel Brown was not a party to the dispute, nor was Henry Garnet, another Eastern New York Anti-Slavery Society member who also was active in the Underground Railroad. Apparently the feud faded, and it likely was forgotten after Torrey left Albany in the fall of 1843.

On March 1, 1842, there was a more serious development. The Prigg Decision by the Supreme Court threatened the security of all blacks in the North. It decreed that states had no right to interfere with the recovery of slaves by their owner. In effect, it overruled the right of a trial by jury in New York State for fugitive slaves, which had been granted by the 1840 state law, and put complete authority of the disposition of a fugitive slave into the hands of the slaveholder or his or her representative. In a March 17 editorial, *The Northern Star and Freemen's Advocate* wrote: "We believe there is much danger and we warn our people to watch." ("Decision of the Supreme Court") The *Tocsin's* warning was more ominous: "Several good citizens in our city have taken the alarm, and are fleeing and are making preparations to flee, as fast as possible to the land of HER MAJESTY" ("Decision of the Supreme Court" *National Anti-Slavery Standard* 189). The more moderate tone of *The Northern Star* is apparent in further cautioning: "We are not, however, prepared to advise our people to assemble and organize associations, for the purpose of self-defense, or to declare their determination to oppose the law of the land" ("Decision of the Supreme Court").

In Troy a meeting, among whose participants was a Troy laborer referred to as "Mr. Fitch," the Prigg Decision was declared unconstitutional and slavecatchers were decried as devils whom all blacks had the right to resist ("Decision of the Supreme Court" *National Anti-Slavery Standard*).

Fortunately, the early fears that the Prigg Decision would result in wholesale reclamations and kidnappings of fugitive slaves and free blacks never materialized. The Supreme Court had left a loophole in its decision when it stated that such reclamations could be only made through the use of federal authorities. As a result, Massachusetts, Vermont, Pennsylvania, and Rhode Island passed Personal Liberty Laws that forbid the use of state officers and jails in cases involving fugitive slaves. This in effect nullified the Prigg Decision because of the difficulties involved in placing all the responsibility on reclamation with the federal government. In addition, Connecticut already had a similar law on the books before the decision. Though New York's law which granted fugitive slaves a trial by jury became moot, its 1840 and 1841 laws that protected free blacks from kidnapping and that forbid slaveholders from bringing slaves into the state, and the Personal Liberty Laws passed by neighboring states, were enough to render the Prigg Decision powerless.

For all of Torrey's faults, he was instrumental in the transfer of runaways into the hands of the area vigilance committees. So successful were they that, before long, a $1,500 reward was offered to Albany police for the apprehension of Brown, Torrey, and their associate, Goodwin. It is surprising that they weren't kidnapped as they earlier had found that Albany Police were attempting to kidnap free blacks and sell them into slavery (Brown 139). Nevertheless, the unabashed conductors published a report of the offer and added that because of their need for funds to help fugitive slaves who continued to seek their aid, they would go to Baltimore for half that sum, provided the money was deposited in a bank in their names (150).

They not only needed funds for fugitives but for themselves. Torrey was not able to support his family, and his wife and children were forced to move back to Massachusetts to the home of his in-laws after living in Albany for about a year (Lovejoy 86–87). Brown, who had left his pastorate in Sand Lake in April 1842, remained in Albany where he was constantly on the move to avoid harassment from anti-abolitionists and fellow Baptist ministers in Albany who were opposed to his methods. To complicate matters, the Whig Party had filed charges against him for what they claimed were libelous statements about Henry Clay

Charles T. Torrey

after Brown distributed a circular that called Clay, among other things, a man stealer.

This was a traumatic period for Brown. His wife Mary, who had been editor of the benevolent magazine *The Golden Rule* and who had opened their house to many fugitive slaves, passed away after a short illness. This forced him to send his two young children to live with his parents in Fredonia. As his biographer wrote, "Mr. Brown was surrounded by men of violence and blood; who, ere the remains of his deceased wife were removed, threatened the destruction of his house—and he often was obliged to seek refuge at night in some habitation of his friends, unknown to his enemies" (Brown 146).

In spite of the turmoil, Brown, Torrey and their associates were successful in assisting many runaway slaves to freedom. The annual report of the Eastern New York Anti-Slavery Society's vigilance committee in 1843 stated: "The persons engaged in aiding fugitive slaves within the bounds of the Eastern N.Y. Anti-Slavery Society's operations are numerous. There are committees in New York, Albany and Troy, whose business it is to aid these 'children of sorrow' on their way. Many of these men engage in these efforts at a great personal sacrifice of time, reputation and money.... Some of them have already spent what little of this world's goods they called their own, and still they can rejoice in these labors of mercy" (*Annual Report of the Committee* 2).

Chapter 11

HEARD IT THROUGH THE GRAPEVINE

If you consult the etymology of the word grapevine, meaning a secret communication, you find it first used during the Civil War as the "grapevine telegraph." However, Wilbur Siebert credits this usage earlier, as a description of the secret communications between conductors of the Underground Railroad (Siebert *Underground Railroad...* 56). Secrecy would seem prudent, considering the illegality of the operation and the efforts made to reclaim fugitive slaves by their masters and slave catchers. However, contrary to popular belief, the Underground Railroad was not always so secret, especially during its earlier years.

The Rev. Abel Brown was among the most notorious of those who flaunted his lawbreaking activities. During the summer of 1843, Brown advertised the following letter in the *Vermont Freeman* and the *Albany Patriot*, whose former name was the *Tocsin of Liberty*:

> Mr. Fernandis:—This is to inform you that the noble Robert Hill reached this city in safety and was safely sent on his way rejoicing. We charge you $25 for money paid him and services rendered, and 56 cents for the letter containing the advertisement. Please send a draft for the same.
>
> Abel Brown, *Forwarding Merchant, Albany.*
>
> P.S. The business is very good this year. Please inform the slaves that we are always on hand and ready to receive them [*Vermont Freeman* 3].

Such candid admissions not only alerted slavecatchers but were a public confession of a criminal act, which made the confessor liable to prosecution. Yet, this was not uncommon at this time, as we have seen in the excerpts quoted from the *Tocsin of Liberty*. And the *Tocsin* was not alone. The *Emancipator*, which had become the publication of the American and Foreign Anti-Slavery Society after the schism of 1840, ran a weekly ad during this period for the Boston Vigilance Committee entitled, "Aid the Fugitive." It asked that food, clothing, and money be sent to 21 Cornhill Street in Boston, care of William Nell, a black supporter of Garrison. It was a reflection of the defiant character of those involved in the Underground Railroad, who had no qualms about admitting to breaking the law because they were obeying the higher law of God ("Aid the Fugitive" 23).

Cooler heads, however, began to question its wisdom. A June 29, 1843, editorial in the *National Anti-Slavery Standard*, the organ of the American Anti-Slavery Society, reported that letters had been received "expressing disapprobation and regret at the frequent exposure through the public print of the modes of escape of fugitives.... The result of this exposure has been to bring slave hunters upon the track of the unfortunate fugitive, and to surround him with the most critical dangers" ("To Vigilance Committees" 15). Illustrating the point of the *Standard* in the corresponding issue of the *Emancipator* was a reprint from the *Albany Patriot* with exactly the kind of article the editorial had opposed. It stated: "In regard to the Canada Transportation Line, via Albany ... 'the cry is still they come'—two, yesterday morning and two this morning...." The article reported that the fugitives were transported in "North River towboats" (*Emancipator* 34).

Such openness endangered not only runaways, but also the agents helping them. The brazenness of conductors like Abel Brown and Charles Torrey would not bring them a just reward. Not long after the *Standard's* editorial, the number of advertisements decreased. Though there were exceptions—six months later, Brown ran an ad asking for woolen socks for fugitive slaves that was printed in the *Patriot* and *Liberty Press* in Utica—the general consensus followed the rationale of Frederick Douglass, who at that time concealed the particulars of his own escape to freedom in the 1855 edition of his autobiography.*

"I have never approved of the very public manner, in which some of our western friends have conducted what they call the 'Under-ground Railroad,'" Douglass wrote in that edition, "but which, I think, by their open declarations, has been made, most emphatically, the 'Upper-ground Railroad.' Its stations are far better known to the slaveholders than to the slaves.... Nothing is more evident, than that such disclosures are a positive evil to the slaves remaining, and seeking to escape. In publishing such accounts, the anti-slavery man addresses the slaveholder, not the slave; he stimulates the former to greater watchfulness, and adds to his facilities for capturing his slave. We owe something to the slaves, south of Mason and Dixon's line, as well as to those north of it; and ... we should be careful to do nothing which would be likely to hinder the former, in making their escape from slavery (Douglass *My Bondage and My Freedom* 323–324).

The bold advertisements were not the only clues the Underground Railroad left behind. A good detective can find evidence simply by looking at the commercial ads in the publications with reports of escaping slaves. An example of this can be found in the *Tocsin of Liberty*. Below the masthead of its March 2, 1842, issue are listed seven business owners who served on one or more vigilance committees in Albany from 1842 to 1845. An eighth business owner, while not appearing on any known vigilance committee roster, is nevertheless identified in a number of sources as aiding fugitive

---

*In his final 1881 edition, however, Douglass recants and reveals the story of his escape; notable exceptions were published reports of vigilance committees in Albany, Troy, and Syracuse in 1856 and 1857.

The Tocsin of Liberty,

Published Weekly, at Albany, N. Y.

BY ELDER ABEL BROWN,

Under the special patronage of the

ALBANY LIBERTY ASSOCIATION.

At $1.50 per annum to Companies of 10,

Or $2.00 the single copy, per mail,

ALWAYS IN ADVANCE.

Devoted to Freedom—Equality—Temperance—Virtue
—Agriculture—Commerce—Legislative Proceedings—
The News of the Day, Foreign and Domestic—The Arts
and Sciences—Trades—Select Miscellany, &c.

OFFICE No. 56 (UP STAIRS,) STATE-STREET.

☞ Ministers of the Gospel, Lecturing Agents, and
others, are requested to act as Agents.

Clergymen who obtain for us two subscribers and send
us FOUR DOLLARS in advance, free of postage, or SIX DOL-
LARS and FOUR subscribers, will receive our paper a
year gratis.

. A liberal commission to travelling agents. Address the publisher, Albany, N. Y.   Jan. 4, 1842.

Those editors who will insert the above, shall have
a like favor from us.

Masthead of *Tocsin of Liberty.* (From *Tocsin of Liberty*, 2 March 1842; courtesy of Rare Books and Manuscripts, Carl A. Kroch Library, Cornell University.)

slaves (Aptheker 81; Douglass *Life and Times...* 272). Also listed are three Temperance houses and one Temperance grocery, frequent stopping places of abolitionists.

These newspapers also supplied the names of agents, who were responsible for their distribution and promotion. Each of the lists in the 1840 *Colored American*, 1842 *Northern Star and Freeman's Advocate*, and the 1844 *Albany Patriot* show known Underground Railroad conductors—making them a convenient key to the grapevine. Does that mean that all those on the list were aiding fugitive slaves? No, but if someone wanted to connect with the Underground Railroad, one of these agents surely would have been a good place to start.

If such advertisements and listings made conductors more vulnerable, they also made them more accessible to their co-conspirators. In an age before phones, letters served as the primary mode of communication outside one's community. Inside the antebellum community, word was spread at gathering places like taverns and through the grapevine at the local barbershop.

Cutting hair was perhaps the free black man's most prudent road to financial security during this period. Census records generally show that the majority of free blacks in upstate New York who had attained some level of prosperity were barbers. But more significant to a study of the Underground Railroad is the inordinate number who were agents or active in organizations that intersected with the Underground Railroad. In Albany, there were at least six such barbers, two of whom were members of the 1856 Albany Vigilance Committee; in Troy, the stationmaster, William Rich, was a barber, and in Schenectady, there was the ubiquitous R.P.G. Wright (*Schenectady Directory...*). Other upstate barbers who were stationmasters included the legendary John Jones in Elmira and George Johnson in Ithaca, one of Harriet Tubman's favorite destinations, and quite likely Uriah Boston in Poughkeepsie. In all, we find at least ten black barbers in Albany, Schenectady, and Troy who may have participated in the Underground Railroad, and farther north, one in Glens Falls and one in Keeseville, Clinton County.

Hairdressing also may have been the fugitive slave's profession of choice because of the respectability it afforded blacks in the community. An examination of the census records of Washington County, New York, in 1850 and 1860 suggests this possibility. In 1850, seven black men listed their profession as barbers, with six of them living in Whitehall, which was a quick trip in a steamer up Lake Champlain to Canada as well as a reputed terminal (Zirblis 70, 72). Only one of the six shows any accumulation of property, all but one fit the profile of a fugitive slave ranging in age between 20 and 33, and not one of them remains in the 1860 census. An individual who bears special scrutiny as a possible conductor is Felix Schuyler of Whitehall, who in 1850 lists his profession as grocer, and in 1860, as a barber. Both censuses show that he has met the property qualification that makes him an eligible voter; in addition, he has increased his personal worth during those ten years.

The security, visibility, and accessibility of black barbers made them leaders in their community and likely Underground Railroad agents. Their shops also were a natural rendezvous for other collaborators, many of whom were in the business of transportation along the waterways.

For instance, in Albany there was Linnaeus P. Noble,* the owner of a towboat line that served the route from New York to Oswego, and E.M. Teall, owner of the Erie Canal Line that operated from New York City to Buffalo—how convenient that R.P.G. Wright's barbershop sat at a stop along the canal in Schenectady (*Schenectady Directory*...). Both Noble and Teall were members of the Albany Anti-Slavery Society with Noble also an officer in the Eastern New York Anti-Slavery Society.

In Troy, Thaddeus B. Bigelow, the president of the Troy Anti-Slavery Society, was for a time the city's customs house officer, which meant he oversaw all merchandise coming in and going out of the port. The society's vice-president Gurdon Grant was a grain dealer whose offices looked out at the Hudson River on 101 River Street, and its treasurer, Pliny A. Moore, Grant's partner in the grain business, was a shipping agent ("Troy Anti-Slavery Society"; *Troy City Directory* 1838–39; 1843).

AGENTS FOR THE PATRIOT.

The following persons are duly authorized to obtain subscribers and give receipts in the Publisher's names.

E. M. K. Glen, Travelling Agent.
Rev. Abel Brown,
J. N. T. Tucker, Syracuse.
Gordon Hayes, Rochester.
Edward Cruttenden, Buffalo.
John R. Hopkins, Esq. Auburn.
Wm. M. Barker, New Haven.
Austin F. Wing.
Linneus P. Noble, Fayetteville.
John McQuarie Lake
Leonard Church, Esq. Shushan.
George W. Durant, Rensselaerville.
Rev. J. P. Miller, South Argyle.
Wm. P. Greene, Ballston.
E. F. Simmons, Cortlandville.
D. Trembly, Trumansburg.
W. S. Ingraham, Cato 4 Corners.
J. Stevens, Quaker Street.
E. W. Goodwin, Albany.
Rev. Mr. Waterbury.
Rev. B. Shaw
George W. Reynolds, Stamford.
Rectus Murch, Esq., Battenville,
Asa W. Cole, Traveling Agent.
Merritt Woodruff, Esq., Silver Lake, Wyoming co.
Alfred Peck, Big Hollow, Green co.
Orrin Hill, Quaker Springs, Saratoga County.
George W. Clark, Victor.
W. Hamlin, Penn Yan.
Rev. O. Shipman So. Hartford, Washington County.
W. E. Richardson, Arcade.
John Roberts, Lockport.
J. C. Norton, Cazenovia.
Z. P. Birdsall, 58 Congress st., Troy.
Agents will make returns, when in funds, as often as once a fortnight.

Albany Patriot agents (from an 1844 issue of *Albany Patriot*).

---

*Noble moved first to New York and later to Syracuse, where he was one of the participants in the Jerry Rescue of 1851.

Advertisement of Eastern New York Anti-Slavery Society officer. (From *Albany Directory and City Register.* L.G. Hoffman: Albany, 1838.)

Bigelow assisted with the incorporation of the city's most important black church on Liberty Street, and Grant was a trustee of the Bethel Free Congregation, which was established for the "spiritual benefit of the boatmen" (Weise 149). Another trustee of the sailors' church in Troy, and for a time its president, was Albany abolitionist William A. Tweed Dale, the treasurer of the Eastern New York Anti-Slavery Society. During part of the 1830s, Bethel's pastor was Fayette Shipherd, close associate of Abel Brown, member of the executive committee of the Eastern New York Anti-Slavery Society, and writer of the 1840 letter to Vermont conductor Charles Hicks that identifies Shipherd as a stationmaster.

Abolitionists also worked on the boats. There are many stories of sailors aiding fugitive slaves, including an Albany man, James Lane, who in 1843 was sentenced to 12 years in prison for aiding fugitive slaves on his ship in Virginia. This author has not learned whether Lane served out his time or died in prison, but C.S. Brown relates in her biography of her husband, Abel, that as of 1849 Lane was still alive and serving time. Other Albany boatmen who sympathized with runaway slaves were Skipper Peter Bradt, Captain John Johnson, who lived at same address as Stephen Myers in 1856, and Myers himself, who was a boatman as early as 1834, and later became a steward, serving on a boat at least as late as 1848.

Then there is Ezra Thurber, the customs officer in Rouses Point, New York, along Lake Champlain at the Canadian border. His house, legend claims, had a tunnel that led to Canada, a story we will take up later.

Another group that drew Underground Railroad agents were lumber dealers. What is especially intriguing about their connection is that their industry not only made the greatest use of the Champlain Canal (a prime getaway for runaway slaves), but that they also made Albany the largest lumber trader in the world at that time (Munsell 221). Lumbermen in upstate New York known to have aided fugitive slaves or to have been vigilance committee members were Noadiah Moore, the Champlain conductor, who owned a lumber mill in Canada (Everest 50); Nathaniel Safford, an officer in the state anti-slavery society and an executive committee member of the Eastern New York Anti-Slavery Society, whose lumber business was located at the port of Albany and who operated a popular Temperance House there; Chauncey P. Williams, a prominent Albany businessman, who dealt in lumber and shipping and was a member of the executive committee of the Eastern New York Anti-Slavery Society; Minos McGowan, a lumber merchant, who during the 1850s was a member of Albany's vigilance committee; and Nathan Colburn, Jr., a lumber dealer and committee member of the Albany Anti-Slavery Society (Brown 116; *Albany Directory ... 1838–1856; Vigilance Committee Office*).

As we have seen, some abolitionists like Brown and Torrey weren't hard to find. Henry Garnet made himself a target on August 16, 1843, at the National Negro Convention in Buffalo. His emotional appeal to the slaves of the South to revolt was reported in many newspapers in the North.

> Brethren, the time has come ... cease to labor for tyrants ... Now is the day and the hour. Let every slave throughout the land do this, and the days of slavery are numbered. You cannot be more oppressed than you have been—you cannot suffer greater cruelties than you have already. Rather die freemen than live to be slaves.
>
> Let your motto be resistance! Resistance! Resistance! [Ripley 410].

Garnet had a stump for a leg like Captain Ahab, but his physical disability did little to quell his emotional strength, and his "Address to the Slaves," of which the above is only a brief excerpt, inflamed the passions of blacks and whites. The *Albany Argus* described the speech as "a dangerous document." Even the *Liberator* condemned it as "treasonous, provocative, and a flight of fancy," and the conventioneers failed to endorse it, but only by a margin of one vote, 19–18 (Pasternak 47). However, the convention brought black leaders closer to the Liberty Party by passing a resolution supporting it.

Less than a month later, Garnet was attacked at his Liberty Street Church in Troy, an incident that will be described later. His fearlessness was demonstrated during another incident in 1848. He was en route to Canada aboard a train when the conductor asked him to get out of his seat and go to a car reserved strictly for colored persons.

> To this I objected, and I returned to the seat which I had first taken. The conductor came back and insultingly ordered me to leave the car. I obeyed his command and at the same time remonstrated against the unreasonableness of his course. But he only replied, "You shall go where I choose to place you." I asked him if I received such treatment on account of any indecorum. He said, "Colored people cannot be permitted to ride with whites on this road, for southern ladies and gentlemen will not tolerate it." This was not a sufficient reason to my mind; and not being accustomed to yield up my rights without making at least a semblance of lawful resistance, I quietly returned towards my seat, when I was prevented by the conductor, who seized me violently by the throat, and choked me severely.
>
> I have been for many years a cripple. I made no resistance further than was necessary to save myself from injury; but nevertheless, this conductor and another person, whose name I do not know, continued to choke and assault me with their fists. A part of the time my legs were under the cars, near the wheels, and several persons were crying out—"don't kill him, don't kill him!" An officer of the road, whose name I am informed is William. A. Bird, said that they would put me or any other person out, whenever they pleased—and that no law could interfere, and that I might as well attempt to sue the state of New York, as to prosecute the company ... I am suffering greatly from my wounds and bruises, so ... that I called in a physician... [Brutal Outrage 110].

The hostility demonstrated in this racial incident shows why the majority of abo-

Henry Highland Garnet. (Courtesy of the Rensselaer County Historical Society.)

litionists and conductors did not want to draw attention to themselves, and it is not surprising that secrecy became such a priority. Though the reports of secret rooms and tunnels have been exaggerated and have led many researchers to question their existence, we should keep in mind that those in the Underground Railroad had good reason for such hiding places. An important factor to consider in regards to their more secretive behavior in later years is the publicity they gave to their early efforts. This forced them to make their grapevine more abstract and to make use of signs like those in the Battenkill Valley that led to Vermont communities like Rupert and Manchester, where the stations had a row of bricks around their chimneys painted white (Siebert 95).

Chapter 12

ROLL IT ALONG

The years from 1843 to 1845 were the heyday of the Liberty Party and may have been the most active period of the Underground Railroad in northern New York. Some insight to its workings in the region during this time was provided by western New York conductor Eber Pettit in his 1879 memoir, *Sketches in the History of the Underground Railroad*. Pettit, a native of Fredonia in western New York, admitted writing from memory, and though his dates of the events more than 30 years later are not precise, the details are a remarkable fit.

Pettit wrote that the "first well established line of the U.G.R.R. had its southern terminus in Washington, D.C. and extended in a pretty direct route to Albany, N.Y..... The General Superintendent resided in Albany. [And] I knew him well. He was once an active member of one of the churches in Fredonia [Abel Brown lived in Fredonia for a time]. Mr. T [Charles Torrey], his agent in Washington city, was a very active and efficient man; the Superintendent at Albany was in daily communication by mail with him and other subordinate agents at all points along the line" (Pettit 34).

Pettit's first recollection of the term Underground Railroad was in a Washington, D.C., newspaper. It referred to runaways who ended up in Albany and told of a young black boy who said that "the railroad went underground all the way to Boston." The article contained an anecdote about a slave owner who had a tobacco plantation near Washington and had lost five slaves. He learned of their whereabouts when he received a newspaper in the mail from Albany, according to Pettit, called the "Liberty Press" [the *Liberty Press* was published in Utica], which reported his slaves' escape via the Underground Railroad (35–36). Pettit may have confused the Utica paper with the *Tocsin of Liberty*.*

The itinerary of the runaways took them on foot to stops at the farms of Quakers on the way to Philadelphia. From there, they took a boat along the Delaware River

*Editor of the Liberty Press, James C. Jackson, also was for a time the editor of the Albany Patriot.

to Bordentown, New Jersey, where they took a train to New York City. Then they were moved on to Albany. A surprising detail about their mode of escape was that it was coordinated with the "liberty" newspaper, that the publication of the runaways' successful flight was actually a ruse. In reality, they were hiding not far from their point of departure. While they waited for the signal to move on, a newspaper article was telling of the runaways' successful escape to Canada and was sent to their masters. This threw the slavehunters off their tracks and enabled them to make a safer getaway.

By the time the fugitive slaves reached Albany, a year had passed since they left their master. Pettit knew this because one of the runaways, Jo Norton, was sent to him. Norton stayed on as a farmhand. Though he had gained his freedom, it was at the cost of leaving behind his wife, Mary. When Pettit later learned that "General" Chaplin had taken up residence in Washington, D.C.,* he suggested they contact Chaplin to inquire about the whereabouts of Mary. Chaplin located her and negotiated a price for her freedom with her master. The thankful Jo raised the money by giving speeches about his daring escape. The family was personally reunited by Chaplin in Utica, and for the first time Jo saw his child, who had been born after his flight (43–45).

A similar case involved Abel Brown, in which he reunited a husband and wife, who had traveled hundreds of miles, shortly before they gave birth to their first child—born free (Brown 190). It was heartwarming successes like these that inspired abolitionists like Brown to push on with their work. "God will not suffer me to rest," he wrote, "while others are deprived of the precious blessings designed by our Heavenly Father for all mankind" (Brown 153).

That fall, Abel Brown toured the Adirondacks. He attended anti-slavery conventions at Ballston Spa, Corinth, and a Baptist Meeting House, five miles from Lake George. Following that meeting, they stayed with a Mr. Richards. Thereafter, Brown was joined by the fugitive slave Lewis Washington, who had become an associate of Brown on the lecture podium. They had dinner with Warren County's Liberty Party president Joseph Leggett and his wife in Chestertown at the Temperance Tavern of Oliver Arnold, the county Liberty Party secretary. From Warren County, Brown and Washington went to Clinton County. Passing through Essex County, Brown was overwhelmed by the scenic splendor—"The beautiful valleys, the immense forests, extending as far as the eye can reach— the huge piles of rocks, the towering mountains..." (179). In Plattsburgh they were met by Noadiah Moore, who took them to their lecture in Chazy, then provided lodging at his home. The next evening Brown lectured in Champlain and the following day at Mooersville. Lectures in St. Albans, Vermont, concluded the appointments, and from there they took the steamboat to Whitehall and the packet boat down the Champlain Canal through Washington County to Albany.

Brown's biography provides no mention of either lecturing or attending anti-slavery meetings in Washington County at any time. Undoubtedly, however, he was well acquainted with its abolitionists, especially considering that Hiram Corliss and William H. Mowry were president and vice-president of the Eastern New York Anti-Slav-

*Chaplin went to Washington, D.C., around December 1844 as a correspondent for the Patriot.

ery Society. Perhaps, because the county already was so well abolitionized and in the capable hands of a leader like Corliss, Brown saw no need. Typical of the outreach going on there is the following letter, which is excerpted, from Hiram Corliss, dated March 21, 1843:

> We have districted our town on the plan of pledging days to labor for the slave from house to house conversing on the subject, obtaining signatures to the Liberty roll, distributing tracts and obtaining signatures to the petition for the abolition of some part of the slave system. I pledged four days, and my place of labor was in a distant part of the town, eleven miles from my residence. Accompanied by Mr. Wilmarth, on the 6th inst, we left home at 9 o'clock and drove to the field assigned us. We commenced by calling on Elder Brand, the Baptist minister of the place. He, Mrs. Brand, and his sons all signed the Liberty roll and petition to Congress to rescind the 21st rule, by which all petitions touching the subject of slavery were left unread and unreferred [The Gag Rule]. We continued laboring from house to house until nearly 9 o'clock in the evening. We then left for home after having obtained 65 names, to the petition, 35 to the Liberty Association, 12 of whom were voters, and now pledged to vote for liberty... [Corliss "Personal Effort..." 1].

Corliss said nothing of the Underground Railroad. If he did discuss it, he would not have mentioned it in a public letter. The devotion to the cause of the northern New York abolitionists did not extend to placing themselves in jeopardy. Most of them were law-abiding, church-going citizens, for whom the reckless actions taken by Brown and Torrey would have been out of character.

Among events that fortified the abolitionism of northern New York and added stations to its Underground Railroad was the organization of the Wesleyan Methodist Connection on May 31, 1843, in Utica. Its 151 delegates represented a broad area that included Massachusetts, New Hampshire, Connecticut, Rhode Island, Vermont, Ohio, Michigan, Pennsylvania, and New York, with two-thirds of them coming from New York. This small but vocal group, led by the Rev. Orange Scott of Vermont and the Rev. Luther Lee, had been protesting for about a decade against Southern Methodists who owned slaves. They could no longer remain in the church as long as it refused to rule against the practice of slaveholding. Among its other leaders was the Rev. Cyrus Prindle, well-known in the Adirondack region, who offered the prayer to open the convention.

The new church's formation was inspired by the founder of Methodism, John Wesley, who abhorred slavery. It did not merely oppose slavery but urged active resistance: "In a word, we desire that every member of the Wesleyan Connection should not only be a zealous advocate of every branch of moral reform, but co-workers, even in the front rank, battling side by side with those who contend with the Lord's enemies" (Matlack Chapter 3). The Utica Convention lasted 11 days and established a denomination comprising 75 or 80 ministers with 6,000 members.

The denomination was organized into six annual conferences, including the Champlain Conference, which actually had met a month prior to the Utica Convention. It included 1,000 members with Adirondack congregations in Hadley (Warren County), Champlain (Clinton County), Jay and Crown Point (Essex County) and Granville (Washington County), as well as at Ferrisburgh in Vermont, and its first

ANTI-SLAVERY CONVENTION.

A meeting of the friends of the slave will be held at Hartford, on Wednesday the 22d inst. at 10 oclock A. M. Distinguished speakers from abroad are expected to be there; and the attendance of Alvan Stewart, esq. will be secured if possible. Let this notice be widely circulated—let the abolitionists secure its announcement from the pulpits in their vicinity, that there may be a general turn out on the occasion. Let every abolitionist be there, with as many of his pro-slavery neighbors as he can persuade to attend. Feb. 6th, 1843.

THOMAS BIGELOW, Jr.,
JOHN STRAIGHT.
ANTHONY McKALLOR,
JAMES P. MILLER,
LEONARD CHURCH,
HIRAM CORLISS.
WILLIAM MOWREY.
Committee.

Announcement of an anti-slavery meeting in Hartford, Washington County, New York. (From *Sandy Hill Herald*, 14 February 1843.)

Noadiah Moore, Champlain, New York. (Courtesy Special Collections, Fineburg Library, Plattsburgh State University.)

president was Cyrus Prindle, then pastor of the Ferrisburgh Church and a known Underground Railroad conductor ("One Hundred and Twenty-Five..." 3–4).

Not long after, additional congregations and circuits also were organized in the hamlets of Corinth in Saratoga County; Darrowsville and Stony Creek in Warren County; Mooers, Chazy and West Plattsburgh in Clinton County; and Cooks Corners in Franklin County. Of these, the Warren County churches have been associated with the Underground Railroad, but it would not be surprising if any or all of these churches participated, considering the mandate of the new denomination.

Farther north, in Clinton County, support for the Liberty Party was growing. However, in the town of Champlain, less than five miles from Canada, a confrontation occurred that showed hostility toward the abolitionists was still active there.

On December 1, 1843, Noadiah Moore, the county's Liberty Party president, led a group from the First Presbyterian Church in publicly condemning slavery at the church's services. The others were Silas Hubbell, a prominent local lawyer who frequently did business in Canada and whose brother was Moore's brother-in-law; Lorenzo Kellogg; O.B. Ashmun, the brother of colonizationist Jehudi; and the church's pastor, the Rev. Abraham Brinkerhoff, Moore's other brother-in-law. Moore offered two resolutions. The first condemned "American Slavery as a sin" and was passed. But the second, which pledged to convince slaveholding Presbyterian brethren in the South to immediately abandon slavery, was not. This resolution was not well received, and "ridicule [was] heaped on" them by some church members (Nye 17).

This action apparently was part of a well-coordinated effort by the county's Liberty Party to force the issue there. Shortly before this, the county Liberty Party had begun publishing their own newspaper, *The Herald of Freedom,* under the editorship of O.B. Ashmun. A monthly, it is not known how long the newspaper was published as only one known remaining copy exists from May 1844, which is listed as number eight from volume one. At the top of the front page, just below the masthead, Moore is listed at the head of the Liberty Party's executive committee that also consisted of Edward Moore of Plattsburgh, Calvin Cook of Clintonville, Ebenezer Drury of Peru, and Anderson Keese of Keeseville. A list of more than 50 individuals who distributed the paper follows them.

The article on the front-page article begins as follows:

"N.M..... the only consistent abolitionist, has turned out at last to be a slaveholder."

At first glance, it seems puzzling because it talks of Moore as a slaveholder, an impossibility because slaveholding was outlawed in the state in 1827. But when one realizes that at the time claims were being circulated in the mainstream abolitionist press by Southern slaveholders that their slaves were better off than many free wage earners in the North, it becomes clear that the article is a piece of satire and that Moore's "slaves" were probably either individuals who worked for him or who were fugitive slaves.

"Their condition now, in 1844," the article continues, "is as follows: five children, one daughter married who has made her escape to Canada; two sons with families reduced to the condition of tradesmen, and still held to labor and service; another, the youngest, working with his father at the same trade; while the next oldest, contrary to the rules of the slave code, and in defiance of his master, has actually entered himself as a student on the Academy and had the audacity the other day of presenting a tuition bill of $6 [about $100 in today's currency] for his master to pay" ("N.M.'s Slaves" 1).

The satire is evidence of the opposition faced by abolitionists in the County. Why it was decided to confront the issue at the First Presbyterian Church in Champlain is not known, other than that Noadiah Moore, the county's leading abolitionist, was a member.* It may have been the motivation for an arson to set fire to the church and cause it to burn to the ground on June 17, 1844 (Nye 18).

Meanwhile, the Eastern New York Anti-Slavery Society held its annual meeting that year in New York City at the Apollo Rooms and drew an enthusiastic crowd of 1,500. The society had good reason to celebrate. Among its successes were the improved finances of the *Albany Patriot,* the distribution of more than 100,000 anti-slavery tracts and publications, an increase of agents lecturing in the field from four to nine, and the tripling of Liberty Party voters. But the greatest cause for celebration was making the northern half of the state entirely safe for fugitive slaves (Brown 186). It also was a cause for celebration that at least 1,000 fugitive slaves had passed through the Northeast that year ("Freedom and Slavery for Afric-Americans" 139).

Although the Liberty Party was making advances in northeastern New York, it

---

Because of the Liberty Party's strong evangelistic bent, it urged its members to confront churches that did not openly condemn slavery.

500 PAIRS WOOLLEN SOCKS WAN-
TED! The Ex. Com. of the East.
New York A. S. Society have made arrangements
so that they can dispose of Woollen Socks, at
seven and a half cents, for a good common acct.
We hope our sisters in the country who know how
to make them will furnish us 500 pairs within
eight weeks.
      The proceeds of them will be applied to supply
the Cor. Sec'ry. and Mr. Lewis Washington, the
excellent colored lecturer, and to aid fugitive slaves.
      Let one and all send immediately to
                        ABEL BROWN,
      Cor. Sec ry of the E. N. Y. A. S. Society
Albany, Jan. 1st 1844.
      ☞ Will the Liberty Press and Country
please insert, once or twice.

Advertisement requesting socks and other aid for
fugitives. (From *Albany Patriot*, 3 January 1844.)

was finding itself becoming increasingly alienated from the Garrisonians and their American Anti-Slavery Society. At the May 16 business meeting of the American Anti-Slavery Society, it condemned the Liberty Party as its enemy and charged the party with attempting to destroy the cause of emancipation with its immoral behavior. It called on all Liberty Party members to leave the party if they wished to bring the end of slavery ("AAS Annual Business Meeting" 199).

Despite the political squabbling, the Underground Railroad continued to roll along. Liberty Party meetings were being held regularly throughout upstate New York, and party membership was growing. The successes of the Underground Railroad inspired the composition that year of perhaps the most famous of all abolition songs, "Get Off the Track."*

> 'Ho the car emancipation,
> Rides majestic through our nation,
> Bearing on its train the glory.
> Roll it along! Roll it along! Roll it along!
> Through the nation.
> Freedom's Car, Emancipation.'
> Roll it along! Roll it along! Roll it along!

*"Get Off the Track" was written by Jesse Hutchinson of the Hutchinsons, America's most famous singing group during the antebellum period. Composed of three brothers, Jesse, John, and Judson, and their sister Asa, they made numerous tours throughout the North and often spent time in New York City.

Chapter 13

DEATH AND TRANSFIGURATION

Whitney Cross, in his classic study, *The Burned-Over District*, attributes the many reforms that occurred after 1830 to the Second Great Awakening. Its revivals, he wrote, focused on an emotional appeal and a fixation on a single, moral problem. They produced a climate that made people susceptible to causes like temperance, abolition, and women's rights (Cross 211–236). It gave them a sense that something big was about to happen, and, as we have already alluded, the period had its share of visions, premonitions, and visitations by God. In Washington County, where abolition and temperance burned in the souls of many, another movement arose led by the Rev. William Miller, who predicted the second coming of Christ and the end of the world, no later than October 1844.

"I found, in going through with the Bible, the end of all things was clearly and emphatically predicted, both as to time and manner," he wrote sometime before 1840. "I believed; and ... I was compelled by the Spirit of God, the power of truth and the love of souls, to take up my cross and proclaim these things to a dying and perishing world" (Himes 12).

Abolitionists fit the profile of the true believers who became Miller's followers. Among them were Theodore Weld's wife, Angelina Grimke, who wrote several prominent anti-slavery tracts during the 1830s, and the Rev. Orrin B. Shipman of Fort Ann in Washington County, who is believed to have aided fugitive slaves and who made an anti-slavery lecture tour through Vermont that summer for the Liberty Party (*Vermont Freeman* 3). But how many abolitionists were followers of Miller is open to speculation. Miller was right about one thing—some significant things were about to happen, so far as the region's Underground Railroad was concerned.

Abel Brown, who would be one of the principals involved, was on a tour through Essex County that summer with his wife Catherine. Like his first wife, she was a devoted abolitionist, and she was also a singer of abolitionist songs. They were expecting a cordial welcome from Judge Gideon Hammond, a leader in the organization of the county anti-slavery society, who had protected abolitionist lecturer Thomas B. Watson from an attack in Westport five years earlier. Brown did not realize, however, that Hammond was a Whig and supporter in the upcoming election of Henry Clay for president, against whom Brown and the Liberty Party had been vigorously campaigning. As a result, Hammond's Baptist Church refused to permit Brown to lecture, forcing him to go to the Methodist Church (Brown 191–193).

Afterwards, on the way back to their hotel, the Browns were confronted by a group of men who pelted them with eggs. More harassment from Whigs followed them at Moriah, Elizabethtown, Keeseville, and Jay. Yet Brown found new hope in the form of a wagonload of Irish Catholics from Clintonville, who came to the meeting in Jay (Brown 194).* It would be the last sign of hope for this martyr to the cause of liberty.

Charles T. Torrey, who had moved to Washington, D.C., to "run the Underground Railroad" (Lovejoy 357), was the other man upon whom fate had cast its net. On June 24, 1844, less than three months after his move, he was arrested for aiding fugitive slaves (Lovejoy 126). The indictment charged Torrey with aiding three slaves owned by a Virginia slaveholder. Torrey, whose reputation had preceded him from his earlier stay in Washington, had made himself a target of authorities, and a trap had been set for him.

While Torrey awaited his trial in prison, the Browns returned home to Troy, where they often provided shelter to fugitive slaves (Brown 190). Also, during this time, they became the legal guardians of a black girl who came to live with them, along with one of Brown's brothers, who came back east from Wisconsin (212). In addition, Brown began doing outreach for the Liberty Party and the upcoming election. At the first rally held at the city courthouse steps, in which he was joined by Lewis Washington and the Rev. Merrit Bates of the Wesleyan Church, they were attacked. For a short time, police officers repelled the mob, and the abolitionists fled to the mayor's house. However, the mayor refused to protect them, and, without police protection, they were forced to flee to the home of Fayette Shipherd. During this jaunt, along Albany Street between Third and Fifth Streets, they were stoned and beaten, and one eyewitness said the mob's intent was to knock Brown down and trample him to death (199).

The following week another Liberty Party organization meeting was held at the Baptist Church near the Rev. Shipherd's home. A mob had gathered but remained outside when it learned that Brown was not in attendance. However, midway through the meeting, Brown arrived, returning from a convention in one of the northern counties. At this point the mob forced itself inside, and when Brown rose to speak, they began to taunt him.

"I know not, but I am as well prepared to die now," he answered them prophetically, "as I should be forty years hence" (203).

The mob returned outside. They began throwing stones through the windows, and people started to leave. Brown pleaded with them to stay but the mob set fire to the church. Fortunately, the mayor arrived with the police just in time.

---

*Few Catholics were abolitionists; its ministry was consumed by the spread of Catholicism rather than the practice of good works.

In the next month, Brown participated in two Liberty party conventions in Saratoga County, the first in Edinburgh, at which money was raised to employ an anti-slavery agent to circulate through the county, and a second in Corinth. His wife, who accompanied him, wrote that the second meeting was held in a large, dilapidated, cold barn, where a large and sympathetic audience gathered to hear the weary Brown, who supported himself with the use of a cane (207).

Following this trip, Brown held abolition meetings in Poughkeepsie. Brown made several trips into the downstate region, whose anti-slavery was of a different character than that north of Albany. A major reason was its large black population, most of whom were descendants of the many slaves who had been there. Consequently, racial prejudice, the underpinning of slavery, was more widespread downstate (Groth 293–345). Slavery was rare in the more northern regions of Franklin, Clinton, Essex, and Warren counties, which may account for their generally more benevolent attitude towards race.* Nevertheless, the large number of free blacks downstate made it an inviting location for runaway slaves, and many legends have been recorded there of the Underground Railroad's operation. Suggestive of this were the fugitive slaves present at Brown's meetings earlier that year in New Windsor, where he stayed with the abolitionist Peter Roe (Brown 182). The strong pro-slavery climate was in evidence during Brown's final trip there. During one meeting, a mob threw liver and rotten meat at him, which he fended off with a board at the suggestion of his associate, the Rev. Charles Van Loon, pastor of the Poughkeepsie First Baptist church.

The time had come for Miller's prediction of the end of the world. After an anti-slavery lecture in Troy during which Alvan Stewart joined him, Brown left for a trip to the western part of the state. He paid Miller's prophecy little heed as his fateful journey began with a train ride to the vicinity of Rochester, where he gave yet another lecture. His next stop was Canandaigua, and he took a train part of the way to a village where he intended to get lodging for the night. But there were no vacancies, and when he attempted to solicit a room at the home of a stranger, he was turned away at gunpoint. Meanwhile, a storm had blown over and the temperature had dropped. Nevertheless, Brown walked the rest of the way during the night to Canandaigua. When he arrived the next morning, he was exhausted and ill, yet fulfilled his appointment at the next convention. Bouts of fever followed in the next days, and on November 1, he collapsed at the home of his friends John and Laura Mosher in Canandaigua (215–217).

During the next week, Brown's condition shifted between apparent recovery and periods of hopelessness. At one point, he rallied and it looked as if he might recover, but then he became delirious and began shouting that a mob was chasing him (219). Perhaps he was thinking of the events of his life and how it turned after he took up the cause in 1834, of how he was knocked down in the streets and cruelly whipped— three times, once receiving more than fifty lashes with a heavy cowskin; of the gang in Pennsylvania that shot at him for helping runaways slaves, when he was with his

---

*In 1790, there were 16 slaves in Clinton County; in 1800, the combined total of slaves in Clinton and Essex counties was 58; in 1810, the combined total in Clinton and Franklin was 32, with Essex County listing none; in 1820, the combined total for all four counties was 12. This is in contrast to the downstate region, whose slaves numbered on average more than 6,000 during the period from 1790 to 1820 (See U.S. Census).

Gravesite of the Rev. Abel Brown, Canandaigua, New York; the headstone has been worn away by time. (Photograph by the author.)

wife, Mary, and their child; of being stoned and splattered with eggs; of the runaways he aided near the Virginia border or hid in his upstate New York home; of leaving on one of his secret missions and Mary commending him to God: "Go my husband, go, for God will be your shield" (185). Perhaps he was thinking of the runaway violinist who could improvise abolition songs on cue; of the old slave whose eleven children had all been sold away; of the fugitive slave families he had reunited; of those who shared his labors—Lewis Washington, Edwin Goodwin, Charles Ray, Shipherd, Garnet, the Rev. Wright and Mr. Wright, Alvan Stewart, Van Loon, the poor Torrey in jail; of the good country people ready to receive the weary runaway—Dr. Corliss, Noadiah Moore, Joseph Leggett, Smith St. John, Peter Roe, and Ellis Clizbe; of his wife, Catherine; his three children; his mother in Wisconsin; his brothers and sisters, and their departed and beloved sister, Cynthia, whom now he was going to join in that time at the end of his world.*

Abel Brown was only 34 when he passed away at the home of the Moshers on November 7. He had sustained beatings, gunshots, and continuous threats to his life, but in the end it was the exhaustion brought on by his ceaseless efforts to destroy slavery that caused his death.

A funeral was held in Canandaigua, where those present expressed a "feeling of profound respect and love [and a] deep and pungent grief" ("Death of Abel Brown" 1). Alvan Stewart delivered the eulogy. In Troy, a funeral also was held, and Henry Garnet was the eulogist.

---

*Brown had two children by his wife, Mary, and one by Catherine; he was one of six siblings, and his older sister, Cynthia, had died in 1840, while serving as a missionary to Indians, apparently west of the Mississippi.

The *American Freeman*, an abolitionist paper in Prairieville, Wisconsin Territory, where Brown lectured on his western tour and where his mother had moved, wrote a lengthy obituary, from which came the following excerpt:

> In every department of the Anti-Slavery enterprise, he exhibited a spirit that could not rest while so much was at stake and so much required to be done— in circulating anti-slavery publications; in urging religious denominations to practice the principles they avowed, and by their presses, influence ministers and benevolent societies to assist our colored brother, who was bleeding in the porch of the sanctuary; in bringing the political parties at the north, from under the thralldom in which they were kept by the slave-power; in assisting, as a member of the vigilance committee, trembling Americans, to the number of *not less than* one *thousand*, to the shelter afforded by a monarchial government from the inhuman monsters walking at large and claiming property in human flesh. He was a pattern to believers—a living argument against unbelief [Brown 225].

However, there would be more discouraging news. A month after Brown's death, Charles Torrey was convicted and sentenced to six years in prison. His trial had been anything but fair, and, although he was guilty, the prosecution made sure of his conviction by getting witnesses to make false statements. It is not clear if the loss of Brown and Torrey affected the Underground Railroad in northeastern New York. Instead of slowing efforts, it may actually have reinvigorated them, like the murder of Lovejoy, though on a smaller, more localized level. If nothing else, it took the attention of slavecatchers away from the region, and, coupled with the trend for greater secrecy, probably sent the Underground Railroad there farther underground.

Chapter 14

A Breach Has Been Made

The death of Abel Brown was overshadowed by the defeat of Henry Clay in the presidential election. The Liberty Party had vigorously opposed Clay because he was a slaveholder, and its opposition was directly responsible for Clay's loss of New York State, which in turn caused him to lose the election. However, it was a Pyrrhic victory because Clay was opposed to the extension of slavery in the west, and his defeat put into office James Polk, who favored both the extension of slavery and the admission of Texas, which would add another slave state to the Union.

The realization of this tactical error had not yet become clear, and members of the Eastern New York Anti-Slavery Society remained optimistic. Its executive committee declared at a meeting, the same day Brown died, that their goal was "to put Albany in the forefront of anti-slavery cities with Cincinnati and Boston" ("Meeting of the Executive Committee..." 11). To accomplish this, it planned to improve and enlarge the *Albany Patriot*, and to hire William L. Chaplin as its correspondent in Washington, D.C.

On December 4–5, the Rev. James P. Miller of Argyle offered the opening prayer at the Liberty Party national convention in Albany and asked God's help for their brothers in prison, most prominently Charles Torrey. Concern also was voiced for Albany boatman James D. Lane, in a Norfolk prison for concealing two female slaves aboard his packet schooner traveling from Norfolk to New York City, and other "associates" in prison for aiding fugitive slaves.*

A lengthy article by the Rev. Miller on the front page of the New Year's issue of the *Patriot* showed that the loss of Brown and Torrey had not discouraged area abolitionists. "A breach has been made, which slavery feels," he wrote, "and at which the monster trembles throughout the length and breadth of his domain..." ("Correspondence..." 1).

---

*These associates included Henry Bush in Washington, D.C; Calvin Fairbank and Delia Webster in Lexington, KY; Jonathan Walker in Pensacola, FL; and Alanson Work, James E. Burr, and George Thompson in MO.

That day a New Year's abolition celebration was held in Granville in a non-descript, A-frame clapboard church with shutters and no spires. Little more than a decade earlier it had been the site of sermons by the Rev. Lemuel Haynes, who had served as its pastor from 1822 until his death in 1833. The proceedings of the rally were reported by Hiram Corliss, who acknowledged the memory of the black minister whose gifts had made the case for the equality of blacks more strongly than any abolitionist.

Guest speaker Day spoke of the urgent need for clergy to speak out against slavery, and warned that those who neglected to do so would be subject to the wrath of God ("For the Patriot"). Corliss praised Day, whom he said was going to remain in the area.

"His plan is to give a number of lectures in each neighborhood," Corliss wrote. "His first lecture is on the duty of ministers, in which he clearly shows that they cannot let the subject [slavery] alone without incurring guilt. In his second lecture, he endeavors to prove that the free states are responsible for all the slavery in the nation, in as much as they have the power to remove it if they wish. His third lecture is on political action" (ibid.).

In Troy, later that month, at a convention in the Rev. Fayette Shipherd's Free Congregational Church, the local party showed its resilience after Abel Brown's death by appointing the Rev. Day as his replacement as general agent for Rensselaer County, and Lewis Washington as an associate agent. President of the convention was Garret Van Hoosen of Hoosick Falls, the Underground Railroad agent identified by Shipherd in his 1840 letter to Charles Hicks concerning the transport of runaway slaves ("Convention at Troy").

The Eastern New York Anti-Slavery Society also was optimistic at its annual meeting on May 7, 1845, in New York City. Guests included James Birney and Alvan Stewart, with Hiram Corliss installed as president, William H. Mowry as first vice-president, and the Rev. Miller as second vice-president for the coming year. Members of the executive committee included: Shipherd; Garnet; the Rev. Pritchett; new *Patriot* editor, James C. Jackson; lumber merchants Nathaniel Safford and Chauncey P. Williams of Albany; *Patriot* Washington correspondent Chaplin; teacher E. P. Freeman of Albany; hat retailer William Mayell of Albany; and two members of the New York Committee of Vigilance, New York City natives Andrew Lester and George R. Barker, who was residing at the Eagle Tavern in Albany ("Anti-Slavery Society" 110).

Among their concerns were the annexation of Texas, the lack of support from clergy, the possibility of Southern secession, and the misrepresentation of the Liberty Party by the Whigs. Henry Garnet urged voters to continue to back Liberty candidates despite the unlikelihood of their election. Voting for a major party candidate, the least of two evils, was morally bankrupt, he declared. He also warned abolitionists to be prepared to make sacrifices: "The first martyrs in all moral reformations are members of the true church of Christ" (110). Elijah Lovejoy and Abel Brown already were counted, and more would follow.

Regardless of the sacrifices, the members of the society were prepared to make them. Like most abolitionists in the North, they believed they were on the brink of ending slavery. The American Anti-Slavery Society, for example, was predicting the end of slavery within seven years. But the published accounts of aid to fugitive slaves had diminished.* Perhaps the prosecution of Torrey and the others, and the experiences of Brown, had made conductors more cautious. Also, the publicity was less important, for the basic network that comprised the Underground Railroad had been forged, and others were ready to take their place.

Prominent among those filling the void was the Rev. Fayette Shipherd, pastor of the Free Congregational Church in Troy. A likely collaborator of Brown's, the Granville, New York native was fashioned out of the mold of the evangelists of the 1820s and 1830s. Son of former U.S. Congressman Zebulon Shipherd, he was ordained in 1826 by Lemuel Haynes and became a follower and acquaintance of Charles Finney. His first church was in Pawlet, Vermont, and from there he went to Troy to assist the evangelist, the Rev. Nathan Sydney Beman, serving as a circuit rider to rural churches near the city. In 1832, he was called by Captain Gurdon Grant to serve the Bethel Free Church in Troy, which was established to minister to the city's boatmen and poor. After some differences with Grant, Shipherd left the church in the latter part of 1834 and moved to Walton in Delaware County, where, in addition to his ministerial duties, he was one of the founding members of that county's anti-slavery society and became its secretary. It was during this period that his wife, Elmina, died and he married his second wife, Catherine (Shipherd "A Legacy..." 17–33). By 1838, at the request of Grant, Shipherd returned to the Bethel Church, where he continued his active role in abolition as Rensselaer County's leading representative in the state society and as a conductor in the Underground Railroad, as we have seen earlier from his 1840 letter to Vermont conductor Charles Hicks. Upon leaving Bethel in 1841, he remained in Troy and formed his own Free Congregational Church, with 72 members of the Bethel Church moving to his new congregation. In order to pay for the lot and get the church built, he negotiated with contractors, borrowed money, and taught school on the side, and the church was completed in 1844 (Shipherd "My Legacy..." 87). Throughout this time, Shipherd continued as a member of the executive committee of the Eastern New York Anti-Slavery Society, which was responsible for the forwarding of runaway slaves.[†]

An insight to the Underground Railroad network in the Adirondacks of northern New York at this time might be derived from Gerrit Smith's journal during his anti-slavery speaking tour through the region from May 27 to June 15, 1845. Smith's first stop was Saratoga, the home of his friends, Edward C. Delevan, the Temperance champion, and Judge Reuben H. Walworth, the state's highest-ranking judicial official. However, so far as its prospects for abolitionist outreach, he wrote, "The village is thought to be about as unfavorable a soil, as Charleston or New Orleans for anti-slavery" ("Gerrit Smith Anti-Slavery Tour" 130).

In Glens Falls, he spoke in the Presbyterian Church. "I have never been in a village, which promises better ... for the anti-slavery cause," he wrote. "Dr. Davis is an

---

*An exception were the annual reports of the Albany Female Anti-Slavery Society, which had been founded at the urging of Torrey in 1843; in 1845, it reported that "We have sustained a monthly meeting for prayer and the execution of plans for the assistance of fugitives on their way to Canada. A number have been furnished with clothing and strengthened with a cup of cold water" ("Report of..." 135).

†Despite the many associations that indicate Shipherd's activity in the Underground Railroad, his two memoirs among his family papers and letters do not mention assisting runaways; the only such references found among those papers were in an 1840 letter from his brother, who was at Oberlin College.

intelligent and decided abolitionist, and I think, that I can say as much for Mr. Wilson. There are other leading men in the village, who will, I think, espouse the good cause.... Among these are Mr. Paddock, Mr. Sherwood, and Mr. Burnham." Warrensburg, about 15 miles to the north, was just the opposite. "There is not one man in all this considerable village, who is called an abolitionist.... The ministers here never speak of the slave in their sermons or public prayers."

Chester, another 15 miles farther north and the home of Joseph Leggett, the Rev. Baker, and Oliver Arnold, drew Smith's praise. "I am much pleased with the people. They are candid and truth-loving. Their ministers are not afraid to plead the cause of the enslaved. Here are abolitionists of the truest class.... Mr. Leggett, Mr. Arnold, and Dr. Pritchard" (ibid.).

The Rev. Fayette Shipherd. (From Bragdon Papers, courtesy of Rare Books and Special Collections, Rush Rhees Library, University of Rochester.)

Following old Route 9 north, Smith's next stop was Schroon Lake where he met with Mr. Warren, Mr. Leland, Mr. Lindsay, A. Smith, and Judge Tyrrell. In Keene, among those attending his lecture were Phineas Norton and Valentine Fuller. He gave three lectures in Elizabethtown, two in the Grove and the other at the Baptist Meeting House. He also met with Jesse Gay and Alfred Ames. At Keeseville, he met "that true friend of the slave, Wendell Lansing," and on the way to Plattsburgh, Calvin Cook of Clintonville and James W. Flack of AuSable Forks. In Plattsburgh, he spoke at the Courthouse in the afternoon and the Methodist Church in the evening. He found few abolitionists in the city of Plattsburgh but met with many in the surrounding communities, including "that wise and steadfast friend of the slave, Noadiah Moore," O.B. Ashmun, Edward Moore, William G. Brown, Horace Boardman, Benjamin Ketchum, George Beckwith, and Henry Hewitt. Clinton County, Smith wrote, "will probably be the first ... in our state to throw off its political shackles and stand forth for the slave" (131).

Considering that Smith would become president in 1848 of the New York State Vigilance Committee, a hybrid organization consisting of members of the New York Committee of Vigilance and agents from upstate New York, the contacts Smith made on this trip should be carefully noted.*

Despite the optimism, pockets of racism remained in the north, even in such abolitionized communities as Union Village. Its intensity can be gauged from a let-

*From 1847 to 1853, the committee reported giving aid to 1,003 runaway slaves in three separate accounts covering about three-and-a-half years during that period (Quarles 154; Campbell 6)

Gerrit Smith. (From Helene C. Phelan, *And Why Not Every Man? An Account of Slavery, the Underground Railroad, and the Road to Freedom in New York's Southern Tier*, Interlaken, NY: Heart of the Lakes Pub., 1987.)

ter written by a resident of Easton, the town bordering Union Village, excerpted in part from the July 10, 1845, issue of the *Albany Patriot* and describing the recent July 4 celebration there.

"In due time some 8 or 10 schools assembled from the different districts in Easton, Cambridge, and one [the Congregational Church] from Union Village.... It being a notorious fact, that the Congregational Church of Union Village is noted for its 'nigger' principles. It was an oversight in the committee of arrangements to invite them under any circumstances; and it was still a greater one to place them at the head of the procession. Why, will you credit me, Mr. Editor, when I tell you they had their 'niggers' all mixed up with the white scholars? They didn't put them at the end, as they should have done, but walked side and side just as if they were white" ("Correspondence of the Albany Patriot" 143). The writer added that "niggers" needed to be taught their place and should be driven off with the Indians!

While such opinions were not common in northern New York, their existence showed how far the anti-slavery cause still had to go, and this became evident in the 1845 election when the Liberty Party showed only a slight gain statewide and an overall decline in northern New York. The lack of significant progress led to a disagreement over whether the party should continue to confine its agenda to the "One-Idea," the abolition of slavery, or whether it should begin to include other issues like land reform, tariffs, and the rights of women in order to attract more voters.

1843–1845 Liberty Party Vote by County in Northeastern New York

County	1843	1844	1845
Clinton	716	410	323
Washington	299	338	268
Essex	123	143	167
Rensselaer	0	181	131
Saratoga	105	119	118
Franklin	87	93	95
Warren	0	118	94
Albany	154	124	72
Schenectady	20	31	20
St. Lawrence	18	468	551

[Hendricks 194–197]

Among those disheartened was party leader Gerrit Smith, who considered leaving the Party. In a May 7, 1846, letter Smith gave three main reasons for this: one, many members of the party were voting outside the ticket for pro-slavery candidates; two, many used products made from slave labor; and three, many attended churches that did not condemn slavery ("Letter to the Liberty Party").

Two days following Smith's letter, Charles Torrey died in a Maryland prison. Even before his trial, Torrey's health had begun to decline in jail. But in the beginning, his attorneys had given him hope that a pardon from the governor might be possible, and committees were formed in the North to assist the funding of his legal needs. Such a pardon, however, was conditioned on Torrey expressing his regret and asking forgiveness for aiding the 400 slaves, whom by his own admission he had helped to freedom. His reply was that "It is better to die in prison with the peace of God in our hearts, than live in freedom with a polluted conscience" (Lovejoy 336). As time passed and the likelihood of a pardon decreased, Torrey became despondent and his health worsened. He became resigned to his fate. Torrey was 33—"His exit ... perfectly calm and peaceful ... without a groan or struggle; and with every indication of a happy state of mind" (Lovejoy 294).

Torrey's body was brought home to Boston, where it was denied a burial by the Congregational Church, for whom he had been a minister. The funeral was moved to the Tremont Temple of Nathaniel Colver. Many expressed grief and anger at Torrey's passing, especially blacks: in Oberlin, they offered sympathy to his wife and children, and condemned the governor of Maryland for not allowing him to go home after the state of his health had become hopeless; in Boston, they voted to erect a monument to him. Torrey was buried at the Mt. Auburn Cemetery in Cambridge, and though the monument was never built, possibly because of Garrison, with whom he had feuded,* his grave frequently was visited by free blacks throughout the antebellum period (Quarles 165).

An issue of growing concern was the vote for free blacks. At the Liberty Party's national convention in December 1844, the Rev. E.C. Pritchett had introduced a resolution stating that: "the disenfranchisement of our fellow colored citizens is a disgrace in this State and we call on our Democratic majority in the Legislature to take the requisite measures for righting this wrong..." ("Liberty Party National Convention").

The push for full Negro suffrage in the state had been developing for years among leaders of the black community. It had been the major focus of the state Negro conventions of 1843 and 1844 in Rochester and Schenectady. Now, abolitionists throughout the state, led by the Liberty Party, were calling for the restoration of full suffrage to blacks to be a topic for discussion at the State Constitutional Convention in 1846.

Regional feeling strongly supported full Negro suffrage. In an April 15, 1846, letter, William Hotchkiss of Chestertown, later elected as a Warren County delegate to the convention, promised to "vote to abolish the property qualification" ("Interesting Correspondence" 2). Leonard Gibbs, who had just moved back to the area after living for six years in New York City and who was elected as a delegate from Washington County, wrote that he was "decidedly and without hesitation" in favor of full Negro suffrage ("Correspondence of the Albany Patriot" 15 April 1846).

*William Lloyd Garrison spoke out against the monument, saying that the money could be put to better use.

Gibbs had been active in abolition circles in New York City, being a member of the executive committee of the American and Foreign Anti-Slavery Society. Legend also suggests his participation in the Underground Railroad there.* Moving back to his native Washington County, he settled in Union Village with his wife and two daughters and became a trustee of the Free Church. He quickly assumed a leadership role with Corliss and Mowry in the county's abolitionism, which may have needed some direction with the apparent break-up of the Eastern New York Anti-Slavery Society.† The county's Liberty Party, however, was still very active, and Union Village continued to be a hub as indicated by a Liberty Party convention held there in 1847 to nominate Jabez Parkhurst and Noadiah Moore as State Supreme Court candidates ("Nominations" 94).

Another regional convention that reflected the county's strong role in northern New York abolition was the Convention of Christians and Christian Ministers at the North Granville Presbyterian Church on September 1. No mention was made of the Underground Railroad, but a number of its participants had an association with it, including Gibbs; Corliss; the Rev. Miller of Argyle; the Rev. Sabin McKinney, Free Church pastor and son-in-law of Corliss, who moved to Fredonia, a major Underground Railroad terminal, the following year; Granville Presbyterian minister, the Rev. J. B. Shaw, whose home in Granville was a legendary stop and who would move to Fairhaven, Vermont, a reputed terminal; and the Rev. Charles Gillette of Granville, who would move to Fort Covington, the home of conductor Parkhurst. President of the convention was the Rev. Lewis Kellogg, pastor of the First Presbyterian Church in Whitehall, another suspected terminal. Among the resolutions passed were that "slavery is a great hindrance to progress of religion in the states in which it exists, that it is the duty of all Christians to do rightfully what they can to remove it, and that ministers ... in this county be requested to preach to their respective congregation ... on the sinfulness of slavery ("Convention of Christians..." Albany Patriot).

Meanwhile the state constitutional convention was in session throughout the summer and decided to put the issue of full Negro suffrage to the vote of a referendum on Election Day. The statewide outcome resulted in 223,834 voting against it and 85,306 voting in favor (Hirsch 423). In northern New York, however, the outcome was much different. The top three pro-suffrage vote tallies in the state came from the region. Clinton County had the state's highest pro-suffrage vote with 72.8 percent and Essex County was right behind with 71.1 percent; in third place was Washington County with 59.9 percent. In all, only ten of the state's 59 counties recorded pluralities over 50 percent, and two more were in northern New York—Franklin and Warren counties (Field 62). This strongly suggests that the region was a safe haven for fugitive slaves and is another strong piece of evidence in support of the legends of the Underground Railroad here, which many have ignored.

---

*Wilbur Siebert lists a Gibbs as an Underground Railroad operative in New York City.
†It is not known by this author when the Eastern New York Anti-Slavery Society disbanded.

Chapter 15

FAT OF THE LAND

Though frustrated by the slow process of politics, Gerrit Smith did not leave the Liberty Party. Instead, he decided to take matters into his own hands. He set aside 120,000 acres of his own land in the Adirondacks and other sections of northeastern and central New York to be parceled into 40-acre homesteads for needy, temperate black men between the ages of 21 and 60. Not only would it give them a new beginning, but it would also qualify them to vote under the state property qualification. Assisting Smith in the process of selecting candidates were Theodore Wright, Charles Ray, and James McCune Smith, all members of the New York Committee of Vigilance.

This was a period of transition for free blacks becoming frustrated with the discrimination they encountered daily. The moral improvement societies were now encouraging blacks to leave the cities and cultivate farms in the countryside, where they could escape much of the prejudice and become self-sufficient.

Austin Steward, the former slave and Rochester businessman who for a time was leader of the Wilberforce Colony, articulated this position in his autobiography:

> I knew many colored farmers, all of whom are well respected in the neighborhood of their residence. I wish I could count them by hundreds; but our people mostly flock to cities where they allow themselves to be made "hewers of wood and drawers of water"; barbers and waiters,—when, if they would but retire to the country and purchase a piece of land, cultivate and improve it, they would be far richer and happier than they can be in the crowded city. It is a mistaken idea that there is more prejudice against color in the country. True, it exists everywhere, but I regard it less potent in the country, where a farmer can live less dependent on his oppressors [Steward 167].

Gerrit Smith himself attended the "Great Meeting of the Colored People in Troy" at the Liberty Street Church in October 1846 to promote his land giveaway along

101

with one of his first recipients, Robert Grooms, who presented potatoes, wheat, and corn that he had grown on his land. Also speaking at the meeting was William Jones, a fugitive slave, who hoped to accept Smith's offer.

"I will go to work for myself. I will cut down my own trees, build my own cabin, plant my own grain, eat the fruit of my own stall," he said to a round of applause. "Once I had to drive the carriage of an old drunken slaveholder, but soon I hope to drive my own team, lead my own horse to water.... We must not be afraid of a big tree. I used to be compelled to clear up ten acres of land a year in the South, and do other work, and get thumped in the bargain. But when I reach my little farm, with my liberty axe I expect to clear up 15 acres annually. I have received so much abuse from white men that once I thought all were my enemies. I was mistaken. God Bless, Mr. Gerrit Smith.... Come off from the steamboats and leave your barbershops. Leave the kitchen, where you have to live underground all day and climb up ten pair of stairs at night. Tomorrow morning I intend to leave for Essex County to see for myself" ("Great Meeting..." 201).

During this time, an open letter from Wright, Ray, and McCune Smith to free black men in New York was being published in newspapers around the state urging them to accept Smith's offer. They also outlined a plan, which they believed potential grantees should follow to achieve success: "Go clear and cultivate" the land and "retain" it, no matter what purchase offer is made for it; practice frugality, self-reliance, trust (of fellow grantees), and temperance. The Temperance movement was particularly vibrant among blacks in upstate New York at this time as evidenced by a recent convention at a town, not named, along the Hudson where 10,000 "persons of color" attended and were "well-treated" by the townspeople ("Correspondence of the Patriot" 203).

Among those who went to Essex County, where a group of blacks had established a colony called "Timbucto" on the Smith lands in the town of North Elba, were Edward and Charles Weeks, sons of John Weeks from the town of Jackson in Washington County. As early as 1827, the Weeks family had lived in the town of Jackson, where several other blacks had farms. That year John Weeks had purchased a half-acre of land, and in 1850 would own a 40-acre farm worth $1,200 (Jones 33). Before going to Timbucto, Edward had married Hannah Dimond at Henry's Garnet's Liberty Street Church (29). However, the Weeks brothers quickly became discouraged by the poor farmland and harsh winter. Charles moved back to Jackson in Washington County, while Edward and his wife, Hannah, moved first to Westport, then to Keeseville, where he became a barber and aided runaway slaves (Jones interview).*

Another black man who settled in northern New York during this time was a "Mr. Fitch," who built a cabin atop a lonely mountain outside Corinth, New York, then called Jessup's Landing. According to a one-page typewritten document attributed to "Mrs. Ellsworth's Scrapbook," Fitch aided fugitive slaves. It states the following:

> In Civil War times West Mountain was on route of the underground railway

*This would not be surprising, considering that Edward and Hannah were on the rolls of the Free Church in Union Village from 1846 to 1856 (Manual... 29).

Scene of black farmers in the fields of Timbucto. (Courtesy of the Adirondack Museum.)

[This is not the West Mountain in Queensbury, Warren County but another mountain south of Corinth].... It is said there was a station about one mile from Ballston Center, near High Bridge. From there, slaves taken over back road, near the Smith farm ... a short distance west of M.G. up through Daniel's School District (past Frink House) through Chatfield Corners and on to Lake Desolation. From this point the route continued down Honse Creek and thru the wilderness to Black Pond, west of Corinth, thence along a blazed trail for about two miles to a little cottage owned by a Negro named Fitch.

His house was an oft frequented station. For a day or two the slaves would rest at the Fitch home and then be guided by their host past Lake Efnor, down the outlet to the Sacandaga River. From here they went through a section known as the Allentown, thence to Newton Farm, Hadley Hill continuing easterly for about five miles to Stony Creek and thence to a cottage near Thurman Station and on to the border.

Mrs. Ellsworth adds that thereafter they may have "traveled through the mountains, and up through Keene, past Cascade Lakes to a station known still as 'Freeman's Station,' which is near the Olympic Bobsled Run on Mt. Vanhovenburg..." ("Mrs. Ellsworth's Scrap Book").*

Although we cannot be certain, a whitewasher named Henry Fitch who lived in

The document ascribed to "Mrs. Ellsworth's Scrapbook" can be found in the archives of the Saratoga County Historian's office.

Troy from 1841 to 1843, and for a time in 1846, may have been both the Mr. Fitch on the mountaintop and the Mr. Fitch, earlier referred to, at the Prigg Decision meeting in Troy.* If so, he may have known some of the Smith grantees, as a number were from Troy.

Fitch likely found support and friendship in nearby Jessup's Landing, the site of Liberty Party meetings held by Abel Brown and "General" William L. Chaplin, who in fact led a convention there in October 1846 to nominate Liberty Party candidates for the upcoming election. The Underground Railroad was in evidence at that convention. Among the participants was Underground Railroad conductor Mason Anthony, who also was president of the county's Liberty Party and who was nominated for the State Assembly. Conventioneers openly admitted aiding runaway slaves, the report mentioning a black woman who had left her master from Georgia and had been hiding in a barn in Jessup's Landing for the previous three weeks. A resolution related to this also was passed: "We advocate ... strict laws preventing citizens of this state from assisting in the *recovery* [author's italics] of fugitive slaves" ("Saratoga Liberty Nominating Convention").

Connections northward may have been made through the Albany Female Anti-Slavery Society, which reported the continual passage of fugitive slaves through the city during this period—"besides the two barrels of clothing sent to Canada, they have distributed considerable quantities to fugitive slaves passing through the city, and have quite a quantity still on hand." Their report also mentioned support of a mission to Canada by the Rev. Cyrus Prindle to minister to fugitive slaves and quoted letters from Prindle that had been published in the *True Wesleyan*. They told of Prindle's visit to Dawn, where he met Hiram Wilson at his manual labor school, and Josiah Henson, who some claim was the model for Harriet Beecher Stowe's Uncle Tom.† He also visited Amherstburgh, which was across the river from Detroit and which he described as "the great western gate to freedom ... [where] thousands have ... inhaled the breath of freedom [and] in some instances when the slave master was in company with them on the same boat that landed them on the Queen's dominions!" ("Third Annual Report..." 31).

By the end of the year, another of the *Albany Patriot's* radical young abolitionists was no more. In December 1846, the colleague of Brown and Torrey, former *Patriot* editor E.W. Goodwin, passed away. His obituary published by the *Patriot* mainly concerned itself with his career as an artist, which included portraits of former President Martin Van Buren and Liberty Party presidential candidate James Birney ("The Late..." 30). It did not mention his part in aiding fugitive slaves that caused a reward to be offered for him, Brown, and Torrey by Southern slaveholders during the years when the *Patriot* was known as the *Tocsin of Liberty*.

The void left by Brown, Torrey, and now Goodwin was taken over by that unflappable blueblood of abolition, "General" William L. Chaplin, who became the

---

*The Prigg Decision of the Supreme Court was thought at the time to threaten the security of runaway slaves living in the North; Fitch's vocal concerns suggest he may have been a fugitive slave.

†Samuel Ringgold Ward, the fugitive slave preacher, who resided first in Poughkeepsie and then moved to Syracuse, had little good to say about the school in his 1855 autobiography. Though he did commend the efforts of the fugitive slaves who had settled Dawn, he was not very complimentary about their children, whose indolence he said had prevented them from prospering as they might have (Ward 194–199).

Patriot editor in 1846. Son of a prominent Congregational minister, the Rev. Daniel Chaplin, and one of the wealthy Lawrences of the prosperous mill town in north-eastern Massachusetts, Chaplin was a graduate of Andover and Harvard ("The Case..." 14). Trained to be a lawyer, he instead turned over his life to social activism, first engaged by the Temperance movement and then moving onto his life's work, the gospel of abolition. Chaplin coupled his anti-slavery work with journalism, first as editor of the *American Citizen* in Rochester, then as the *Patriot's* Washington correspondent where he observed slavery first hand and, to his revulsion, a number of Congressmen's mixed children, who also were their slaves.

As editor of the *Patriot*, Chaplin was confronted by a fragmented Liberty Party, with many party members, including his colleague and former *Patriot* editor James C. Jackson, joining a new, more moderate wing called the Liberty League. It sought to move away from the "One-Idea" approach and broaden the political agenda. Another difficulty was the apparent dissolution of the Eastern New York Anti-Slavery Society, which had been a major source of support for the *Patriot*. He also was forced into double duty as the newspaper's primary agent. An account of one of his trips through Washington and Warren counties was published in the *Patriot* in 1847. His first stop was Union Village, about which he had very favorable comments, followed by Whitehall, about which he did not. From Whitehall, he traveled to Luzerne in Warren County, where he praised his audiences, and on his return, addressed a meeting in Glens Falls, where he also found support ("Labor Abroad" 86).

During this transition period, the New York Committee of Vigilance was reorganized. Theodore Wright, one of its founders and guiding forces, passed away at the age of 50 in May 1847, and his father, R.P.G. Wright, the Schenectady barber, only two months later. The Quaker Isaac T. Hopper became NYCV president, and during the first six months that year, it aided 166 fugitive slaves (Quarles 154). Also, in October, a National Negro Convention also was held in Troy at Garnet's Liberty Street Church with 68 delegates from nine states, 46 of them from New York. Following the defeat of the Negro suffrage referendum in New York, it focused on the issue of creating wealth among blacks through land ownership and commerce. Education was given a high priority in achieving these ends, and committees on education and the development of a national Negro press were appointed (Bell 15–17).*

Another event that year involved the meeting of two men whose importance has enlarged enormously with the passing of time. In his 1881 autobiography, Frederick Douglass provided an account of his first meeting with John Brown, which is as fascinating as its subject and measures the man as well as any account before or since.

"[Brown] was a respectable [wool] merchant in [Springfield, Massachusetts] and our first place of meeting was at his store," Douglass wrote. "This was a substantial brick building, on a prominent, busy street. A glance at the interior, as well as at the massive walls without, gave me the impression that the owner must be a man of considerable wealth...."

---

*An interesting sidelight to the convention is the mention of the Northern Star, Stephen Myers' newspaper. Apparently, it still was in publication, though this author has not seen any issues after January 1843. Another reference to a later publication date is in The Black Abolitionist Papers, which reports the last issue of the Northern Star in June 1849, as a joint effort with S.R. Ward's Impartial Citizen (Ripley 39).

Douglass was in for a surprise, however, when brought to Brown's home.

> Every member of the family, young and old, seemed glad to see me, and I was
> made much at home in a very little while. I was, however, a little disappointed
> with the appearance of the house and with its location.... In fact, the house
> was neither commodious nor elegant, nor its situation desirable. It was a small
> wooden building, on a back street, in a neighborhood chiefly occupied by labor-
> ing men and mechanics; respectable enough to be sure, but not quite the place,
> I thought, where one would look for the residence of a flourishing and suc-
> cessful merchant. Plain as was the outside ... the inside was plainer. Its furni-
> ture would have satisfied a Spartan.... My first meal passed under the misnomer
> of tea ... beef soup, cabbage, and potatoes; a meal such as a man might relish
> after following the plow all day ... the table announced itself unmistakably of
> pine and of the plainest workmanship. There was no hired help visible. The
> mother, daughters, and sons did the serving and did it well.... In [this house]
> there were no disguises, no illusions, no make believes. Everything implied
> stern truth, solid purpose, and rigid economy. I was not long in company with
> the master of this house before I discovered that he was indeed the master of
> it, and was likely to become mine too if I stayed long enough.... His wife believed
> in him, and his children observed him with reverence. Whenever he spoke his
> words commanded earnest attention. His arguments, which I ventured at some
> points to oppose, seemed to convince all; his appeals touched all, and his will
> impressed all. Certainly I never felt myself in the presence of a stronger reli-
> gious influence than while in this man's house.
>   In person he was lean, strong, and sinewy, of the best New England mould,
> built for times of trouble, fitted to grapple with the flintiest hardships. Clad
> in plain American woolen, shod in boots of cowhide leather, and wearing a
> cravat of the same substantial material, under six feet high, less than 150 pounds
> in weight, aged about fifty, he presented a figure, straight and symmetrical as
> a mountain pine.... His head was not large, but compact and high. His hair
> was coarse, strong, slightly gray and closely trimmed, and grew low on his fore-
> head. His face was smoothly shaved, and revealed a strong square mouth, sup-
> ported by a broad and prominent chin. His eyes were bluish gray, and in
> conversation they were full of light and fire. When on the street, he moved
> with a long, springing racehorse step, absorbed by his own reflections.... Such
> was the man, whose name I had heard in whispers ... Captain John Brown...
> [Douglass 277–279].

That evening Brown described his long-held dream of leading a large-scale slave
revolt in the South. His idea was to organize a guerilla army that would undertake
missions into the South from somewhere in the Allegheny Mountains. Having lived
in Ohio and Southwestern Pennsylvania, he knew the area well and told Douglass:

> God has given the strength of the hills to freedom. They were placed here for
> the emancipation of the Negro race; they are full of natural forts, where one
> man for defense will be equal to a hundred for attack; they are full also of good
> hiding-places, where large numbers of brave men could be concealed, and baffle
> and elude pursuit for a long time.
>   I could take a body of men into them and keep them there despite all efforts
> of Virginia to dislodge them ... My plan is to take at first about twenty-five
> picked men, and begin on a small scale; supply them with arms and ammuni-
> tion and post them in squads of five on a line of twenty-five miles. The most
> persuasive and judicious of these shall go down to the fields from time to time,

as opportunity offers, and induce the slaves to join them; seeking and selecting the most restless and daring [Stavis 66–67].

Brown added that in time he would expand his forces, who would liberate slaves in large numbers, sending those who did not join them north by the Underground Railroad. Brown made such a strong impression on Douglass that a continuing friendship developed, and Douglass admitted that Brown had an even stronger influence on the militancy of his views that developed progressively thereafter (Douglass 282).

John Brown as he looked when he met Frederick Douglass.

That same year, Brown met another black man with whom he became close friends. Willis Augustus Hodges had been a farmer in Virginia—the free son of a white Southerner and a black woman—and was one of the foremost supporters of black agriculture in the North. He and Brown became friends after Hodges began publishing the black newspaper, *The Ram's Horn*, in 1847, and had actually met at the newspaper's office in New York City. Hodges subsequently published "Sambo's Mistakes," a satirical essay by Brown in which he posed as a black author who criticized Northern blacks for their submissive response to racism (Hodges xli-xliii). Both Hodges and Douglass would remain among Brown's strongest supporters right up until the last days before Harpers Ferry.

Hodges was one of only 200 or so blacks who actually emigrated to the northern New York wilderness (Gurnet G4). Most of them were Smith grantees. Hodges had purchased his 200-acre plot overlooking Loon Lake, using funds from the sale of *The Ram's Horn* (Hodges xliv). He arrived in Franklin County on May 12, 1848, with his family and eight others, where they formed a colony called Blacksville not far from the Smith lands in North Elba. It was probably Hodges who gave Brown the idea to go and see how Smith's grantees were doing (Blankman 35–36).

When Brown first gazed upon the cloud-piercing Adirondack peaks, he said he felt the presence of God. But he also found the struggling black farmers in Timbucto huddled together in crude, dilapidated wooden shacks with stovepipes for smokestacks. After returning to Springfield, he wrote Smith, offering his services to move to North Elba and help them.

"I am something of a pioneer," he wrote. "I grew up among the woods and wild Indians of Ohio, and am used to the climate and the way of life that your colony finds so trying. I will take one of your farms myself, clear it up and plant it, and show my colored neighbors how much work should be done; will give them work as I have occasion, look after them in all needful ways, and be a kind of father to them" (Hearn 17).

Willis Augustus Hodges

Brown was facing another business failure among the many that plagued him throughout his life. He showed up at Smith's mansion after several days on horseback from Springfield, Massachusetts, dressed in a ragged homespun shirt, holey boots, and a shabby Sunday dress jacket soiled with mud and blood. Nevertheless, his farming knowledge and passion impressed Smith, and they agreed upon an arrangement in which Brown would move there and assist the black farmers (Renehan 19–20).

In October 1848, John Brown sent the struggling farmers of Timbucto and his friend, Willis Hodges, barrels of pork and flour, and in May 1849, he moved his family from Springfield, Massachusetts to North Elba. They first rented a small house, a two-story dwelling with the second story unfinished and little more than an attic. After a trip back to Springfield to tie up the loose ends of his failing wool business, he and his sons bought the farm in North Elba that would be his eventual resting place.

Chapter 16

EXODUS

The movement among free blacks for land came about the same time that a major new national political party with an anti-slavery position was organized. Formed by a coalition of Democrats, Whigs, and Liberty Party members, it called for the non-extension of slavery into new states rather than immediate abolition. Its candidate in the 1848 election was former president Martin Van Buren, and its slogan was "Free Soil, Free Labor, Free Speech, and Free Men." However, while many of its leaders voiced opposition to slavery, they also confessed privately to a belief in the inferiority of blacks and the desirability of segregation (Foner 242–243). In fact, although the party professed to be anti-slavery, it failed to include a provision for the support of the rights of blacks in its political platform, to which all abolitionists hitherto had been firmly committed. However, with the Liberty Party no longer a force in national politics, partly as a result of the split caused by the Liberty League, anti-slavery voters had no other viable option.

Early in the spring of 1848, the Rev. Jermain Loguen of Syracuse, the former fugitive slave and Underground Railroad conductor, made an exploratory trip into the Adirondacks to enlist local abolitionists to aid Gerrit Smith's land grantees. After his trip, Loguen wrote a report to James McCune Smith, describing the land grants in Essex County as good for farming and those in Franklin County valuable for timber. Referring to the latter, he noted the increased number of sawmills in the region.

Loguen also issued a warning about the con games played by some locals with blacks who had gone to claim their land. They were leading claimants to the wrong plots, which often were worthless parcels on some remote hilltop, and offering to buy them at a very cheap price. He advised recipients not to sell their land and that they could identify it by marks on the trees made by surveyors. However, in order to protect themselves, Loguen suggested that recipients find trustworthy individuals to assist them and mentioned the following: Jesse Gay and Alfred S. Spooner in Elizabeth-

The Rev. Jermain Loguen

town; Uriah Mihills in Keene; J. Tobey, Jr., in Jay; Wendell Lansing in Wilmington; William M. Flack in AuSable Forks; the Merills in Merillville; and Rensselaer Bigelow in Malone ("Gerrit Smith's Land" 1).

Continuing runaway slave traffic in the area was reported by the Rev. Cyrus Prindle, the ubiquitous Wesleyan-Methodist preacher whose travels took him through Vermont, northern New York, and Canada. He was quoted in the *Green Mountain Freeman* on March 5, 1848, that "by the Underground Railroad, in which I have some interest, we have been doing the past fall, a large business" (Zirblis 86). The Albany Female Anti-Slavery Society, which had an interest in Prindle's activities, confirmed the continuing traffic in its sixth annual report: "Our Society during the past year has, as formerly, aided the Canada Colonization scheme, but has directed its efforts more particularly to the relief of fugitives passing through" ("Annual Report of the Albany Female A.S. Society" 1).

One means by which these fugitives may have journeyed between New York and Albany was reported in the same issue of the *Patriot*. It told of the *Armenia*, a "neat, swift, little day-boat from New York to Troy." It could make the trip from New York to Albany in nine hours, and "nothing on the river is likely to slip by her in any fair contest." The safety of its passengers was assured by "Capt. Tallman ... who makes it his study to oblige and render secure all who commit themselves or their property to his care." And the boat's design was marked by a novel "improvement" that made it more amenable for the passage of fugitive slaves:

> One thing we notice, which is new in the arrangement of steamboats: the table is set on the first deck instead of below, as is usual.... A light, airy saloon, of a hot or a dark day, is altogether more comfortable than a close and dungeon-like place. But the most incriminating evidence was the identity of its steward—none other than Stephen Myers ["Comfort and Economy for the Traveller" 2–3].

Myers as we already know had long been aiding fugitive slaves and apparently was still publishing the *Northern Star and Freemen's Advocate*, which sometimes published accounts of the fugitive slaves it had helped. Not only was Myers a social and political organizer, journalist, and speaker, but he also could cook, as the article testified—"a man who knows as well as any other, how to cater successfully for the tastes of those, who are not wholly insensible to creature comforts. He really does up the thing, with the support of his assistants, in just about the best style. Stephen has had a long experience in the culinary department, and can't be beat by white folks" (ibid.).

A memoir from these years outlined a route very similar to the one described by Mrs. Ellsworth. It was written in 1849 by Lydia Frances Sherman, who lived in Hadley in northern Saratoga County, just across the Hudson River from Lake Luzerne in Warren County.

"The first station after leaving Saratoga," she wrote, "was in Greenfield at the house of Mason Anthony, a good Quaker abolitionist. Friend Anthony would bring the escaped man after dark to our house in Hadley. The next night my father would take him to the house of Uncle Henry Beach, in Luzerne, Warren County, six miles away. From that station he would be taken to a place near Lake George, and so on" (Sherman 1–2).

The Sherman route also corresponds to one that could have connected to the Rev. Thomas Baker of the Darrowsville Wesleyan-Methodist Church, mentioned in Chapter One. At this time, he is believed to have been working with John Brown, who by then had moved to North Elba. Lyman Epps, who came to Timbucto from Troy with his family and who was five

1856.

DAY BOAT FOR

ALBANY & TROY

LANDING [EACH WAY] AT

Nyack, Grassy Point, West Point, Newburgh, Poughkeepsie, Kingston Point, Bristol, Catskill, Hudson, and Coxsackie.

MEALS SERVED ON BOARD.

THE FAVORITE STEAMER

Armenia,

CAPT. SMITH,

WILL LEAVE FOOT OF CANAL & SPRING STREETS,

EVERY

MONDAY, WEDNESDAY & FRIDAY,

AT 7 O'CLOCK, A. M.

Returning,—Leave TROY at 6, and ALBANY at 7 o'clock,

EVERY TUESDAY, THURSDAY, AND SATURDAY,

Passengers by this Boat will arrive at Albany in ample time to take the Evening Trains of Cars for Saratoga, Whitehall, Rutland, Burlington, Montreal, and the West.

A Baggage Master will accompany the Steamer each way to Check Baggage FREE.

E. H. TRIPP, Printer, 272 Greenwich Street, N.Y.

Advertisement of the *Armenia*, a steamboat on which Albany stationmaster Stephen Myers served as steward. (From "An American Time Capsule, Three Centuries of Broadsides and Other Printed Ephemera," in the Rare Books and Special Collections Division of the Library of Congress.)

when Brown moved to North Elba, remembered Brown assisting fugitive slaves. "After John Brown come, they got him to help em' into Canada," Epps said, adding that Brown transported his passengers in an ox-cart (Thompson 303).

Brown also was in frequent contact during this time with Willis Hodges in nearby Blacksville, where fugitive slaves also were reported to be passing through (Hodges xlvi-xlvii). Brown made numerous trips to Springfield, which gave him additional opportunities to rendezvous with runaway slaves in Whitehall, the hometown of his wife, Mary. One of his friends there was Ralph Richards, a school principal from Whitehall, who had been vice-president of the Washington County Liberty Party in 1846 (Johnson 370).

Overall, despite the interest created by the Smith land grants, this was a relatively slow period for the Underground Railroad in New York State. For example, the New York State Vigilance Committee reported assisting only 151 fugitive slaves in 1849 (Campbell 6). But as the year 1850 began, things changed with the talk of a new, stronger fugitive slave law. Senator Andrew Mason of Virginia introduced the bill on January 3, and a debate began that lasted through the summer. Some Northerners attempted to add a clause that guaranteed fugitive slaves a trial by jury, but this failed, and it became evident that a law which threatened the freedom of fugitive slaves and jeopardized those who assisted them was about to be passed.

Of course, activity along the Underground Railroad increased. During that summer, a Washington correspondent to the *New York Express* reported: "The runaway slaves have been so numerous of late in these parts, under the instigations of the abolitionists here and elsewhere, that the owners of this species of property have become very much alarmed, and hence are disposed to remove them to safer parts of the United States or to sell them to slave traders" ("An Exciting Slave Case" 131). One incident involved the coachman of President Fillmore, who had assumed the presidency after the sudden death of President Zachary Taylor in May of that year. The coachman's wife, children and grandchildren were sold to a slave trader for auction. Fortunately, the president, General Winfield Scott, and a number of senators and citizens contributed the funds to purchase their freedom.

Earlier that month, a fugitive slave case of national prominence took place in the nation's capital involving "General" William L. Chaplin, who had moved there after publication of the *Patriot* stopped sometime in 1848. He had been purchasing freedom for slaves with money provided by Gerrit Smith and was being watched by authorities in Washington. Four policemen were waiting in ambush one night as Chaplin and two slaves of a Southern congressman fled in his carriage about six miles outside the city. One policeman pushed a rail fence between the spokes of the hind wheels while the others grabbed the bridles of the horses. Chaplin whipped his horses furiously but to no avail, as the rear wheels of the coach had been blocked. One of the fugitive slaves apparently fired the first shot, and, while the police subdued Chaplin, an exchange of shots followed. Two of the policemen and both fugitives were wounded, and one of the fugitive slaves was able to escape. Chaplin and the other fugitive, however, were arrested and put in jail ("Another Martyr to Liberty" 131).

In the *North Star*, Frederick Douglass wrote:

> We have seen him, heard him, and know him; and if our brother had been seized at our side by a ferocious tiger, we could not feel more keenly than we now do for William L. Chaplin.... As to what will be the fate of Mr. Chaplin, the prospect seems now too dark—too fearful to contemplate.... He is too distinguished a mark to be allowed to escape the inhuman clutches of slavery. Yet something ought to be done. If money can bail him, it should be forthcoming. But if this will not do, there should be petitions circulated in all directions.... The time has come for action... ["Arrest and Imprisonment..." 134].

A mass convention was called the next week in Cazenovia with both Douglass and Gerrit Smith, along with 2,000 others, to plead for Chaplin ("Cazenovia Convention" 138). At the meeting a circular from the Chaplin Fund Committee was distributed. It listed as its members such notable abolitionists as Samuel May, Joshua Giddings, Salmon Chase, Francis Jackson, and John Greenleaf Whittier. The circular stated that $20,000 was needed to provide Chaplin with the proper legal defense ("*Circular...*" 22 August 1850).

Five months later, Chaplin was freed on bail of $25,000, equivalent to $500,000 today, and given a hero's welcome in both Syracuse and Boston. He said if faced with the choice of helping fugitive slaves again, that he would rather be dead than refuse ("The Chaplin Meeting" 14). Chaplin owed his life to Gerrit Smith, who had personally contributed more than $12,000 to his bail fund (Harlow 291–293), and because Chaplin did not return to Maryland to face trial, Smith forfeited his money. In addition, his lawyer, Lysander Spooner, was not paid. It had been hoped that Chaplin would stage a lecture tour to help pay for some of his legal costs. Instead, little was heard from him thereafter, and it left some with less respect for him. Apparently, he settled down with his wife, Theodosia Gilbert, the business partner of his close friend and fellow abolitionist, James C. Jackson, whom he had married while in prison.

On August 26, 1850, the second Fugitive Slave Law was passed by the Senate, and on September 18, it passed in Congress by a vote of 109–75. Not one Southern congressman voted against it, though 15 abstained. It was a provision of the Compromise of 1850 that included outlawing the slave trade in Washington, D.C., and slavery in California, as well as extending slavery into the territories of Utah and New Mexico.

The new law put the handling of fugitive slave cases solely under federal jurisdiction, and not only denied alleged fugitive slaves the right to a trial by jury, but denied any testimony by them on their own behalf. All that was required for the arrest of an alleged fugitive slave was the identification of the fugitive by two witnesses who confirmed under oath that the individual was indeed a fugitive from slavery. It also punished those aiding fugitive slaves with a fine of $1,000* and six months in jail for each offense. Adding force was a $1,000 fine imposed on federal marshals who failed to follow an order to arrest a fugitive slave; these marshals also were made liable for the value of any slave who escaped from them. Furthermore, it encouraged a prejudicial review of the cases by judges by paying them $10 for those cases in which a fugitive slave was turned over to the claimant and $5 for those in which the burden of proof was not satisfied.

It frightened not only fugitive slaves who had settled in the North but also free blacks who feared the law's disregard for the rights of the accused would increase the activity of kidnappers. "It is impossible to describe the anguish, terror and despair which fill the minds of our colored fellow-citizens," Garrison wrote in *The Liberator*. "They are very naturally wrought up to the highest pitch of desperation, and are determined to sell their lives and liberty as dearly as possible. They are now generally armed. It will be an evil hour—probably his last hour—whenever the slave hunter shall visibly make an effort to seize his victim in this city. Boston is not New York..." ("The Slave Catching Law" 159). Garrison was referring to the seizure in New York of James

---

*Based on the year 2000, this is approximately $20,000 (The Inflation Calculator).

THE FUGITIVE BILL!

THE PANTING SLAVE!

FREEMEN TO BE MADE SLAVES!

Let every colored man and woman attend the GREAT MASS MEETING to be held in

ZION CHURCH,

Church street, corner of Leonard, on

Tuesday Evening, October, 1, 1850.

for your Liberty, your Fire-side is in danger of being invaded! Devote this night upon the question of YOUR DUTY in the CRISIS.

Shall we resist Oppression? Shall we defend our Liberties? Shall we be FREEMEN or SLAVES?

By order of the Chairman of the Committee of 13.

Fugitive Slave Law meeting in New York City. (From *National Anti-Slavery Standard*, 10 October 1850: 78.)

Hamlet, a fugitive slave from Maryland, whose case was widely publicized as the first arrest under the new law.

Fugitive slaves were in such haste that they left behind many of their worldly possessions. They had good reason, considering the increased activities of kidnappers, like the attempt in Providence, Rhode Island, to kidnap Henry "Box" Brown ("Attempt to Kidnap a Colored Woman" 143). A general climate of hysteria had developed among blacks in the North. Both free and fugitive made a hasty pilgrimage to Canada. Among them were Frederick Douglass, Jermain Loguen, and Harriet Tubman. Henry Garnet, another fugitive slave who had gained prominence, was arrested under the jurisdiction of the law. As soon as he was released by the presiding judge, he left the country and did not return for five years.

Reports of the exodus of blacks were widespread. The *Buffalo Republic* stated that "a party of 51 colored men, women, and children from Pittsburgh under the command of B.G. Sampson ... crossed the Ferry at Black Rock into Canada. They were all armed 'to the teeth,' and on their way to Toronto.... When they landed on the British side, they paraded on the beach and again swung their hats and gave shouts of joy mingled with song. It is said, that one hundred left Pittsburgh in this party, but 49 dropped off and remained in the States for the present. It is also stated that 1500 have already organized and are on their way to Canada from the States..." ("Slave Emigration" 2).

In Toronto, a correspondent wrote, "The numbers who will take refuge under this species of ostracism, will no doubt, far exceed those of the captured. Indeed it is impossible to say to what extent this emigration may not be carried, as but few negroes in the free States will be secure from the meshes of the new law, which is so framed that by a little hard swearing a planter may successfully claim almost any negro as his property..." ("Fugitive Slaves in Canada" 3).

A Utica dispatch reported, "Sixteen fugitive slaves on a boat for Canada, passed through this city yesterday. They were well armed and determined to fight to the last" ("Slave Catching in New York..." 159).

One of the more horrible results of the law took place in Syracuse. A fugitive slave, his wife, and infant child were riding a canal boat. After being told in jest that his master was about to board the boat to apprehend him, the fugitive slave cut his throat, then jumped off the boat with his wife and child. The parents survived; their child did not ("Attempted Suicide of a Fugitive").

Some groups left en masse, like black congregations in Buffalo, Rochester, and Detroit, where 130, 112, and 84 members respectively of a single Baptist church in each city fled in fear, many leaving their belongings behind (Landon 25–26).

And those who did not leave armed themselves in preparation for resistance. They did this at the urging of white abolitionists like Gerrit Smith, who wrote an address for fugitive slaves to their fellows in the South: "We cannot furnish you with weapons," it read in part. "Some of us are not inclined to carry arms, but if you can get them, take them, and before you go back with bondage, use them if you are obliged to take life—the slaveholders would not hesitate to kill you, rather than not take you back into bondage." It was made public on August 30 at the aforementioned Cazenovia Convention, which was attended by 30 fugitive slaves, among whom were the singing Elmore sisters ("Cazenovia Convention" 138).

TO THE FRIENDS OF THE FUGITIVE.

Alarmed at the operation of the new Fugitive Slave Law, the Fugitives from slavery are pressing Northward. Many have been obliged to flee precipitately, leaving behind them all the little they have acquired since they escaped from slavery. They are coming to us in increasing numbers, and they look to us for aid. Oppressed by the tyranny of a heartless and God-defying government, who will help them? Their first and most earnest desire is for *employment*. That is the greatest charity which finds it for them. Help us, then, all you who are friends of the fugitive, to extend to them this charity, this simple justice. Let all, who know, or can learn of places which may be filled by these men, women and youths, give information by letter or otherwise, to ROBERT F. WALL-CUT, or SAMUEL MAY, Jr., 21 Cornhill, Boston.

Friend, whoever you are that reads these lines, this appeal is made to *you*. Cannot you find, or procure, one or more places where the hunted slave may abide securely, and work through the winter? We want you to attend to this AT ONCE.

N. B. Many of the fugitives come very poorly provided with clothing; and those who have garments of any kind to spare, will be sure to confer them on the suffering and needy by sending them, marked For fugitives, at 21 Cornhill, as above.

Advertisement requesting aid for fugitive slaves. (From *The Liberator*, 25 October 1850: 171.)

In New York City, more than 1,500 citizens filled the Zion African Methodist Episcopal Church to hear William P. Powell, the proprietor of the Colored Sailors' Home, denounce the law and hear others vow to fight to the death to remain free.

"My colored brethren, if you have not swords, I say to you, sell your garments and buy one," said John Jacobs, a fugitive slave from South Carolina. "They said they cannot take us back to the South; but I say under the present law, they can; and now I say unto you, let them take only your dead bodies."

The Rev. Charles Gardner seconded Jacobs, cautioning his black brethren to be on guard but not to be passive: "Take the life of every man that attempts to deprive you of your liberty" ("Meetings..." 78).

A call was made for members to join a secret committee to prevent the rendition of fugitive slaves under the supervision of Powell, and the meeting concluded with the announcement by Charles Ray that funds had been raised to purchase the freedom of James Hamlet, the law's first victim (ibid.).

More reports of blacks in arms came from the October 24 *Green Mountain Freeman*, referring to Oswego, New York, and Springfield, Massachusetts. In the latter, where about 50 fugitive slaves resided, thousands gathered at a town hall meeting to discuss the suspected presence of slave-catchers. A pledge of resistance to the new law was made and a resolution passed that called the law "unconstitutional" ("Victims..." 2).

Proceedings of the Colored Citizens of Lansingburgh in relation to the Fugitive Slave Law.

At a meeting of the colored citizens of Lansingburgh, held at the African Methodist Episcopal Church, in Pitt street, Oct 6th, 1850, FRISBY WAY was called to the chair, and JAMES HALL appointed Secretary. The meeting was held to consult together for their own safety, since the passage of the man catching law has taken place The meeting was called to order by James Hall. Prayer was offered up by Rev. Mr. Owens. The meeting being organized, the Chairman stated the object. There was a committee of three appointed, consisting of E. Tillman, John See and Columbus Jones, to draft the resolutions.—After the committee had retired, Mr. Rich of Troy addressed the meeting, in a warm and impressive manner. He was followed by Mr. Mead of Waterford, Mr. Owens of Troy, and many others. The committee returned after an absence of some time with the following resolutions, which were adopted.

Resolved, That we will repudiate any law that has for its object the oppression of any human being, or seeks to assign us to degrading positions.

Whereas, we hold to the declaration of the poet, that, "Who would be free, himself must strike the blow, and that, "resistance to tyrants is obedience to God," therefore,

Resolved, That we welcome to our doors every one who claims for himself the position of a man, and has broken away from the Southern house of bondage, and feel ourselves justified in using every means which the God of love has put in our power to sustain our position.

And whereas active vigilance is the price of liberty, we therefore resolve ourselves into a vigilant association, to look out for our brothers, and also for the oppressor when he shall make his approach, and that measures be taken forthwith, to organise a committee to carry out the object of the association.

Fugitive Slave Law meeting in Lansingburgh, New York, pledges to aid fugitive slaves. (From *Lansingburgh Democrat*, 8 October 1850.)

With all the talk of violence and the reports of many slavecatchers in Boston, President Fillmore sent a large contingent of calvary and artillery there.

Closer to northern New York, a Fugitive Slave Law meeting was held in Lansingburgh, Rensselaer County, at the African Methodist Episcopal Church. Frisby Way chaired the meeting, and William Rich was the primary speaker. The group resolved that "We welcome to our door everyone who ... has broken away from the Southern house of bondage ... that [if his] Master or his minion presume to enter our dwellings and attempt to rescue any of our brethren who he may call his slaves, we feel prepared to resist his pretension" ("Proceedings...").

In the Adirondacks, we find accounts of emergency meetings in Jay, Essex County, and Union Village, Washington County.

At the former, participants included: Wendell Lansing of Wilmington and Uriah D. Mihills of Keene, both of whom were singled out by Jermain Loguen during his trip to the Adirondacks; and Roswell Thompson of North Elba, two of whose sons would be killed at Harpers Ferry. The meeting, held at the Baptist Church, was chaired by James Kimball, Esq., and its resolutions included the following pledge to aid fugitive slaves: "We cannot withhold our approbation from alleged fugitives for using any degree of resistance necessary to prevent resubjection to tyranny from which he has escaped" ("Meeting in Jay" 2).

At the latter, a "large and enthusiastic" meeting was held. Speaking were Erastus Culver, Leonard Gibbs, Free Church trustee John Masters, and attorney James Lourie ("Spirit of the Washington County Press" 15 October 1850: 2). Among the resolutions was the following: "In view of the enormities of the present Fugitive Slave

Law, its opposition to the spirit of the Constitution framed to establish Justice; and *in view of the good character of those in our midst who have escaped from Slavery* [italics added], that we will obey God who commands us to hide the outcast and obey the dictates of the Golden Rule—and *never* whatever pains and penalties we may suffer, assist into remorseless Slavery those who in our midst may be claimed as Fugitives from the Southern prison-house, but defend to the extent of our duty as Christians, citizens and men" (ibid. 22 October 1850: 2). Tensions only worsened in Union Village, for on October 22, one of the area's leading abolitionists and a member of the village's founding family, William H. Mowry was stricken and died at the age of 39.

Despite the determination and strength of the abolitionists in northern New York, total resistance to the Fugitive Slave Law was not a view shared by everyone. The *Sandy Hill Herald* reprinted a glowing account of a pro-law meeting from the *Washington County Post.*

Spirit of the Washington County Press.

The Union Village *Journal* contains the proceedings of the "Anti-Fugitive Slave Law Meeting" alluded to last week. The Resolutions breathe the sentiments of the North, save, perhaps, the following, the spirit of which we view as anti-Republican. All civil laws, however cruel and oppressive in their operations, should be obeyed. The remedy is with the People: they should correct the evil through the ballot-box; and not countenance the spirit of open rebellion against the Government. But to the resolution :—

Resolved, In view of the enormities of the present Fugitive Slave Law, its opposition to the spirit of the Constitution framed to establish Justice; and in view of the good character of those in our midst who have escaped from Slavery, that we will obey God who commands us to hide the outcast and obey the dictates of the Golden Rule,—and never, whatever pains and penalties we may suffer, assist into remorseless Slavery those who in our midst may be claimed as Fugitives from the Southern prison-house, but defend to the extent of our duty as Christians, citizens and men.

Report of Fugitive Slave Law meeting during which a strong commitment is made to aid fugitive slaves. (From *Salem Press,* 22 October 1850: 2.)

Held in old Cambridge at the Academy Hall on November 22, 1850, several resolutions in support of obedience to the law and the supremacy of the union were passed. One stated that "we recognize the provisions of the Constitution relating to the recovery of fugitive slaves from service, as binding on us all as good citizens, and we emphatically deny that we have any intention of breaking our plighted faith with our brethren of the south; that the privileges surrendered by them, in the admission of California as a free State and the establishment of free territorial government for Utah and Mexico, and the suppression of the slave trade in the district of Columbia, are more than equal to any concessions made by the north" ("The Fugitive Slave Law" *Sandy Hill Herald* 2).

Nevertheless, the number in the North pledging resistance to the law was large enough to show that enforcing it would not be easy. On December 18, 1850, abolitionist Henry C. Wright wrote an open letter to *The Liberator* on the "duty of the people of the North to incite and assist the slaves of the South to escape from slavery," appealing for new recruits to the cause of abolition. A God who permits slavery is unjust, he wrote, condemning those who would use the name of God to justify it: "The priests and churches say, God requires slaves to obey their masters, and us to be subject to the powers that be," he wrote. "My answer is—I cannot and will not ... if what you call God requires slaves to obey their masters, or me to submit to and help execute a slaveholding Constitution and the Fugitive Law, I spurn his authority and his worship" ("Duty of the People of the North..." 8).

Only three months after the passage of the law, it was estimated that more than 3,000 American blacks had fled to Canada. It was only the beginning of a mass exodus that would continue throughout 1851, and of a continuing migration that lasted right up through the Civil War (Landon 23). While the second Fugitive Slave Law was a grave setback for abolitionism, it proved to be the beginning of the end for slavery.

Chapter 17

IN SEARCH OF THE PROMISED LAND

Fugitive slaves continued to pour into Canada. But some, like a writer in the *Montreal Courier*, questioned the wisdom of their mass emigration. "A certain number of this class of persons may be very useful," it declared, "but the influx of a large number would be very undesirable. They would not readily find employment for which they are fitted, and the surplus would inevitably fall a burthen on the community..." ("Fugitive Slaves in Canada"). Robin Winks in his seminal study, *The Blacks in Canada*, found this to be true: As the numbers of runaways swelled, prejudice grew among Canadians, and the Promised Land became increasingly less idyllic.

During the early years of migration, runaways were welcomed with open arms. Though they struggled to survive at first, life as free men was better than slavery, and with persistence many found success. In 1837, when Hiram Wilson was sent to Canada by the American Anti-Slavery Society to investigate their condition, he estimated there were 10,000 runaways, who were described as loyal, well behaved, and law-abiding (Landon "Documents: Records..." 199).

Wilson, who became perhaps the foremost fugitive slave missionary in Canada, was well known in northeastern New York. He attended the 1838 Albany convention, was married by Fayette Shipherd in Troy, was visited by Abel Brown in 1842, was given support by local abolitionists, and was identified by Frederick Douglass as the agent to whom he forwarded runaways (Douglass 272).* He remained in Canada until after the Civil War, and, as one observer wrote, "managed to keep himself free from the care of riches, by giving to the needy, as fast as he earned it" (Drew 32).

Like many abolitionists, Wilson looked upon his work as a sacred mission. In 1841, he founded the fugitive slave community of Dawn in western Ontario. His fervor is evident in his description of his efforts:

*Among those who contributed to his mission were Thomas C. Green of Saratoga County and the Albany Female Anti-Slavery Society ("Matters and Things").

On securing the lot and obtaining the Deed, for which I paid $800 of God's gold. I looked upon the ground as emphatically 'Emanuel's land'—called a few persons, white and coloured ... and consecrated the ground to the Lord....

After a tedious walk to Detroit and back, via Chatham, 140 miles through dissolving snow, rain, and mud, partly by moon and starlight, for the purpose of seeing Royal Weller and widow Lovejoy, I shouldered an axe, called a few colored men to my aid, cut away the brush, cleared off a beautiful building spot, chopped the logs, and in 3 days got my house up as high as the joice, 20 by 26 feet. It stands where once stood an Indian wigwam, the old stakes of which I pulled up with my own hands....

Our prospects, brother, are glorious. The merciful designs of Heaven towards the bewildered outcast will surely be accomplished, and we have but to struggle on a little longer, assured that the victory will be ours though we die in the struggle for God and humanity [*Friend of Man* 11 Jan. 1842].

Despite his struggles — his wife died in 1847, and he was constantly on the brink of poverty ("Letters from Hiram Wilson" 344–349)—he maintained his optimism. In an 1854 letter to *The Liberator*, he emphasized the hospitableness of western Canada for black people, pointing out that sections of Canada West were not as cold as upstate New York ("Fugitives in Canada" 80).

Wilson was a promoter of Canadian emigration and a person who saw hope even in the most desperate situation. More objective were the observations of Samuel Ward, who was the chief agent of the Anti-Slavery Society of Canada, which formed in Toronto in 1851.

In his 1855 autobiography, Ward described the kind of prejudice faced by blacks there and the people who were likely to display it.

"Canadian Negro-haters are the very worst of their class," he wrote. "This feeling abounds most among the native Canadians, who, as a rule, are the lowest, the least educated, of all the white population ... I do not mean that it is confined to them; nor do I mean to say that it is universal, without exception, even among this class—others exhibit it, and some of that class are among the freest from it....

"In many cases, a black person traveling, whatever may be his style and however respectable his appearance, will be denied a seat at table d'hôte at a country inn, or on a steamer."

Ward noted, however, that when discrimination occurred at schools or the polling place, Canadian authorities were quick to stop it. This probably was due to the high moral fiber of the leaders, who followed the example of England, and which Ward was quick to recognize. It was also because Canadians strictly followed their laws, which prohibited any sort of discrimination.

"One thing I have here the greatest pleasure in saying: I never saw the slightest appearance of [prejudice] in any person in Canada recognized ... as a gentleman.... Therefore, in every town of Canada, and especially in Toronto, I see what I saw in but extremely few and exceptional cases in the States—viz., that among gentlemen, the black takes just the place for which he is qualified, as if his colour were similar to that of other gentlemen."

Despite the prejudice among the lower classes, Ward also noted the prevalence of miscegenation among them, which was rare and strongly discouraged in the U.S., even by most abolitionists.

"And now for an anomaly. Fugitives coming to Canada are, the majority of them, young, single men.... Coloured young women are comparatively scarce; and, in spite of the prevalent prejudice, they marry among this very lower class of whose Negro-hate I have said so much. Hence, while you get so much evidence of the aversion betwixt these classes, you see it to be no strange thing, but a very common thing, for a black labourer to have a white wife..." (Ward 143–151).

Many blacks corroborated Ward's description of prejudice in Canada during interviews with Benjamin Drew in 1855 and Samuel Howe in 1863. Nelson Moss, who lived in London, West Canada, said, "I have lived in a slave State all my life until seven years ago. I am now forty-five. I lived three years in Pennsylvania, in which State I suffered more from prejudice than in Virginia, and there is a great deal here in London, but not so much as in Pennsylvania" (Drew 153).

The Rev. L. C. Chambers, of St. Catherines, said: "The prejudice here against the colored people is [a great deal] stronger than it is in Massachusetts. Since I have been in the country, I went to a church one Sabbath, and the sexton asked me, 'What do you want here to-day?' I said, 'Is there not to be service here to-day?' He said, 'Yes, but we don't want any niggers here.' I said, 'You are mistaken in the man. I am not a "nigger," but a negro'" (Howe 45).

G. F. Simpson of Toronto, said, "I must say that, leaving the law out of the question, I find that prejudice here is equally strong as on the other side. The law is the only thing that sustains us in this country" (ibid.).

Perhaps an accurate appraisal of the conditions faced by blacks, whether free or runaway, would be this sober statement from Howe's report: "The refugees in Canada earn a living, and gather property; they marry and respect women; they build churches and send their children to schools; they improve in manners and morals—because they are free men" (Landon *Henry Bibb* 447).

Though Canada was an obvious destination for runaway slaves, it was not necessarily better than many communities in the North, other than that it was out of the reach of slavecatchers. In Toronto, there were reports of slavehunters tracking down fugitive slaves in 1840. As a result, blacks formed vigilance committees and published notices warning newcomers (Hill). What was closer to reality was that while most blacks claimed the North American continent as their homeland, they were out of place here no matter where they ended up, even in Canada or some abolitionized community like Union Village.

A story of prejudice that may surprise some occurred in Fulton, New York, an Oswego County village that was a major terminal on the Underground Railroad. William G. Allen, a professor at McGrawville College in Cortland and a quadroon (the racist term for a person who was one-quarter black), had developed a close friendship with Mary King, a student at the school and the daughter of a Wesleyan-Methodist minister in Fulton, the Rev. Lyndon King. In the beginning his relations with her family were cordial, and her father approved their friendship. However, the disapproval of his sons and wife, Mary's stepmother, and the revelation of the couple's intention to marry changed her father's mind. Allen was informed that he was no longer welcome at the King home if he had intentions of marrying King's daughter, and the couple moved their next meeting to the home of a friend. There a mob, armed with a pole, buckets of tar and feathers, and a large, empty barrel spiked with nails into which they intended to place a tar-covered Allen, surrounded the house while the couple was inside and ordered Allen to come out. In fear of his life, Allen remained inside until some abolitionist friends arrived and escorted him out.

After rescuing Allen, however, they suggested that he give up thoughts of marriage to Mary. In the intervening weeks, Allen received letters from Mary in which she broke their engagement. Little did he know that she was being coerced and that she was a virtual prisoner in her own house.

After a period of time, the couple secretly reunited and eloped to England, where they were married and where Allen wrote a book about this experience, *The American Prejudice of Color*. The irony and shock of this affair is that this community was actively involved in the Underground Railroad. In reference to Mary King's stepmother, Allen wrote, "...though not lacking a certain benevolence—and especially that sort which can pity the fugitive, give him food and raiment, or permit him at her table even ... Mrs. King ... finally resorted to such violence of speech and act, as to indicate a state of feeling really deplorable, and a spirit diametrically opposed to all the teachings of the Christian religion...."

"I judge not mortal man or woman," Allen wrote in true Christian spirit, "but leave Mrs. King, and all those who thought it no harm because of my complexion, to abuse the most sacred feelings of my heart, to their conscience and their God" (14).

Blacks could not be certain of their place in American society because prejudice was liable to appear out of nowhere in places they might least expect it. This sense of displacement might be inferred from the itinerancy of free blacks in Washington County, New York, though it was an area strongly sympathetic to their cause, during 1850 to 1860.*

Out of 307 blacks in Washington County accounted for in the 1850 census, only 57 remained in the census records of 1860. Thirty-three of those individuals were in three towns: Whitehall (a jumping off point to Canada), and Easton and Greenwich, two towns with Underground Railroad terminals. Fourteen of those 33 were reported living in Greenwich, the site of Union Village, where nine of those 14 had moved from another town in the county. Other interesting associations regarding the black population were found there. The 1840 census shows only ten blacks living in Greenwich, with none in the households of Free Church members. But in 1850, the year of the second Fugitive Slave Law, the census shows 28 blacks living there with six white households that included blacks. Of the six, five were members of the Free Church, with the sixth being the older brother of William H. Mowry. They included Free Church trustee William H. Mowry on Church Street; trustee Henry Holmes on Church Street; trustee John T. Masters on Main Street; deacon Abel Wilder on Washington Street; and Pardon Bassett, whose wife Mary Bailey Bassett was a Free Church member, on Main Street.

It is unlikely that the blacks listed as living with white families in Union Village were fugitive slaves. This would be too risky. In fact, all were born in New York. But

*Actual census figures show 350 and 259 blacks in the county for 1850 and 1860 respectively. However, the author was able to identify only 307 and 250 of them through personal observation of the census records, so the data is based on those numbers. See Appendix V for more details on the black population in the Town of Greenwich.

it is well known among historians of the Underground Railroad that fugitive slaves preferred shelter with other blacks, and it seems unlikely to be a coincidence that six white households in Union Village with connections to the Free Church suddenly would show blacks in their households, the same year the second Fugitive Slave Law was passed. A plausible explanation is that the church mobilized as a result of the new law.

Fugitive slaves, or at least family members of fugitive slaves, also were members of the Free Church. Listed on the church rolls from 1837 to 1851 was Priscilla Weeks. She and her sister, Susan, married the well-known fugitive slave brothers, John and Charles Salter. The Salters had fled from Maryland and arrived in Washington County around 1846. Their intention had been to go to Canada, but Hiram Corliss persuaded them to stay, assuring them that the local abolitionists would protect them from slave-catchers (Thurston 71–72).

Census records clearly show its transient nature and a shift of the county's black population to the town of Greenwich. The 1855 New York State census shows 55 blacks living in the town of Greenwich, an increase of nearly 100 percent from 1850 when there were 28, and an increase of nearly 500 percent from 1840 when there were only ten. However, most of these individuals did not remain long. Of the 55 individuals in 1855, only five had lived in the town in 1850. This may be the result of the movement of fugitive slaves, who may have taken relatives who had lived in the county to Canada or more remote areas. The census of 1860 showed a similar pattern with 58 blacks in the town but only 11 remaining from 1855, and only five from 1850.

The transient nature of the black population illustrated in the town of Greenwich suggests that fugitive slaves from the South may have been seeking the havens of sympathetic areas. A July 29, 1856, letter of Union Village Free Church member Diantha Gunn to her fiancée also suggests a larger number of blacks locally than indicated by census records: "Yesterday, a little colored child was buried, in this goodly town which boasts so many warm hearted abolitionists, so many true friends to the poor colored man, and in the procession which followed it to the grave, I could distinguish no white faces, not one." The implication here is not that whites were not supportive [obviously, they were in a town with "so many true friends to the poor colored man"] but that the number of blacks was so large that if there were any whites in the procession, she didn't notice.

Another statistic that speaks directly to the presence of the Underground Railroad in Union Village is that among 128 black individuals listed in the town of Greenwich from 1850 to 1860, 14 were listed as born in Maryland and one in Virginia, where conductors like Torrey and Chaplin operated. Not only may some of them had relatives still in slavery, but they also could have drawn fugitive slaves to the area.

One also might expect a move northward of free blacks to safer and more remote communities in the Adirondacks, as well, though the census records don't indicate this—except for a dramatic increase in the numbers in Franklin County, which showed three free blacks in 1840 and 62 in 1850—the community of Blacksville might be the cause. Still, those are small numbers, and they decreased to 19 in the 1860 census. In Essex County, there was a fairly significant increase in the number of blacks from 1850 to 1860, more than doubling their numbers from 50 to 123, perhaps attributable to the stir created by Timbucto. However, only a handful of black families remained in Timbucto after 1850, which may have contributed to John Brown leaving for several years after 1851 for a business opportunity in Ohio. Nearby Clinton County only showed a slight increase from 112 in 1850 to 128 in 1860. In any case, the accuracy of census records is questionable, especially in relation to blacks. Furthermore one would expect that fugitive slaves would avoid being listed in the census (Cramer 1–2).

The same problem was found with census data related to the numbers of blacks in Canada during the antebellum period. Contemporary accounts claim four to five times the number listed in the census records—1861 records show 13,566 (Winks 234)—with about nine blacks out of every ten being a fugitive slave (Ward 154). In addition, to avoid being listed some fugitive slaves may have neglected to report they were runaways or even may have attempted to pass themselves off as white (Winks 235). The transient nature of the black population was another obstacle.

Blacks were a group in transition both in the North and the South, especially after the passage of the second Fugitive Slave Law. They were searching for a place to call home, but the rampant and sometimes subtle prejudices on account of color proved daunting. Some few blacks did find their place, but many more did not. This inability of blacks to find a home here would give rise to a colonization movement later in the decade started by blacks, among whose leaders were Henry Garnet and Henry Bibb.

Itinerancy Among Blacks in Washington County from 1850 to 1860

Town	Number in 1860	Remained from 1850	Moved here in 1860 from within county
Argyle	9	3	1
Cambridge	6	2	0
Easton	30	9	0
Kingsbury	31	1	1
Salem	17	4	0
Fort Ann	22	2	0
Fort Edward	4	1	1
Greenwich	58	5	9
Jackson	24	1	2
White Creek	11	3	0
Whitehall	34	7	3

While most blacks searched for a place to call home, one black man, finally, after 12 long years, returned home in January 1853. Solomon Northup had tried to escape several times during his enslavement, but all it brought was more hardship. His extraordinary tenacity kept him alive, and he never gave up hope that someday he would regain his freedom. In 1852, Northup befriended a sympathetic, non-slaveholding white carpenter named Bass. Northup persuaded him to mail a letter to a friend in Saratoga. It was brought to the attention of lawyer Henry B. Northup of Sandy Hill, whose father had manumitted Solomon's father. Northup obtained a commission from New York State Governor Washington Hunt and within a short time went to

Bayou Boeuf to bring Northup home under the jurisdiction of the 1840 New York State law that safeguarded free black citizens from being kidnapped into slavery.

According to the newspaper account, "Mr. Northup found Solomon on a cotton plantation, who, as soon as he saw him, ran to him and called him by name ... thus, and by other means, satisfying his master that he was a free man, who immediately delivered him up ... he is now with his family, a wife and two children, at Glens Falls" ("H.B. Northup, Esq..." 2).

Following his return to freedom, Northup's book, *Twelve Years A Slave*, was published. It put him in demand as a speaker at abolition meetings, and some believe he began to participate in the Underground Railroad with Methodist minister the Rev. Lame John Smith of Hartland, Vermont (Siebert 98–100). Northup disappeared around 1855, and it has never been determined where he went or when he died. One possible location may have been Constantia in Oswego County, where his brother was living.

THE SANDY-HILL-HERALD.

TUESDAY MORNING, JAN. 25, 1853.

H. B. NORTHUP, Esq. returned to this village on Thursday evening, with Solomon Northup, the colored man about whom so much has been said and written within the past few days.

Solomon, about twelve years ago, was hired as a teamster, at Saratoga Springs, by a company of travelling actors; and during their perigranations found himself in Washington City, where he was kidnapped, carried to New Orleans and sold into slavery— from whence he was taken to the swamps of Louisiana, up Red River, where he remained until liberated through the agency of Mr. Northup.

Announcement of the return of Solomon Northrup from slavery. (From *Sandy Hill Herald*, 25 January 1853.)

Chapter 18

VOICES CRYING IN THE WILDERNESS

In Union Village, the Fugitive Slave Law energized the abolitionists. The Rev. James P. Miller of Argyle organized a major new convention, and the featured speaker was the renowned English orator and activist in the cause of freedom, George Thompson, perhaps the man most responsible for the end of slavery in the British Empire. Thompson, who had been elected to Parliament in 1847, had made a two-year lecture tour in the U.S. that began in 1833 and included stops in Albany and Troy. He provoked riots and was in danger of losing his life several times, yet he persisted, leaving the U.S. in January 1836 ("George Thompson, M.P." 32). Now 15 years later, in need of money and with the North in an uproar over the passing of the second Fugitive Slave Law, he expected more receptive audiences.

Thompson arrived first in Boston, where he met with his friend, William Lloyd Garrison. At one of his first engagements, he encountered an unfriendly mob of proslavery Whigs at Fanueil Hall. But numerous stops thereafter along the New England coast from Rhode Island to Maine met with success ("Mr. Thompson at Springfield" 35). A two-month tour through New York State followed, organized by Abby Kelley Foster, a staunch Garrisonian and former enemy of the now almost defunct Liberty Party, which had barred the participation of women at its meetings.

Foster saw an opportunity to reconcile the divided abolitionist forces. Gerrit Smith had also sent signs that he was ready, publicly praising Garrison, calling him "the best and greatest as well as the earliest abolitionist in the country" (Harlow 296). This effort at bringing greater solidarity among abolitionists prompted Foster to include stops on Thompson's tour in many former Liberty Party strongholds, including Union Village and Syracuse.

On the way to New York State was a stop in Springfield, Massachusetts. At this time, the rescue of the fugitive slave Shadrach Minkins had sent the region into turmoil. Minkins, who had escaped from Virginia during the summer of 1850 and settled in Boston, had been arrested under the jurisdiction of the Fugitive Slave Law the week before. He was awaiting trial at the federal courthouse when a large band of blacks forced their way in. While authorities stood by without resistance, they freed him. The sentiments of many in Boston were reflected in Garrison's report of the incident in *The Liberator*, stating, "We defy the Fugitive Slave Bill, its framers and upholders, together with the devil and all his works. Freedom for all, and for ever!" ("The Arrest..." 30).

In response, President Fillmore issued a proclamation calling on citizens to assist in Minkins' recapture and commanding authorities to arrest and prosecute those involved in his rescue. The reaction of public support for the president may have ignited the riot that followed when Thompson, Wendell Phillips, and others spoke in Springfield. Thompson was pelted with eggs and the windows of his hotel room smashed, but the commotion served to create the publicity that drew large audiences to his lectures in New York ("Mr. Thompson at Springfield" 35).

Tall, handsome, electrifying on the podium, and an indulger in the opiate laudanum, the 47-year-old Thompson was a worthy attraction. Accompanied by George W. Putnam, who wrote a report of the convention for *The Liberator*, Thompson left on a train to Troy. They were met by one of the Wilburs of Easton and stayed overnight in Schaghticoke. The next morning, on February 20, 1851, "Friend" Wilbur took them to Union Village and the house of Leonard Gibbs ("George Thompson in Union Village" 35).

The convention opened in the morning with Abby Foster and her husband, Stephen, speaking at the "Free" Church. Thompson joined the Fosters and another guest speaker, Sojourner Truth, who was on her first lecture tour, in the afternoon. He "gave a thrilling and most humorous account of the Springfield mob. The high expectations which the renown of Mr. Thompson had excited were in that one speech more than realized," Putnam reported. At the close of his lecture, Mrs. Foster introduced Truth, who had come from Northampton and who gave a short talk in "her peculiar manner ... and was most kindly received by the audience, who pressed around her to purchase her books." In the evening, after a hymn from the choir, Thompson spoke for two more hours, holding the audience "spellbound," according to Putnam, as "he analyzed the subject of American slavery" (ibid.).

In attendance, at his first anti-slavery convention, was 19-year-old Aaron Powell of Columbia County. Powell would return to Washington County as an anti-slavery lecturer on a number of occasions from 1856 until the end of Civil War. Years later, in his autobiography, Powell wrote his impressions of Thompson at the convention:

> His face was radiant with good cheer, and his voice melodious and the most eloquent I had ever listened to. It seemed to me then well nigh incomprehensible how any one would come from such mobocratic confusion and uproar, attended with great risk of personal violence, and yet bring to us so much geniality and spiritual sunshine!
>
> [His speeches] abounded especially with humorous sallies and anecdote, carrying the convention, his pro-slavery hearers and others, enthusiastically with him [Powell 12, 20].

Powell had some interesting comments about Sojourner Truth, whom he described as "a woman of much native intelligence, of powerful voice, with great originality of expression, which combined with her peculiar dialect, a quaint humor, and picturesque appearance, made her always a welcome speaker at anti-slavery meetings" (Powell 17).

He also related an incident that demonstrated her powers of intuition. During an interlude between speakers, Truth approached Powell and placed her hand on his head.

"I'se been a lookin' into your face," she said to him, "and I sees you in the futur,' pleadin' our cause!" (Powell 16).

The next day, the Fosters, Gibbs, Putnam, and Erastus Culver, who had moved to Brooklyn, spoke prior to Thompson, and in the evening Thompson gave the closing speech: "No man who believes slavery is wrong will sit still or keep silent while it exists! It is all hypocrisy," he declared in a true oratorical flourish. "While trumpet-tongued you boast your love of liberty ... you deny it to three millions of men! Give liberty to the slave, and show to God and the world that you rightly ... deserve it yourselves. At your monstrous inconsistency the tyrants of the earth mock and hold you in derision, and Hell itself laughs in triumph to see the unspeakable meanness and hypocrisy of your nation" ("George Thompson in Union Village" 35).

A constitution also was submitted at the convention for a new anti-slavery society that took in Washington, Saratoga, and Rensselaer counties. The "Old Saratoga District Anti-Slavery Society" was well represented by women from Union Village and Easton in Washington County, and nearby Quaker Springs in Saratoga County ("Trip to Northern New York" 46). It was evidence of the changes taking place as well as of the reconciliation of Liberty Party supporters with the Garrisonians, who had supported the joint participation of women in anti-slavery meetings with men since it became an issue around 1840. One last development was the announcement by the Rev. Miller that he was moving to Oregon ("George Thompson in Union Village" 35).

Sojourner Truth

Miller's departure and the new anti-slavery organization signaled the rise of a new generation of activists in Washington and Saratoga counties from the farming communities of Easton and Quaker Springs, who were joining with the old guard in Union Village. Nevertheless, Dr. Corliss and Leonard Gibbs continued as key members, and with this new generation, they would continue to operate the Underground Railroad. A year following Thompson's visit, the Old Saratoga District Anti-Slavery Society's first annual meeting brought the most illustrious abolitionist of all to Union Village—William Lloyd Garrison.

The announcement of the meeting

signed by Samuel Wilbur was published in *The Washington County Journal*. The Liberty Party, once Garrison's foe, was now a non-factor. Joining him was Boston abolitionist Parker Pillsbury.

A lengthy account of Garrison's trip, during which he also stayed in Albany, appeared in the March 19, 1852, issue of *The Liberator*. The opening section is a fascinating commentary, looking back today, on the promise of the railroad—the overground railroad.

"To travel two hundred miles without the slightest fatigue," he began, "and with a rapidity and in a manner that ancient kings and conquerors would have parted with half their sovereignty to enjoy is something still to boast of though an every day occurrence.... It seems but the other day since the proposition was under discussion for building the first railroad in this country—not exceeding thirty miles in length; and the way it was treated as visionary, and ridiculed and resisted, is now past credibility ... and the number of railroads in the land is not easily enumerated, reaching in extent some ten or twelve thousand miles—with others projected ... covering as great a distance ... from the Atlantic to the Pacific—the traveling to be, on that long route, at an average speed of not less than twenty-five, probably in a few years not less than forty miles an hour" (Trip to Northern New York" 46).*

Garrison then quoted a passage from Scripture, which showed perhaps a softening of his anti-clerical position and an accommodation to the devout Christians of Washington County, whom he knew would be anxious to read his comments.

Before coming to Washington County, Garrison and Pillsbury stopped in Albany, where they spoke at City Hall in opposition to colonization, for which a bill was being proposed in the state legislature to provide funding. That evening they stayed with tailor William H. Topp, whose shop Garrison described as being "one of the handsomest ... and [having one of the] best locations in the city..." (ibid.). Topp was at the time operating Albany's Underground Railroad terminal with Stephen Myers and a group of black men that included John G. Stewart, Charles B. Morton, William P. McIntrye, William H. Matthews, Primus Robinson, George Morgan, Dr. Thomas Elkins, and Benjamin Cutler (Johnson 61). They likely were working with the New York State Vigilance Committee, which from January 1851 to April 1853 reported aiding 686 fugitive slaves (Quarles 154). Topp, who along with Myers, represented Albany at the National Negro Conventions during the 1850s, also may have talked with Garrison about colonization, which continued to be a major topic of discussion at the Negro conventions.

Garrison and Pillsbury also visited with Lydia Mott, who was becoming more visible in local abolition circles and also was known to have been aiding fugitive slaves during this time (Douglass 272).

The next day they arrived in Union Village. Garrison said there were two "special" reasons for his visit: one, because of a broken promise he had made to attend a similar meeting the previous year; and two, to visit with the people who had given such a warm welcome the year before to his good friend, George Thompson. Five meetings were held at the Free Church. The principal speakers at every meeting were Garrison and Pillsbury, who were directed to "state [their] principles, expound [their]

The transcontinental railroad was completed in 1869.

doctrines, defend [their] measures, and expose the folly and wickedness of [their] accusers" because in that region "they were everywhere spoken against as infidels and disorganizers" (ibid.).

The audience listened attentively to Pillsbury explain why political action would not end slavery and to Garrison attack colonization. Though many in the audience probably disagreed with Pillsbury, they were polite and posed no opposition. However, they were in total agreement with Garrison, and the last four of eight resolutions made by the society dealt specifically with colonization. The first four resolutions, however, dealt with religion and politics, both of which were to some degree at odds with their guests. They included first and foremost: "That the anti-slavery enterprise is pre-eminently a religious movement. By the term 'religious,' we do not mean that it is devoted to the advocacy of any particular theological creeds ... but we mean that it is founded on the highest and holiest impulses operating in human nature ... [that it is based on the great principle of] love to God and love to man" (ibid.).

Garrison and Pillsbury stayed with Leonard Gibbs during their visit, and illustrating the transition that was occurring in abolition politics, Garrison said that the former Liberty Party leader was "carefully examining the ground occupied by Garrison's American Anti-Slavery Society." In closing his report, Garrison wrote: "Long, gratefully, pleasantly, shall we remember our visit to Union Village, and our attendance at the first annual meeting of the Old District Anti-Slavery Society" (ibid.).

The *Washington County Journal* took little notice of the visit of this illustrious celebrity. It reported shortly after Garrison's departure that: "We must confess ... that entertaining no sympathy for the views which (that gentleman is) understood to hold, we have felt little desire to attend" ("The Abolition Convention" 2).

What Northerners who had been cool to abolition were taking notice of was a book by Harriet Beecher Stowe, who had seen the evils of slavery firsthand. A few weeks after Garrison's visit to Union Village, her book, *Uncle Tom's Cabin*, was published. Compelled to write the book after the passage of the second Fugitive Slave Law, she had moved to Maine from Cincinnati, where her father, Lyman Beecher, had been president of the Lane Seminary and had inspired a number of prominent abolitionist ministers. Prior to its publication, the book had been serialized for nine months in the abolitionist newspaper, *The National Era*. It met with immediate and astounding success. Three thousand copies sold the first day, and within ten days, a second edition went to press. The publisher was barely able to keep up with the demand. The story had universal appeal, and all sorts of people took to it. By August, an unauthorized dramatic version was being staged to sell-out crowds in Troy, New York, and within a year, more than 300,000 copies had been sold worldwide (Downs 80).

Stowe's intention had not been to attack the South. She believed that the evil of slavery lay within the system and not with those who perpetuated it. She drew heavily on moral and religious sources. A clear example of this is the following passage spoken by a character in the book, Mrs. Shelby, the wife of a Southern slaveholder, who had difficulty accepting slavery:

> My view of Christianity is such that I think no man can consistently profess it
> without throwing the whole weight of his being against this monstrous system

of injustice that lies at the foundation of all our society, and, if need be, sacrificing himself in the battle. That is, I mean that I could not be a Christian otherwise, though I have certainly had intercourse with a great many enlightened and Christian people who did no such thing; and I confess that the apathy of religious people on this subject, their want of perception of wrong that filled me with horror, have engendered in me more skepticism than any other thing [Turner 73].

Stowe's book probably did not add to the earnestness of the abolitionists, for they already shared her point of view, but it did bring many converts to the cause. Its great contribution was that it succeeded in doing what the abolitionists with their meetings and tracts had failed to do—make the horrors of slavery real to the common everyday person in the North whose life was untouched by slavery. It was a new voice that cried out to people whom the abolitionists could never hope to reach, and in many ways, as Lincoln later acknowl-

Report of William Lloyd Garrison in attendance at an anti-slavery meeting in Union Village, which the newspaper did not wish to attend. (From *The Washington County Journal,* 26 February 1852.)

edged during the Civil War, it was "the book that brought on this big war" (Downs 82).

Chapter 19

TO THE RESCUE

Among the incidents that bear witness to the organization of the Underground Railroad were the rescue or protection of fugitive slaves seized or nearly seized by slave-catchers. Not all of them were successful, and the failure of some has been cited by Larry Gara as evidence of the lack of organization in the Underground Railroad (Gara 114). Nevertheless, many were successful, though few of those involved in the Underground Railroad were trained in such activities. Most occurred after the passage of the second Fugitive Slave Law, but one little-known rescue took place much earlier in January 1837 in Utica, N.Y.

Two fugitive slaves from Virginia, Harry Bird and George, who had been in Utica since the previous September, were arrested by local law enforcement officials on a warrant presented by a representative of John Goyer of Woodstock, Virginia.* Alvan Stewart, who lived in Utica, was secured as their attorney, and the case immediately took a favorable turn because it was to be tried by Judge Chester Hayden, who had publicly condemned the mobbing of abolition meetings. The hearing was set for the morning, and the judge agreed to Stewart's request for a postponement until 6:30 that evening. In the meantime, he also allowed Stewart to counsel the runaways in the back room of his office rather than returning them to jail. During the day, a great commotion arose outside. About a half-hour before the hearing, as darkness fell, a mob of both black and white men assembled and went into the judge's office. A signal was given, and the lamps were extinguished. Armed with clubs, the mob rushed for the room where the runaways were being held. They were met by law enforcement officials and other citizens guarding the prisoners but overpowered them and set the runaways free. The *Oneida Whig*, which had been condemning the mob violence used against the abolitionists, was quick to condemn the abolitionists for their similar actions (Item 123).

After the Prigg Decision in 1842, local officials were under no obligation in matters involving fugitive slaves.

The use of force to rescue or protect fugitive slaves moves a great distance from the early strategy of moral suasion, and this early rescue attempt in Utica shows that such militance had roots at a very early period in upstate New York.* After the passage of the second Fugitive Slave Law, many in the North saw no other alternative. The first widely publicized incident occurred in 1851 when there was a surge of activity involving slavecatchers. Numerous kidnappings of blacks occurred, many of them who were free, with much of this activity centered in southern Pennsylvania near its borders with Delaware and Maryland (May *The Fugitive Slave Law...* 18). A celebrated case that made national headlines occurred in the town of Christiana, only a short distance from Maryland. A slave owner from Maryland was killed and several others injured during an attempt to retrieve his slaves under the jurisdiction of the Fugitive Slave Law with the aid of a federal marshal. William Parker, whose house concealed the fugitive slaves and who killed the slave owner, was a former slave himself who had escaped from bondage. After the Civil War, he wrote an account of the incident.

"Kidnapping was so common [in southeastern Pennsylvania] that we were kept in constant fear," Parker wrote. "We would hear of slaveholders or kidnappers every two or three weeks; sometimes a party of white men would break into a house and take a man away, no one knew where; and, again, a whole family would be carried off. There was no power to protect them, nor prevent it" (Parker 161).

"These fellows consorted with constables, police-officers, aldermen, and even with learned members of the legal profession, who disgraced their respectable calling by low, contemptible arts, and were willing to clasp hands with the lowest ruffian in order to pocket the reward that was the price of blood. Every facility was offered these bad men; and whether it was night or day, it was only necessary to whisper in a certain circle that a negro was to be caught, and horses and wagons, men and officers, spies and betrayers, were ready, at the shortest notice, armed and equipped, and eager for the chase" (281).

As a result, blacks and sympathetic whites in the area were in constant vigilance. To alert others of impending danger, Parker's wife blew a horn, and neighbors, both black and white, gathered in the hundreds and hurried over to show their support of the fugitive slaves. Though they usually didn't interfere, their arrival weakened the resolution of the rendition party.[†]

While slavehunters were not as commonplace in upstate New York, their appearance was not unusual, as earlier noted. The new Fugitive Slave Law also had increased their activity there. For instance, there were renditions in western New York of the cook, Daniel, and farmhand, Harris, and in Poughkeepsie of a tailor named John Bolding that occurred shortly before the Christiana incident. Daniel was freed by Judge Albert Conkling on a legal technicality and Bolding's freedom was purchased by friends. However, the unfortunate Harris was sent back to slavery ("Judge Conkling's Decision" 2; May *The Fugitive Slave Law...* 19).

In the Adirondacks, a well-documented attempt at a fugitive slave rendition occurred the same month of the Christiana incident, in Glens Falls, involving a black

*In 1839, a prominent central New York lawyer, Jabez Hammond of Cherry Hill, suggested a plan to Gerrit Smith to train an army of blacks to lead a slave revolt in the South, an idea similar to that of John Brown (Aptheker 455).
†Rendition was the term used to describe the apprehension of fugitive slaves.

barber named John Van Pelt and his fugitive slave wife, Lucretia. She had escaped from her master, who was from Georgia, during a trip north in 1846 and married Van Pelt the following year. At the time of the attempted rendition, she was 23 and he was 30.

Samuel Boyd, who as an eight-year-old boy met the slavehunter, told the story more than 70 years later. One morning, he and Add Stoddard, the son of chiropractor Joseph Stoddard, were skating on the sidewalk when they were approached by a man wearing a heavy fur coat, whom they saw get off the stage at the corner of Park street.

"My son," he said to Boyd, "can you tell me where John Van Pelt lives?"

"Oh, yes," Boyd said, and started to show him when Add brushed him aside and said, "He don't know where he lives. I'll show you."

Stoddard, who was a year older and wiser, sent the slavehunter in the wrong direction. He had heard that slavehunters might be looking for Van Pelt's wife. Stoddard then went to his father, and in less than an hour, the Van Pelt family was on their way to safety (Boyd 8).

Van Pelt accompanied his family to Prescott, Canada, and then returned to Glens Falls. He attempted to negotiate with the slavehunter for the price of his wife's freedom. However, he was unable to raise the $600 that was demanded. As a result, Van Pelt sold his barbershop and moved to Canada ("Another Fugitive Slave Case" 2). It is significant that the Van Pelts went to Prescott because it is directly across the St. Lawrence River from Ogdensburg, which is at the end of the old military road that originated in North Warren County and which was possibly the last leg of a western Adirondack route developed by the Rev. Abel Brown.

This incident was reported in the *Glens Falls Free Press* which commented:

> Here was one of our neighbors, colored, to be sure, but none the less a man for that, who had lived in this village some two years, and by his industry and good behavior, merited what he was receiving, the cordial support of our citizens. He was upright and inoffensive in all his transactions ... and to all appearances, was as much entitled to a residence here with his wife, as any one of us. But by the law of the Union, in the face of the idea that "all men are created free and equal," he had been compelled to flee to the Queen's dominions..." [ibid.].

The Van Pelt episode was only one of a continuing series of attempted slave renditions in upstate New York, which continued until the Civil War. Perhaps the most celebrated attempt occurred in Syracuse only weeks after the Glens Falls incident. Leonard Gibbs was there attending the Liberty Party convention. The party was now for the most part concentrated in central New York with some isolated groups in northern New York like Chestertown ("Liberty Party Convention"). Just four months earlier, Daniel Webster, then U.S. Secretary of State, had given an address there and threatened the abolitionists of the city.

"Those persons in this city who mean to oppose the execution of the Fugitive Slave Law are traitors! traitors!! traitors!!!" Webster declared. "This law ought to be obeyed, and it will be enforced—yes, it shall be enforced; in the city of Syracuse it shall be enforced, and that, too, in the midst of the next anti-slavery Convention, if then there shall be any occasion to enforce it" (May *Some Recollections...* 373).

Webster was hated by the abolitionists. While a senator, he made an important

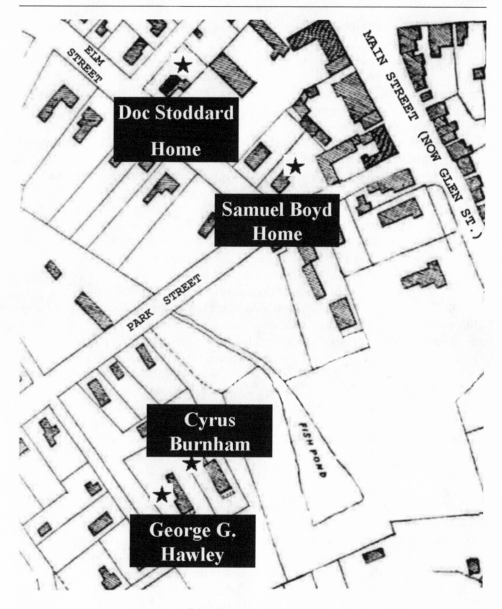

(Map by the author.)

speech six months prior to the second Fugitive Slave Law's passage during which he vowed "to support the Bill with all its provisions to the fullest extent." And after he was appointed Secretary of State, he had renewed this vow (ibid. 347).

The convention was in session when a messenger interrupted with news that a runaway had been taken into custody. Webster had made good on his threat. William Henry, a black carpenter who had been living in Syracuse for a number of years and known to all as "Jerry," had been seized by law enforcement officials and taken to the City Hall where he was charged with theft under the jurisdiction of the Fugitive Slave Act of 1850. Liberty Party officials designated Gibbs and Gerrit Smith as Jerry's defense attorneys.

The first thing Gibbs did was demand that Jerry's shackles be removed. A man is innocent until proven guilty, he insisted. Gibbs also demanded that the revolver in the possession of the claimant's agent should be surrendered. As people squeezed into the courtroom, the commissioner decided to adjourn to a larger room. As they filed out, with the help of sympathizers, Jerry escaped into the streets and made a run for it. But he was still partially shackled, and the police caught and beat him severely. They placed Jerry under guard in a back room.

Gibbs with two additional lawyers but minus Smith, who was backstage helping to plan a rescue,* continued the hearing. As he raised the point that the claimant needed proof that Jerry was indeed a slave from Missouri, the mob that had gathered outside began to throw stones through the windows. The commissioner called for an adjournment, but before the authorities realized the severity of the situation, the mob was at the door of Jerry's holding room with a battering ram. The guards fled, and Jerry was carried to friends who took him into hiding.

The next day, eighteen abolitionists were arrested. At the same time, the agent of Jerry's owner who had taken him into custody was arrested and charged with kidnapping. It was five days before Jerry was hustled out of Syracuse to the village of Mexico, where he stayed in hiding for more several days. He then taken to Oswego, a port on Lake Ontario, and hid there for several more days. Finally he was put on a boat that took him safely across the lake to Kingston, Canada (ibid. 373–384).

The charges against the abolitionists were eventually dropped—the accused having the good fortune of being in the court of Judge Conkling, a personal friend of Gerrit Smith—and no one ever tried to seize a fugitive slave again in Syracuse, where it is estimated 1,500 fugitive slaves were assisted after the passage of the Fugitive Slave Act of 1850 (Loguen 444).

Among other efforts by abolitionists to help fugitive slaves to gain their freedom was the use of the court system. The New York Committee of Vigilance and later the New York State Vigilance Committee worked with attorney Horace Dresser to free many runaways. Assisting the process was the 1841 state law that conferred immediate freedom upon any slave brought into the state. It was responsible for 38 such cases that were successfully pursued by the New York State Vigilance Committee from 1851 to 1853 (Quarles 154). A case of this type that made headlines in 1852 involved the Brooklyn law firm of Union Village native Erastus Culver. A young lawyer from Culver's firm, who also was a Union Village native, future President Chester Arthur, successfully defended a family of eight slaves who sought their freedom after being brought into New York from Virginia by their owner. It was the first of a series of civil rights cases involving free blacks and fugitive slaves that Culver's law firm would success-

*Drs. Hiram Hoyt, James Fuller, R. W. Pease; Gerrit Smith, Samuel J. May, John Thomas, Charles A. Wheaton, Samuel R. Ward, Samuel Thomas (Cazenovia), Linneas P. Noble, (Fayetteville), Washington Stickney, (Canastota,) William Crandall, R. R. Raymond, Caleb Davis, Montgomery, Merrick, Abner Bates, James Davis, J. M. Clapp, C. C. Foot, (Michigan), James Baker, Jason S. Hoyt, Edward K. Hunt, George Carter, Peter Hollinbeck, James Parsons, Lemuel Field, William Gray, and J. W. Loguen were listed as those at the meeting by Loguen, who added that there also were others, whom he failed to recall (Loguen 408–409).

fully represent. In this case, the slaveholder Jonathan Lemmon, enroute by boat to Texas, had taken his slaves off the boat to a boarding house in New York. A free black man had discovered this and petitioned one of the justices of the Superior Court of New York for their freedom (May, *The Fugitive Slave Law*, 24).

But even lawyers and judges who were sympathetic to runaways were not always successful because there were many in law enforcement who assisted slavecatchers, such as New York City constable Tobias Boudinot. In one case in which Culver attempted to intervene, three fugitive slaves had been taken into custody in New York City. The runaways were the brother and nephews of the prominent black minister, the Rev. J.W.C. Pennington, himself once a fugitive slave. Two days later, a service was held at the Rev. Pennington's church at which Judge Culver was a speaker. He said that the authorities had lied to him at the fugitive slaves' hearing. They told him the alleged runaways did not desire counsel and freely admitted that they were the fugitive slaves who had escaped from Virginia. With the help of Mrs. Pennington, Culver found the prisoners in the lock-up. Contrary to what the marshal had said, they did desire counsel and a trial. But before Culver could obtain a writ of habeas corpus, the fugitive slaves were taken away. It made him so angry, he said, that he felt like tearing down the city courthouse ("Three Fugitive Slaves, Arrested..." 87; "Man-Hunting in New York" 7). This incident occurred during the time of the more famous Anthony Burns rendition in Boston when pro-slavery advocates were attempting to capitalize on the passing of the Kansas-Nebraska Act in 1854, which allowed all future states west of the Mississippi the right to permit slavery, in effect nullifying the Missouri Compromise.*

A well-represented vigilance committee had been in place in Boston at least as early as 1843, as indicated by the ads they placed for a time under the name The New England Freedom Association, in newspapers like the *Emancipator*, asking for donations for fugitive slaves. These ads resumed after the passage of the second Fugitive Slave Law. In 1851, Thomas Simms, a runaway from Georgia, had been arrested in Boston. A large, menacing crowd had surrounded the courthouse while Simms was being tried, and an armed brigade had been appointed as a precaution. However, the vigilance committee's efforts at judicial intervention failed, and Simms was returned to slavery. In the case of Burns, the committee was determined not to allow it to happen again, but only a portion was willing to use force.

Burns's whereabouts had been learned by authorities when he inadvertently wrote Boston next to the date on a letter he sent to his brother, a slave in Virginia. He had been charged with robbing a jewelry store ("Right and Wrong in Boston" 5). It was a false charge that permitted his arrest by city officers, who had no jurisdiction under the Fugitive Slave Law. Burns was arrested and taken directly to the federal courthouse where a federal marshal was waiting with a warrant for his arrest. The vigilance committee called a public meeting, but they were divided on the issue of using force. Those in favor made an appeal to Worcester for help. Thomas Higginson, a

---

*The events surrounding the Kansas-Nebraska Act will be covered later—suffice to say that the Missouri Compromise guaranteed that states west of the Mississippi River and north of Missouri would not permit slavery; the Anthony Burns rendition which followed on its heels was viewed by abolitionists as a carefully timed political move by pro-slavery forces within the federal government to weaken them.

leading abolitionist there, in turn sent a request for help to Martin Stowell, who had been involved in the Jerry Rescue. Acting without the sanction of the committee, those in favor of using force met with Stowell and Higginson to create a plan.

They decided to use a public meeting that would discuss the abolitionists' options at Fanueil Hall, featuring Wendell Phillips and Theodore Parker, to draw attention away from the rescue attempt. Those making the rescue attempt, a small group, mainly blacks, met with Higginson in the basement of the Tremont Temple Baptist Church. Just before their attack began, the Fanueil Hall meeting was interrupted with news that it was underway. A crowd of hundreds rushed over to the courthouse just as the rescuers began assaulting its doors with a battering ram. Little did they know that the federal marshall had stationed 50 deputized officers inside as a precautionary measure. They were able to hold back the door, though Higginson—who was injured—and a black man briefly got inside. During the course of the melee, one account stated that 30 or more shots were fired by the crowd, some of which were aimed into the court-room. According to that account, a deputy officer, James Batchelder, was shot and killed by a blunderbuss (a type of shotgun), which literally tore his bowels out. This account also said that the deputized officers succeeded in stopping the mob with clubs only. However, another account said only the police fired shots. In any case, the attack was repulsed. Shortly after, two military units were summoned with the approval of President Fillmore (Campbell 124–128; "From the Boston Traveller...").

During Burns's prosecution, thousands of protesters gathered outside the courthouse, but the presence of the military discouraged any further violence. Rather, a shocked crowd, estimated at 100,000, watched as Burns was escorted through the streets of Boston by the military and put aboard a ship bound for Virginia. For Burns, the return to slavery was only temporary. A Boston church raised money to purchase his freedom, and less than a year later he was back a free man once again.

Two weeks after the rendition, the committee issued a letter with a brief report of their activities in which they accounted for assistance to 230 fugitive slaves since the passage of the Fugitive Slave Law.* Though some of its members had been part of the attempt to rescue Anthony Burns, they stated that their official policy was not to support the use of force (Letter. Boston). It would make some of its members like Samuel Gridley Howe and Thomas Higginson even more resolute in the future.

Saratoga Springs was often referred to in accounts of the day as a frequent vacation spot for Southern slaveholders, and at least one report in *The Liberator* in 1853 stated that "very many ... slave-hunters are here ("Letter from Henry C. Wright" 137). It is not surprising then that slavecatchers posed a constant threat to nearby Washington County. One local history states that "persistent" attempts were made by slavecatchers to return the fugitive slave, John Salter, to slavery (Thurston 72). Though events had moved the nation close to civil war, slavecatchers were still lurking in the area as late as 1858. The *People's Journal* in Union Village reported that "a number of Slave hunters were prowling about the town of Easton, endeavoring to arrest some of the Fugitives from Oppression who have sought refuge in that town, and employment whereby to gain an honest livelihood in a free country.

---

*A May 22, 1858, letter from Stephen Myers of Albany to Francis Jackson, president of the Boston Vigilance Committee, indicated that Myers was working with the committee in forwarding runaways.

"Fortunately," the report continued, "the kidnappers were baffled in their vile attempt and accomplished nothing by their ill-timed and unwise movement, save to awaken the jealousies and arouse the anger of the Quakers against Slavery, Slaveholders, and all Kidnappers under the Fugitive Slave Law. Accordingly, on the 18th inst. they held a large and enthusiastic Indignation Meeting, at which Francis M. Tobey, Esq., presided. A Committee of Vigilance in each School District was appointed. Resolutions to obey God rather than man in the matter of harboring the Fugitive, and pledging themselves to use all means in their power to rescue any Fugitive who should be kidnapped, were passed.

"The meeting was ably addressed by L. Gibbs, Esq., and others, in condemnation of the Fugitive Slave Law and the kidnappers, and in favor of all needed aid and protection to the Fugitive Slave in his glorious struggle for personal Liberty and Freedom from the oppression of the Slaveholder, and the tyranny of unrighteous laws" (*People's Journal* 22 April 1858).

John Salter may not have been the only runaway who was being sought at the time. He also had two brothers, Charles and William, who were living in the county. The 1860 federal census showed John living in the town of Jackson with property worth $2,000 and a personal worth of $800; his brother, Charles, also was living in Jackson. The youngest brother, William, was listed in the 1855 census in the town of Greenwich with his wife, Martha, on a farm valued at $400. That census indicated that he was a native of Maryland and had been living in the county for 11 years, which means that at least one of the brothers had come to the county as early the mid-1840s (*U.S. Federal Census* 1860; *New York State Census* 1855).

Perhaps the last celebrated fugitive slave rescue occurred in Troy, New York, in April 1860. It involved Charles Nalle (pronounced "Natallee"), a Virginia slave who had fled in 1858. He had found a respectable job as the carriage driver of Uri Gilbert, Troy's wealthiest man, and a room in the home of another fugitive slave, William Henry. However, Horace Averill, a local journalist, revealed his whereabouts and authorities seized him. Henry, a member of the local vigilance committee, secured the legal services of attorney Martin Townsend, then mobilized his associates for a rescue attempt. Among those joining them was Harriet Tubman, who apparently had been in the area visiting a cousin.* It was Tubman who led the band and gave the signal to take Nalle when he left the federal office building in the custody of federal marshals. Some accounts claim Tubman was the first to rush the group and physically grappled with the marshals, actually clutching onto Nalle. Inspired by her fierce display, the mob surrounded and beat the marshals, setting Nalle free. A chase followed during which officials again gained custody of Nalle, but in the end the vigilantes were triumphant, and they were able to spirit Nalle to a hiding place in Niskayuna. There he remained for the next month while a group from Troy negotiated for the sale of his freedom, finally paying $650 to his former owner (Christianson 30–35). Today, a bronze plaque commemorating his rescue from federal marshals on April 27, 1860, adorns the wall of the National City Bank building at the northeast corner of First and State streets.

*Two early local accounts of the Nalle rescue fail to identify Tubman as the woman leading the rescue; one of them, Hayner, said she was a scrub woman named Mary Haynes, who worked at a local bank (Hayner 705; Weise 225–226).

Chapter 20

FAMILY MATTERS

One could say that the Old Saratoga District Anti-Slavery Society was a Wilbur family operation. One of the three vice-presidents was John Wilbur (the nephew of Easton's legendary conductor Esther Wilbur); the secretary was Samuel Wilbur (Esther's grandnephew); the treasurer was Job Wilbur (Esther's husband); a member of the committee to circulate anti-slavery literature was Phebe T. Wilbur (Samuel's wife); and a second vice-president, Joseph W. Peckham, was a relative ("Trip to Northern New York" 46).

The leader of the Wilbur clan was a woman, Esther Wilbur, second wife of Job Wilbur, and mother of Job H. and Charles Wilbur. A sickly woman with a vigorous spirit, she was, as her eulogist wrote, "the friend of all—the widow, the fatherless, the destitute and the trembling fugitive, [a woman whose] heart always beat in sympathy with their necessities, and [who extended] an open hand to render all the aid in her power" ("Obituary" *National Anti-Slavery Standard*).

When the movement for immediate emancipation began during the 1830s, many Quaker meetings discouraged active participation in abolition societies. Apparently, this was the case in Easton where there were two meetings, the older one in South Easton and the other in North Easton, whose house was built in 1838 on land donated by the Wilbur family. The story of its first abolition meeting, which occurred sometime around 1850, was preserved in the memoirs of Oren B. Wilbur.

John Wilbur, Jr., Esther's cousin by marriage, was caretaker of the house. Unsympathetic to abolitionists, he banned their meetings. One morning after the Quaker services, Esther Wilbur remained alone in a pew. John wanted to close the house but waited. Finally, growing impatient, he spoke up.

"Esther, I want to close the meeting house now and thee will have to go."

Esther remained seated.

"John," she replied, "thee can lock up the meeting house, but I have not finished my worship so want to stay a little while longer" (Wilbur).

North East Meeting House. (Photograph by the author.)

After several more attempts to persuade her to leave, John became frustrated, locked the doors, and went home. But apparently he forgot that the door on the woman's side of the house was locked from the inside. When it came time for the anti-slavery meeting, Esther simply unlocked it. Thereafter, John decided it was no use to stop the anti-slavery meetings. In any case he wasn't about to argue with Esther again, and so the North Easton Friends Meeting opened to any anti-slavery society that wished to use it (ibid.).*

The Wilburs joined the anti-slavery efforts of their brethren in Quaker Springs, just a short distance from the other side of the Hudson River, to form the Old Saratoga District Anti-Slavery Society. They installed Hiram Corliss as president and Leonard Gibbs as a member of the executive committee. The membership included a substantial number of women. In addition to Esther were her niece, Phebe; Sarah and Deborah Wilde, and Eliza Shove of Quaker Springs; and Almy Corliss, the wife of Hiram ("Trip to Northern New York" 46).

Perhaps another way to unravel the mysteries of the Underground Railroad might be to explore the family connections that were used to forward fugitive slaves. An examination of the Old Saratoga District Anti-Slavery Society, for example, shows that it was, in a manner of speaking, a family affair. In addition to Job and Esther Wilbur,

---

*An 1853 letter written by L.M. Hoopes at the Easton Library states that the North Meeting House hosted a lecture by the famed black abolitionist, Sojourner Truth; other notes at the library state that Lucretia Mott was a guest speaker. Others who spoke there included Charles Burleigh in 1855, Aaron Powell on several occasions between 1855–1856, and Henry C. Wright in 1864 (National Anti-Slavery Standard 9 June 1855, 13 Dec. 1856; The Liberator 1 April 1964).

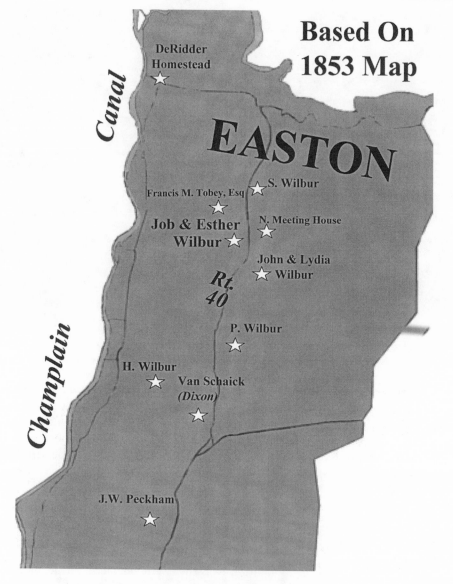

**Based On
1853 Map**

Canal

DeRidder
Homestead
★

EASTON

★S. Wilbur

Francis M. Tobey, Esq ★
★
Job & Esther   N. Meeting House
Wilbur ★   ★

John & Lydia
★ Wilbur

*Rt.
40*

P. Wilbur
★

H. Wilbur
★   Van Schaick
(Dixon)
★

Champlain

J.W. Peckham
★

(Map by the author.)

a number of others in Easton and Quaker Springs have been identified as conductors. In Easton, these include Humphrey Wilbur, the son of Job and stepson of Esther ("Memorial to Henry Wilbur" 10) and likely his cousins, Samuel and John, Jr.,* who were officers in the district society; in Quaker Springs, there were Cornelius Wright (Caldwell) and Isaac Griffen, the uncle of the Wildes, also members of the district society. Griffen was said to have hidden the fugitive slaves in his cellar. One time, a

---

*There were several John Wilburs. This is not believed to be the John Jr. who resisted Esther in opening the meeting house to anti-slavery.

fugitive slave died there of smallpox and infected the entire Griffen family, causing the death of two of his children (Griffen 7).

Quakers maintained close relations with other Quakers in the various regional meetings (Meader-Nye interview). They undoubtedly were in contact with the Quakers at the Peru Meeting; the Chestertown Leggetts, who had relatives in Quaker Springs; the Quaker Meeting of the Anthony family in the town of Greenfield, Saratoga County; and the Quaker Street Friends in Duanesburg, Schenectady County, whom legend claims also worked the Underground Railroad (Phillips 24). It is reasonable to assume that these neighboring meetings could call on each other for assistance in forwarding fugitive slaves.

In Clinton County, by far the largest Underground Railroad clan was the Keese family. Stephen and Samuel Keese, father and son, rode at the head of the posse of abolitionists coming to the organizational meeting of the county anti-slavery society in 1837 (Everest *Recollections* 59–60). At least 27 abolitionists in the county were Keeses or related to the family through marriage, and all but three of them were officers in their respective community societies (Keese 10–25; "Clinton County Convention"). Their ties also link to Saratoga County, where a Keese married William Shepherd of Quaker Springs, a member of the district society, and to Vermont, where Nathan C. Hoag of Ferrisburgh, a relative of William Keese's wife, Lydia Hoag, sometimes collaborated with Rowland T. Robinson (Everest *Recollections* 58). The Hoag family was well represented in the county's anti-slavery movement, showing five Hoags as members of local societies, including Embree E. Hoag, who was secretary of the West Peru Anti-Slavery Society ("From Peru").

In the northern section of the county, the Noadiah Moore family represented another, smaller clan of abolitionist leadership, but one that may have reached out in a number of directions. A place to start might be Moore's law apprenticeship with Zebulon Shipherd of Granville, who was a prominent lawyer and for a time a member of the U.S. Congress. Not only was Shipherd designated as a vice-president during the early years of the state society, but he also was the father of Underground Railroad conductor, the Rev. Fayette Shipherd, who was forwarding fugitive slaves north from Troy during the time that Moore was taking them to Canada.

The evidence for a connection with the Rev. Shipherd is only circumstantial, but there may have been another connection in central New York through the avenue of family. Shipherd's daughter, Katherine, married the wealthy George Chandler Bragdon of Oswego County, whose father, George Bragdon, was an active Underground Railroad conductor and collaborator with conductor Asa Wing (Wellman 1).

In any case, our narrative earlier had referred to Shipherd as the likely successor to Abel Brown, and he may have taken up those responsibilities at that time. For some reason, he left his free church in Troy in December 1846 and was unemployed for several months until receiving an invitation from Stephentown, which is in eastern Rensselaer County not far from its border with Massachusetts. He remained there until May 1849 when he moved to a church in West Nassau just a short distance from Stephentown. This is an extremely rural and mountainous area and right along a route from Rensselaer County to the Berkshires mapped out by Sand Lake historian Judith Rowe, who believes a fugitive slave named Isaac Tinley settled in Stephentown and became a blacksmith (Rowe interview). This route also is identified in a 1901 article, which also claims that a community of blacks took up residence in the surrounding mountains ("Berkshire's Old Underground Railroads" 7). Though there is no record or other evidence of Shipherd forwarding runaways while living in this area, it is conceivable that he was aiding runaway slaves during this time. Another puzzling matter that might lead one to believe he was working in the Underground Railroad at the time, is that his family continued to reside in Troy. After 1851, Shipherd moved first to Jefferson and then Oswego County, where he lived until 1858; the latter the site of perhaps the heaviest runaway slave traffic in the state during that time. He finally ended his days in Oberlin, where he moved in 1858 and reunited with his brother, who in an 1840 letter to Fayette had confessed that he was helping runaway slaves (Shipherd 98–102; Letter from John Jay Shipherd). Apparently, such things ran in the family.

Other Underground Railroad connections to the Moore family linked his brother-in-law, the Rev. Abram Brinkerhoff, pastor of the Champlain Presbyterian Church, who joined Moore in his public stand against slaveholders in the Presbyterian Church in 1843; another member of that group, Silas Hubbell, was the brother of Moore's brother-in-law; and finally, there was Moore's son-in-law, the Rev. Ovid Miner, who married his daughter, Eliza, in 1834. His is a story worth telling.

Born 1803 in Middletown, Vermont, Miner apprenticed as a printer for seven years at the *Northern Spectator* in East Poultney, Vermont, the same newspaper where Horace Greeley later apprenticed in 1826 and with whom he struck up a life-long friendship. Miner operated newspapers in Castleton until 1825 and in Middlebury until 1829, when he came under the spell of a revival and gave up his journalism career for the ministry. In 1834 he went to Peru, New York. The following year, we find him contributing a letter to Elijah Lovejoy's religious newspaper, the *St. Louis Observer*, reporting the dedication of a Congregational Church in Peru: "The Temperance cause is strong here.... There are good appearances in other parts of the county. Fifty-five were admitted to the Keeseville Church yesterday" ("Peru, N.Y." 1). Miner also mentions other letters that he had contributed to the newspaper. In 1836, he undertook a revival in Ticonderoga, and one history book reported him to be "a thorough abolitionist and vehement against slavery, for which some opposed him, and he finally went west to Oberlin" (Cook 93). He also collaborated with Nathaniel Colver in the formation of anti-slavery society in the same town.

That same year, he moved to Penn Yan, a prosperous town in the Finger Lakes region. During the next 19 years, there is some uncertainty about what he was doing. Having a family, it is likely that he remained in Penn Yan or Syracuse, the two locations his Middlebury College alumni records indicate he lived. However, records also show long periods when his occupation is listed as a lecturer, which suggests it was his custom to be a circuit rider. This could explain the reference about him going to Oberlin; it also could explain the letter in the Rev. Abel Brown's biography of Brown meeting a the Rev. Mr. Miner in Prairie Village, Wisconsin, during the summer of 1843 (Brown 171).*

Miner also is referred to by the Rev. Luther Lee, who lived in Syracuse for a short

---

*The Rev. Miner referred to is identified as a Baptist minister; Miner was a Presbyterian. However, another minister referred to in the same sentence is identified as a Presbyterian. It is possible that Brown made a mistake.

time in 1843, and again from 1852 to 1855, and who aided hundreds of fugitive slaves during those years (Lee 331). His recollection of Miner shows him to be a man who indeed was active in the Underground Railroad. Note, also, that Lee spells his first name Obed rather than Ovid.

"There was a gentleman—one of our true men—by the name of Obed Miner," Lee wrote. "He left town to go as far west as Lyons (near Rochester) on business, and a telegram was received, sent from Lyons, as follows: 'There will be a fugitive slave on the train which will pass Syracuse at eight o'clock this evening'" (334).

The letter was signed "O.M."

"All knew that if the 'O. M.' represented Obed Miner there was business to be attended to, but most believed it to be a game of our enemies; but it was thought best to be on the safe side, and at the right time the bell sent its pealing call, thrilling the air for miles. The result was, when the train arrived there were a thousand men on the track, and the way into the depot was closed up. The conductor, learning what the demonstration meant, came out upon the platform and stated that, upon his honor, there was no slave on board of his train, and that he would not carry a fugitive back to bondage" (ibid.).

Lee also gave some rather interesting details about the operation of the Underground Railroad in Syracuse.

"Precaution was taken against any surprise by slave-catching officers. A signal was arranged. A particular ring of a very far-sounding bell in the Congregational church told the people for four and five miles that help was wanted for a fugitive slave, and they would come rushing down from Onondaga Hills in a manner that meant business" (ibid.).

Lee also explained the city's attraction to fugitive slaves.

"[It] was a convenient shipping-point. I could put them in a car and tell them to keep their seats until they crossed the suspension bridge, and then they would be in Canada.... [And] it cost nothing to ship fugitive slaves from Syracuse to Canada. From all other points their fare had to be paid; if they could get to Syracuse they went free the rest of the way. The fact was, I had friends, or the slave had, connected with the railroad at Syracuse, of whom I never failed to get a free pass in this form: 'Pass this poor colored man,' or 'poor colored woman,' or 'poor colored family,' as the case might be. The conductors on the route understood these passes, and they were never challenged" (332).

In Union Village, the family or families that formed the "Free" Congregational Church developed a close-knit network. First among its families was the Mowry clan: William H. Mowry and wife, Angelina; Ann Caroline Mowry and husband, Henry Holmes; Mary Mowry and her husband, John T. Masters; Jane Mowry, daughter of William H., and her husband, Deodatus Haskell—all were members of the Free Church, with the husbands serving as trustees. Then there was the Corliss clan: Hiram and two of his wives, Susan, who died in 1843, and Almy, who died in 1858; his son, Albert, who was an associate pastor of the church; his daughter, Mary, and her husband, Cortland Cook; his son, George H., and his wife, Phebe; and his daughter, Elizabeth, who married one of the church's pastors, Sabin McKinney (*Manual* 32; *Corliss-Sheldon Families...*). The move of Corliss's daughter and her husband to Fredonia in 1847 provides an interesting connection, for Fredonia was a major Underground Railroad terminal under the supervision of Eber Pettit, who was discussed earlier.

Regarding surnames, Bigelow is one that merits a closer look, appearing eight times among the region's anti-slavery societies. For starters, there are two Bigelows who were members of the Free Church: Horace, who was a trustee (*Manual* 32), and Erastus, who left a substantial endowment to the church at his death (Thurston 58); in Hartford, Washington County, there was Thomas, an officer in the county society and a Liberty Party candidate ("Washington County Anti-Slavery Society"); other Washington County abolitionists were Dr. I.S. Bigelow, one of the founding members of the county society ("Spirit of the Times..." 3), and Anson Bigelow, who signed the anti-Nebraska petition ("Anti-Nebraska Meeting"); in Troy, the president of the anti-slavery society there in its formative years was Thaddeus B. Bigelow ("Troy Anti-Slavery Society"); in Clinton County, there was an A. Bigelow, whose house in Keeseville is an alleged Underground Railroad stop; and finally, Lucius Bigelow was one of Vermont's leading conductors in Burlington (Zirblis 71).

Family collaboration was not uncommon. There was the MacDougall family of Elizabethtown in Essex County that collaborated with John Brown; in Hadley, New York, the Sherman family in Saratoga in which father, mother, uncle, and grandfather worked together in forwarding the runaways; and another little known example of the Underground Railroad running in the family, that of the Rev. Jermain Loguen, the fugitive slave minister in Syracuse, and his wife's parents in Busti, Chautauqua County, both of their homes being frequent refuges for runaways (Bailey 56).

Perhaps the most natural relationship to involve family members in the Underground Railroad was father and son. Among them Mason Anthony and his father, Elihu, who were joined in their efforts by their cousins, the Allens, and the Keeses, who passed their anti-slavery legacy from grandfather, John, to father, Samuel, and finally to the younger son, John. But the most significant father-son relationship in New York State abolition may have been that of Richard P.G. Wright and his son, the Rev. Theodore Sedgwick Wright.

R.P.G. Wright lived in Schenectady for more than 40 years, moving there from Massachusetts after living in Providence, Rhode Island, where his son was born as a free man. Whether R.P.G. was born free or slave is not known, but he was an early advocate for civil rights among blacks and in 1817 "under great anxiety, took a journey to Philadelphia" to protest African colonization (Woodson 87–88). He also was in the forefront of education for black youth and his son was the first black graduate of Princeton. Wright was a respectable and prosperous barber in Schenectady who attended many of the Negro conventions and was an early member of the American Anti-Slavery Society, a vice-president of the state society, and a member of the New York Committee of Vigilance, making the long trip from Schenectady to attend its meetings. We know he was involved in the Underground Railroad on the basis of a letter mentioned in the Eastern New York Anti-Slavery's executive committee report of 1843. How active is a matter of conjecture, but it is worth noting that both his barbershop and home were only a short walk to the boarding docks for packet boats on the Erie Canal (*Schenectady Directory...*), and one would expect that a man who was "most tenderly attached" ("Obituary" *Albany Patriot* 133) to his son, who was the president of the New York Committee of Vigilance, perhaps the most important Underground Railroad organization during the antebellum period, would be more than casually involved.

The life of the Rev. Wright, the son, was inspired by the earlier efforts of his father. In a speech before the annual convention of the New York State Anti-Slavery Society in 1837, Wright referred to the inspiration of his father. His father's opposition to colonization caused the younger Wright to publicly oppose the pro-colonization views of the president while he was at Princeton and led to his incarceration (Woodson 88–89). In addition to being president of the New York Committee of Vigilance, the model on which the Underground Railroad was patterned, the Rev. Wright also was on the executive committee of the American Anti-Slavery Society and the American and Foreign Anti-Slavery Society that formed after the American Anti-Slavery Society split. In addition, he was vice-president of the American Missionary Association, which formed in 1839 to help fugitive slaves and other slaves who had been freed and were living out of the country. His staunch opposition to African colonization culminated in the tract, "The Colonization Scheme Considered," which he co-authored with Samuel Cornish (Gross 135). Perhaps Wright's greatest contribution was his mentorship to Henry Garnet, for whom he served as a kind of surrogate father. Of the relationship between Wright and Garnet, Dr. James McCune Smith wrote, "They were one in life"; and black educator Alexander Crummell wrote that Wright "looked upon him as his own son in the gospel" (ibid.). His death at the early age of 50 in 1847 was a blow to New York's black community and may have had a bearing on the death two months later of his own father.

Chapter 21

GO WEST, YOUNG ABOLITIONIST

"When we open a newspaper, the first thing that greets our eyes is 'Nebraska.' If in a railroad car, the noise of the whistle is almost drowned out by some windy politician crying out 'Nebraska.' Meet a friend in the street and instead of 'Good morning,' he yells out 'Nebraska'" (*Sandy Hill Herald* 2).

A strong push began in Congress in 1854 to enact a law that would allow citizens in the territories of Nebraska to decide whether or not to permit slavery. The question of whether the territory of Nebraska, which then included the present states of Kansas, Nebraska, North and South Dakota, Colorado, and part of Wyoming and Montana, would become slave or free was a new battlefield in the escalating political war between pro- and anti-slavery forces. For the latter, it had not been an issue, as they had assumed the Missouri Compromise of 1820 had permanently decided that all land north of the 36° 30" latitude line would be free. But the South with its greater influence in the federal government was gaining support because of the increasing radicalization and civil disobedience of the abolitionists. The South worried that if the Missouri Compromise endured, the addition of more states in the West would provide the free states with enough of a majority to eventually legislate the end of slavery.

Five months of debate followed in Congress, and on May 23, 1854, the Kansas-Nebraska Act passed by a narrow margin of 113–100. It was a great victory for the South and a horrible day for the abolitionists. "The deed is done—the Slave Power is again victorious," declared *The Liberator*. "A thousand times accursed be the Union which had made this possible!" ("The Nebraska Bill Passed..." 82). The *Albany Evening Journal* accurately described the situation when it lamented the division among the abolitionists.

"There is in the North a great—nay—a gigantic Party for Freedom. It comprises four-fifths, at least, of all the voters this side of Mason and Dixon's Line. It has, any day, a majority of half a million, in the Union. Its members have only to unite, to be invincible and overwhelming. [But] the irresistible party of Freedom is frittered between 'Free Soil Whigs' and 'Free Soil Democrats,' 'Independent Democrats' and 'Silver Grays,' and twenty other subdivisions, each bent, not only upon having its own way ... Yet each has proved, by years of experience, that this [plays] directly into the hands of Slaveholders" ("Friday Evening..." 2).

Though anti-slavery sentiment now was felt generally by a majority of those in the North—for example, only two upstate New York congressmen voted in favor of the Kansas-Nebraska bill ("New York..." 2), the division in the "party for freedom" that began with the schism of 1840 continued to be a problem. By 1854, only a fringe element of the Liberty Party remained—mainly those in central New York who would elect Gerrit Smith to Congress that fall—and abolitionists were split among various political groups. Underscoring this division was the unity and power possessed by the Southern slaveholders, whose overrepresentation in key positions of the U.S. government since the nation's inception had given their region an inordinate amount of influence. The following analysis made in 1859 illustrates this.

• The Presidency had been held by Southerners and slaveholders for 48 out of the nation's 71 years
• The Speaker of the House had been held by Southerners for 45 years
• The Secretary of State had been held by Southerners for 40 years
• The Attorney-General had been held by Southerners for 42 years
• The Secretary of the Navy had been held by Southerners in 16 of the 18 previous years
• The Supreme Court was—and had been for many years—comprised of a majority of Southerners ("What the South Has Had" 2)

This advantage held by the South continued, though its states were represented by only a little more than 40 percent of the nation's population by the Civil War, and it had been clearly demonstrated in the series of political victories gained by the South since the start of the abolition movement. This began with the repression of the rights of free blacks in the South. It was followed by a series of prohibitions, including the Gag Law and the censure of abolitionist mail that suspended parts of the bill of rights, and restrictions on the rights of free blacks in the North that included increasing discrimination and limitations on their suffrage. Finally, victories like the Supreme Court's Prigg Decision and the second Fugitive Slave Law were enlarged by the opportunity to extend slavery with the Kansas-Nebraska Act.

The new bill spawned many protest meetings throughout the North, among them a mass meeting held at the McFadden residence in Argyle, Washington County. More than 400 citizens had signed a petition calling for the meeting. James Thompson, town supervisor for Jackson in 1842 and 1848–49, and a former postmaster and tavern owner, was chairman. Among its resolutions were declarations that the North should be freed of any agreement to permit slavery in territories north of Missouri's southern border (36° 30") and that it should unite to oppose the existence of slavery in any existing territory or new state, whether north or south of that borderline. A resolution also was passed, calling for the repeal of the Fugitive Slave Law.

Among the speakers were Henry Northup, the man who freed Solomon Northup; Leonard Gibbs; and Judge Culver, direct from Brooklyn, speaking far longer than anyone "in his usual felicitous style" ("Proceedings..." 2).

The county sent ten delegates to the state Anti-Nebraska convention in Saratoga, among them two designated as abolitionists, notably Leonard Gibbs, who also attended a later "Convention of Seceders" in Auburn, a prelude to the first organizational efforts of the Republican Party that took place in Ballston Spa on October 6, 1854, under the leadership of General Edward Fitch Bullard of Saratoga (Sylvester 200).

Whether it was radical dissent as displayed in Boston or Syracuse, or merely law-abiding political action as shown in the many mass meetings, it was evident that the anti-slavery mood had become widespread and vehement throughout the North. Now that the sides were drawn, the first skirmish over slavery was brewing in Kansas. It was five years after the famous California Gold Rush, and "Go West, Young Man" was already part of the vernacular. The new law stimulated a similar stampede of settlers from East to West to defend their right to determine whether the territories would become slave or free.

The Emigrant Aid Company, organized by Eli Thayer of Worcester, Massachusetts, began recruiting free-staters for the move from New England to Kansas even before the law was passed. The first group arrived in August 1854 and formed the town of Lawrence, Kansas, and by the end of the year, it had 700 settlers. Before Northerners could muster any sizable settlement movement in the territory, however, thousands of pro-slavery Missouri residents moved in and set up a second residence in Kansas for the purpose of voting in a pro-slavery government. On the day of the first elections in March 30, 1855, 5,000 armed, pro-slavery residents of Missouri invaded Kansas and took control of the election precincts. All pro-slavery candidates but one were elected to the legislature and that one resigned in protest. When the territory's governor, Andrew Reed of Pennsylvania, protested to President Pierce, he was removed. The stage had been set for what would be the prelude to the Civil War (Macy 150–154).

Lending substantial support to the burgeoning conflict in Kansas were two Northern cities that had become the centers of militant abolitionism, Boston and Syracuse. Among the generous individual supporters were Gerrit Smith, and Theodore Parker and Samuel Howe of Boston. In northern New York, the Free Church in Union Village gave financial support ("Anti-Slavery Indifference").

That summer, a convention of "Radical Abolitionists" met in Syracuse. It resolved to secede from the Union if necessary to end slavery. President of the convention was longtime New York Committee of Vigilance member James McCune Smith; other leading members were Gerrit Smith, Frederick Douglass, Samuel May, Arthur Tappan, William Goodell, and Jermain Loguen. Also attending was John Brown, who had moved back from Ohio to North Elba and whose sons had moved their families west to homestead in Kansas. They had been drawn into the conflict and had been writing to their father, urging him to join them. Brown brought one of the letters that was read aloud by Gerrit Smith. It stated that large armed groups of pro-slavery vigilantes were coming into Kansas from Missouri to intimidate the settlers and that the free-staters, who were showing a lack of resolve in the brewing confrontation, needed more support. Brown offered his services to fight for freedom in Kansas and asked for contributions to assist his efforts. Frederick Douglass and some others endorsed Brown, but the convention did not give full endorsement. Rather, the hat was passed and $60 was raised, though it is likely that Gerrit Smith, who contributed $16,000 overall to the Kansas cause, and others contributed additionally behind the scenes ("Radical Political Convention" 3; Renehan 87; Frothingham 100).

About this time, the success of Union Village native Erastus Culver in civil rights cases involving blacks in New York City and his position as a judge in Brooklyn had catapulted him to national prominence. How prominent may be indicated by his position as the featured speaker at the West India Emancipation Celebration of the New York Anti-Slavery Society, among a group that included the illustrious William Lloyd Garrison, in July 1855 ("West India Emancipation").

One month later in Syracuse, at the inauguration of the Republican Party in New York State, Culver, who was in attendance as a Whig Representative, was called to the floor and made a vigorous speech in support of it. "By the authority vested in me as a Judge," he said in conclusion, "by the people of the State of New York, I pronounce the Whig and Republican parties one. 'And what people have joined together, let not demagogues put asunder!'" ("Inauguration of the Republican Party in the State of New York" 3). From that day, Culver would be a diehard Republican.

Events of that period show the climate of growing anti-slavery feeling that existed throughout the state: in Saratoga Springs, the den of Southern vacationers, a group of free black workers at the hotels had organized to protest their treatment as second-class citizens; in Mexico, Oswego County, 3,000 gathered to dedicate a monument to Underground Railroad conductor Asa Wing, who died the previous year; and in Olean, Cattaraugus County, there was the report of Silver Grays, those who advocated obedience to the Fugitive Slave Law, aiding fugitive slaves. The latter report also indicated a similar incident in Albany. It concluded, "[the] best way to cure Northern men of their veneration for this most odious piece of legal barbarism is to consign one of its victims to their hospitality" ("Coloured Gentleman..."; "Monument..."; "Silver Grays...").

The time was ripe for John Brown to embark on the road that he believed was his destiny and that would immortalize him in American history. After making repairs on his house and stocking it with supplies for his family, he left North Elba in a wagon loaded with rifles and ammunition. He reached Kansas in October. By November, the free-staters had set up their own government and drafted a constitution that prohibited slavery. Also that month, a free-stater was killed in a dispute with a pro-slavery settler over a land claim. The murderer escaped the authorities, but a free-stater who threatened to kill him was taken into custody only to be freed after the law enforcement officer was threatened by a free-state mob. On December 18, three days after the free-staters had approved their constitution that prohibited slavery in the territory, a confrontation occurred in Lawrence that involved the sheriff whose authority had been usurped by the mob. The town had been alerted and set up its defenses; among those prepared to fight were Brown and his sons. Before any hostilities occurred, however, the governor intervened and brought the matter to a temporary resolution.

On the national front, President Pierce took action. In a message to Congress, he characterized the free-staters as unlawful revolutionaries, and following his lead,

John Brown as he looked when in Kansas.

authorities in Kansas issued indictments against free-staters who participated in the confrontation in Lawrence, among whom were Brown and his sons. Now calling himself "Captain," Brown transformed himself into a self-appointed military leader and began to commandeer a band of anti-slavery proponents that included his sons. In May 1856, word came that another invasion of Lawrence by forces from Missouri was imminent. Brown and his band went to help, but they were too late and Lawrence was burned to the ground (Macy 156–159).

Enraged, Brown vowed to inflict a savage blow that would strike fear into the hearts of the pro-slavery forces and regain the momentum for anti-slavery. After going off alone to talk to God— Brown claimed that he communed with God and saw visions that guided his actions—Brown led his sons on a secret expedition the night of May 23, 1856. They surprised three pro-slavery families and broke into their cabins near the Pottawatomie Creek. Armed with broadswords, Brown's sons brutally hacked five settlers to death, cutting off the hand of one and the arms of another. Among them were James P. Doyle and his two sons. Brown spared the youngest son at the plea of his mother. Mahala Doyle later gave testimony regarding the murders to the authorities in Missouri, which was published on June 21, 1856, in the *Leavenworth Herald*.

"He said if a man stood between him and what he considered right, he would take his life as coolly as he would eat his breakfast," Doyle said. "His actions show what he is. Always restless, he seems never to sleep. With an eye like a snake, he looks like a demon" (Oates 144).

In the national headlines, another event that occurred overshadowed it. Charles Sumner, the senator from Massachusetts, who had strongly condemned the pro-slavery Kansas faction, was beaten with a cane by South Carolina Congressman Preston Brooks in the very halls of Congress. Nevertheless, news of the "Pottawatomie Massacre" appeared in many Northern newspapers, and both pro-slavery and free-state forces condemned the massacre. Additional warrants went out for the arrest of Brown and his sons, who managed to evade capture and went on a looting spree during which he also freed some slaves.

At the same time, pro-slavery forces in Kansas captured his sons, Jason and John, Jr., the latter who was beaten severely with rifle butts. They later killed his son, Frederick, during hostilities in the Osawatomie section and pillaged the Brown homestead there. Murdering and pillaging occurred on both sides, and during the next few months, Brown and his band participated in a number of clashes with pro-slavery forces, which were now under the direction of the federal government. In all, about 200 individuals lost their lives (Oates 126–146; Renehan 95–97). Fortunately, none of the Brown women were harmed.

Now on the run, Brown managed to evade capture, but from that time on, he was a renegade. He would return to North Elba only for brief periods. The remainder of his life was devoted to traveling around the country to raise money for his holy war against slavery.

Chapter 22

NEVER HALF WHAT IT IS NOW

During the first week of March 1854, Frederick Douglass visited Washington County, New York.* It was reported to *The Liberator* by Hiram Corliss and provides a revealing look at the state of abolition in northern New York. Corliss, then 61, wrote that the meeting was called by the "Free Democrats," and remarked that despite the political chaos among abolitionists and the growing support in northern New York for the more moderate Republican Party, "Anti-slavery with us was never half what it now is..." ("Letter from Dr. Corliss" 55).

Douglass lectured in South Easton, Galesville, Lakeville, Shushan, Coila, Cambridge, and twice in Union Village. By then the editor of his own abolitionist newspaper and renowned for the first version of his autobiography, Douglass was expressing anti-slavery views that were becoming increasingly more militant. A contemporary description of Douglass in 1850 illustrates what Washington County residents saw when he came to the county:

> Frederick Douglass is nearly six feet tall, and well proportioned ... He is a mulatto ... has crisped hair which is marked with a few silver threads ... and compressed lips, which show the unyielding firmness of the man. He has a habit of twitching the muscles of the mouth when he become excited, as though a speech was breaking out of it in silent syllables ... He is courteous ... gentlemanly ... [and] entirely free from affectation.... As an orator he ranks with the best speakers in Congress.... While but few of our educated men have such a command of classical English ... a still smaller number can equal him in eloquence and originality... ["Frederick Douglass" 156].

Corliss didn't comment on Douglass's appearance, but focused on setting the scene and the substance of his message:

*Douglass may also have ventured to Clinton County ("Lectures..." 72).

NOTICE.

We learn that FREDERICK DOUGLASS, the world-renowned Fugitive Slave, will hold a series of Meetings in this vicinity, during the first week in March. His appointments are as follows:

On Wednesday, Eve. March 1, Union Village.
On Thursday, " " 2, Lake.
On Friday, " " 3, Shushan.
On Saturday, " " 4, Coila.
On Sunday, Afternoon, " 5, S. Easton, Quaker Meeting-House.
On Monday. Eve. " 6. Galesville.
On Tuesday " " 7, Union Village.

Free Democratic League Meeting, on MONDAY EVENING, meet at Harts Hotel. A general attendance solicited.

By order of Ex-Committee.

Notice of Frederick Douglass's lectures in Washington County, 1854. (From *The Journal*, Greenwich, NY, 1854.)

Mr. Douglass's first meeting was appointed for the evening of the first day of March [at the Free Church], but owing to a delay on the railroad, he did not arrive until nine o'clock," Corliss wrote. "[Nevertheless] Miss Holley [Sallie] who was at my house at the time, went and lectured. After Miss Holley had closed her lecture, the audience called out Leonard Gibbs, Esq., who spoke for nearly an hour with his usual ability and great power ... A choir of colored persons then sang a song, and while they were singing, Mr. Douglass came into the house. He made a short speech, and the meeting adjourned. The meeting was good, and well-pleasing to all.

Corliss continued to report on Douglass's other meetings.

Two of Douglass's meetings, the one on Sabbath afternoon at the Quaker meeting-house in South Easton, and the one in our village on Tuesday afternoon at the Baptist meeting-house, were very great, filling those large houses to a perfect jam.... The impression on the minds of the people, by his meetings, was very good indeed. Those I heard were full of great truths, sound logic, and enforced by vivid illustrations.... He gave, in one of his lectures, an account of his conversion from a belief that the Constitution of the United States was slaveholding ... His arguments ... were ... quite insufficient to vindicate a constitution, made by the representatives of a slaveholding people, and that Constitution too, forbidding Congress in one of its articles to pass any law for twenty years restricting the foreign slave trade, and in another article giving to slaveholders forever the three-fifths representation....

That comment by Corliss indicated a shift in his political views. Having been a Liberty Party man, he almost certainly had supported at one time the view Douglass was presenting. But now Corliss actually admitted to being a Garrisonian. If a leading Liberty man like Corliss had come to terms with Garrison, this shows that a healing of the wounds created by the schism of 1840 had to some degree taken place. Corliss's commentary also shows that being an abolitionist was no longer so controversial. More and more people in the North were seeing the light, so to speak. Most had probably read *Uncle Tom's Cabin*, which though having little immediate political effect, was gradually seeping into the national consciousness. As historian James Ford Rhodes wrote, "It is often remarked that previous to the [Civil] war the Republican party attracted the great majority of school-boys ... the youth of America whose first ideas of slavery were formed by reading Uncle Tom's Cabin..." (as quoted by Siebert 324).

The book probably reached more easily into the homes of ordinary folks in the remote hamlets of northern New York than the preaching of abolitionists. The grow-ing Wesleyan-Methodist Church was serving such communities. In 1853, the St. Lawrence Conference and its congregations at Bucksbridge, Rossie, Pierpont, Lisbon, Morely, and Brookdale became part of the Champlain Conference, and the denom-ination also had added such communities as Long Lake, and Brant Lake in Warren County; Keene and Wilmington in Essex County; and Keeseville, and North Chit-tenden in Clinton County ("One Hundred Twenty-Five Years..." 4–7).

While warfare raged in Kansas in 1856, abolitionist speakers toured the North. Almost two decades had passed since the years of the mobs and threats of violence against the abolitionists. So much had occurred: the fight in Congress over consti-tutional rights; the appearance of slavecatchers in northern New York; the struggle in the state for Negro suffrage; the imprisonment and martyrdom of northern New Yorkers who aided fugitive slaves; the Fugitive Slave Law of 1850; the publication of *Uncle Tom's Cabin*; the repeal of the Missouri Compromise; the battle in Kansas over the expansion of slavery; and the formation of the Republican Party. Support for the South had almost completely eroded in the North. As Henry Stanton observed that year after a lecture in Rhode Island, the men who led the mobs against him in the 1830s were now leading the cheers (Stanton 28).

Among the prominent exhorters in the Northeast were Aaron Powell, Charles Burleigh, Henry C. Wright, Charles Remond, Sarah Remond, Susan B. Anthony, and William Wells Brown. After Frederick Douglass, Wells Brown was probably the most prominent black writer in the nation during this time. During summer of 1856, he spent two weeks in Washington County, where he lectured and performed at the Free Church in Union Village. A fugitive slave, he took his name from the Quaker family that helped him during his escape to freedom in 1834. He also was active as an Underground Railroad conductor in Buffalo, admitting to helping as many as 69 fugitive slaves escape to Canada in a single year (Coleman 49). In 1847, his fugitive slave account, *The Narrative of William Wells Brown, A Fugitive Slave*, was published and sold 8,000 copies within two years (Gara 123).

During Wells Brown's visit, he presented his one-man fugitive slave play that Diantha Gunn described in an August 19, 1856, letter:

> On Monday evening attended recitation of an anti-slavery drama, written by William Wells Brown ... who was a slave until nineteen years of age, when he made his escape from slavery. He was in England at the time of the fugitive slave law was passed and dared not to return lest he should again be taken into slavery. Some English ladies therefore, made a bargain with his master, pur-chased him, that he might return to his family in this country, and gave him his name. He is quite a smart man. Has lectured two Sabbath evenings in our church.

Nevertheless, though a majority in the region was opposed to slavery, the anti-slavery fervor had moderated to some degree. Aaron Powell, probably the most active abolitionist speaker in the region during this period, referred to this during a tour that took him from Washington to Clinton and finally to St. Lawrence County from November 1856 to January 1857, about which he sent periodic reports to the *National Anti-Slavery Standard*.

Joining Powell were the black lecturers from Massachusetts, Charles and Sarah Remond, who were brother and sister. Charles, a longtime crusader for abolition, was the first black hired as a lecturer by the American Anti-Slavery Society in 1838. In 1847, he issued a call for all slaves to resist their masters and, during the latter part of 1850s, typically addressed his audiences about prejudice on the basis of color, arguing that its origin resulted from the need to justify slavery.

"In Washington County," Powell wrote, "we held meetings in South Easton, North Easton and Union Village, ten meetings in all.... I have heretofore attended meetings and lectured in those towns, but in no instance have the audiences been as limited in numbers; never have they manifested so much indifference, such coldness of spirit" ("Letter from A.M. Powell" 13 Dec. 1856: 3).

Powell attributed this to the recently completed political campaign, which he believed had left the people tired of politics ("Anti-Slavery Indifference" 3).

"At North Easton, we held meetings in the Friends Meeting House and in the Wilbur District. Of our friends there, who have a continued and increasing interest in uncompromising freedom, and to whom we are indebted for cordially proffered hospitality are John and Lydia Wilbur; Abel and Hannah Thomas; Job and Esther Wilbur.

"At Union Village meetings were held in the Congregational Church," Powell wrote. "Its pastor, the Rev. Mr. Shattuck, is one of the few liberal and outspoken clergymen rarely to be met with. Though he was induced to vote for Fremont, I am informed that he has since the election, on Thanksgiving Day, preached a radical sermon in favor of disunion. Our friend Leonard Gibbs, also Dr. Corliss, I understand, refused to engage in the late political contest. Aside from the exceptions named, the anti-slavery of Union Village seems to be mainly of a political or compromising character" ("Letter from A.M. Powell" 13 Dec. 1856: 3).

"We have at South Easton some of the best friends of our movement," Powell wrote, concerned because his last lecture there two years earlier drew a large audience. He wondered if it were the result of the recent growth of the Republican Party and its moderate anti-slavery views. Powell noted that Jacob Pratt, formerly a strong abolitionist from Easton, had moderated his views and attempted, unsuccessfully, to prevent them from returning to another anti-slavery meeting at the South Meeting House (Ibid.).

From Washington County, Powell and the Remonds went to a convention at the Union in Peru, Clinton County, where Susan B. Anthony joined them. On the way, they were met by Stephen Keese Smith in Keeseville, of which Powell wrote, perhaps with some exaggeration but with poignancy, that Keeseville's "moral atmosphere, in relation to slavery, is not very unlike that of South Carolina." He mentioned a local Republican who considered abolitionists like Powell and his fellows who preached disunion as traitors who should be hung. Powell did, however, praise Wendell Lansing, the editor of that village's newspaper, the *Northern Standard* ("Letter from A.M. Powell" 27 Dec. 1856: 3).

At the convention, the president was the county's earliest and most vocal abolitionist, Samuel Keese. Many of the officers and committee members were Keeses or their relatives, similar to the make-up of the Old Saratoga District Anti-Slavery with its many Wilburs. One of the three major issues of concern was the growth of slavery as a result of the prejudice against color ("Anti-Slavery Convention..." 3).

More interesting, as well as ironic, was an incident that followed in Plattsburgh, where they were scheduled for meetings. At the Cumberland House, where they stayed, they were confronted by the very prejudice that they had been addressing during their lectures. The Remonds were refused a place for dinner in the public dining room on account of the complaint of another guest. When this was brought to the attention of the proprietor, he apologized and set up a private table for them. The next morning, the proprietor made sure they were seated in the public dining room ("Letter from A.M. Powell" 27 Dec. 1856: 3).

While the Remonds held meetings in Champlain, Powell and Anthony went to Malone in Franklin County. Powell called the audience there "attentive and respectful," but the turnout was poor and mainly women and children. He added that the Republicans there were not supportive, but speculated that some of the lack of participation may have been because an agent of the American Bible Society was also holding meetings at the various churches. Another disappointment was that none of the churches there invited them, which is puzzling, given the Underground Railroad legends associated with its Congregational Church.

In Potsdam, the Remonds joined Powell and Anthony, and had very good meetings. A former Garrison associate, Silas Leonard, made arrangements for their meetings, and the Remonds were invited to stay at the home of the editor of the Republican newspaper, *The Northern Freeman*. Powell and Anthony stayed at the residence of a man named Jackson. In Ogdensburg, their presence was met with mixed results. Again, they were confronted by racial prejudice when the Remonds were turned away at the Webster House, the home of U.S. Senator Preston King.* It was disheartening, but it was foreshadowing of the future difficulties blacks in America would to face long after slavery was abolished ("Letter from A.M. Powell" 10 Jan. 1857: 3).

Meanwhile, the Free Church in Union Village continued its anti-slavery mission, holding regular abolitionist meetings and lectures. Among its causes was that of the Rev. John Fee of Kentucky, who probably came to the awareness of the church in 1851 when he made public a shocking appeal for aid to build an anti-slavery church in of all places, Kentucky. He had written that year to the *Pennsylvania Freeman* that he had organized a small congregation of 13 members in Bracken County and another church in Lewis County in areas of non-slaveholding farmers. He said he had one "colored" member and that several other "coloreds" had attended services. He was requesting $150 to build the church.

"We ask that they (the stewards of the Lord) will give, either by sending directly to me," he wrote, "or through the Rev. George Whipple, Secretary of the American Missionary Association, New York" ("Abolitionism in Kentucky" 1).

We know Fee's appeal reached the Free Church because its 1860 *Manual* states that it "sustained a mission church in Kentucky" and, later in the same paragraph, that it assisted the Rev. John Fee (*Manual* 11). In January of 1857, Fee wrote a letter to the Rev. Simon Jocelyn in regards to support he had been receiving from the church and Dr. Corliss.

"By last mail I received from each of you, a line in reference to an enclosed check of $50, from Hiram Corliss of Union Village, N.Y," Fee wrote. "Brother Corliss is an

---

Later legend claims this house was an Underground Railroad Station.

old correspondent—helped build the church edifice in Bracken County—deeply sympathizes with our whole movement here—wants to do through his church [the Free Church], most, if not all the supporting of a pastor here in Kentucky. He will do this through your Society. He expects from the pastor of the church, they shall aid, and from myself something for every monthly concert. I shall leave most of this for that Pastor. By this means he expects to interest his church members and induce them to give more than they would otherwise do. I suggested to him that he aid the church here through you. That will keep up the union between you and the two churches— awaken sympathy and interest in all" (Letter from John G. Fee...).*

The Free Church's *Manual* also states that "a pro-slavery mob burned the house of worship and broke up the operations" (*Manual*... 11). This occurred during the summer of 1857 when Fee was nearly lynched. During church services, a mob of 30 men entered the church with pistols drawn and rushed up to the altar. Cursing and ranting, they struck Fee on the head and dragged him outside. They forced him to walk two miles and considered hanging him, but instead they asked him to promise never to re-enter the county. Fee refused. He insisted he only would obey God. They marched another seven or eight miles during which two members of his congregation joined him in support. As they went, more threats were made on Fee's life, but finally the mob dispersed and released Fee and the others. Two weeks later, Fee reported that the temporary building where he had given his last services also had been burned. He said his church members were scared and that his health was poor ("The Latest Kentucky Mob" 129; "The Assault Upon the Rev. John G. Fee" 130). "My condition is at present perilous," he wrote, "...I am worn down with continued riding, am not vigorous in health and am pressed with care, but have the rest of faith. I hope that God is my friend, and will overrule all for good, and give me wisdom and grace. Pray for me" ("Mob Violence Still Prevailing in Kentucky" 152).

Somehow, Fee persisted and continued to minister to poor blacks in the South up through the Civil War. After the war, he founded Berea College, the first school of higher education in Kentucky to admit blacks. The Free Church did not desert him either; as their *Manual* stated, "now it is assisting to a considerable extent that devoted and dauntless man of the same state (Kentucky), the Rev. John G. Fee, in his worthy educational enterprises of religion and reform" (*Manual* 11).

These years after the Kansas-Nebraska Act were a period of apparent apathy in abolition. Although the fervor of earlier years had waned, overall support for the end of slavery was greater than ever and had gained converts among those from all walks of life in the smallest and most remote hamlets. The Underground Railroad was firmly in place, and most local tales that recount its existence probably date from these later years. While runaway slave traffic may have not been as heavy in the northeastern region, with most runaways using routes through central and western New York, there is no doubt many there were ready to help.

*Letter courtesy of Marion B. Lucas, Department of History, Western Kentucky University.

Chapter 23

ALL ABOARD!

The surge of emigration to Canada by both fugitive slaves and free blacks following the passage of the second Fugitive Slave Law slowed by 1853. While many sympathizers were ready to assist them on the Underground Railroad in northern New York, central New York was the primary destination of most fugitive slaves who had come through Philadelphia, New York, and even Boston, where their vigilance committee worked with Stephen Myers in Albany (Ripley 407, 410). The Liberty Party, which originated in central New York, still maintained a presence there. It also provided closer access to fugitive slave communities in Canada through the ports of Pultneyville (north of Rochester), Oswego, and Port Ontario, as well as St. Lawrence River crossing points in north-central New York like Cape Vincent and Ogdensburg.

By mid-decade, the numbers apparently increased again. For example, during the summer of 1854, Hiram Wilson reported that "fugitives are coming over and calling daily" ("Fugitives in Canada" 80). A June 10 dispatch from the *Chicago Tribune* testified that they were being assisted by the organized machinery of the Underground Railroad: "Its trains run through our streets regularly, but notwithstanding its passenger business has increased at a rate equal to that of any other 'upper ground' road ... We can assure its friends and the public that its business, above all expectations, is still increasing at a most astonishing rate ... A large corps of trusty conductors have been secured, the stations well fitted up, and the officers and passengers on the road furnished with 'irons' to be used against all who may have the audacity to interfere with trains or passengers" ("Underground Railroad" 15).

In Montreal, an attempt by Southern slaveholders to induce a Canadian official in Montreal to act as a slavecatcher was exposed by the *Montreal Gazette* on January 13, 1855 (Landon 36). This indicates the probability that fugitive slaves were coming on a fairly regular basis, and if so, may have come by way of northern New York. Gary Collison, author of *Shadrach Minkins: Fugitive Slave to Citizen*, who has done extensive research of the black population in Montreal during this time, found a total of 228 blacks in the 1861 census. A large percentage probably was fugitive slaves, as Collison found that 39 of the 44 males who admitted that they were born in the U.S. were from the South (Collison 206). Furthermore, he believes that the true total of blacks in Montreal was closer to 400 as had been reported in the *Montreal Gazette* during this time. As Robin Winks stated in his seminal work on blacks in Canada during the antebellum period, fugitive slaves in Canada often did not convey their true identity: "No accurate figures can be given for the number of fugitive slaves in the whole of the British North American provinces, or for the total number of Negroes. Many attempted to pass for white when in the Canada's, many were not enumerated, and census takers might reasonably have confused fugitive American with free American blacks, since the former often claimed the status of the latter, especially because of their misplaced fear of extradition" (Winks 235).

A more precise and revealing indicator of fugitive slave traffic in the region was the Albany Vigilance Committee broadside of 1856, which stated that they had assisted 287 fugitive slaves from September 1855 to July 1856. The broadside, which made an appeal for assistance from the local community, also listed the names of the vigilance committee members. General Agent and Superintendent was Stephen Myers, and among those assisting him were William H. Topp, the prominent black tailor and friend of William Lloyd Garrison; Thomas Elkins, a local black medical professional; and Reverend John Sands of the second Wesleyan African Church on Third Street in Arbor Hill. The committee also was distinguished by its integrated composition, with four of its twelve members being white. The committee spent more than $600 assisting the fugitive slaves during the nine-month period and reported that one group of 16, which it had assisted, had successfully reached the Stamford Township near Niagara Falls in Canada. The Vigilance Committee at that time maintained an office at 198 Lumber Street, now Livingston Avenue (*Vigilance Committee Office*).

While in all likelihood the majority of those fugitive slaves who headed to Canada were sent west to Syracuse and vicinity, based on the Loguen autobiography that states he aided about 1,500 fugitive slaves from 1851 to 1859, there also is a likelihood that some were sent north to join family members who at the time may have been living there temporarily. Meanwhile, upstate New York conductors were advertising their accommodations for runaways. The Syracuse Fugitive Aid Society requested "that all fugitives from slavery coming this way may be directed to the care of the Rev. J.W. Loguen; also, that all moneys subscribed or contributed or subscribed be paid directly to him as UGRR conductor; and that all clothing or provisions contributed may be sent to his house, or such places as he may designate" (To the Friends...").

The advertisement admitted that the work of housing and moving fugitive slaves had always been the work of a few individuals and that since 1850 most of the work had been done by Loguen, a former fugitive who knew how to fill the needs of fugitive slaves as well as how to ensure their safety.

In Troy, New York, a meeting of the Vigilance Committee at the Liberty Street Church reported in 1857 that it had assisted 55 fugitive slaves during the previous year and directed that all contributions be sent to William Rich ("Public Meeting"). Among other members of the committee was William Henry, who provided board to the fugitive slave Charles Nalle and who was among the leaders of the group that participated in the rescue of Nalle.

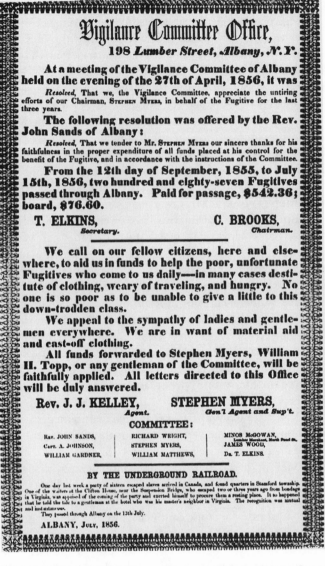

Vigilance Committee Office,

198 Lumber Street, Albany, N.Y.

At a meeting of the Vigilance Committee of Albany held on the evening of the 27th of April, 1856, it was

Resolved, That we, the Vigilance Committee, appreciate the untiring efforts of our Chairman, STEPHEN MYERS, in behalf of the Fugitive for the last three years.

The following resolution was offered by the Rev. John Sands of Albany:

Resolved, That we tender to Mr. STEPHEN MYERS our sincere thanks for his faithfulness in the proper expenditure of all funds placed at his control for the benefit of the Fugitive, and in accordance with the instructions of the Committee.

From the 12th day of September, 1855, to July 15th, 1856, two hundred and eighty-seven Fugitives passed through Albany. Paid for passage, $542.36; board, $76.60.

T. ELKINS,
Secretary.

C. BROOKS,
Chairman.

We call on our fellow citizens, here and elsewhere, to aid us in funds to help the poor, unfortunate Fugitives who come to us daily—in many cases destitute of clothing, weary of traveling, and hungry. No one is so poor as to be unable to give a little to this down-trodden class.

We appeal to the sympathy of ladies and gentlemen everywhere. We are in want of material aid and cast-off clothing.

All funds forwarded to Stephen Myers, William H. Topp, or any gentleman of the Committee, will be faithfully applied. All letters directed to this Office will be duly answered.

Rev. J. J. KELLEY,
Agent.

STEPHEN MYERS,
Gen'l Agent and Sup't.

COMMITTEE:

REV. JOHN SANDS,	RICHARD WRIGHT,	MINOS McGOWAN, Lumber Merchant, North Pearl St.
Capt. A. JOHNSON,	STEPHEN MYERS,	JAMES WOOD,
WILLIAM GARDNER,	WILLIAM MATTHEWS,	Dr. T. ELKINS.

BY THE UNDERGROUND RAILROAD.

One day last week a party of sixteen escaped slaves arrived in Canada, and found quarters in Stamford township. One of the waiters at the Clifton House, near the Suspension Bridge, who escaped two or three years ago from bondage in Virginia, was apprised of the coming of the party and exerted himself to procure them a resting place. It so happened that he told the tale to a gentleman at the hotel who was his master's neighbor in Virginia. The recognition was mutual and instantaneous.

They passed through Albany on the 13th July.

ALBANY, JULY, 1856.

Broadside reporting the efforts to aid fugitive slaves by the Albany Vigilance Committee. (Courtesy of the American Antiquarian Society, Worcester, MA.)

It was shortly after the Troy report that Albany lost one of its most important conductors. William H. Topp, the prominent black tailor, community leader, and friend of William Lloyd Garrison, died on December 11, 1857, at the age of 45. Topp had been in poor health with lung problems for six months, and his death was not unexpected. "Numerous are the heroic adventurers from the scenes of Southern oppression," his obituary stated, "who have thanked God and taken fresh courage, and who refer with blessings to his memory for his generous and self-sacrificing aid in the hour of their greatest need" ("Death of William H. Topp" 3). The obituary also praised him for his efforts devoted to improving the status of blacks and for his achievements as a businessman.

The Underground Railroad in Albany carried on. It had evolved into an operation like that in Syracuse, being supervised by one man—Stephen Myers. He had been its superintendent for a decade or more and had developed contacts throughout the northeast. In his April 1858 "Circular to the Friends of Freedom," Myers reported that he had assisted 121 fugitive slaves during the prior five months. Another letter to Francis Jackson, president of the Boston Vigilance Committee, enumerated another 66 in the following month. In addition to fugitive slaves coming from New York, he also was receiving numerous fugitive slaves from New England conductors

Jackson and Thomas Harley in Springfield, Massachusetts. He also had developed a wide range of financial contributors, attracted through his contacts among leading New York State politicians, who included New York Governor Edwin Morgan, U.S. Senator William Seward, and *Albany Evening Journal* publisher Thurlow Weed (Ripley 410).

In New York City, Judge Erastus Culver continued to do his part. A slave named Jeems was discovered stowed away aboard a ship in New York harbor. But instead of making preparations to return him to his master in South Carolina, police officers took him ashore and placed him in safekeeping with the intention to collect a reward or sell Jeems to slave traders. However, their plans were discovered and brought to the attention of Culver, who issued a writ of habeas corpus and had Jeems brought to his house.

To the Friends of the Fugitives from Slavery.—The Members of the Syracuse Fugitive Aid Society find it no longer convenient, nor necessary, to keep up their organization. The labour of sheltering those who flee from American tyranny, providing for their immediate wants, and helping them to find safe homes in this country or in Canada, must needs devolve, as it always has devolved, upon a very few individuals. Hitherto, since 1850, it has been done, for the most part, by Rev. J. W. Loguen. He, having been a slave and a fugitive himself, knows best how to provide for that class of sufferers, and to guard against imposition.

Mr. Loguen has agreed to devote himself wholly to this humane work, and to depend, for the support of himself and family, as well as the maintenance of this Depot on the Underground Railroad, upon what the benevolent and friendly may give him.

We, therefore, hereby request that all fugitives from slavery, coming this way, may be directed to the care of Rev. J. W. Loguen; also, that all moneys contributed or subscribed may be paid directly to him; and that all clothing or provisions contributed may be sent to his house, or such places as he may designate.

Mr. Loguen will make semi-annual reports of his receipts of money, clothes or provisions, and of the number of fugitives taken care of and provided for by him; and he will submit his accounts, at any time, to the inspection of any persons who are interested in the success of the Underground Railroad.

SAMUEL J. MAY,   WILLIAM E. ABBOTT,
JAMES FULLER,   LUCIUS J. ORMSBEE,
JOSEPH A. ALLEN,   HORACE B. KNIGHT.
Syracuse, September 17, 1857.

Notice advertising Rev. Jermain Loguen as the Syracuse Station master. (From *National Anti-Slavery Standard*, 3 Oct. 1857.)

Under New York State law, any slave brought into the state was automatically free. If the police had kept Jeems aboard the ship, Culver would not have been able to act. However, under the state statute, Culver was able to release him. The next day the case on return of the writ came up in open court, and the attorney for the slaveholder appeared.

"The writ is defective in this point," the attorney charged.

"Yes," said the judge, "we will amend that."

"Here is another error," said the counsel, who pointed out additional errors, but the judge overruled him.

The attorney then asked that Jeems be brought before the court.

"Oh," said the judge, "he was discharged last night."

The attorney was helpless to do anything further, and as Jeems made his escape to havens northward, Culver had his captors arrested on charges of kidnapping and conspiracy, setting their bail at $3,000 for the first charge, and $1,500 for the second ("Too Good to be Lost"; "Interesting Slave Case" 3). The story made the mainstream press, inspiring a satirical commentary slanted in favor of Culver's action in the *Peo-*

ple's Journal of Union Village, which only five years earlier under the same management had shown disdain for Garrison.

In the midst of southern slaveholders at Saratoga Springs, another judge may have been conveniently looking the other way. Reuben Walworth, the state's highest-ranking judge, who in 1851 had married a slaveowning woman from Kentucky, employed a live-in black maid named Dolly, who had come from Kentucky with his wife. An outspoken Temperance advocate, Walworth had been less supportive publicly of abolition. But this stance had drawn criticism from friends like the esteemed Gerrit Smith. Considering that Walworth also had established friendships with William Lloyd Garrison and Wendell Phillips, it would not be surprising if the legend were true that Dolly was hiding fugitive slaves in Walworth's empty wine cellar (Britten 231).

In Johnsburg, Warren County, another conductor had set up roots. The Rev. Enos Putnam, a Wesleyan-Methodist circuit rider, whose travels had taken him throughout the Adirondacks since the church's formation, had bought a farm, which had become an Underground Railroad outpost, and was building a church. Due north about 30 miles was a black man living in a hut on Ethan Mountain, near the hamlet of Igerna and the Warren County border with Essex County. Mr. Cutler's place was a stopover for fugitive slaves near the start of an old military road that began in Igerna and led all the way to Ogdensburg (Rist 9–10), where they could take a ferry across the St. Lawrence River into Prescott, Canada.

With all the advertisement and support for the Underground Railroad, one might expect that runaway slaves now had little to fear in the North. But apparently that wasn't the case, for in 1859, abolitionists were lobbying for a Personal Liberty Law to make slavehunting a crime. Among the state's leaders in this movement were lecturer Aaron Powell, who was president, and Leonard Gibbs, who was a member of the state executive committee lobbying for its passage. The consideration of such legislation indicates that slavecatchers continued to pose a threat.

As the inevitable climax approached in 1859, two of northern New York's most devoted abolitionists passed away: Noadiah Moore of Champlain, New York, succumbed at the age of 70 on February 9, and Esther Wilbur of Easton met her maker on May 23 at the age of 67.

"She was one of the earliest to espouse the antislavery cause," Joseph Peckham wrote in her obituary that appeared in the *National Anti-Slavery Standard*, "and although possessed of but a frail physical organization, yet no one in this country has rendered that hated cause more efficient service....

"Through her efforts mainly ... the Friends meeting house at North Easton was first opened to anti-slavery meetings, some eight or ten years since, and from that time its doors have been kept open to the anti-slavery laborer.

"The numerous petitions that went up to Albany, during the past winter, from this town, for a Personal Liberty bill, were first put in motion through her efforts.... A long illness had led up to Esther's death in 1859, but she continued during her last days to work for the cause of anti-slavery.... At a meeting of the Saratoga Anti-Slavery Society held in North Easton on June 5, 1859, 13 days after her death, it was resolved in part that 'the anti-slavery cause has lost one of its most clear-sighted, radical, and intrepid supporters...'" ("Obituary" 3).

Moore was perhaps the first and foremost abolitionist in Clinton County. As Stephen Keese Smith, another of the county's leading abolitionist said some years later, "Noadiah Moore ... first came to The Union and stirred us up to work in the anti-slavery cause. His place was a station in the Underground Railroad in Champlain, about seven miles from Canada. He went with the Negroes to Canada and looked out for places for them to work" (as quoted in Everest *Recollections* 57).

As always, death signals the end of one era and the beginning of a new one. John Brown sensed that his destiny was to prepare for a new age. Two years earlier, he had gone to Torrington, Connecticut, to retrieve the tombstone of his grandfather, whom he had long venerated for his service in the American Revolution. He wanted the tombstone placed at his own grave. Steamboat operator James Allen of Westport remembered transporting the stone when it arrived at his wharf. Brown took it to a stonecutter and had the name of his son Frederick, who had died in the Kansas war, inscribed on the reverse. He then left it on the porch of his house in North Elba (Royce 482–483).

About to set into motion his plan to free the slaves, he knew the odds were against him, and during his last visit to North Elba, in the summer of 1859, Brown etched his initials on the tombstone. When he said good-bye to his family, he told them to place the stone near a huge boulder behind which the snowcapped peak of Mt. Marcy towered in the distance (Ibid.). Perhaps Brown likened himself to the heroic and majestic figure that the tallest peak in the Adirondacks embodied.

Chapter 24

MARCHING TO IMMORTALITY

The growth of the Republican Party and the increasing hostility in the North for the South set the stage for John Brown at Harpers Ferry. It was left for him to resound the march to the Civil War. For several years he had been making preparations for his unilateral assault on the South, which he had envisioned two decades earlier. His original plan was to set up headquarters in the Allegheny Mountains, with which he had become familiar when he had lived in Pennsylvania and Ohio and worked as a farmer and postmaster during the 1830s. From there, he planned to wage guerilla warfare with 100 or so able men, many whom he expected to be fugitive slaves, and send paramilitary missions into the South to free slaves.

Brown managed to attract six financial sponsors who provided money for his military operations. They later became known as "the secret six." Five came from the Boston area—Franklin Sanborn, Thomas Wentworth Higginson, Dr. Samuel Gridley Howe, the Rev. Theodore Parker, and Luther Stearns. The sixth was Gerrit Smith. All, like Smith, were men of high distinction: Sanborn, a writer; Higginson, a Renaissance man, minister, reformer, editor, swashbuckling romantic; Howe, the soldier of fortune husband of Julia Ward Howe and pioneer in caring for the blind; Parker, a radical minister who was an early advocate for using force to end slavery; and Stearns, a highly successful businessman who operated an Underground Railroad station and always carried arms, and who provided weapons to the free-staters in Kansas and to Brown at Harpers Ferry (Renehan 8).

Brown's plan evolved over time. By 1858, he had set his sights on the arsenal at Harpers Ferry. Once it was taken, he hoped to enlist the aid of slaves in neighboring communities and raise the army that would retreat into the Allegheny Mountains and begin guerilla warfare. In July 1859, he left North Elba for the last time. With his band of revolutionaries and family members, he went to Maryland and rented a farm under the name of Isaac Smith about five miles from Harpers Ferry. There they prepared for the moment to strike, hopefully with surprise. But at a public meeting in August 1859, an associate named Gen. J.J. Simons said that a plan was in operation to invade the South with an army of blacks and free the slaves. As a result, lynch mobs in the South terrorized blacks in the coming weeks, discouraging the hoped-for rebellion (Johnson 194–196).

Brown's mission had been delayed once already, the year before, when another associate leaked his plans. Despite the attempts of some like Frederick Douglass, who met with him only days before the assault on Harpers Ferry and tried to discourage him, he was not about to turn back and resigned himself to the martyrdom he often said that God had intended for him. Newspaper headlines that reported smashing victories by the Republican Party in the states of Ohio and Pennsylvania the week before his assault on the arsenal, which began on October 16, probably fortified this resolve.

Volumes have been written about Brown and Harpers Ferry. What proves insightful regarding the abolitionist perspective in northern New York is the coverage provided by local newspapers. By this time, the telegraph had been in use for more than a decade; however, only the newspapers in Albany and Troy indicate that they were using it. So, we find little about the insurrection in northern New York papers until more than a week later.

The *National Anti-Slavery Standard*, a New York City weekly, offered this information in its October 22 edition nearly a week after the assault began. The text is of interest as much as for its depiction of when and how the news was received—at first, for example, it was thought to be a slave insurrection.

"The people of this city were startled by the telegraphic announcement, in the evening papers of Monday, that an insurrection of slaves had broken out at Harper's Ferry," it stated. "The first reports were so confused that it was scarcely possible to understand the origin of the affair or to measure its consequences" ("Slave Insurrection in Virginia" 3).

The article, referring to Brown as "Captain," summarized the events, beginning with his arrival on the scene more than a year earlier to examine the area. Brown, along with 21 young men who ranged in age from 20 to 32, had taken the great-grand-nephew of George Washington hostage and captured the arsenal. But after the first day, without help from local slaves, vigilantes surrounded them. Later accounts reported that the vigilantes were liquored up and began firing haphazardly in the direction of the arsenal as if it were shooting practice. A favorite target was the body of one of Brown's men, who had tried to escape, floating in the Shenandoah River (Renehan 200). Before long, the vigilantes were joined by the state militia and then by the Second Calvary sent by President Buchanan under the command of Robert E. Lee. It was only a matter of time before they stormed the arsenal and took Brown and the rest of the survivors into custody. Ten of Brown's men were killed, two of whom were his sons, Watson and Oliver, and five escaped.

The *Standard* article included an interrogation of Brown that asked questions such as whether he expected aid from the North and whether he expected to kill anyone. To the latter, he replied: "I did not wish to do so, but you forced us to it." It also reported that among Brown's papers were found letters of support from Frederick Douglass and Gerrit Smith (ibid.). Douglass soon fled to Canada for a brief period for fear of prosecution, and Smith checked himself into a sanatorium, claiming mental illness. For the rest of his life, Smith would deny all complicity with John Brown.

In upstate New York, a report appeared the same day in the October 22 issue of the *Troy Daily Whig*. "Old Brown, the leader," it reported, "is a small man with white head and beard, and cold-looking grey eyes. When not speaking, his lips are compressed, and he has the appearance of a most determined man." Another item described the state of affairs in Harpers Ferry afterwards; "The town and neighborhood are filled with persons of all descriptions who are running about with government arms in their hands, some of whom are intoxicated and disorderly, and occasionally arresting innocent parties without cause." Another stated that, "It is a remarkable fact that not a single slave joined the party of insurgents." Also included was the following statement from John Brown on the day of his capture: "My name is John Brown. I am well known. I have been known as Old Brown of Kansas. I'm from Litchfield County, Connecticut. And have lived in diverse places. Two of my sons were killed here today and I am dying too" ("The Late Insurrection at Harper's Ferry" 2).

In Washington County, the first account appeared in the October 27 issue of the *People's Journal*, the Union Village newspaper. "At last we have more definite information as to the origin of the outbreak at Harper's Ferry," the report began. Down farther, it referred to Brown's hardships in Kansas: "Brown was one of the victims of the Border Ruffian Invasion from Missouri. He was robbed of his property, maltreated, his house was burned, and three of his sons were murdered in cold blood....* None but a madman could seriously expect that twenty men could make head against the whole union, and none but those whose sense of justice was blunted by deep passion could fail to see that they were committing a crime against the innocent men, women, and children, which would inevitably meet, and justly deserve, universal condemnation." The paper's source for the article was the *Albany Evening Journal* ("The Trouble at Harper's Ferry" 2).

Generally, the *People's Journal* cast Brown in a sympathetic light and showed other indications of its strong Republican character. One was an article that detailed the overrepresentation of Southern individuals in the presidency, cabinet, supreme court, and highest ranking congressional position in comparison to the North, i.e., the slaveocracy; another was harshly critical of President Buchanan. Again, these articles were attributed to the *Albany Evening Journal*.

However, there were those in Washington County who took the opposing view.

The *Sandy Hill Herald*, which had berated *Uncle Tom's Cabin* when the book was first published ("Uncle Tom's Cabin" 2), stated that, "We did not allude to this terrible affair last week, for the reason that we hoped it might turn out that none but a few misguided men were engaged in it; but the confession of Brown and the papers found in his possession prove beyond a doubt that it was a concerted plan, to carry out the 'irrepressible conflict' doctrine of William H. Seward and the Republican leaders.... The Republicans seek to screen themselves by saying that Brown is crazy. If Brown and his followers were crazy, how happens it they were in correspondence with

---

Only one of Brown's sons was murdered in Kansas; the other two died at Harpers Ferry.

many of the most eminent Republican in this and other States?" ("The Harper's Ferry Outrage" 2).

The *People's Journal* countered two days later: "The attempt to connect the Republican party with Old Brown's mad outbreak is a necessity of the Sham Democracy.... The Slaveholder ... sees an army in seventeen crazy fanatics and magnifies three black men with a pitchfork into five hundred insurgents in line of battle" ("No Go" 2).

Such point-counterpoint between the newspapers continued right up through and after Brown's execution. However, it was Brown himself who won the battle in the court of public opinion. Though his wounds were serious, he survived to stand trial. It was the turning point of his life. Brought to the courtroom lying on a cot, he arose and delivered several dramatic monologues that were widely publicized. One was later pointed to by Ralph Waldo Emerson as one of the two greatest American speeches along with Patrick Henry's famous "Give Me Liberty or Give Me Death" oration.

Brown made this speech just before sentencing when offered the opportunity to speak on his own behalf. He stood and spoke without notes, quoted here in part:

> Had I so interfered in behalf of the rich, the powerful, the intelligent, the so-called great, or in behalf of any of their friends ... or any of that class, and suffered and sacrificed what I have in this interference, it would have been all right.... I believe that to have interfered as I have done, as I always have freely admitted I have done, in behalf of [the almighty Father's] despised poor, I did not wrong, but right. Now, if it is deemed necessary that I should forfeit my life for the furtherance of the ends of justice, and mingle my blood further with the blood of my children, and with the blood of millions in this slave country whose rights are disregarded by wicked, cruel and unjust enactments ... Let it be done [Fleming 98].

A brief item in the *Salem Press* (NY) reported his conviction and sentence to be hung, but added that his execution was doubtful, offering no explanation (*Salem Press* 8 Nov. 1859).

Perhaps this statement was made because of the widely circulated rumors that a plot was being hatched to rescue Brown. One of the first individuals to suggest such an undertaking was Leonard Gibbs of Union Village in a letter to Gerrit Smith.

"I am distressed on account of poor, unfortunate Capt. John Brown. He must not be executed if it is possible to save him," Gibbs wrote in his letter dated October 27, 1859. "He cannot in Virginia be successfully defended. No jury dare acquit him, no judge dare favor his acquittal or Executive dare pardon him. All that can be gained by counsel is delay. *Delay till Brown's rescue can be effected*" (underlined by Gibbs).

Gibbs goes on to say that he is a man of limited means, but he is appealing to Smith because he has the means to finance such an undertaking.

"Please consider the cause of poor Brown," Gibbs concludes, "and do not let him die on the gallows" (Letter from Leonard Gibbs...).

Considering that Smith had entered an asylum after suffering a nervous breakdown, he may not have read this letter until much later, and even if he did, he was in no condition to act upon it.

Overall, opinion was pretty much divided in the North. Even in Essex and Clinton County, closest to Brown's home, newspapers were split on their opinion. The two "Black Republican" newspapers, the *Northern Standard*, published in Keeseville by Wendell Landing, and the *Plattsburgh Sentinel*, supported the noble martyrdom of Brown, but the *Plattsburgh Republican* stood diametrically opposed.

For example, on November 12, it called Brown's actions "a wanton and unprovoked outrage"; on November 19, it condemned the Black Republicans for trying to turn Brown's crimes into the acts of a saint and confidently predicted that history would judge him fairly "in the records of the Kansas midnight massacres, as well as the murders at Harpers Ferry" ("The Hostile Camps" 3; "A New Saint" 2).

The plot to rescue Brown was considered by a number of sympathizers but never materialized, perhaps because Brown himself asked that it not be undertaken. The night before his execution, Brown gave the jailer a note that prophesied: "I, John Brown, am now quite certain that the crimes of this guilty land will never be purged away but with Blood" (Fleming 100).

The next morning, they took Brown to the scaffold in a wagon. Seated on his empty coffin, his hands bound, he said to the driver, "This is a beautiful country. I never had the pleasure of seeing it before" (Ibid.).

Around the scaffold, 1,500 armed soldiers were stationed with another 1,500 guarding the roads in case a rescue attempt was made. The noose was placed around his neck and a hood over his head. Brown was forced to wait 12 endless minutes for the troops to maneuver into position. Then the trapdoor sprung, and John Brown hung in the gentle, sunny breeze.

At the hour of Brown's death, church bells tolled throughout the North. Public prayer meetings and speeches praising him were held that day in all the centers of abolitionism and Republicanism. In Albany, there was a 100-gun salute; at the Free Church in Union Village, there was a public indignation meeting; and in nearby Glens Falls, the bell at the Universalist Church tolled ("Notice..."; "A Bell Tolled" 2).

The *Plattsburgh Republican* meanwhile repudiated the demonstrations and asked, "Could anything be more disgraceful, more repugnant to all ideas of good citizenship, more at war with our ... relations to a sister State of the Confederacy?" "(A Scandalous Proceeding" 2).

Brown's body was delivered to his wife, Mary, by an army escort and then taken by train to Philadelphia. A large crowd had gathered at the train station, and, fearing that the body might be stolen, authorities used an empty coffin to draw the crowd away, then secretly loaded the coffin with Brown's body onto a boat for New York City. There his body was transferred into another coffin, and Mary Brown and her escorts, among whom was the noted Boston abolitionist, Wendell Phillips, began the procession by railroad to North Elba.

The farther North they went, the more likely it was that Brown was considered a hero. In Troy, Rutland—where they spent the night—Vergennes, and back across Lake Champlain to Westport, New York, church bells tolled and people gathered in the streets (Oates 357). It was reported in the *People's Journal* that the party passed through Washington County on Monday evening, apparently on the Rutland Railroad that passed from Troy to Eagle Bridge to Salem and onto Rutland, Vermont (*People's Journal* 8 Dec. 1859). At Vergennes, the party was taken by coach to the ferry across Lake Champlain. The remainder of the journey was made by carriage.

The procession stopped overnight at Elizabethtown, where an honor guard stood watch over the coffin at the village courthouse. From there, they took the long last leg of the trip up the mountain roads in the sleet and rain to the Brown farm in North Elba. On December 8, John Brown was laid to rest. In his eulogy, Phillips said that Brown "has loosened the roots of the slave system; it only breathes—it does not live—hereafter" (Oates 357).

As one poet had written that same week, John Brown's soul was marching on, and it would lead the march to the Civil War. It is not for us to judge the life of John Brown. He was a man of extremes, both good and bad; a complicated, able, deeply religious man, who never found his place until he reached the scaffold. Whatever has been and will be said, no one can deny that his mission in life was gloriously fulfilled.

PART II

The Underground Railroad Stops in Eastern New York from New York City to Canada

Everyone asks—how can you be certain that a house was a station on the Underground Railroad? The answer is, you can't. Verifying an Underground Railroad site is like finding the proverbial needle in a haystack. However, a good detective can sift the evidence and often come up with information that can satisfy the legal criterion of beyond a reasonable doubt.

Many claims for Underground Railroad sites begin with the renovation of an old house. Someone finds a hidden room or space that includes an artifact like a water pitcher or an old shoe, or even a manacle, and the story is passed to a real estate agent, and so on the story builds until it becomes a legend. An example of this in northern New York was the Judge Tyrrell house along Route 9 north of Chestertown in Warren County. Renovation of that home some years ago brought the discovery of a hidden room with a cot, a dresser, a washstand, a water pitcher, a candle, a folded sheet, a blanket, and a bible. The discovery that Tyrrell had abolitionist sympathies and local lore that fugitive slaves used old Route 9 fuels the speculation that this home was a stop. However, this is still speculation, and the house can be classified

Judge Tyrrell House, Route 9, Town of Chester, Warren County. (Photograph by the author.)

only as a "possible" station that requires further research before upgrading it to "probable."

Before beginning our survey of possible Underground Railroad stops from New York City to Canada, a hierarchy of criteria needs to be established upon which to evaluate the authenticity of a site. The following list includes five criteria with four subcriteria. Any combination of these criteria obviously increases the chance of authenticity.

Site Criteria

1. First-person contemporary account
2. Membership in a vigilance committee
   a. Membership in an anti-slavery society, church, or political party
   b. Participation by the individual as an officer, board member, or editor of the organization's publication
3. Third person account
   a. Oral family legend
   b. Family associations (genealogy)
4. Local legend
5. House history

The first criterion and most reliable source is a first-person contemporary account that states a resident of a house was a conductor or agent, either by the participant, or a relative or friend of the participant. The second criterion is membership in a vigilance committee. The sole purpose of these committees was to aid fugitive slaves, so membership implies participation in the Underground Railroad. Subcriteria of this category are membership in an anti-slavery society, church, or political party, which would be made more compelling by a second subcriterion of participation as an officer, board member, or editor of the organization's publication. Some may object that simple membership in an anti-slavery society does not mean participation in the Underground Railroad. However, coupled with a local legend about their house, this adds up to compelling evidence. The third criterion, which is less compelling but still worth scrutiny, is a third-person account by someone who learned from someone who personally knew of another's participation—for example, an oral family legend, which we also can deem a subcriterion. The last two and least compelling criteria are local legend, emanating from the files and reports of local historians; and house history, which is provided with a property deed. Both are in the realm of hearsay. While they merit consideration and can be considered "possible" Underground Railroad sites, their veracity is questionable and should only be taken seriously when combined with other factors.

This author's research method has matched local legends regarding houses and individuals with contemporary accounts that report the individual's abolitionist activities. Appendices with lists of individuals who have some alleged or known connection with abolition or the Underground Railroad are provided to help researchers for various counties in the northern New York region, as well as the downstate area. Old maps were also used to pinpoint the residences of prominent abolitionists. If the owner of a house with a legend attached is not known, then this author attempted in some cases to learn the identity of the house's owner during the abolition period to determine if that individual was an abolitionist. To help the researcher and the traveler in search of discovery, the author has included maps, which were created based on period maps and other information.

This study began with Washington County and then incorporated the other counties in the Adirondack region. Because Albany and Troy were so crucial to the development of the Underground Railroad there, some attention has been devoted to them. Also, some scrutiny has been given to New York City because it was the gateway for most fugitive slaves entering not only New York State but also New England. Less attention has been given to more peripheral areas like St. Lawrence County and the downstate county region. A book would be needed to adequately cover New York City, as well as the downstate counties, which have a rich Underground Railroad history waiting to be revealed. It is hoped that the information provided about the downstate region and New York City will be useful to others who wish to more fully develop its story. Just as the organizational structure of the anti-slavery societies and the Liberty Party were broken down by county, this section will examine the various stops and participants according to county. It is a convenient way to identify the various stops and the leading participants.

Chapter 25

STOPS IN
NEW YORK CITY

The homes of New York Committee of Vigilance members, who comprised the leadership of the New York City's Underground Railroad, were clustered in lower Manhattan. In 1850, there were more than 500,000 people living in its already teeming environs, nearly more than double what it had been in 1835, and by the beginning of the Civil War, more than 800,000. New immigrants, including runaway slaves, were arriving daily, and blacks were drawn to Manhattan because of the abundance of menial jobs as domestics, launderers, carpenters, whitewashers, garbage men, and chimney sweeps. Though there was no black ghetto, many blacks lived in or near the Five Points slum area, where most new arrivals settled. It was described at the time as "inhabited by a race of beings of all colours, ages, sexes, and nations" with "the vilest rabble, black and white mixt together" (Burrows 480, 482). But in the years approaching the Civil War, most blacks gravitated to the fifth and eighth wards on the west side of lower Manhattan below Houston Street (Walker 5). Census records also show that although the overall population of the city increased by 400 percent from 1830 to 1860, the population of blacks showed no increase (ibid. 6–7).

An examination of city directories of the period shows that the leading vigilance committee members lived within a close radius of a circular area bordering the fifth, sixth, and fourteenth wards. David Ruggles, the early leader and stationmaster, lived at various addresses during his years in New York, all within the center of this area. He also operated a bookstore in this vicinity at 36 Lispenard Street, the same address for a time of the law office of Horace Dresser, the vigilance committee's lawyer. The store was only a few doors down from the Zion African Methodist Episcopal Church, the largest black congregation in the city. Other key vigilance committee members surrounded Ruggles. Among them, Charles Ray and William P. Johnson, who shared an address for a time at 153 Orange Street, east of Ruggles; the Rev. Theodore Wright, who lived on 2 White Street at the intersection with Broadway, almost exactly between Ruggles and Ray; and Dr. James McCune Smith, who had at least two different residences in the fifth ward, at 151 Read Street and 15 N. Moore Street, to the west of Ruggles. Vigilance committee member Thomas Downing also lived in the fifth ward, at 245 Broadway, and owned a popular oyster house restaurant at 5 Broad Street near Battery Park south of city hall, which was near the business district. It is believed he hid fugitive slaves there. Another committee member who lived in the business district was Thomas Van Rensselaer, of 122 Water Street (*The New York City Directory*).*

In 1847, the New York Committee of Vigilance was renamed the New York State Vigilance Committee and Isaac T. Hopper, a white man, was installed as president. Hopper had been a member of the old New York Society for Manumission and had been aiding fugitive slaves for many years. Disowned by the Friends Society for his abolitionist activism, he had worked closely with Ruggles, who had left New York in 1841 after a dispute with other members of the committee over finances. Hopper's home was on the west side of the Bowery at 110 Eldridge, only a half-dozen blocks west of Charles Ray. Another white abolitionist was Washington County native Leonard Gibbs, who lived about a half-dozen or so blocks north of Hopper at 22 Second Street from 1840 to 1845. Two prominent white abolitionists who moved from New York to Brooklyn after the riot of 1834 and who participated in the Underground Railroad were Arthur and Lewis Tappan.

An individual who may have been a member of the committee, but if not was certainly associated with them, was William P. Powell, proprietor of the Colored Sailors' Home at 330 Pearl Street. He organized an emergency vigilance committee at the city Fugitive Slave Law meeting on October 1, 1850, which was attended by long-standing committee members Charles Ray, Samuel Cornish, and the Rev. John T. Raymond ("Meeting..." 78). Powell's address was listed in the New York City directory at 61 Cherry Street.

The offices of a number of businesses were known to have assisted in hiding fugitive slaves on occasion. Among them were the sugar refinery of Dennis Harris on Duane Street, which was called by one contemporary, "a sort of Grand Central Station of the Underground Railroad" (Johnson 289), and the *National Anti-Slavery Standard* newspaper, which shared office space with Isaac T. Hopper's bookstore at 143 Nassau Street. An interesting story involving a runaway refers to both of them.

One morning a crowd was chasing a runaway. His owner was attempting to reclaim him after a judge at the city court had freed him. William Johnson, who may have been the same man as the vigilance committee member, joined the chase. The runaway dashed into a bakery and disappeared into the basement. The crowd was puzzled, but on seeing a doorway, they headed through it. It led to the engine room of the *Standard*, where the crowd was rebuffed by a huge man who was the engineer.

"Where's that Negro?" the crowd cried.

"Negro?" the engineer said. "I don't know anything about any Negro. Now, unless you have some business with me, you better get out!"

---

*The addresses given are based on listings in the New York City Directory from various years and do not necessarily reflect a permanent address throughout the antebellum period—e.g., Wright shows an earlier address at 28 John St. and W.P. Johnson shows an earlier address at 69 Leonard Street (The Colored American 3).

Isaac T. Hopper. (From L. Maria Child, *Isaac T. Hopper: A True Life*, Boston: John P. Jewett and Co., 1853.)

As the crowd turned around, he gave the newspaper and Johnson a knowing glance. The runaway had been hidden in a small crawl space in an upper story. He stayed there a couple of days before an attempt was made to move him to Harris's

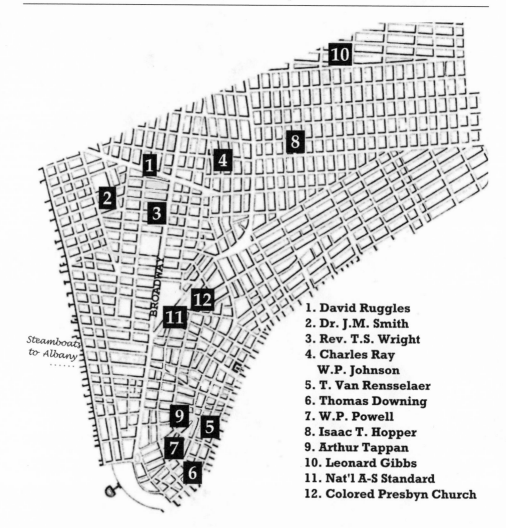

1. David Ruggles
2. Dr. J.M. Smith
3. Rev. T.S. Wright
4. Charles Ray
   W.P. Johnson
5. T. Van Rensselaer
6. Thomas Downing
7. W.P. Powell
8. Isaac T. Hopper
9. Arthur Tappan
10. Leonard Gibbs
11. Nat'l A-S Standard
12. Colored Presbyn Church

Map by the author.

sugar refinery. He was put in a packing box, which was placed on a cart outside the office. The police, who had been suspicious all along, were watching the office. They demanded that the box be opened, and they arrested the runaway.

The next day, after a plan was put in place by the abolitionists, the runaway, represented by John Jay, was brought to court.* A large group of abolitionists gathered in the courtroom and as soon as the judge again dismissed the charges, they surrounded the runaway and escorted him into the hallway, where he was able to slip out unseen to a back entrance where a carriage awaited. Before anyone knew he had left the building, he was on his way to Canada, where he arrived in a few days (Johnson 288–290).

*The grandson of John Jay, the former Supreme Court Justice, and son of William Jay of Bedford in Westchester County.

Other locations that likely served as refuges where runaways could receive assistance were Arthur Tappan's store at 122 Pearl Street just one street north of Van Rensselaer's residence; Theodore Wright's Colored Presbyterian Church at the corner of Frankfort and William streets, better known as the Shiloh Church,* which was about a block and a half from the office of the *National Anti-Slavery Standard*, and about a block away from the office of Samuel Cornish's *Colored American* newspaper, which was published from 1837 to 1841. Other locations in the business district that were friendly to the slave included Horace Dresser's later law office at 89 Nassau Street; Leonard Gibbs's law office at 18 Wall Street; the office of the *Ram's Horn*, the newspaper published by Thomas Van Rensselaer and Willis Hodges at 141 Fulton Street; and the offices of the American Anti-Slavery Society across the street from its newspaper, the *Standard*, at 138 Nassau Street.

One other address that merits listing is the Plymouth Church of Henry Ward Beecher in Brooklyn, where Charles Ray sent runaways who needed a place to hide (Ray 25). The church, built in 1847, was destroyed by fire in 1849 and rebuilt by January 1850.

---

*In 1851, the Church moved north to Prince Street in the eighth ward, when the Rev. J.W.C. Pennington was pastor; Henry Garnet took over as pastor there in 1855.

Chapter 26

STOPS IN THE
MID-HUDSON REGION

As discussed in Chapter 13, abolitionism in the downstate region was of a much different character than that north of Albany. An important reason was that slavery—whose underpinning was racial prejudice—was considerably more prevalent there before statewide emancipation in 1827. To get an idea of how great the difference in attitude towards race was between the regions, one only needs to compare the results for the downstate counties in the 1846 state referendum on equal suffrage for blacks. While every county in the Adirondack region but Saratoga registered pluralities of 50 percent or more in favor of full voting rights for blacks, the largest plurality of any Mid-Hudson county south of Albany was Columbia County with 8 percent in favor. Ulster, Westchester, and Greene counties all registered totals in the neighborhood of 4 percent, Rockland a meager 3 percent, and Putnam a shockingly low 2.3 percent in favor of equal suffrage for blacks (*The Tribune Almanac* 44).

In all likelihood, most runaways moved up the Hudson by boat from New York City; the rest came on foot, through Philadelphia and New Jersey. The first New York counties along this route were Rockland on the west side of the river and Westchester on the east side. One local legend states that Edward Hesdra in Nyack, Rockland County, worked with an agent in Jersey City, New Jersey. Hesdra's home was near the reservoir on Main Street, east of Highland Avenue. Another Nyack resident, John W. Towot, also is believed to have been a conductor, working with the Tappan brothers. His deeds are commemorated in a plaque at the local African Methodist Episcopal Zion Church (Zimm 697).*

In Westchester, claims have been made for the homes in Bedford of William Jay

---

*There are a number of AMEZ churches in the region, including churches in Tarrytown, Peekskill in Westchester County; all may have played a role in the Underground Railroad.

Possible Underground Railroad Stops in the Mid-Hudson Region

(Map by the author.)

and in Peekskill for Henry Ward Beecher, who summered there during the 1850s and moved there permanently in 1861. Locals claim Beecher had built a secret tunnel leading from his house to nearby MacGregory Brook. Another Peekskill stop near the brook at 1112 Main Street had a secret stairway that led to a secret room. It was the home of John Sands, a member of a Quaker group in the town that helped runaways. He bought the house in 1839 from Hawley Green, a black barber, who remained in Peekskill and also is alleged to have aided runaways. In addition, Peekskill locals claim their AMEZ Church had a secret room where they hid runaways (Brothers interview). Lore also claims runaways could find aid from Quakers John Carpenter in Scarsdale and Moses Pierce in Pleasantville (Hall E1).* A romantic legend involves a black community in Harrison, in the southeastern part of the county, where fugitive slaves may have settled and which also may have collaborated with Quaker James Mott of Purchase, the father-in-law of Lucretia Mott (Caro 64–65).

In Orange County, the Underground Railroad legends are surprisingly plentiful, thanks to Roger King, who found many in old, local newspaper accounts and put them all in his fascinating little book, *The Underground Railroad in Orange County, N.Y.: The Silent Rebellion.*

"Hiding people became easy and a way of life in Orange County in the 1850's," King wrote. "Hence, a frenzy developed with opposing sides—those who harbored and abetted slaves, and those who were violently opposed ... [The Fugitive Slave Law's] enactment produced a society that took shape in mountains, caves, ledges, tunnels, secret passages, root cellars, homes, wagons, and on the railroad itself. The railway 'Erie' became so popular that it was the backbone of any quantitative movement in the mountains north of New York City..." (King 3).

King presents an interesting body of folklore that reveals the extraordinary experiences of very ordinary people. According to him, most of the runaways came to Orange County up a line that led from Philadelphia through northern New Jersey. Apparently, the runaways were sent to the Bull family of Walton Lake, who sometimes took them to the village of Chester and hid them in the barn of Presbyterian minister the Rev. James Washington Wood. From there, they were sent either to Goshen on the Erie Railway or to Newburgh, where the Alsdorfs, a black family of dance teachers, harbored them. An alternate destination was the Cornwall home of Peter Roe, who, it may be remembered, was a friend of Abel Brown and active in anti-slavery circles.

Another King story concerns two men in Goshen who operated businesses out of the same building. W.M. Vail, a grocer and shipping agent, rented out his upstairs office to Dr. Graham, a dentist. They were next to the railroad station, and runaways often got off the train and went straight to Vail's store. Vail was one of the organizers of the local Republican Party, and Graham was a Democrat. But both hated slavery, and this passion united them in the Underground Railroad. They had a system, which used a bell attached to a wire that led from Vail's store to the dentist's office and which Vail could ring in case of trouble. Mathias Droyer, a prominent black citizen, also assisted them in their efforts.

One day in 1858, a family of runaways got off a freight train and came to the

---

They may have been part of a Quaker trunk that began with Isaac T. Hopper in New York City.

store. They had come from Maryland, mostly on foot with slavecatchers in pursuit. Vail hid them in his cellar, then called Droyer to help find a safer place. But before they were moved, two men, one a slave owner and the other a federal marshal, came into town and headed straight for Vail's store. They demanded that Vail turn over the runaways, but Vail denied the charge and rang for Graham. He pretended to come down by chance, but he immediately defended Vail. When the slavecatchers learned that Graham was the president of the local Democratic Club, they were persuaded that he was telling the truth. After diverting the slave catchers in another direction, Vail called Droyer, who arranged for the runaways to be forwarded to Newburgh, and then organized an armed reception committee for the slave catchers, whom they expected to return once they realized they had been duped. When the slave catchers finally returned, they got off the train only briefly. The site of the armed mob convinced them to get back on the train and never to come back to Goshen again (King 20–22; 25–28).*

The stories King tells are very personalized and detailed. Some deal with federal agents using torture in their interrogations to find runaways, as well as backwoods people murdering agents. It makes one wonder why these incidents were never reported considering the scrutiny the press was giving to the renditions of fugitive slaves. It also is surprising considering the political and social disposition of the region regarding blacks. One of the more interesting pieces of information is the distribution of passes to runaways to ride the Erie Railroad by its director, A.S. Murray of Goshen, and the liberty taken by one of his conductors, a Mr. Willett, in allowing runaways free rides on his trains. This shows the crucial role played by the transportation industry in the success of the Underground Railroad.

The next county on the way to Albany is Dutchess. Among its settlers were a large number of Quakers. The county had many Quaker meetings and was home to a well-respected Quaker boarding school at Nine Partners. The county also had several prominent black leaders who were activists in abolition and civil rights. These factors probably contributed to the 1840 declaration by the county society that it would "do all in our power to assist those of our brethren, coming through this county, who may have thus far escaped the iron grasp of tyranny, by giving them meat, money, and clothes, to enable them to prosecute their journey to a land of liberty ("The Second Anniversary..." 35).

Blacks and Quakers in the county worked together, according to local lore. In Baxtertown, the largest black community in the county and where some fugitive slaves are believed to have settled, Joe Collis is alleged to have worked with Quakers in the nearby Dutchess County town of Oswego, also known at one time as Freedom (McCracken 106). Another route involving Dutchess Quakers may have connected with the Quakers in Westchester who worked with Isaac Hopper; this line ended with David Irish at Quaker Hill in the southeastern part of the county (Barbour 72). One other alleged Quaker stop was at the home of Stephen Haight near the Nine Partners Boarding School, in a direct line north of Quaker Hill (McCracken 281).

Poughkeepsie, the largest community in the county, was the home of the county anti-slavery society as well as home to several prominent black leaders. David Ruggles

*King tells two versions of the story with different endings; the first ending likely apocryphal.

Dutchess County.

We find in the Poughkeepsie Journal of June 3d, an account of the second anniversary of the Dutchess County Anti-Slavery Society. The following are among the resolutions adopted.

Resolved, That we collectively and severally will use all the means in our power, by printing, writing, speaking, and subscribing money, to forward the anti-slavery cause in this county.

Resolved, That we collectively and severally will do all in our power *to assist* those of our brethren, coming through this county, who may have thus far escaped the iron grasp of tyranny, by giving them meat, money and clothes, to enable them to prosecute their journey to a LAND OF LIBERTY.

Dutchess County Anti-Slavery Society pledge to aid fugitive slaves. (From *Friend of Man*, 1 July 1840: 151.)

had close ties here, representing Poughkeepsie at the National Negro Conventions in 1833 and 1834 with the Rev. Nathan Blount, the city's AMEZ minister.* the Rev. James N. Mars, who succeeded Blount as the city's AMEZ pastor in 1839, represented the city at the Black State Convention in Albany in 1840, was an agent for the *Colored American*, and undertook a mission for the Wesleyan-Methodist Church to minister to fugitive slaves in Canada in 1846. But the most prominent black resident was probably Uriah Boston, a prosperous barber.

Boston was the leader of the black community's annual Emancipation Day celebrations on August 1 to commemorate the British abolition of slavery during the early 1840s. He attended the first black state convention in Albany in 1840 with Mars and was an agent for the *Northern Star and Freemen's Advocate*. Boston was a proud man noted for his fashionable appearance. He frequently wrote letters to newspapers, one in 1840 to the *Colored American* in which he exhorted his fellows to "Action, Action, energetic, untiring, and continued action" in elevating their status. In another 1853 letter to *Frederick Douglass's Paper*, he criticized Douglass for calling barbering a servile profession, and two years later in the same paper endorsed disunion (Groth 362; 375–376).

County abolition also was favored for four years with the radical Charles Van Loon. Pastor of the First Baptist Church in Poughkeepsie and friend of Abel Brown, he was a vice-president of the Eastern New York Anti-Slavery Society in 1845. His close relationship to Abel Brown suggests his participation in the Underground Railroad, and like Brown, his intense involvement in abolition affected his health, leading to his death of a stroke in 1847 at the age of 28. Another abolitionist whose activities merit further scrutiny was Samuel Thompson, one of the county society managers and a vice-president of the state society. Thompson also was listed as a vice-president at the formation of the Eastern New York Anti-Slavery Society.

On the whole, Dutchess County was not very sympathetic to anti-slavery; however, there was a devoted clique of abolitionists, white and black, and a fairly large black population—more than 2,000 listed in the censuses between 1840 and 1860—from which a reliable Underground Railroad developed.

The same cannot be said for Ulster County, which except for an unsubstantiated report of a fugitive slave community at a place called Eagles Nest in the town of Hurley, has so far yielded no evidence of Underground Railroad activity. However,

*From 1839 to 1841, Samuel Ringgold Ward was pastor at the Congregational Church in Poughkeepsie; however, he spent much of that time as a lecturer for the American Anti-Slavery Society. Commenting on the anti-slavery feeling in the region, he said in 1851 that "most places on the Hudson River" are "thoroughly and hopelessly pro-slavery" (Groth 296).

Ripley's *Black Abolitionist Papers* identify a Kingston barber, Thomas Harley, who worked with Stephen Myers in the Underground Railroad. Harley moved to Springfield, Massachusetts, in 1853, but Ripley does not indicate if Harley was active in the Underground Railroad while he was living in Kingston (Ripley 410).

North of Ulster is Greene County. The village of Catskill had a large black population, and in 1836 David Ruggles addressed the British Emancipation celebration at the Baptist church there. An interesting resolution of that meeting was the expression of regret for the "unworthy course pursued by the colored friends of Albany, who have condescended to celebrate this day in a steamboat excursion and frolic, while our brethren of the South are crying to be delivered from the iron that enters the soul" ("Catskill, N.Y."). The county had a number of anti-slavery societies that met regularly during the late 1830s, and in 1839, the county society reported more than 200 members with Colonel William W. Edwards of Hunter as president ("Greene County Anti-Slavery Society" 7). So far as the Underground Railroad in this county, this author has not as yet received any information. However, considering that it was home to two agents of the *Northern Star and Freemen's Advocate*—Martin Cross of Catskill and William Thompson of Athens—an agent for the *Albany Patriot*—Alfred Peck of Big Hollow—publications with ties to the Underground Railroad, and a vice-president in the Eastern New York Anti-Slavery Society, Jabez Hubbard, it would appear that some kind of organization probably was in place.

Moving to Columbia County, we come to an area where many of its earliest settlers were Quaker seamen from New England. Their progeny gave rise to Quaker meetings in Hudson, Ghent, and Chatham. Though this author has not explored the Underground Railroad there, residents have assured him that it was active, pointing to Coeymans, which is just north of its border with Albany County. After 1850, one county resident, Aaron Powell, rose to prominence in abolitionist circles. Powell became a lecturer for the American Anti-Slavery Society and a correspondent for the *National Anti-Slavery Standard*. In 1859, he spearheaded a statewide movement to pass a Personal Liberty Law in New York State that would safeguard the rights of fugitive slaves, and in 1866, he was made editor of the *Standard*. Nine black delegates also represented the county from the city of Hudson at the 1840 Black State Convention. Considering the Quaker influence and the early political awareness of the black community that included two agents for the *Northern Star and Freemen's Advocate*—Joseph Pell and William Green of Hudson—it would not be surprising that residents there were aiding fugitive slaves.

Chapter 27

Stops in
Albany County

As early as 1831, an organized effort was being made in Albany's black community to aid fugitive slaves.* Just as New York City was the major gateway for fugitives who passed through the Northeast, Albany served as the primary gateway for fugitives passing through northeastern and central New York. Thousands of fugitive slaves probably passed through Albany in that 30-year period prior to the Civil War.† During the early 1840s when Abel Brown and Charles Torrey were working the line, there apparently were two separate vigilance committees assisting runaways. One representing them and the Eastern New York Anti-Slavery Society, and the other representing Myers and the *Northern Star and Freemen's Advocate*. It is not known who was the more active, though it is doubtful there were any more active conductors than Torrey and Brown. After the demise of the Eastern New York Anti-Slavery Society and the Liberty Party, Myers's group carried on, and what was earlier exclusively a black group became integrated in the 1850s.‡

Four lists help to identify the individuals who comprised the Underground Railroad here. They are the members of the Executive Committee of the Eastern New York Anti-Slavery Society, the members of the Albany Vigilance Committee, and those individuals in the black community identified in William Henry Johnson's autobi-

---

*An editorial in the January 3, 1843, issue of the Northern Star and Freeman's Advocate.

†Based on an extrapolation of the numbers of fugitive slaves reported to have been aided by Myers in 1856 and 1858, and by the Albany Vigilance Committee during 1842, the number would be over 10,000 for the 30-year period—Myers reported aiding 287 runaways during a nine-month period starting in 1855, and 187 runaways during a seven-month period starting in 1857; the Eastern New York Anti-Slavery Society reported the Albany Vigilance Committee aided 350 runaways during 1842 (Vigilance Committee Office; Ripley 410; Annual Report of the Committee). However, those reports probably reflected periods of unusually high traffic.

‡ The Albany Female Anti-Slavery Society also reported that it was aiding fugitive slaves during the late 1840s.

Underground Railroad Stops in Albany, N.Y.

1. Vigilance Committee Ofc.
2. Thomas Elkins
3. William Gardner
4. Minos McGowan
5. Thompson Temperance Hs.
6. Mrs. Dilzey Dennison
7. Chauncey P. Williams
8. Mott Sisters
9. Tocsin of Liberty
10. E. NY Anti-Slavery Society
11. N. Star & Freeman's Adv.
12. Nathaniel Safford
13. Tappan Townsend
14. William Tweed Dale
15. William H. Topp
16. Rev. Abel Brown
17. Benjamin Cutler
18. Richard Wright
19. James Woods
20. E.W. Goodwin

(Map by the author.)

ography. These lists are far from all-inclusive, but they do provide a roadmap from which to start.

The executive committee of the Eastern New York Anti-Slavery Society included: lumber dealer Nathaniel Safford, also president of the Albany Anti-Slavery Society; lumber merchant Chauncey P. Williams; William Mayell, of the Mayell family who were hatters; A.O. Wilcox, innkeeper; E.P. Freeman, teacher; Christopher Hepinstall, a leather dealer, William Crapo, a grocer; Benjamin Lattimore, black grocer and son of Benjamin Lattimore, who died in 1839 and was president of the African Temperance Society; Samuel H. Hammond, an attorney; Tappen Townsend; Homer Martin; and *Albany Patriot* editors and agents, James C. Jackson, E.W. Goodwin, William L.

Chaplin, Abel Brown, and Charles T. Torrey—all residing in Albany. It also included a number from other localities, including: Henry Garnet, Fayette Shipherd, Preston Sheldon, and Benjamin Snow of Troy; Dr. C.H. Gregory, Sand Lake; Smith Griffin, Nassau; Isaac Aiken, Greenbush; Rev. E.C. Pritchett, Union Village; Andrew Lester and G.R. Barker of New York City, and members of the New York Committee of Vigilance. Interestingly, Barker, one of the founding members of the NYCV, listed an Albany address for a time at the Eagle Tavern ("Anti-Slavery Society" 110; "Eastern New York..." 7).

The second list is the Albany Vigilance Committee, which listed members by the wards they oversaw: first ward, Benjamin Cutler; third, William Richardson; fourth, Tappan Townsend; fifth, Timothy A. Gladding; sixth, E.P. Freeman; seventh, John Rogers; eighth, William Sherwood; ninth, Thomas R. Richardson; and tenth, Hiram Martin (*Albany Patriot* 2 April 1845).

The Johnson list included: Stephen Myers, John G. Stewart, and Charles B. Morton, the proprietors of the *Northern Star and Freeman's Advocate*; tailor William H. Topp; barber William H. Matthews, Temperance grocer Primus Robinson, Dr. Thomas Elkins, George Morgan, William P. McIntrye, and Benjamin Cutler (Johnson 61). Cutler is quite possibly the same person as the Mr. Cutler who built a mountaintop home in rugged northern Warren County where he aided fugitive slaves. He also served on the predominately white Albany Vigilance Committee.

The final list is taken from the 1856 Broadside that reports 287 fugitive slaves being aided in the prior nine months and consists of the following: Stephen Myers, William H. Topp, Thomas Elkins, Charles Gardner, Captain John Johnson,* Richard Wright, William Matthews, Rev. John Sands, Rev. J.J. Kelley, Minos McGowan, C. Brooks, and James S. Wood.

Included in this chapter is a map that identifies possible refuges for runaway slaves. Only a handful have been located that still remain; a more thorough investigation may yield more. They include: the headquarters of the Albany Vigilance Committee in 1856 at 198 Livingston Avenue, then called Lumber Street. This house, whose current identity has not yet been verified, was the home of Stephen Myers from 1856 to 1857. Myers shared the house with a Captain John Johnson, who lived there from 1856 to 1859 and who also is listed on the 1856 Vigilance Committee broadside as a member of the committee. Other Vigilance Committee members whose houses possibly remain from the antebellum years include: William Gardner at 49 Second Street in Arbor Hill; Tappan Townsend at 138 Hamilton near the Empire State Plaza; and William Tweed Dale, a school principal who was treasurer of the Eastern New York Anti-Slavery Society, at 173 Madison, around the block from Townsend. Two other possible locations include the 39 and 81 Columbia Street homes of E.P. Freeman and Chauncey P. Williams.

The full story of Myers and his life, which has yet to be told, would likely reveal much of the Albany operation still clouded in mystery. Myers worked on steamboats for many years and it is probably by this means that he was able to transport so many runaway slaves. This mode of travel is corroborated by Charles Ray. As we can see

---

*Johnson's first initial is A. on the broadside, but the city directory shows a Captain John Johnson sharing the vigilance committee office as a residence with Myers.

from the map, it was a short walk to many who were sympathetic to aiding runaway slaves. In addition, downtown Albany had more than its share of Temperance houses, which gladly opened its doors to teetotaling abolitionists and temperant black men in search of freedom. Among them were Nathaniel Safford's Temperance House at 280 N. Market Street; Richard Thompson's Colored American Temperance House at 142 S. Pearl Street; A.C. Churchill's Temperance House at 10 Hudson Street; G.T. Hill's Temperance House at the corner of Steuben Street and Broadway; and the Delevan House in downtown Albany, which apparently took its name from the prominent Temperance advocate, E.C. Delevan, of Saratoga County. A portrait of the latter appeared in January 27, 1847, issue of the *Albany Patriot*, an excerpt of which follows:

> The Delevan House is five stories high; and as to its length and breadth, I dare not give an opinion; I think it is one of the largest in the State. It is situated close by the railroad, so that "the weary traveler," on getting out of the cars from the East or West, or landing from the boat, is but a few steps from the most comfortable, the most genteely managed, and in short, "the most desirable hotel in America"... ["The 'Delevan House'" 47].

Myers, who was a Temperance advocate himself and who even had a Temperance Society named after him in Lee, Massachusetts, developed a vast network of co-conspirators who helped finance his operations, many of whom were obtained through the influence of the publisher of the *Albany Evening Journal*, Thurlow Weed. Some of these individuals were identified in a December 17, 1858, letter from Myers to New York City lawyer John Jay and included Moses H. Grinnell, Robert B. Minturn, Simeon Draper, Edmund Morgan, John Alsop King, James W. Beekman, and John P. Cummings of New York City; James S. Wadsworth of Livingston County in western New York, and William Newton of Albany (Ripley 409–411). Myers, who frequently traveled to New York City in the course of his work on the steamboats, apparently made many personal connections with the New York City business community.

Another element that apparently played a role in Albany's Underground Railroad was the lumber industry. As alluded to earlier, during the 1850s Albany was the largest importer of lumber in the world, and a number of lumber merchants were members of the vigilance committees. Lumber Street, the location of Stephen Myers's vigilance committee office, led directly down to the lumber district along the banks of the Hudson. The following description of the area reveals how extensive it was.

"With the completion of the Erie and Champlain Canals, and the construction of the Albany Basin and Pier, the wharfs were first used for the storage of lumber. When increased imports from Canada and the West demanded greater storage facilities, slips were dug from the canal towards the river and the lumber piled along their banks.... During the decade from 1840 to 1850, the receipts [from this trade] increased from 124,173,383 feet of boards and 784,310 feet of timber, the total value of which was $2,142,636, to 425,095,436 feet of boards and 3,039,588 feet of timber with a total value of $6,806,213 [approximately $140 million in 2001]" (Howell and Tenney 612).

While lumber was the largest, it was not the only significant resource fueling Albany's busy port. The role of the business community, especially the shipping industry, may be another key to unraveling the mystery of Albany's Underground Railroad.

ALBANY ANTI-SLAVERY OFFICE,

No. 3 Lark St., Arbor Hill.

CIRCULAR TO THE FRIENDS OF FREEDOM:

The hundreds of fugitives that have fallen to my care during the last twelve years, have required a great deal of labor and expense to make them comfortable. They are sent to me by the Underground Railroad, south of Albany, and in many cases they come poorly clad and are greatly in want of clothes, such as coats, pants and under garments, both males and females. Whatever is sent, clothes or money, shall be faithfully used for that purpose. We have received some articles of clothing and money in this city, and from abroad, from ladies and gentlemen, for which they have our thanks. We devote all our time to the care of the oppressed who come among us. Our pay is small, but yet we are willing to continue to do what we can for them. From the 1st of November, 1857, to April 1st, 1858, the number of fugitives which passed through Albany, in this time, was 121. Paid $2 for passage each, amounting to $242. We have arrivals every few days from Southern oppression; we forward them to the next depot, and from there they are forwarded to Canada. If any information is wanting concerning how many come through from time to time, they can address a line to the Albany papers.

All letters or packages must be directed to S. MYERS, or to the Anti-Slavery Office, Albany. Any articles of wearing apparel can be sent by express. A general report will be given through the Albany papers every six months. My books and accounts can be inspected by the friends of the cause, at any time they wish to see them. Those that arrive now at this time of the year are in want of warm clothes, and especially the children. If there should be farmers wanting help, either men or women in the house, they can be accomodated by sending to this office. We consider it safe for them to go into the country, and it saves expense. We have sent quite a number in the country during this season and the last, and they write to us that they make good help.

P. S. Ladies and gentlemen will please, when they receive these circulars, to send them to their friends, for we are in want of material aid.

WM. HARRIS, ASSISTANT,   S. MYERS,
    and Travelling Agent.   Superintendent Underground Railroad.

Report of S. MYERS, Superintendent of the Underground Railroad:

MONEYS RECEIVED BY S. MYERS. By subscriptions and by Agents, $206,34. From the 1st November, 1857, up to April 1st, 1858, we have not received enough to meet the necessary expenses of the Underground Railroad. We make an appeal again to the friends of freedom to be generous towards aiding those destitute fugitives from slavery. WM. HARRIS is an Agent sent from this office, and is duly authorized to collect funds for the Underground R. R. He forwards all subscriptions faithfully to this office.

[From the New-York Tribune.]
From Our Own Correspondent.

ALBANY, March 29, 1858.

Eight passengers per Underground Railroad passed through this city during the last week, in the direction of the North Star. Why don't somebody call the attention of Mr. Stephens, or Mr. Toombs, or "Extra Billy" Smith to this incendiary? The North Star is clearly unconstitutional; as decidedly so as the Dismal Swamp or any other device which tends to lessen the value by decreasing the security of a peculiar species of property. If the President has not the power to remove this troublesome meddler with vested rights, he should make up a case and take it before the Supreme Court, where he would find no difficulty in obtaining a decree to "put out that light" or to remove it to a Southern point or to prevent its shining, except on cloudy nights, when it can't be seen. Either would answer the purpose. I have carefully examined the Constitution of the United States and the Resolutions of '98, and can find no warrant in either for this Northern aggression. Mr. Myers, the efficient agent of the Road, reports a remarkably prosperous business for this season, so far.

Broadside reporting efforts by conductor Stephen Myers in Albany to aid fugitive slaves. (Courtesy of Boston Public Library.)

Though men were the dominant players, the Albany Female Anti-Slavery Society, whose formation was inspired by Abel Brown and Charles T. Torrey, and the sisters Lydia and Abigail Mott, who operated a clothing store on Maiden Lane in downtown Albany, also aided fugitive slaves. Mrs. Dilzey Dennison hosted another stop, according to her granddaughter, Mrs. Aaron Oliver, at 7 Cross Street, now Sheridan Place, a short, one-block byway off Sheridan Avenue (African-Americans in Albany, Box I, Folder 25).

It will take a great deal more research to fully develop the network that comprised Albany's extensive Underground Railroad. Most of its stops were eliminated during the course of the city's urban redevelopment. Abel Brown's residence at 209 Green Street, which was approximately across the street from the *Urban Voices* weekly newspaper, has been supplanted by a housing development, and we have as yet found no address listed for Charles Torrey. But the information provided here should give researchers a good start.

For stories about fugitive slaves who passed through Albany, see the fascinating collection of brief vignettes in Appendix III, compiled by Albany researchers Paul and Mary Liz Stewart.

Chapter 28

STOPS IN
RENSSELAER COUNTY

Today in Troy, most Underground Railroad landmarks like the old Liberty Street Church are gone. For some years before its destruction, it had been used as a laundromat, but all that remains is a vacant lot at the corner of a rundown alley. Along with it, William Henry's residence is but an empty plot of grass; Fayette Shipherd's Free Church and the Bethel Church are gone; the buildings where William Rich had his hairdressing salon and residence have been torn down; and the location of Abel Brown's home is unknown. Fortunately, a couple of houses do remain. As of this writing, the 153 Second Street residence that may have been the home of fugitive slaves Lewis Washington, from 1845 to 1847, and John H. Hooper, a laborer who lived there from 1847 to 1888 and listed by Wilbur Siebert as a conductor, is for sale.* When this author contacted one of its former owners some years ago, he learned of remnants of a tunnel that once led from its basement—the owner had seen it himself. This tunnel may have led to the river only a few blocks away and may corroborate the many legends of Underground Railroad tunnels in downtown Troy that led to the river. The other building known to have housed an Underground Railroad conductor was the Trojan Hardware Company building at 137 Fourth Street, where Henry Garnet resided during part of his eight years in Troy.

But as to the tunnels, is there any substance to them? Troy was an important shipping center during the antebellum period. Whereas in Albany the major industry was lumber, in Troy a major enterprise was textiles. For example, in 1830, the Ida Mills cotton and weaving factory employed 100 women and children spinning yarn and weaving cloth, and the Troy Cotton and Woolen Factory employed 80 (Weise *History...* 161–162). This may be relevant if the claim is true that runaways hid in ships

---

It has not yet been verified if this is the actual house, but it is the correct location.

194

Alleged John Hooper house, 153 Second Street, Troy, New York. (Photograph by the author.)

among the cotton bales in order to make their escape, and which may have led to the development of an Underground network in the cotton shipping industry. Troy's shipping industry also had more direct links to northern New York than those in Albany. By 1850, it had 46 barges and 120 ships available, 25 of the latter that ran to Whitehall along the Champlain Canal. Business interests in Troy also were extensively involved in shipping along Lake Champlain (205–206).

The link between transportation and the Underground Railroad is a natural one. In Troy, a concrete connection began with the formation of the Free Bethel Church in 1832, founded to serve the boatmen and others who worked along the river and the canals. Among its organizers was the evangelist and abolitionist the Rev. Nathan Sidney Beman of the First Presbyterian Church, and its first pastor was the Rev. Fayette Shipherd. Also, one of the church's first two officers was grain dealer Gurdon Grant, who was vice-president of the Troy Anti-Slavery Society and whose business offices, like the society's president, Thaddeus Bigelow, were located at the port of Troy. Local legend associates the Underground Railroad with Bethel, of which Shipherd was the pastor when he wrote the letter about forwarding runaways to Vermont because the Champlain Canal was closed.

White abolitionists also connected with the black community. The Rev. Beman and Bigelow were among the organizers of the Liberty Street Church, the most important black church in Troy during the antebellum period. Dedicated in 1834 by New York City Underground Railroad leader the Rev. Theodore Wright, it was used only as a Sunday School until 1840, when Bigelow and black citizens William Rich, identified as Troy's stationmaster, and Alexander Thuey were named trustees ("His-

Liberty Street Church, Troy, New York, an underground railroad stop. (Courtesy of Rensselaer County Historical Society.)

tory of Bethel..."; Weise *Troy's One Hundred...* 130). A year later, Henry Garnet became its pastor.

A story involving Garnet and the Underground Railroad took place at the church shortly after he gave his famous "Address to the Slaves" speech in Buffalo in 1843. He had received a group of runaways at his Liberty Street Presbyterian Church, where he also ran a school for colored children and adults. As usual he hid the runaways in the basement, but before they were able to resume their journey, his church was surrounded by an angry mob. Apparently, locals knew of his Underground Railroad activities, and as his speech had been widely reported, it probably had stirred up anger. It never was explained in the story what happened to the fugitive slaves, only that they were driven away. Perhaps they escaped through some trapdoor or tunnel. The house on 153 Second Street was only a few blocks from the church, so perhaps a tunnel led there from the basement of the church. In any case, the mob burst in and grabbed Garnet. They dragged him outside, and repeatedly beat and spit on him, took his crutch, and left him in the street. Garnet, who lived a number of blocks away, had to crawl home (Pasternak 38).

This incident is reminiscent of the Troy mob that stoned and beat Abel Brown, who lived in Troy the last six months of his life. On the other hand, Troy was home to many who supported abolitionism, as Brown's widow wrote:

> Here we were cheered and sustained by many kind and Christian friends....
> Here—we often held meetings in the reform churches and at a public hall ...
> [and] often had the pleasure of affording shelter and relief to many a weary
> and heart-stricken fugitive.... [An] exceedingly interesting case occurred, in
> which a very shrewd and intelligent slave, had been directed on his way to the
> care of Mr. Brown, and in a few weeks his wife was restored to him. She had
> traveled hundreds of miles, with the simple direction of Mr. Brown's address.
> After spending a week with us, she was conveyed to her husband, at a place
> some distance north of Albany.... Such was their joyful meeting, that they
> remained in silence for some minutes, pacing the room to and fro, and then
> each burst into a flood of tears.... One week only elapsed, when they were
> cheered by the addition of a freeborn child, their first and only offspring [Brown
> 190].

In contrast to Albany County, the rural areas of Rensselaer County played a more significant role in the Underground Railroad. Among the most militant of abolitionist communities was Sand Lake, about 15 miles west of Troy in the foothills of the Berkshire Mountains. Not only was it home to the Franckean Synod, a group of radical abolitionist Lutheran ministers, who broke from their denomination and who legend claims were devoted conductors—including the Rev. Nicholas Van Alstyne, the Rev. H.L. Dox, and the Rev. John D. Lawyer—but its Baptist Church was the last congregation served by Abel Brown, from May 5, 1840 to April 3, 1842, before moving to Albany and devoting full time to the cause of abolition.

Sand Lake historian Judith Rowe has been researching the Underground Railroad in her locality for many years. She believes that the Sand Lake's old glass company, which got its sand from Lanesboro, Massachusetts, near the New York border and which owned a glassmaking factory in Durhamville in central New York, transported slaves in empty barrels between the locations (Rowe interview). The company's owner, Isaac Fox, also was a founder of the village Baptist Church. An important clue to her hypothesis is an article that appeared in the January 1901 issue of a monthly called *Berkshire Hills* published in Pittsfield, Massachusetts. The article describes three Underground Railroad routes that led out of Rensselaer County into Massachusetts, one that would have led from Sand Lake. Another key piece of information that clearly points to Sand Lake as an Underground stop was the membership of resident Dr. C.H. Gregory in the Eastern New York Anti-Slavery Society's executive committee.

At least one other rural location in the northern part of the county was a stop for fugitive slaves. Hoosick Falls, near Washington County, was the home of Garret Van Hoosen, to whom Shipherd forwarded his 1840 letter for Hicks. Van Hoosen also was the president of the county Liberty Party in 1845 ("Convention at Troy").

A truly revealing document that sketches the Underground Railroad as it was in

Public Meeting.

At a public meeting held in the Liberty st. Church, Sept. 15th, 1857, by the Vigilant Committee of the Underground Railroad, Rev. JONATHAN C. GIBBS was called to the Chair, and the following business transacted:

The Acting Committee reported fifty-five persons having passed through under their care since the 15th day of September, 1856,—one year,—and having expended one hundred and twenty-five dollars for their passage.

The Committee return their thanks to the public for the assistance so promptly rendered, in affording shelter, food and means, whereby they were able to make glad the hearts of the afflicted.

The report was received and adopted.

Resolved, That the thanks of this meeting be tendered to the Committee for the prudent and faithful manner they performed their trust; and also, that WM. RICH be the receiver of such means as are sent to him for the fugitive.

The following persons were appointed to act for the ensuing year: Philip Owens, Charles Hagerman, Wm. Henry, Capt. Hawkins, Wm. Bishop, Southy Bingham, R. Schoonmaker.

The meeting then listened to an Address from Rev. Mr. Crawford, of Nantucket, and then adjourned, subject to a call of the Acting Committee.

Report of the Troy, New York, Vigilance Committee. (From *Troy Daily Times*, 6 October 1857.)

Troy in 1857 was a published report by the Troy Vigilance Committee for that year. "The Acting Committee reported fifty-five persons having passed through under their care since the 15th day of September, 1856— one year—and having expended one hundred and twenty-five dollars for their passage." Further down in the report, it tendered thanks to the committee, "and also, that William Rich be the receiver of such means as are sent to him for the fugitive." The other members of the committee were the Rev. Jonathan C. Gibbs, pastor of the Liberty Street Church; Philip Owens, a whitewasher, who lived on 320 Congress Street; William Henry, a furnace man, at 26 Division Street; Captain Hawkins, probably Zebedee at 37 Green Street; William E. Bishop, a whitewasher, at Church Street near Ferry; R. Schoonmaker, also a whitewasher at 129 William Street; Southy Bingham, a cook at 146 Third Street; and Charles Hagerman ("Public Meeting"; *Troy City Directory* 1857).* Whereas the vigilance committee in Albany had become integrated, every member in Troy was black.

William Rich, identified as Troy's stationmaster, had been a leading member in the black community for more than 20 years, having been chairman of the publishing committee for the Union Meeting of Colored People of Albany, Troy and vicinity in 1837, one of the founding trustees of the Liberty Street Church in 1840, president of the Prigg Meeting in 1842, and active in the Negro conventions. He was born in Massachusetts in 1804 and resided in Troy for many years at 29 Elbow (today Fulton Street). His hairdressing salon in 1857 was at the Troy House.

One other revealing piece of information about Troy's Underground Railroad was provided in correspondence in 1896 and 1897 between historian Wilbur Siebert and Martin Townsend, a former congressman from Troy and the lawyer who defended Charles Nalle. Townsend wrote these letters, when he was 89 and very feeble, in response to a query from Siebert. In one, Townsend writes: "Fugitives from slavery always traveled from Troy to Canada with perfect safety—whether by steamboat and Lake Champlain—by suspension bridge [a bridge crossing at Rouses Point, New York, into Canada]. When they reached Troy they only needed money to pay their fare for the rest of their voyage. Five left for suspension bridge [even though] John M. Mott, U.S. Marshall, [was] in the same railroad car, [and] knew of the character of his fellow travelers as they were."

*The addresses were not included in the report but obtained in the Troy City Directory for that year.

Underground Railroad Stops in Troy, N.Y.

(Map by the author.)

Townsend's explanation of how this could occur is completely different from some of the stories about federal marshals we have heard from the downstate region.

"A man was held in Auburn Prison for crimes," Townsend wrote. "Mott was waited upon by a Southern man and told he would be on hand on the day when the prisoner's sentence [would be completed and]* would explain with papers to show him to be his slave. Mott got the Governor to pardon the alleged slave and when the claimant arrived his chattel was not in Auburn. Mott was a Buchanan man Democrat but he was humane."

In another letter, dated April 1, 1897, from Siebert, Townsend identified whitewasher John Hooper, the man who for many years lived at 153 Second Street, as an Underground Railroad agent. In an entry dated April 3, Townsend has added to Siebert's correspondence: "Hooper was a fugitive from the Eastern Shore of Maryland and an acquaintance of Fred Douglass" (Townsend letters).

These words, missing from the original, are suggestive of the meaning intended and added by the author.

Chapter 29

STOPS IN
WASHINGTON COUNTY

One can still see the same rolling farmland, green foothills, and quaint villages in Washington County. It has not changed much since the days of Hiram Corliss, and although few residents remember his name, most do know that the Underground Railroad was active here. Until recently, however, even the local historians said that there was little more they could learn because it was secret and nothing was written down. Nevertheless, new stories continue to emerge. It makes people feel connected to something heroic if their home was a part of the Underground Railroad, and though few can prove their homes were stops, abolitionism as we have now learned was more active here than most of its modern residents had ever dreamed. Therefore, the legends should not be taken too lightly.

We begin our journey through Washington County along Route 40, the old Coach Road, which runs parallel to the Champlain Canal, and enter the farm country of Easton. Here oral tradition, kept alive by the unpublished memoirs of Oren B. Wilbur, has identified a number of homes as stops. Untouched by urban development, many of these rural homes still remain. We first come upon the former Van Schaick home, now owned by Ron and Helen Dixon, on the western side of Route 40 at the intersection with Waite Road. Residents say it has a small room above the attic near one of the chimneys and is reached by a disappearing stairway that can be raised from above or lowered from below. A little farther up the road, on the other side, is a former Wilbur family house, for years the Albert and Dorothy Slocum farmhouse, now owned by the Pratt family. It is said to have a long kitchen chamber in the back of the house hidden by a lintel and into which one can enter by removing a loose plank. A little farther up Route 40, on the western side, is the Esther and Job Wilbur farmhouse, set away from road at the end of a long dirt driveway.

Underground Railroad Stops in Washington, Saratoga, & Warren Counties

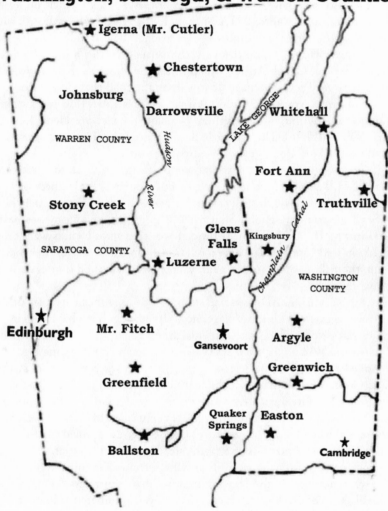

(Map by the author.)

One episode from Oren B. Wilbur's memoirs involved a runaway named Frank, who reached their home deathly sick with pneumonia. He arrived with a cane, which he used to fight off bloodhounds. He had by now left the slavecatchers far behind. The Wilburs nursed him back to health. Frank liked it there and took a job with the Wilburs as a farmhand. He never had a surname as a slave. Now as a free man, he decided to adopt one, calling himself Frank Quaintance, because as he said, "It was through the quaintance of the good Wilbur family that I am still alive and comfortable." Frank died only a couple of years later, but left behind the cane with which he fought his way to freedom (Wilbur).

Back across Route 40, kitty-corner to the Wilbur driveway, is the North Easton Meeting House, where Esther had her celebrated confrontation and where Sojourner Truth, Aaron Powell, and other abolitionists came.

Local legends also have associated other homes, some of which no longer exist, with the Underground Railroad. These include the Aaron Barker house with a hidden room near the attic that could only be reached by a trapdoor in the cellar ("A Pre-Revolutionary House"), and the Van Rensselaer-Schuyler house along Route 113 near the Champlain Canal. An 1853 map of Easton shows as many as four Saratoga District Anti-Slavery Society officers living along the road that is now Route 40: treasurer Job Wilbur; secretary S. (Samuel) Wilbur, Francis Tobey (Job and Esther's neighbor) and several J. Wilburs—one of them probably the vice-president, John ("Trip to Northern New York" 46). There is little doubt that along this small stretch of Route 40 existed a close-knit Underground Railroad terminal.

One other existing site in the town of Easton sits at the bottom of the Schuylerville Hill along Route 113 near the Hudson River and is now owned by Dr. Edwin Sullivan. Ironically, this substantial nine-bedroom home was the residence of the former slave owner, General Simon De Ridder. But this irony has basis in historical tradition. The explanation behind this is that slave owners were more familiar with blacks and continued to have a relationship with the slaves they manumitted. As a result, their slaves often settled nearby, and this made their homes desirable stops for fugitive slaves.*

Leaving Easton, fugitive slaves had several options as to the next leg of their journey. An obvious one was Union Village, now Greenwich. It probably was not unusual for fugitive slaves to go straight to Greenwich, especially before 1850, which was the period when the Wilburs became active. Perhaps its most intriguing legend is that a tunnel linked the many abolitionist homes in the Park Street area, in those days known as Church Street. Though this cannot be confirmed, local historian Helen Hoag, who lived in Greenwich for more than 70 years, said she had known about it ever since she was a child. Most recently, Robert Huffman of 1 Cottage Avenue, whose 1890 house is almost directly in the path of these houses, claimed that he found what appears to have been a portion of a tunnel leading from his cellar.

A quick survey of that section of the village shows that nine abolitionists, eight of whom were members of the Free Church, resided within less than a block of each other during the 1850s. Among them, on the even numbered side of the block are the former Henry Holmes house, still on 18 Park Street, the Erastus Bigelow house, which was at the present 8 Park Street, and the former William H. Mowry house, still at 6 Park Street, which was said to have a secret chamber under the wing of the house that could accommodate 30 people ("Jesse Williams"). The Mowry house is right around the corner from the Huffman house. Across the street from Bigelow on the odd-numbered side was the home of Edwin Wilmarth, mentioned in the Liberty Party outreach letter by Hiram Corliss.

Directly across the street from the Huffman house is the home at 150 Main Street of Leonard Gibbs, ardent abolitionist and host to Thompson and Garrison. In this

---

*In Washington County, there also is the Goodman Farm in Fort Ann; in Saratoga County, the Dr. Davis house on Middleline Road in the town of Ballston, and the Gansevoort Mansion in Gansevoort.

Underground Railroad Stops in Union Village

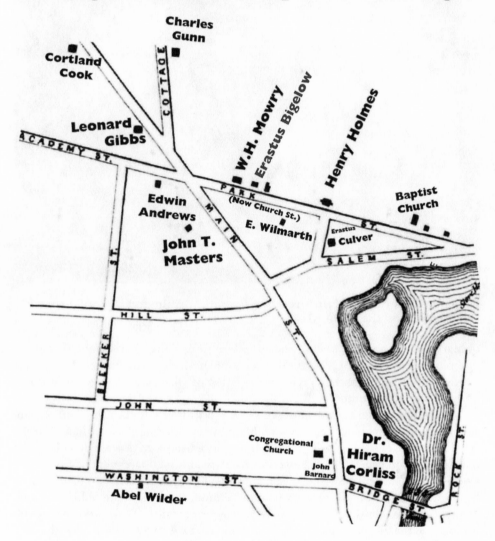

Charles
Gunn

Cortland
Cook

COTTAGE

Leonard
Gibbs

ACADEMY ST.

W.H. Mowry

Erastus Bigelow

Henry Holmes

PARK
(Now Church St.)

Edwin
Andrews

MAIN

E. Wilmarth

Erastus
Culver

Baptist
Church

John T.
Masters

SALEM ST.

HILL ST.

ST.

BLEEKER

JOHN ST.

Congregational
Church

John
Barnard

Dr.
Hiram
Corliss

ROCK ST.

WASHINGTON ST.

BRIDGE ST.

Abel Wilder

(Map by the author.)

house, now known to everyone in the village as the chiropractor's house, the legend of the Underground Railroad lives more vividly than in any in all the county—"the Mystery House, haunted by the escaping black man; with dark secret places and stealthy whisperings, hasty coverings into friendly wagons for further flight to the North," as one local writer described during the 1930s ("When Greenwich Was...").

Across the street from Gibbs on Academy Street is the former Edwin Andrews house, which now serves at the town hall. Andrews was the only non-member of the Free Church among these abolitionists, but he was one of the founders of the county anti-slavery society and very active in the early years of the movement. Around the corner from him is the former house of Edwin T. Masters, entrepreneur and husband

Leonard Gibbs House, Main Street, Greenwich, Washington County, New York. (Photograph by the author.)

of Mary Mowry, and the house is now the Evergreen Bank. Also among this group of abolitionists were C.S. Cook, the son-in-law of Dr. Corliss, who lived on Main Street a little west of Gibbs, and C. J. Gunn, the father of Diantha, who lived a few doors up from the Huffman house.

According to the legends, fugitive slaves most often stayed in the Corliss mansion that was several blocks east, just off Main Street on Bridge Street adjacent to the small bridge that crosses the Battenkill. It has since been torn down, but a picture of it can be seen on page 17. Corliss, whose office was around the corner on Main Street where he also had his residence prior to the building of the mansion, is alleged to have sent runaways on their way by boat to Vermont from the shore of his backyard. This is possible, considering that there is only one small section of the Battenkill, just outside the village, where there are any rapids. Legend also alleges that the Free Church's parsonage on 28 Main Street, which still remains and is a realty office, hid fugitive slaves (Ibid.).

The road north out of Greenwich led to Argyle, another small village rife with Underground Railroad legend. The site of the county's first anti-slavery meeting and the county poorhouse, it may have been aiding fugitive slaves as early as 1833. One woman fleeing slavery gave birth to twin boys, Austin and Horace, at the poorhouse during this period.*

Interestingly, no records exist of persons of color entering the poorhouse from

*Austin and Horace lived at the poorhouse until 1851 and 1852; what happened to Horace after that is not known. Austin lived out his life in Washington County and served in the Civil War. He died in 1918 and his obituary listed his age at 85; however, various documents show different dates of birth, and according to census records, he was 11 in 1850, which means that the more likely birth date of the twins was 1839 (Doolittle B1).

1834 to 1859, the period of the Underground Railroad. We know about this woman, however, because her son, Austin, remained in the county, served in the Civil War, and lived out a life of about 85 years, so his story became well-known. The lack of records regarding blacks in the poorhouse during this period is puzzling, especially when one considers that the number of blacks in the county then was consistently about 300 persons, many of whom were itinerant, poor, and illiterate—people who would be expected to make use of the poorhouse (Hulslander; Crannell). Adding to this are the anti-slavery associations of two poorhouse superintendents, Ransom Stiles and Anthony McKallor.

Stiles, president of the village and town supervisor in 1839, had underground tunnels leading from his home. During the 1950s a 500-foot-long underground passage was found and seen by numerous persons during excavation of his house along the main street of Argyle (MacMorris 97). Because he was perhaps the village's most prominent citizen during much of the abolition period—he would be elected its president again seven more times in the next 13 years and serve again as town supervisor (Corey 50–51)—his involvement in abolition is extremely compelling evidence that a trunk of the Underground Railroad passed through Argyle.

McKallor, a Liberty Party candidate and elder of the abolitionist Argyle Presbyterian Church, also was the town's supervisor from 1830–32, justice of the peace in 1841, and a member of the Argyle Academy's Board of Trustees (Corey 51–52, 54).

Additional evidence linking Argyle to the Underground Railroad was passed on to Underground Railroad researcher Jesse Williams in the 1950s by Mrs. Roscoe Ellis, who claimed that the old Coach Road leading from Union Village to Argyle was used. The Poorhouse is in this vicinity, and the homestead of Anthony McKallor was directly along this road, near the former South Argyle Presbyterian Church. Also, according to Mrs. Ellis, the neighboring homes of David Hall and Alexander Armstrong on this road were used to hide John Salter, the fugitive slave whom slavecatchers attempted to apprehend in 1858 and on several other occasions ("Jesse Williams").

From Argyle, the fugitive slave could have moved northeast to Granville or northwest to Sandy Hill, now Hudson Falls. More likely, the route to the latter would have bypassed Union Village and Argyle and continued along the Champlain Canal. According to local lore, there were several stops in the Hudson Falls area, two with oral family legends set close to parts of the canal. Margaret Whipple said in 1963 that her ancestor, Horace Dibble, hid a fugitive slave in the woodshed outside his house in Dunham's Basin, a house owned in 1963 by the Woodell family (Sullivan 11). This may be one of those legends that developed from a haven by happenstance, a home that a runaway stumbled upon by accident and was given assistance. The second house is located in the eastern end of the village near one of the feeder canals. Formerly the house of the Van Vranken family, the house now at 49 Burgoyne Avenue originally was located closer to the canal on the opposite side of where it now sits. Former owner Thomas Van Vranken was told by his grandmother that the family at one time had two sets of leg irons in their possession and that the section of the house in which fugitive slaves were harbored was in the basement. Van Vranken added that his father worked along the canal and that his extended family includes black members (Van Vranken interview). A third rumored stop in Hudson Falls is the 1823 brick house at 24 Pearl Street (real estate agents noted a trapdoor in the porch as evidence);

a fourth is the Dr. Fine house on the corner of Clark and North Oak Street, across from Margaret Murphy Elementary. That house, long the residence of physicians, was occupied in 1853 by Dr. E.G. Clark. Regarding these homes, we have only rumor to suggest their use as stations. Their proximity to the residence and office of Henry B. Northup, the attorney who retrieved Solomon Northup from slavery, may be a factor, though he is not known to have participated in the Underground Railroad. All four require more evidence before they can be classified as anything other than pure legend.

Another rumored site in Hudson Falls was the former Mead house on Moss Street (Route 4) near the Hudson Falls cemetery. This site is in the rural town of Kingsbury, where the stories of the Underground Railroad have remained as vivid to residents as those in Easton and Greenwich. This probably is because of the two colorful artifacts that were discussed in Chapter One, the old Underground Railway Guideboard on Vaughn Corners Road in front of the old Doubleday house, and the Stone Chair about a half-mile way. Delilah Chesterman, who grew up in the Doubleday house, offered another intriguing piece of area folklore. She said that as a girl she used to ride her horse along a nearby trail that led directly to Fort Ann and that was called by locals "the Underground Railroad." She had no idea where the name came from (Calarco).

This trail led in the direction of the Goodman farm. About four-and-a-half miles from the guideboard sign at Vaughn Corners Road and only about a half-mile from the Champlain Canal, the Goodman farm was originally owned by Colonel Drury Wray, a British army officer who built the farmhouse in 1773 and who, according to the 1790 census, owned seven slaves. In 1853, Origin Goodman purchased the house. According to the Goodmans, who still own the farm, there was a hidden room in the attic that was removed during renovation.

The farm was only a short distance from the village of Fort Ann and the Old Stone Library, which legend claims was a station. Built in 1825, it was owned and possibly built by the Rev. Orrin B. Shipman, who was an anti-slavery lecturer for the Liberty Party and who was probably related to Hiram Shipman, a Fort Ann tanner and village official who was elected president of the Fort Ann Anti-Slavery Society when it organized in 1835. Hiram also was listed as a vice-president of the county anti-slavery society in the report of its annual meeting in 1836 and attended the Washington Union Baptist Association meeting of 1838 that strongly condemned slavery ("The Work Goes Bravely On"; "Washington County Anti-Slavery Society 1836"; "Minutes").

Though we have little to report of legendary stations in Whitehall, it was a likely destination for the fugitive slaves leaving Fort Ann because it was the final gateway to Canada. However, there were other alternatives. Among them could have been the Free-Will Baptist Church in the sparsely-populated town of Putnam, which was serviced for a number of years by the black minister Charles Bowles and whose northernmost point was the site of a small community of blacks on land called Black Point owned by Prince Taylor, a black Ticonderoga cook, tailor, and surveyor.

Other sites, perhaps somewhat off the beaten path of the Easton-Union Village-Champlain Canal circuit, were rumored stops in the towns of Cambridge, Granville, and Hartford. In the latter town, Mrs. Howard Hanna writes that a station with a hiding place in the basement behind a fireplace was halfway down the street before

Earlier view of the Goodman House. (From archives of Warren County historian's office.)

you get to the present Head Start building (Hanna). To be sure, there were strong-minded abolitionists in Hartford, including John Carlisle, Colonel John Straight, the Rev. Amos Tuttle, and the Rev. John B. Shaw.

The latter minister, who ministered to several churches in the county, including the Congregational Church in Hartford, resided in Granville. A letter from Arthur Dougan, who lives in Cleveland but maintains the family home in Granville, claims his house was home to the Rev. Shaw. It sits in front of the Mettawee River, which empties into the Champlain Canal, and is not far from the homestead where Leonard Gibbs grew up.

"We have a house in Truthville," Dougan wrote, "which is reputed to have been a station on the Underground Railroad. Built before 1825, enlarged in 1831, it was owned before the Civil War by the Methodist minister of North Granville.... We have a basement space, which once had a door, which is thought to have been a hiding place" (Dougan letter).

The house is also near the hamlet of Slyboro, along County Route 23, which legend claims harbored fugitive slaves (*Granville Sentinel*), and which is the location of the Northup homestead where Solomon Northup's father worked as a slave.

In Cambridge, several homes merit further investigation. These include two houses on the old Turnpike Road: the old Wheelhouse, possibly the home of county anti-slavery society vice-president Elijah Wells, and a house now owned by William Zachary just south of the Wheelhouse, which has a crawl space room whose walls are papered with clippings from the time of the Civil War. Zachary said the house originally was owned by J.W. Peckham, possibly the same individual who was a member of the Saratoga District Anti-Slavery Society and who wrote the Esther Wilbur obituary. A third home in the village with a reputed connection is located on 98 East Main Street and dates to 1840. Allegedly, it has a "secret room" off the bathroom that once led to a tunnel connecting with a neighboring house (Country Properties Real Estate).

Despite the intriguing circumstances related to these homes in Hartford, Granville, and Cambridge, all connections to the Underground Railroad remain in the realm of pure speculation. There are others, as well, that have been brought to the attention of this author but which can make even less compelling claims. It will take time to turn rumor and wishful thinking into fact, but there is little doubt that more Underground Railroad stops, whose authenticity will be proven, are waiting to be discovered in Washington County.

Chapter 30

STOPS IN
CLINTON COUNTY

One cannot get much closer to the Underground Railroad's Promised Land than Clinton County. On its eastern border, a rolling countryside flattens out along the coast of Lake Champlain, a landscape with orchards reminiscent of the Finger Lakes. Going west and south, the land rises into forested foothills that lead up to the peaks of the Adirondack range. Settlers came to this region in significant numbers around the turn of the 18th century. Many were from New England and some were sea captains who also settled in other eastern New York communities, such as the Columbia County village of Hudson or the Washington County town of Easton. They came to grow crops, raise livestock, and engage in the lumber trade. It wasn't until later that Clinton County's maple sugar and apple orchard industries sprung up.

But what about the stops along the Underground Railroad? Do any of them still exist? Local historians Emily McMasters and Addie Shields, who followed up on McMasters's research, deserve the credit for mapping out the county route. It began in Keeseville, a small town on the southern border bisected by the Ausable River, with one side of the town in Clinton and the other in Essex County. There a man named Bigelow had a station, and his house remains alongside the river just northeast of the village bridge. A blue plaque with yellow lettering stands outside.

Northwest of Keeseville were the homes of Stephen Keese Smith and Samuel Keese, only three-quarters of a mile from each other. Only Smith's farmhouse remains, on Union Road just south of the village of Peru, and behind it is the barn where he hid the runaways. A blue plaque also stands out front. Smith said he spent about $1,000 of his own money in providing food, clothing, and other necessities for the runaways (Everest 57). Now owned by Richard Stafford, the house is just a short distance from Route 22 and the beginning of a line of stations that led to Noadiah Moore and the Canadian border.

Stephen Keese Smith farmhouse, Peru, Clinton County, New York. (Photograph by the author.)

There also were secondary routes. A house which may have been part of such a route and which may have housed slaves for indefinite periods as hired hands belonged to John Townsend Addoms in the town of Plattsburgh, just south of Beekmantown. Addoms was a circuit rider for the Methodist Church and the son of John Addoms of Cumberland Head, who ran a Sunday school here (Shields). While Townsend Addoms has not appeared on any listings of anti-slavery meetings, he did sign the petition that called for the organization of the county anti-slavery society.

Though the Townsend-Addoms house no longer remains, its significance was understood when it was torn down in 1979 and care was taken while renovating the site to document the various tunnels found in the basement below by the current owner of the property, Eugene Pellerin. That year, Shields interviewed a number of locals about the house's use as a station. Among them were John Banker, born in 1899, Stella Hildreth Sanger, born in 1901, and Minnie Wright, born in 1910 (Shields Item 7, 6–9).

"Why, of course," Banker said, referring to the house, "all of us old folks knew that."

Mrs. Sanger, a friend of the Collins, descendents of Julia Addoms Collins, Townsend Addoms's daughter, said that family members told her that runaways sometimes stayed there and worked for a time. Mrs. Wood, a friend of Lorena Collins, Townsend Addoms's great-granddaughter, revealed that, "There were passages from the various cellars [and] under a long table was a secret door that led to a dry cistern. I've heard stories of lawmen coming down the lane and whoever was sheltered getting under the table, opening a trap door and descending into the cistern."

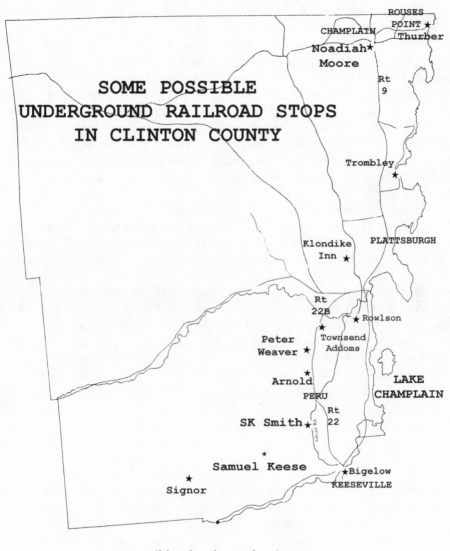

SOME POSSIBLE
UNDERGROUND RAILROAD STOPS
IN CLINTON COUNTY

ROUSES
POINT ★
CHAMPLAIN   Thurber
Noadiah★
Moore

Rt
9

Trombley
★

Klondike   PLATTSBURGH
Inn ★

Rt
22B
★ ★ Rowlson
Peter   Townsend
Weaver ★   Addoms

★
Arnold
PERU
Rt
22
SK Smith★

★
Samuel Keese
★   ★Bigelow
Signor   KEESEVILLE

LAKE
CHAMPLAIN

(Map by the author.)

McMasters also knew of the Townsend Addoms site and also claimed that the "White Pine Tea Room," now occupied by the Klondike Inn on Route 22, was a station. The latter is along the main route that led north to a string of alleged stations. McMasters also identified the Chittendon's place, "now gone," which was identified by Nathan Weaver, son of Peter Weaver, one of the county's leading abolitionists. A short distance north is the Ira Rowlson farmhouse, whose original owner had been Amos Barber (Shields Item 14; Everest *Pioneer Homes* 21). Farther up the road is the Dawson house, a site which Shields believes was a stop because of the cluster of black families who lived nearby, some of them descendents of the slaves of Judge Thomas Treadwell, who manumitted them in 1794 (Shields).

Parallel to Route 22 is Route 9, which takes the traveler to the village of Champlain. This was the residence of Noadiah Moore, the county's most active abolitionist, whose home unfortunately was destroyed by fire in 1873 (Patrick). However, a short distance south of the village is a red house with white shutters. Built around 1810, it is five or so miles from the Canadian border. Current owner Robert Trombly has an 1857 deed that shows it was sold that year by Charles A. Moore to Lewis Kellogg, a known abolitionist. It is not known, however, if Noadiah had any relation to Charles Moore or anyone else who owned the house.

Shields also believes that the Bruno Trombley house, a small cabin nestled in a small bay along Lake Champlain between Chazy Landing and Cumberland Head, was a station. Not far from the cabin lived Ephraim Hoag, who was a cousin of Nathan C. Hoag, one of Rowland T. Robinson's collaborators across Lake Champlain in Ferrisburgh, Vermont.

Wilbur Siebert also claimed that an Underground Railroad station operated in Rouses Point. The source of his information was Martin Townsend of Troy, who wrote that "fugitives arriving in Troy were forwarded either to the Niagara River or to Vermont and Lake Champlain to Rouses Point" (Siebert *The Underground Railroad: From Slavery to Freedom* 126).

No local histories or historians have identified any abolitionists in Rouses Point. However, there is a legend of uncertain origin that claims "General" Ezra Thurber was the stationmaster there. His brick house built in 1818 remains today, and its current owner, Les Mathews, said renovation of the house in the last decade revealed remnants of a tunnel. Mathews claims that he has heard stories that the tunnel once led across the Canadian border, which before 1843 was only a mile away.*

Many people scoff at these claims, but one should consider Thurber's background before rejecting them so easily.

The son of one of Rouses Point's earliest pioneers, Ezra Thurber was among the most prominent men in the county during the early part of the 19th century. He was the leader of the local militia, vice-president of the first county fair, and, most important in considering his role as an Underground Railroad conductor, customs officer at Rouses Point for more than 30 years (*Plattsburgh Republican* 28 May 1842). In 1817, he hosted a celebrated visit by President Monroe (Broadwell III).

Another factor was Thurber's conversion to the Baptist faith in 1824, after which he became the church's deacon and leading financial sponsor (Broadwell V). The church to which he belonged was the restoration of a congregation that had been dissolved during the War of 1812. It was originally founded by the Rev. Nathaniel Colver, Sr., who was ordained in the barn of Ezra's brother, John (Hurd 266) and whose son, Nathaniel, Jr., became one of the nation's leading abolitionists as pastor of the Tremont Temple in Boston. Considering the active participation of the Baptist faith in abolitionism, especially in upstate New York, and Thurber's position as customs officer, it is plausible that he could have been an Underground Railroad conductor.

A book that would be useful for further investigation of other homes in the county that may have been Underground Railroad stops is Allan Everest's *Pioneer*

---

*In 1816, construction of an American military fort had to be halted when it was learned that the site was actually on Canadian soil. Ever after called "Fort Blunder," it was finally completed in 1843, but only after the necessary boundary adjustment was made.

General Ezra Thurber House, Rouses Point, Clinton County, New York. (Photograph by the author.)

Homes. If we cross-reference a list of names of participants in anti-slavery meetings, members of the Liberty Party, subscribers to the *Herald of Freedom*, and those identified by Gerrit Smith as abolitionists following his 1845 visit with the names of individuals or families listed in Everest's book, we find 24 additional homes that could have been stops on the Underground Railroad.*

Among the most compelling are the Peter Weaver House and the Weston House in Schuyler Falls, the Barber Homestead on Barber Road in Beekmantown, both Pliny Moore's farmhouse and homestead in Champlain, and the Ransom Tavern and Julius Hubbell home in Chazy. Weaver was one of the vice-presidents of the county society and a leading member of the Liberty Party, having been its candidate for state assembly in 1846. The names of both Weston and Barber account for four anti-slavery members each, the former of the West Peru Anti-Slavery Society, and the latter of the Beekmantown Anti-Slavery Society. Pliny Moore was the father of Noadiah. His homestead has remained in his family to the present; his farmhouse was passed first to his daughter and her abolitionist minister husband, Abraham Brinkerhoff. After 1835, the house was passed to the Nye family, whose son married Noadiah Moore's daughter. Ransom of Chazy was a member of the county anti-slavery society, and Hubbell, whose brother was abolitionist Silas Hubbell, married Moore's sister. The suggestion that those homes or any of the others were Underground Railroad stations is speculative, but they are a starting place for further study.

*See Appendix VI.

There is no way to know if many runaways came to the remote borders of Clinton County. We do know that anti-slavery sentiment was very strong in this remote outpost to freedom, and the likelihood of further discoveries is strong.

Chapter 31

STOPS IN
SARATOGA COUNTY

In the history of abolitionism, Saratoga County is better known for the kidnapping of a free black man, Solomon Northup, by slave catchers than any of the deeds of its Underground Railroad conductors. In fact, the county's anti-slavery profile resembles the counties downstate. For example, only 17 percent of its voters supported full Negro suffrage in the 1846 referendum (*The Tribune Almanac...* 44), and it had a fairly large slave population during the period before statewide emancipation, averaging nearly 500 resident slaves during that time (*U.S. Federal Census* 1790–1820). The difference, however, was that the county had a dual personality with regard to slavery. In Saratoga Springs, the county's most populated community, the view was very pro-slavery; in the rural areas, abolitionism and the Liberty Party were strong.

The Underground Railroad had two lines running east and west of Saratoga Springs. The western route was actually part of the same route that led into Washington County from Rensselaer County along the Champlain Canal. It passed through Quaker Springs, which had a Quaker Meeting, where a number of the officers of the Old Saratoga District Anti-Slavery Society lived. The homes of Isaac Griffen and Cornelius Wright were stops. As to their exact location, or whether they still exist, this author has not yet determined. Though most runaways along this route probably continued north along the canal and into Washington County, they also had the option of going to the town of Gansevoort on the way to Warren County. Bernard Shaw, a resident of Gansevoort since 1920, remembers hearing stories as a boy about runaways who didn't go all the way to Canada, but settled there. Legend claims the Gansevoort Mansion, the home of Revolutionary War General Peter Gansevoort, was a stop. Northumberland historian Georgia Ball said the General had slaves, but that when they were freed, they stayed on to work for the Gansevoorts, making the mansion a likely stop (Calarco 1).

The eastern route led up from Schenectady County—possibly the home of the black abolitionist R.P.G. Wright on Ferry Street, or other blacks in the city such as John Wendell and Francis Dana, or abolitionists in the Union College community—to the present Middleline Road in the town of Ballston. Outside the first stop, on the left going north, a marker is posted. Originally the home of Dr. Sam Davis, a former slave owner, it had a hidden room under a stairway, about three feet by five feet, that was discovered by a recent owner, Ruth Center. Not much more is known about the authenticity of the location, but local legend claims that Davis later became an abolitionist after freeing his slaves (Briaddy 69). Several other stops are rumored to have existed in the town, according to local historian Kathy Briaddy. One of them may have been the residence of Temperance leader E.C. Delevan, which was near the Davis house. The author does not know if the Delevan residence still exists, nor has he confirmed or located any other stops in the town of Ballston.

In the town of Milton, the old Shep Morey residence on Route 67 north of the North Milton Cemetery is believed to have been a stop. Former Milton town historian Dorothy Alsdorf wrote that the grandmother of a friend told her of a secret room there that sheltered fugitive slaves. She was told that Morey would transport slaves at dusk in wagons filled with hay (Alsdorf). The town was the site of many anti-slavery meetings, and the Baptist Church, predominant in this part of the county, supplied a number of the leaders in the town and county anti-slavery societies. During the summer of 1839, the abolitionist poet John Greenleaf Whittier attended an anti-slavery meeting in the town at the Stone Meeting House Baptist Church. Its pastor, the Rev. Wilkin, was active in the societies, and two members of its congregation were officers: George Benton, president of the Greenfield Center Anti-Slavery Society, founded July 4, 1838, with 84 members (*Friend of Man*), and Sam Benton, vice-president of the Saratoga County Anti-Slavery Society, founded on February 15, 1837 ("From the Plains of Saratoga").

From Morey's, it was only a short distance to Greenfield and the home of Mason Anthony, whom we know was aiding fugitive slaves as early as 1838. Another rumored stop was the Wayside Inn on Wilton Road. Current owner Karen Shook says a tunnel leads from the inn to the house across the street. Lydia Frances Sherman, who lived in nearby Hadley, also the home of Cornelius Dubois, the county anti-slavery society president in 1837, provided additional confirmation of this route in her 1849 memoir. She recalled an incident involving a fugitive slave who was helped by her family:

> At one time we kept a fugitive about the house several days before we dared pass him along, as a reward for his capture was posted in every village and at every post office, and plenty of pro-slavery men were eager for the reward. Fortunately it happened that just at that time my married sister came home on a visit, bringing with her a young infant. They dressed the slave in woman's clothes, with a heavy veil, put in his arms a large doll, well wrapped up to look like a baby, and my mother drove with him to Grandfather Wilcox's....
>
> On their way they had to pass through the village of Luzerne, and the ten minutes spent in transit caused ... much anxiety, for fear that some friend might stop to speak to them.... The most anxious time was when they had to go over the Sacandaga River and the North River, which were close together and were crossed by covered bridges, where they must drive slowly... [Sherman 1–2].

Runaways continuing north also may have stopped and rested with Mr. Fitch, whose mountaintop hut overlooking Efnor Lake near Corinth has been discussed. The notes of Mrs. Ellsworth's scrapbook are not the only description of the route to his cabin. A survey done by the WPA stated that fugitive slaves "were hauled by wagon at night [from Ballston], each wagon covered with straw, up to Lake Desolation in the Mooleyville district. Here they were kept until the next night or possibly moved on the same night across through the woods to Black Pond and down toward the Lake." The survey added that after resting with Fitch, they would be taken by him to the Sacandaga River and on to Thurman where another stop was located (letter from Rachel Clothier).

Some might think the story to be little more than romantic folklore. However, locals swear Fitch existed and even claim the remains of his cabin still exist. This author explored the location, following the directions of Mrs. Francis Reed, who remembered the location from childhood, and I found a short wall of rocks in the middle of a dense section of woods near the summit of a hill overlooking Efnor Lake, and they did look like the remnants of other old foundations previously seen. They are not far from a trail now used by snowmobilers, and a tree has grown up from within the foundation.

On the western shore of Sacandaga Lake, created out of the Sacandaga River in 1929, is Edinburgh. The former home of Liberty Party candidate Henry Noyes, it also was the site of anti-slavery meetings led by the Rev. Abel Brown. Another of its abolitionists was carpenter and postmaster John Barker. His home built in 1847 served as the town's post office and his father was one of the founders of the local Methodist Church. Current owner Dona Robinson, who has turned the building into an antiques and consignment store, was removing shelves when she noticed an opening to a hidden room that turned out to be big enough to stand in. Stories had been

John Barker House, late 19th century photograph, Edinburgh, Saratoga County, New York. (Courtesy of Dona Robinson.)

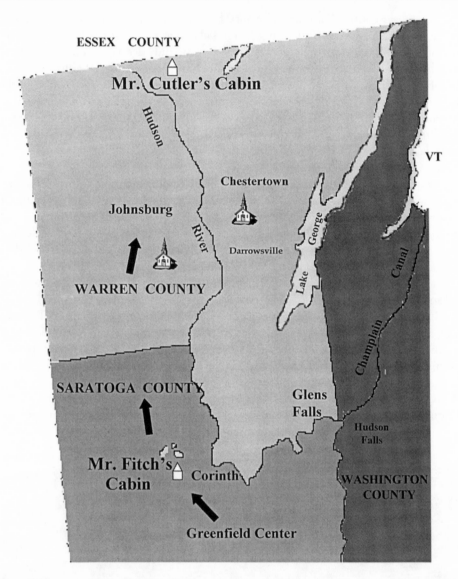

Possible route from Fitch to Cutler showing UGRR stops in Saratoga and Warren counties. (Map by the author.)

passed down that such a room had existed in the current post office across the street, but upon further investigation, she learned that her store was the post office of legend from 1849 to 1857 (Robinson interview).

Abel Brown held one of his last conventions in Edinburgh in September 1844.

"Indeed this is a grand Convention," he wrote, "a new era in Saratoga Abolitionism. The house is still full, and the audience has just voted unanimously to stay another hour, and hear another Liberty speaker. The friends have concluded to raise $100 to employ an anti-slavery agent to go through the county to circulate tracts, papers, petitions, etc. and to lecture and wake up the people to the interests of Liberty. We have called another Convention, to meet in Corinth, week after next. Liberty is progressing" (Brown 206–207).

As already mentioned, fugitive slaves could have continued from Edinburgh along a road that eventually joined roads leading to Ogdensburg.

Other possible Underground Railroad stops in Saratoga County include the Van Aernew house, now on the property of the Saratoga Standard Breds farm in Malta, and the already-reported stories of former slave Dolly Smith operating a station out of the cellar of the Judge Reuben Walworth mansion in Saratoga Springs. Certainly there are readers out there who can supply more.

Chapter 32

STOPS IN
WARREN COUNTY

Warren County was a sparsely populated, backwoods county during much of the antebellum period. But this also made it vulnerable to reform, and it became noted for Temperance, because one of its most prominent citizens, Dr. Billy J. Clark, founded the nation's first Temperance society in Moreau, just south of its border in Saratoga County. Prominent among its earliest settlers were Quakers, who founded Glens Falls, the county's largest community. This marked the county with a strong anti-slavery sentiment, though it was slow to organize anti-slavery societies. Nevertheless, as Samuel Boyd wrote of Glens Falls, "the village became a station on the so-called underground railroad, which aided any fugitive slave to reach the Canadian border and freedom. Many of our prominent citizens knew all the ropes and helped pull them" (Boyd 8).

The first documented account of an anti-slavery society meeting in Warren County was on October 30, 1845, in Queensbury when the Queensbury Liberty Party Association was formed. Elected as officers were Charles Williams, Esq., president; George Hawley, Amos Wells, and L.R. Satterlee, vice-presidents; and A.T. Willson, secretary. The meeting's featured speaker was a Dr. Davis, who "started with the proposition that the 'peculiar institution' robs the people of the North both of their money and their liberty; and although, there were in attendance those who do not act with us, and some who have been hitherto hostile, yet not one will the dispute the proposition..." ("Glens Falls" 2).* Though this was the first anti-slavery meeting we have found on record, it is highly unlikely it was the first such meeting, for as early as 1840, the New York State Anti-Slavery Society lists A.G. Hawley of Warren County as a vice-president ("List of the Officers..." 200). Hawley is probably Glens Falls store-keeper A. Hawley, whose family was among the most prominent members of the city's

This Dr. Davis could not have been Dr. Sam Davis of Ballston, because he died in 1840.

First Presbyterian Church (Hawley), although it could have been his nephew George, who had the middle initial "G."

The most direct route to Canada for fugitive slaves traveling the western trunk in northern Saratoga County was along the roads that led to Ogdensburg. However, this was a rather arduous trek through the wilderness. Warren County, where there were sympathetic souls nearby, was a logical place to stop for runaways to refresh themselves. In South Glens Falls (which actually is Saratoga County), at least two homes have been rumored for many years to have been stops. One of them has some circumstantial support; the other has only a trapdoor. The more likely of the two is the house of the Rev. John Folsom, the guiding force behind the formation of the First Presbyterian Church in Glens Falls. The house, which is near the Hudson River and looks out on the great falls of Glens Falls, is reported to have had evidence of slave pens in the cellar. If this is true, it would mean that the Rev. Folsom not only had slaves there, but also kept them in shackles. This seems unlikely, especially considering that Folsom died 12 years after statewide emancipation and that his son-in-law, George G. Hawley, later became active in the abolitionist movement. In any case, the house was sold at Folsom's death in 1839 to Julius H. Rice. A lumberman, Rice bought the Gerrit Smith Eagles Nest property in Hamilton County, which also has been rumored to have been an Underground Railroad stop, from Cyrus Burnham, another lumberman and an abolitionist from Chestertown, who had bought it from Smith in 1849 (Hochschild 63). The other house is the Parks-Bentley Mansion, also along the river and the home of the Moreau Historical Society, which insists it was a stop on the Underground Railroad, though they have no evidence but the existence of a trapdoor leading to a crawl space under the first floor.

In Glens Falls, we already know about Dr. Joseph Stoddard, who lived on Exchange Street, and Rufus Boyd who lived on Park Street, from Samuel Boyd. Also, a Quaker station is said to have existed at Jay Street (Mason 44). Another possible Glens Falls station, and the only alleged station that as yet is known to still exist in the city, is the Dr. Hiram McNutt house on 12 Bacon Street, where a former owner claims to have found a hidden room that could be reached from a crawl space. McNutt was president of the Warren County Medical Society in 1863 and delegate to the state medical society, among whose founders was the region's most prominent abolitionist, Dr. Hiram Corliss of Washington County (Holden 304). Coincidentally, McNutt turns up as the original owner of another house with long-rumored claims to being an Underground Railroad stop in Warrensburg (*Warren County Book of Deeds* 192).

Northwest of Glens Falls is the village of Lake Luzerne, the residence of Henry Beach, which has not been identified, whom Lydia Frances Sherman identified as assisting with runaways. Legends of Underground Railroad activity also come out of the Gage Hill area there. A couple of houses make this claim, and, during the excavation of a barn at one of them, a room was found in the ground. Farther north, in the hamlet of Stony Creek, locals claim fugitive slaves were hidden in nearby caves (LaGrasse 24). Runaways guided by Mr. Fitch may have passed through Stony Creek and then headed north to Johnsburg or Chestertown. In Johnsburg on Garnet Lake Road lived the Wesleyan-Methodist minister Enos Putnam, whose story was told in Chapter One.

Chestertown, which was northeast of Johnsburg, on the other side of the Hud-

John W. Leggett, Chestertown, New York. (Courtesy of Craig Leggett.)

son, was the most abolitionized community in the county. Its leading abolitionist was the Quaker Joseph W. Leggett. His house, which family legend claims as a stop, is located a couple miles south of the village along Route 9, a little north of the Darrowsville Wesleyan-Methodist Church where the Rev. Thomas Baker harbored runaways. Leggett was the first person on record in the county to show a commitment to abolitionism, being listed as an agent for the New York City-based abolitionist newspaper, the *Emancipator*, in 1836 (*Emancipator* 18 August 1836).

In 1843, Leggett and his wife dined with the Rev. Abel Brown and Lewis Washington at Oliver Arnold's Temperance Tavern (Brown 178). He also met with Gerrit Smith in 1845 ("Gerrit Smith Anti-Slavery Tour" 130) and later appears as the president of the Warren County Liberty Party in 1846 ("Notice"). His son, Benjamin Franklin Leggett, as one might recall, wrote that he saw fugitive slaves at the house late at night ("History of the Chestertown Leggett Homestead"). An interesting coin-

NOTICE—A meeting of the Warren County Liberty Party Association will be held at the house of James I. Cameron, at Caldwell, on the 16th day of April inst., at 1 o'clock P. M., for the purpose of selecting some suitable person to receive the support of the Liberty Party voters of Warren county, at the ensuing election of Delegates to the State constitutional convention. By order of
                                   J. W. LEGGETT, President.
A. T. WILLSON, Sec'y.   apl 7

Announcement of Warren County Liberty Party meeting. (From *Glens Falls Republican*, 8 April 1846.)

cidence was the discovery among the papers at the Leggett House of a receipt for services from Dr. Hiram McNutt, the alleged Underground Railroad conductor.

In the village of Chestertown, Oliver Arnold's Temperance Tavern, where Abel Brown and Gerrit Smith refreshed themselves, remains as a private residence.* North of Chestertown is a stop not far from the county's border with Essex County along Route 9. Owned by the Walkup family, the Judge Tyrrell house was never suspected of being a stop on the Underground Railroad until owners made an excavation during remodeling of a porch that was built onto the house in the late 1850s. They discovered an entrance that could be reached only by way of a crawl space outside. In it, they found tin lanterns the size of a cup with handles and a floor that opened to a separate cellar and the room described in the introduction to Part Two. Judge Tyrrell, one may recall, was mentioned by Gerrit Smith during his tour of the Adirondacks in 1845 as a supporter of abolition.

Another stop not far from the Tyrrell house was in the extinct community of Igerna. There the abandoned Perry House, one of the county's oldest existing buildings, stands in the foreground of a thickly forested Adirondack peak. A former stagecoach stop, area residents claim it was a stop on the Underground Railroad. They also claim that a black mountain man named Mr. Cutler built a barn and cabin on Ethan Mountain, which sits behind the house, a couple of miles away. Cutler, the legend claims, was joined by fugitive slaves who sometimes stayed in the area for extended periods. What adds to the legend is that a military road passed through Igerna and went all the way to Ogdensburg ("Chester to Canton Road" 9–10). It may have been the route used by the Van Pelt family in Glens Falls to make their escape (Fish interview).

The identity of Cutler is unknown; what is known is that he settled on the mountain during the years approaching the Civil War (Ibid.). It is possible, however, that

*Arnold was listed as a vice-president of the state anti-slavery society, representing Warren County, in 1841 ("Annual Meeting" 186).

Perry House, Igerna, Warren County, New York. (Photograph by the author.)

Remnants of Mr. Cutler's cabin, Town of Chester, Warren County, New York. (Photograph by the author.)

he was a black laborer from Albany named Benjamin Cutler, who in 1845 was a member of the city's Liberty Party Vigilance Committee and who was identified by William Henry Johnson of Albany as an Underground Railroad agent. Benjamin Cutler first appears in the Albany City Directory in 1825 and is listed as a man of color. However, after 1832, the designation of color is no longer applied to him. He also could have been John Cutler, a man of color who first appears in the Albany City Directory in 1852. The second Cutler was a barber who listed the same residence as Benjamin Cutler in 1854, but is no longer designated as a man of color and has changed his name from Cutler to Cutter. At first glance, it might appear that John Cutler and John Cutter were different men. But when one factors in the unusualness of the name Cutter, the fact that both Cutter and Cutler were barbers, and that Cutter moved into the residence of Benjamin Cutler, who also apparently made an effort to conceal his race, it seems likely that Cutler and Cutter were one and the same. Both men disappeared from the Albany City Directory after 1855 (*Albany City Directories 1825–1856*), so it is possible that it is one of these Cutlers who moved to Igerna and became the man of legend.

The remnants of Cutler's cabin, looking much like those of Mr. Fitch's cabin, remain today in the middle of a thickly wooded area on Ethan Mountain, as can be testified to by this author, who was taken there by local residents Martin Fish and Art Perryman in 1999.

Chapter 33

STOPS IN ESSEX
AND FRANKLIN COUNTIES

Essex and Franklin counties are the most mountainous sections in New York State and provide some of its most scenic vistas. God's country, to paraphrase John Brown. A place where fugitive slaves, most likely, would be free from the worry of slave catchers. The problem was that it posed other obstacles, as the hopeful farmers at Timbucto discovered—how to survive. Few fugitive slaves settled in this region, and the number who passed through was probably small as well. But there were some, and most of those were probably drawn by the stir surrounding Gerrit Smith's land scheme.

A good place to start piecing together the area's Underground Railroad network is the report of Jermain Loguen after his visit to the Adirondacks to enlist supporters for Smith's land grantees. Loguen named the following individuals as persons from whom grantees could seek assistance: from Essex County, Jesse Gay and Alfred S. Spooner in Elizabethtown; Uriah Mihills in Keene; J. Tobey, Jr., in Jay; Wendell Lansing in Wilmington; and William M. Flack in AuSable Forks (Clinton County); from Franklin County, the Merill family in Merillville, and Rensselaer Bigelow in Malone ("Gerrit Smith's Land" 1).

In Essex County, there was a large county anti-slavery society and societies in Jay, Moriah, Ticonderoga, and Crown Point. An emergency meeting that pledged to aid fugitive slaves in opposition to the Fugitive Slave Law of 1850 was held in Jay a couple of weeks after the law's enactment. But except for the John Brown home outside Lake Placid, now a state museum, the only locality in the county this author has found that makes claims for Underground Railroad stops is Schroon Lake. A short distance north of the village is a large white house with a stone foundation at the corner of Routes 9 & 74, and another a little farther north on the same side of Route 9, which the local historical society claims were part of the Underground Railroad.

Rumors and hearsay tell of this but nothing more substantial exists.

One location that researchers are almost certain was a stop and which some believe still exists is the Wendell Lansing farm in Wilmington. A founder of the Washington County Anti-Slavery Society in 1834, the region's first such society, Lansing came to Keeseville and started the *Essex County Republican* in 1839. In 1846, he left the newspaper business for eight years to devote his time to his farm in Wilmington. It was there, his 1887 obituary stated, that his "homestead on the hill was one of the depots of the famous 'Underground Railroad' for escaped slaves ... [and] a headquarters for colored men and abolition lecturers" ("The Late Wendell Lansing" 2–3). As of this writing, area researcher Don Papson is trying to track it down.

Meeting in Jay.

At a meeting of the citizens of Jay, Keene, North Elba, St Armand and Wilmington at the Baptist Church, in Jay, Oct 16th, 1850 for the purpose of expressing their views of the recent acts of Congress in relation to the slave question, James Kimball, Esq. was chosen Chairman and E P Newell and N C Boynton Secretary. After the reading of the "fugitive slave law" and some preliminary remarks, the following persons were appointed as committee on Resolutions to wit :

from Jay, Daniel Blish, Hiram Newell, " Wilmington, Wendell Lansing, Rogers Bikok ; Keene, U D Mihills, Joseph Hillman ; North Elba, Iddo Osgood, Roswell Thompson ; St Armand, D C Skiff, E G Titus.

Report of Fugitive Slave Law meeting in Jay, Essex County, New York. (From *Keeseville Republican*, 26 October 1850.)

Timbucto might appear to some to have been a haven for fugitive slaves. However, this was not the case, according to Amy Godine, a writer who has done extensive research on the colony. While some grantees were fugitive slaves, Godine said that it wasn't Smith's intention to seek runaways for grants. In other words, Timbucto was not what might be described as a terminal, though there is little doubt that on occasion John Brown did aid some fugitive slaves while living in North Elba.

In Franklin County, at least three homes may have been stops. The evidence for the Jabez Parkhurst residence in Fort Covington, just south of the Canadian border, is by far the most compelling. His involvement in abolitionism when combined with the local testimony of his activities as a conductor, revealed in Seaver's book and related in Chapter One, present an extremely convincing case. A lawyer, Parkhurst was very active in anti-slavery meetings. He attended the organizational meeting of the St. Lawrence County society in 1837 and the important regional meeting of the state society in Albany in 1838. He was president of the Franklin County society and a vice-president of the state society. From the inception of the Liberty Party he was a strong supporter and is listed as an agent for the *Albany Patriot*. In 1846 he was a Liberty Party candidate for Congress, and in 1847 he participated at a meeting in Union Village with Noadiah Moore, which named him and Moore as Liberty Party candidates for the state supreme court that year.*

There also is the Major Dimick home on the road between Malone and Fort

---

*In his book, The Abolitionists, Gerald Sorin lists Parkhurst as one of the 100 most prominent abolitionists in New York State, quite a distinction considering that it includes New York City, where a number of the nation's most prominent abolitionists lived.

Wendell Lansing (From Duane Hamilton Hurd, "History of the Champlain Valleys and Adirondacks," *Essex County Republican Annual for the Year 1891*, W. Lansing and Son.)

Covington—Dimick being named by Seaver as an agent—and the Harison house on Webster Street in Malone. Bill Burns, current owner of the Harison house, said that the house's former owners told him that the remnants of shackles left by runaway slaves were found in the house's basement. The house is across the street from the site of the home of the Rev. Ashbel Parmalee, pastor of the Malone Congregational Church, whose lore claims it harbored fugitive slaves and was visited by slavecatchers (Whitaker).

While Parmalee was sympathetic to the cause of blacks, his mentor being the the Rev. Lemuel Haynes, he also was an ardent supporter of the Colonization Society, as least as late as 1838. We know this because he attended the early organizational meeting of the county's anti-slavery society and confronted its organizer, Thomas Canfield, on the issue. In any case, Parmalee's successor as pastor in 1845, Silas Woodruff, also was active in abolitionist meetings, and the story that a tunnel led from the church to other locations in the village's business section has steadfastly remained part of the church's folklore.

In 1974, an excavation of an underground room may have provided some corroboration to the stories of tunnels in Malone. The room was found by workers during construction at the Malone Junior High. It had walls of heavy slab stone construction and was completely sealed without any sign of a door. It measured six feet by 12 feet and was eight feet high with an arched brick roof. The floor was four feet beneath the surface of the ground. In addition to the tunnel leading from the Congregational Church, some claim another tunnel led from the Harison house to a station at Coolidge Court. From there, it was believed to have proceeded to the present site of the Armory on Main Street, the former site of Foote's Tavern. This tunnel would have passed near the underground room. Unfortunately, the room was demolished when a new wing was constructed for the school (Russell).

Another location in the county named in a 1968 article was the Sawdon place in Constable, which Canfield said had the county's most active society in 1838. The article stated that Constable was a stop on the way to Huntingdon, Canada, and said it was station number 206 in a network of stations that apparently began in the South. This is only time this author has come across any reference to the numbering of stations. However, the article does not supply a reference. Such numbering would imply a high level of organization. It is not known if the Sawdon house still exists.

Other fugitive slave activity in the county is reported in Blacksville, the community founded by Willis Augustus Hodges, and in Bloomingdale, which is not far from Saranac Lake. According to Frederick Seaver, three fugitive slaves settled in

Major Dimick House, Franklin County, New York. (Courtesy of Debbie Manor.)

Bloomingdale, and one of them, John Thomas, was located by his former master. Slave catchers actually were sent to the Adirondacks to recover him but turned back when warned that the locals in Bloomingdale were prepared for a fight to the death (Seaver 644).

Chapter 34

STOPS IN
ST. LAWRENCE COUNTY

St. Lawrence County was nearly untouched by slavery and practically devoid of persons of color. For example, the 1810 census showed only five slaves in the county, and the 1820 census showed eight; the largest total of blacks in the county during the antebellum period was 60 in 1830. A largely rural county, its view of the slavery question was almost entirely influenced by the position of its churches. Settled later than the other counties, it was fertile ground for the Wesleyan-Methodist Church, and many of that denomination's earliest churches were organized here. The county is important to a consideration of northern New York's Underground Railroad because it represented a final destination before entering Canada for many slaves who found themselves in such counties as Warren, Essex, Franklin, and even Clinton County, the latter especially after the completion in 1850 of the Northern Ogdensburg Railroad that ran from Rouses Point to Ogdensburg.

Coming from northeastern New York, runaway slaves likely would have come either from Clinton or Franklin counties, possibly on or along the route of the Northern Ogdensburg railroad. This would have taken them directly through Brasher Falls, where lawyer Calvin T. Hurlburd moved and built his house around 1841 (Hough 271). The son of the town supervisor of Stockholm, Hurlburd was one of the county's most prominent men during the antebellum period and was elected to the state legislature that same year. A ruling elder in the Presbyterian Church, he championed the cause of moral and educational reform. He joined the Republican Party at its formation, and in 1863 he was elected to Congress, where his first speech was in support of the Emancipation Proclamation (Curtis 259; Hough 477). With a biography like that, it's not surprising that his house is alleged to have been a stop on the Underground Railroad. The current owner of the house, Patrick McGreevy, a retired schoolteacher, said that an addition to the cellar was built to hide fugitive slaves (Savage).

Underground Railroad Stops in
the Western Adirondacks

(Map by the author.)

Heading west from Brasher Falls toward Canada, the runaway slave could have found a temperance tavern and grocery, about four miles southeast of Waddington and about five miles north of the route of the Northern Ogdensburg Railroad (Durant 282). It was owned by Anson Chamberlain and later by his son, Methodist minister Ralph Chamberlain, whose granddaughter, Helen Chamberlain, said that he was a conductor (*Rural News*). According to former Waddington town historian, Pauline Tedford, the Chamberlains hid runaways on the third floor in closets under the eaves.

The Chamberlain house could have been a jumping off point to a final destination before reaching Canada. One possibility was the Ogden Island home of the wealthy Ogdens, the founders of Waddington. The house of this family, who for a time owned slaves, included mysterious underground chambers whose purpose was unknown but which gave rise to speculation about their use for the Underground Railroad. This may have some substance, considering the reports of slavehunters prowling the St. Lawrence riverboats. Another possible location along the river was the Meyers home on Point Rockaway. According to Tedford, slaves were hidden in a small stone building on the edge of the estate to await boats to take them across to Ontario; one local told her that children would take soup down to the fugitive slaves (Terpin).

Valera Bickelhaupt, Hammond town historian, said that oral tradition claims

Hurlburd House, St. Lawrence County, New York, an alleged stop on the Underground Railroad. (From Samuel W. Durant, *History of St. Lawrence County*, Philadelphia: L.H. Everts and Co., 1878.)

Chamberlain House, St. Lawrence County, New York, an alleged stop on the Underground Railroad. (Courtesy of Jane Layo, Town of Waddington historian, from Pauline Tedford and Tom Fife, *Waddington, St. Lawrence County, N.Y.: A Look at Our Past*, Town of Waddington, 1976.)

Ogden House, an alleged Underground Railroad stop in Waddington, St. Lawrence County, New York. (Courtesy of Jane Layo, Town of Waddington historian, from Pauline Tedford and Tom Fife, *Waddington, St. Lawrence County, N.Y.: A Look at Our Past*, Town of Waddington, 1976.)

fugitive slaves sometimes lived for periods on some of the many uninhabited islands in the St. Lawrence, subsisting on hunting and farming (Bickelhaupt letter).

Other locations near this line alleged to have aided runaways were the Norman Dayton house in Canton, noted for its cupola, a square-shaped architectural feature. Dayton raised horses and traveled to Alexandria, Virginia to sell them. On occasion he would return home in the company of a fugitive slave ("Old Canton and the Underground Railway"). Also, the Bucks Bridge Methodist Episcopal Church, whose pastor and founder, the Rev. John Byington, was a devoted abolitionist, is believed to have been a stop—until locals discovered this and forced Byington to move to Morley, where he founded another church (Terpin).

Runaways coming along the Old Military Road out of Warren County, or the road from Edinburgh in Saratoga County, may have come upon the John Johnson house on the Somerville-Gouverneur Road. One night, one of his children got up for a drink of water and went downstairs to find three black men lying in front of the fireplace, the first black men he had ever seen. Terrified, he fled to his father and mother who told him there was nothing to fear, but that he should never divulge what he had seen [as revealed by one of Johnson's sons] (Corbin 105). Johnson, who moved to Gouverneur in 1821, was one of the trustees of the county's first Methodist Church erected at Somerville in 1846. Referred to as a "Nigger stealer," "he [would make] a night's drive always returning before the household was up in the morning, and but an accident, none but the faithful mother would have had knowledge either of the fact or cause of his absence [route went through Rossie to Hammond]" (Laponsee).

Two houses in South Hammond, enroute to the St. Lawrence River, are alleged to have been stops. The Webster house on Route 37 is supposed to have contained a notebook in the attic that had entries referring to the Underground Railroad, but it has since been misplaced (Terpin). The Cushman house on Rock Island Road has very compelling evidence of being a stop. Its owner, Myron Cushman, was a tailor who moved to the town of Gouverneur in 1840 and was the first Liberty Party voter in the town (Terpin). According to the local history books, "he was one of the old directors and conductors of the Underground Railroad, the dividends of which were the keeping of a free table for all runaway slaves and Abolition lecturers, for many years" (Corbin 55).

John Johnson, Gouverneur, New York (From *Centennial Souvenir History of Gouveneur, Rossie, Fowler, Hammonds, Edwards, DeKalb*, Jay S. Corbin, compiler, Watertown, N.Y.: Hungerford-Holbrook Co., 1905.)

Myron Cushman, South Hammond, New York (From *Centennial Souvenir History of Gouveneur, Rossie, Fowler, Hammonds, Edwards, DeKalb*, Jay S. Corbin, compiler, Watertown, N.Y.: Hungerford-Holbrook Co., 1905.)

The last possible stop along a direct line in the Underground Railroad that led from Gouverneur was the Chapman house in Morristown, which sits alongside the St. Lawrence River (Terpin). Augustus Chapman moved to Morristown in 1823 and went into the real estate business. He also began to export goods to Canada. By 1830, his business interests had prospered so that he was able to buy a bank in Ohio; and in 1854, he established the Oswegatchie Bank in Ogdensburg. Chapman also had interests in an insurance company, a steamboat company, a couple of railroads, and another bank in Oswego, as well as a role in the organization of the American Express Company. A vestryman of the Presbyterian Church, he was a Whig and later upon its formation, a Republican (Durant 376). His political affiliations, his religious devotion, and his business connections suggest that the rumors of his participation in the Underground Railroad may have some basis.

Research into the Underground Railroad in St. Lawrence County is still in its early stages. Though there were few black colonies in the immediate vicinity of the St. Lawrence River, the county's easy access to Canada make it a likely alternate route, and it is hoped this information will be useful for those who wish to unravel the mysteries of its participants and those forgotten stories awaiting discovery.

Appendix I

Delegates to the Organizational Meeting of the New York State Anti-Slavery Society, Utica, October 21, 1835*

Adams, E. C.
Adams, J. W.
Addington, S. H.
Alexander, R.
Alexander, W.
Anderson, P. A.
Andrews, F.W.
Andrews, J.
Andrews, J. M.
Armstrong, W.B.
Arthur, Rev. W.
Atwater, M.
Avery, C.
Avery, G. A.
Avery, O. F.
Avery, Rev. C.
Avery, Rev. I. F.
Avery, W.
Bacon, R.
Bailey, M. S.
Bailey, S. J.
Baker, E.

Baker, T. C.
Barber, A. D.
Barbour, A. D.
Barnes, E.
Barnes, H. P.
Bascom, C.
Basset, B.
Beadle, C. R.
Beckwith, S. M.
Beebee, A.
Beebee, S. J. M.
Beebee, T.
Beebee, W. M.
Beeman, A. G.
Beeman, Rev. S.
Benham, J. M.
Berrien, H.
Bingham, Dr. D.
Bingham, H.
Blackford, W. H.
Blair, Dr. A.
Bliss, Dr. S.

Bliss, L.
Bliss, S.
Blodgett, Rev. H.
Bloss, J.
Blossom, T.
Bowen, I.
Bradford, S. S.
Bradley, Esq., J.
Brayton M.,
Brayton, G.
Brewster, Hon. H.
Bridges, M.
Bright, T.
Brooks, Rev. A. P.
Brown, O. C.
Brown, R.
Browson, I. C.
Bryant, S.
Buchanan, W.
Buckmaster, T. O.
Bunce, J.
Burnell, J. C.

Burnett, Dr. M.
Burr, A. I.
Burr, W.
Burrows, D.
Bush, C.P.
Bush, O. N.
Bushnell, L.
Butler, B.
Butler, B.
Butler, G.
Butler, G.
Buxton, W.
Cadwell, E.
Campbell, E .
Canfield, E.
Canfield, J. A.
Carver, S.
Cassem, J. M.
Caulkins, C.
Cherry, P.
Childs, Rev. E.
Childs, Rev. W.

*This list of 590 participants was taken at Peterboro, the day after the convention met in Utica where it was broken up by a mob. It is believed that as many as 1,000 anti-slavery supporters were in attendance on the first day.

237

Childs, S. D.
Clapp, Rev. R.
Clapp, Rev. R.
Clark, A. H.
Clark, C. A.
Clark, Dr. W.A.
Clark, E.
Clark, E.
Clark, J.
Clark, J.
Clark, O.
Clark, Rev. D
Clark, W.
Clark, W. M.
Clark, W. M.
Cobb, N.
Cobb, N.
Cole, H. S.
Cole, S.
Coleman, A. E.
Collum, C. R.
Colver, Rev. N.
Conklin, O. P.
Cook, Dr. C.
Copland, Jr., J.
Corey, F.D.
Corliss, Dr. H.
Cornell, S.
Cotton, W.
Cragin, J.
Crandall, Rev. J. L.
Crane, E. B.
Crane, H.
Crane, Jr, I.
Crane, Rev. A.
Crocker, C.
Crouch, D.
Cunningham, R.
Dana, F.
Davidson, G.
Davis, S.
Davis, T.
Dean, Jr., G.
Debnam, R.
Deforest, A. R.
Delong, J. C.
Demming, Rev. R. R.
Dewey, W.
Diamond, L. M.
Dickinson, G. L.
Dixon, J. R.
Dodge, J.
Dohah, G.
Doolittle, J. I.
Dorr, W. S.
Dorrence, G.
Dwight, G. A,

Eddy, E.
Eddy, H.
Elder, Jr., W.
Ellicott, S.
Ellinwood, R.
Elmer, H.
Elmer, H.
Ennis, Rev. A.
Erving, W.
Everts, W.
Fairchild, Rev. E.
Farwell, W.
Farwell, W.
Fish, B.
Fisher, S.
Fitch, J. S.
Flay, Sr. M.
Flint, A.
Flint, P.
Foot, esq., J.
Foot, H.
Foot, H.
Foot, Rev. H.
Foote, C. C.
Forest, Rev. R. De
Forset, D.
Foster, C.
Foster, D.
Foster, G. D.
Foster, R. I.
Foster, Rev. I.
Fox, J. W.
Frank, Dr. A.
Freeman, A.
Frissett, A.
Frost, Rev. J.
Fuller, Rev. W.
Fulton, Rev. I. I.
Gale, W. S.
Galusha, E. B.
Galusha, M.
Gates, W.
Gates, W.
Gaylord, W. M.
Gemel, G.
George, A.
Gilbert, A.
Gilbert, W.
Gillet, J. C.
Gillett, J. W.
Gilliam, C. W.
Gilman, J.W.
Gionard, E.
Gloucester, J.
Goit, W.
Goodrich, Rev. C.E.
Gould, A.

Gould, R.
Gould, W. F.
Grant, C.
Grant, L.
Gray, A.
Gray, F. A.
Gray, F. A.
Gray, W. H.
Green, Jr., W.
Green, R.
Green, Rev. B.
Green, Rev. G.
Gregory, S. H.
Grey, Rev J.
Gridley, Rev. S. H.
Griffin, E.
Griffin, J. F.
Griffin, J. S.
Griffith, Rev. J.
Gross, G.
Groves, B. S.
Groves, Rev. J. B.
Guest, J. P.
Guest, J. P.
Gunn, L. C.
Guy, A.
Had, Rev. A. G.
Hadley, A. K.
Hadley, W. H.
Hall, E.
Hamblin, W. D.
Hamilton, S.
Hammell, W.
Hammond, H. L.
Harrison, Rev. M.
Hart, Rev. J. A.
Hathaway, J. C.
Hathaway, S. R.
Havens, O. H.
Havens, O. H.
Hawley, Rev. S.
Hays, G.
Headly, I. T.
Herrick, E.
Higby, E. M
Higgins, J. W.
Hinsdale, A.K.
Hitchcock, A.
Holbrook, D. A.
Holbrook, Dr. A.
Holcomb, E.
Holdrige, W. A.
Holister, D.
Hollister, A. J.
Hollister, G. A.
Hotchkiss, A.
Hough, S. P.

How, F. S.
Howell, W.
Hunt, A.
Hunt, S.
Ingersol, Rev. A
Ingersol, Rev. J.
Iverson, Jr., H.
Jackson, J. C.
Jackson, R.
James, T.
Jones, J. F.
Jones, Rev.
Judd, Dr. E.
Judd, J. S.
Judson, C.
Keep, J.
Kellogg, Dr. A. H.
Kellogg, J. G.
Kellogg, L.
Kellogg, L. S.
Kellogg, P.V.
Kellogg, Rev. H. H.
Kellogg, S.
Kellogg, T.
Kendall, O.
Kenmore, C. H.
Kennedy, D.
Ketchum, J.
Ketchum, J. M.
Knowled, Rev. C.J.
Kingsbury, Esq., A.
Laden, J.
Lambert, E. A.
Lamson, L.
LaRow, G. L.
Lathrop, A.C.
Lattimore, S. J.
Lawrence, L.
Lawson, G.
Leavitt, Rev. J.
Lee, E.
Leland, M. W.
Lewis, E.
Lewis, E.
Lewis, Esq., E.
Lightbody, S.
Loomis, Dr. E.
Loomis, H. G.
Loomis, Z.
Lord, C. B.
Losey, M. S.
Lovell, V.
Lovell, V. S.
Lowring, M.
Lyman, I. B.
Lyman, J. T.
Lyman, R.

Lyman, S.
Lynus, David
Mann, J.
Marsh, E.
Marsh, E. A.
Marsh, Mr.
Marsh, P. W.
Marsh, S.
Marshall, C.
Marshall, E. F.
Marshall, J. T.
Martin, J.
Martin, Rev. J. H.
Martin, T. M.
Marvin, N.
Mattoon, C. N.
McAll, B.
McCord, J. P.
McFarland, R.
McFarland, T.
McKellur, A.
McLane, C.
McViccar, J.
Meade, S.
Merrell, Rev. E. H.
Metcalf, J.
Miller, Esq., G.M.
Miller, G.
Miller, N.
Miller, T.
Miller, W. G.
Mills, I.
Mills, Rev. A.
Mitchell, C. C.
Miter, J. I.
Moore, E.
Moore, L. M.
Morse, W.
Mosher, A.
Mosher, C.
Mosher, J.
Myrick, Rev. L.
Nash, H.
Needham, G.
Neely, A.
Newland, H.
Nichols, S. S.
Northrop, A.
Northrop, Gen. J. A
Northrup, J.A.
Norton, A.
Norton, I.
Norton, Jr., I.
Nuby, A.
Orvis, Esq., Rev. S.
Palmer, R. C.
Palmer, R. R.

Parker, J.
Parker, J. H.
Parker, J. M.
Parker, O. F.
Parker, Rev. O.
Parmele, S.
Parmelee, C. F.
Parmelee, Jr., C. S.
Parmelee, Rev. A.
Patterson, E.
Payson, E. H.
Pecenix, H.
Perine, S. M.
Perry, Dr. D.
Perry, Mr.
Peters, R.S.
Pettibone, P.
Pettibone, Rev. I.
Phoenix, S. F.
Pitts, Dr. T.
Pixley, I.
Platt, I. S.
Platt, L.
Pocock, G.
Pond, L.
Pool, A. A.
Pool, Rev. E. E.
Porter, F. D.
Powel, J.
Powell, Rev. T.
Powell, T.
Pratt, J. W.
Pratt, R.
Prentiss, J. G.
Prentiss, M.
Prescott, 0.
Prescott, J.
Prescott, Mr.
Prince, L.
Prince, L.
Ramis, C.
Randall, H.
Ransom, W. B.
Rawson, P.
Rawson, S. A.
Rawson, S. A.
Rawson, W. B.
Raymand, A.
Reed, J. A.
Reid, W. W.
Reynolds, E.
Rice, Dr. F.
Rising, L. P.
Roberts, Esq., S. B.
Roberts, R.
Robinson, A.
Robinson, H. N.

Robinson, J. F.
Robinson, Rev. R.
Rogers, E.
Rogers, W. L.
Root, C.
Roundy, T.
Rowe, E.
Ruggles, D.
Rumsey, A. B.
Sage, O.
Savage, A. S.
Savage, K.
Savage, Rev. A.
Savage, W. J.
Sawtell, S.
Sayre, B.
Sayre, J.
Scofield, A.
Scovill, J. F.
Sears, E.
Sedgwick, Rev. A.
Seymour, A.
Seymour, A.
Seymour, R.
Seymour, R.
Shapley, D.
Shapley, N.
Shaw, Rev. J. B.
Shepard, M. L.
Sherman, G.
Sherman, H. B.
Sherrill, Dr. N.
Shipherd, Rev. F.
Sibley, L. W.
Skinner, L. A,
Skinner, S. H.
Skinner. J.
Sleeper, Esq., R.
Smell, R.W.
Smith, A. B.
Smith, A. B.
Smith, Dr. J.W.
Smith, G. K.
Smith, H.
Smith, L.
Smith, N.
Smith, Rev S. S.
Smith, Rev. C.
Smith, Rev. M.
Smith,W.
Snow, B.
Snyder, J.
Snyder, Rev. H.
Southworth, F.
Spalding, Rev. G.
Spear, S.
Spencer, E. M. S.

Spencer, F. A.
Spoor, Rev. J. W.
St. George, G.
St. Johns, W. P.
Stanford, E.
Stanley, S.
Stedman G.
Stevens, A. H.
Stevens, O.
Stevenson, T.
Stewart, A.
Stewart, Dr. S. W.
Stillson, E.
Stone, O.
Storrs, S.
Strong, E.
Swift, R.C.
Talman, J.
Tappan, L.
Temple, J. F.
Thomas, A.
Thomas, B.W.
Thomas, D.
Thomas, J.
Thomas, R. C.
Thomas, T.
Thompson, Esq., D.
Thompson, Jr., L.
Thompson, S.
Thurber, I.
Thurber, P.
Tibbitts, J.
Tibbitts, W. K.
Tompkins, Rev. W. B
Towers, W.
Townsend, Esq., J.
Townsend, Jr., J.
Trotter, J. T.
Tryon, J.
Tucker, H. D.
Tucker, M.
Tucker, Rev. M.
Turner, F. E.
Tyler, R.
Van Dresser, R.
Van Valkenberg, D.
Vanderheyden, J.
Vannerman, D. C.
Vorhis, S.V.
Wait, John
Waldo, G.
Waldo, J. H.
Walker, C. I.
Walker, E.
Walker, R.
Waod, J.
Ward, E. O.

Ward, F. B.	Wattles, J. O.	White, G. H.	Wood, J.
Ward, H. P.	Weaver, L.	White, N.	Wood, J.
Ward, J. J.	Wells, A.	Whittelsey, C.	Wood, J. W.
Ward, O.	Wells, J.	Wilbour, D. C.	Woodworth, F. C.
Warner, H.	Wells, Rev., S.	Wilcox, M.	Worcey, W. H.
Warner, J. E.	Wetmore, Rev. O.	Wilcox, Rev. L.	Worden, O. N.
Warner, Rev. W.	Whaley, S.	Williams, A.	Wright, F.
Warriner, A.	Wheeler, Rev. E.	Williams, R. G.	Wright, Jr., E.
Waterbury, C.	Wheeler, Rev. W.	Wilson, W. Z.	Yates, Esq., W.
Watson, Esq., T. B.	White, B. D.	Wolcott, C. D.	

Delegates from Other States

Massachusetts

Col. George H. Leavitt
Rev. George Storrs
Seth Strong, Esq.

Ohio

Phileman Bliss
Moses Breck
Albert Bliss
Hart Leavitt

Appendix II

ANTI-SLAVERY SOCIETIES IN NORTH-EASTERN NEW YORK (BEFORE 1840)*

Abbreviations: FOM = Friend of Man; E = Emancipator

Society	Date of Org'n	Newspaper Ref.	Additional Info
Clinton (Beekmantown)	4/37	FOM 7/26/37	at Beekmantown
Essex	7/37	FOM 8/9/37	at Westport
Franklin	10/36	FOM 11/17/37	orgd by N. Colver
Schenectady	4/38	FOM 5/2/38	by Stewart & Chaplin
Adamsville (Wash Co)	6/37	FOM 7/5/37	by Weld w/45 members
Albany	4/35	E 5/19/35	Phelps & Thompson w/200 mbrs
Albany Young Men's	2/38	FOM 1/24/38	
Albany City (1839)			
Ballston Spa		FOM 9/36/38	
Bangor (Franklin Co)	1/38	FOM 2/28/38	by Thomas Canfield
Champlain Ladies		FOM 11/20/39	raised money for state society
Charleston	6/38	FOM 6/6/38	by J.G. Duryee
Chesterfield (Clinton)		FOM 9/27/36	
Constable		FOM 2/28/38	most active in Franklin County
Crown Pt (Essex)	6/39	FOM 7/24/39	opposition here
East Nassau (Rensselaer)		FOM 9/12/39	visited by A. Judson
Fort Ann	8/35	E 10/20/35	by Weld
Galway	6/38	FOM 6/6/38	by J. Duryee w/35 mbrs
Gouverneur	10/38	FOM 6/19/39	139 mbrs in June '39
Greenbush (Rensselaer)	4/35	E 6/19/35	by Phelps & Thompson
Greenfield	6/38	FOM 7/18/38	orgd w/84 members
Greenwich (Wash Co)	7/35	E 8/35	known as Union Village A-S Soc.
Hartford		FOM 9/21/ 36	Weld here June, 60 new mbrs
Jackson (Washington)		FOM 9/27/38	
Jay (Essex)	3/37	FOM 6/1037	by Watson w/80 mbrs
Keeseville		FOM 7/26/37	

*From an Appendix of The History of the New York State Anti-Slavery Society by Alice Henderson, Ph.D. dissertation, University of Michigan, 1963; four additional entries from other sources.

Lundy Society (Albany)	1833		female, colored society
Malone		FOM 2/28/38	
Milton (Saratoga)	6/38		by Duryee w/100 mbrs
Moira (Franklin)	1/38	FOM 2/28/38	
Moriah (Essex)	10/36	FOM 11/3/36	by Pritchett
Parishville (St. Lawrence)	10/37	FOM 8/8/38	
Peru (Clinton)		FOM 7/26/37	
Peru Female	12/35	*Plattsburgh Republican* 1/38	
Petersburg (Rensselaer)		FOM 3/1/37	
Plattsburgh	11/37	FOM 12/6/37	by G.R. Parburt, 60 mbrs
Quaker Springs (Saratoga)	3/36	E 4/36	
Rensselaerville		FOM 4/25/38	by Judson, 90 mbrs
St. Lawrence County	8/37	FOM 10/4/37	by Stewart & Chaplin
Ticonderoga	3/37	E 3/16/37	by Colver & Miner, 204 mbrs
Troy	4/35	E 5/19/35	150 members
W. Chateaugay (Franklin)	3/36	FOM 2/28/38	
W. Granville (Wash Co)	6/36	FOM 7/21/36	78 members
W. Peru	4/37	FOM 4/26/37	by Pritchett
Washington County	11/34	*The Liberator* 1/36	

Appendix III

FUGITIVES FROM SLAVERY WHO PASSED THROUGH ALBANY; A LIST COMPILED BY PAUL AND MARY LIZ STEWART*

The following fugitives from slavery passed through Albany's Capital Region on their way to Canada or other locations, or in some cases took up residence there. Some of the names and stories are taken from the *Memoir of Rev. Abel Brown* by C. S. Brown (1849), some from the papers of Wilbur Siebert, and some from articles by others using various resources. Some were contributed by email from other researchers on the Underground Railroad. This list is an ongoing project by Paul and Mary Liz Stewart to identify fugitives from slavery who passed through the Capital Region.

Mr. Moses Viney, along with a friend, took his freedom by flight on Easter morning 1840 from Maryland. He came through the Albany area, spent time in Troy, and finally settled in Schenectady. He came to be a first-rate coachman and owner of his own coach taxi service. Originally encountered by us in *Tales of Old Schenectady* by Larry Hart (1975), this is a somewhat well-known local story. Mr. Viney worked for many years as the driver of Eliphalet Nott, the long time president of Union College in Schenectady.

Mr. Charles Nalle took up residence first in Sand Lake, then Troy, but was betrayed by someone he trusted, causing his capture. The intervention of perhaps a hundred people allowed his second escape. His slave master was

Paul and Mary Liz Stewart are co-founders of the Underground Railroad History Project in Albany, New York, which researches, identifies, celebrates and works to preserve the Underground Railroad story in the Capital Region. The group provides a walking tour of downtown Albany's Underground Railroad story and organizes an annual conference. Go to their web site at www.ugrworkshop.com for an updated list of "Fugitives from Slavery Who Passed Through Albany."

his own half-brother. This is a widely known story thanks to its inclusion in Sarah Bradford's *Harriet Tubman: The Moses of Her People*.

Mr. Moses Roper escaped from slavery in Savannah, Georgia. He traveled six days as a steward on the ship *Fox* and arrived at New York City. He continued by boat to Poughkeepsie and then by land to Albany. He later traveled to England to assure his freedom. The story is from the *Memoir of Rev. Abel Brown* and originally appeared in *The Tocsin of Liberty*, the abolitionist newspaper published from Albany in 1842. It also appears in the papers of Wilbur Siebert.

Mr. Jo Norton traveled from the South to Albany but, upon hearing that many others who escaped from his area had been captured, went to western New York. This story appears in papers of Wilbur Siebert and is cited from materials of Eber Pettit.

Miss Harriet Jacobs was repeatedly lied to and abused by her master. She escaped and hid in a crawl space in her free grandmother's house for seven years. She finally escaped north but continued to be pursued. She came to the Albany area while working as the caretaker of a wealthy woman's child. Harriet Jacobs's autobiography was entitled *Incidents in the Life of a Slave Girl*.

William and Catherine Harris and their child escaped slavery in South Carolina. Their journey took them through Philadelphia, New York, and Albany. They met misfortune somewhere along the Erie Canal when their child was drowned, and we don't know if they reached Canada. This story was originally published in a Syracuse paper of the period, the *Syracuse Tribune*, October 26, 1850.

Mr. Lewis Washington, after his escape from slavery, took up the cause of abolition and preached around the region and in New England. He also spent time in Albany, Troy, and in Peterboro. He is mentioned in detail in the *Memoir of Rev. Abel Brown*.

Harriet Tubman was a fugitive slave and activist who led many other slaves to freedom. She continued her work despite a bounty on her head for her work. She did this in spite of seizures that plagued her because of having been struck on the head by a slave overseer as a child. She visited Troy and helped rescue Charles Nalle from capture in 1860. She is well-known and widely written about. A major work about her life is Sarah Bradford's *Harriet Tubman: Moses of Her People*.

Mr. George Lewis came to Albany by night with his pursuers not far behind. He was able to secure passage secreted on a boat down the Hudson to New York and finally to Boston. This story is told in a pamphlet by Austin Beares and reprinted in Charles Blockson's *Underground Railroad: First Person Narratives of Escapes From Slavery*.

Walter Freeman was a carpenter by trade and formerly a slave of the Honorable Mr. Badger, Secretary of the Navy under President Harrison. He is known to have worked to purchase his own liberty and that of his wife and six children, paying $2,550. His story is mentioned in the *Memoir of Rev. Abel Brown*, and also told in part in *The Black Abolitionists* by Benjamin Quarles.

Charles Nelson was enslaved as a personal servant to a couple who honeymooned in the North. They left him in Schenectady while taking an excursion to Niagara Falls. He decided to flee for his freedom there and went to Vermont. This story was shared with us from Jane Williamson of the Rokeby Museum of Vermont from their records of fugitives who came to that farm.

John Williams and Martha Williams had already escaped slavery and come as far north as Hudson, where they found employment at the home of Charles Marriot. After the "Prigg" decision they considered it unsafe to stay in the North and went north to Vermont and possibly to Canada. This story was shared with us from the Jane Williamson of the Rokeby Museum of Vermont from their records of fugitives who came to that farm.

Jeremiah Snowden escaped from slavery in 1844 and passed through the Albany area en route to Vermont from Westchester County. This story was shared with us from Jane Williamson of the Rokeby Museum of Vermont from their records of fugitives who came to that farm.

Simon was a slave in Maryland who escaped to Pennsylvania. In the spring of 1837 he came north through our area and to Vermont. This story was shared with us from Jane Williamson of the Rokeby Museum of Vermont from their records of fugitives who came to that farm.

Phillip and Benjamin, fugitives from slave owner Cheney Hutton, came up to Albany on the *People's Line* steamship. One was a market man and teamster; the other was a first-rate field hand. This story is mentioned in the *Memoir of Rev. Abel Brown*. It originally appeared in *The Tocsin of Liberty*.

Miss Leah Brown fled from slave owner Mrs. McDonald, who held the rest of her family in bondage and set a bounty of $100 for her return. This story is mentioned in the *Memoir of Rev. Abel Brown*. It originally appeared in *The Tocsin of Liberty*.

Mary Anne fled from Dr. Stewart, who sought her return to bondage. She was assisted by friends, and her passage took her through Albany. This story is mentioned in the *Memoir of Rev. Abel Brown*. It originally appeared in *The Tocsin of Liberty*.

Rev. Mr. James Beulah was a licensed exhorter of the Methodist Episcopal Church and a slave for 30 years. He and his wife and children finally fled slavery. The swamps and woods were their hiding places for weeks until they came to Albany. This story is mentioned in the *Memoir of Rev. Abel Brown*. It originally appeared in *The Tocsin of Liberty*.

Levi fled from Mrs. Margaret A. Culver, who placed a bounty of $100 on him. He was sought by slavehunters while in Albany but managed to escape to Canada. This story is mentioned in the *Memoir of Rev. Abel Brown*. It originally appeared in *The Tocsin of Liberty*.

Joseph Rogers, age 21, escaped from Charles Bryant, a dry goods merchant in Baltimore, in 1843. He ran away because he was about to be sold. His father and mother already had been sold south to Georgia. His story is shared in the Executive Committee Report of the Eastern New York Anti-Slavery Society in 1843.

Mr. Evans, age 22, had been a sailor for eight year when he fled from William Howard. His journey to Albany began on a boat to Baltimore in 1843. His story is shared in the Executive Committee Report of the Eastern New York Anti-Slavery Society in 1843.

Isaac Hinson fled to Albany in 1843. His master was John Groom, a lawyer in Elkton, Maryland. He came with **Jane**, his wife, and **Charles**, his son. His story is shared in the Executive Committee Report of the Eastern New York Anti-Slavery Society in 1843.

Fester Dixon fled to Albany in 1843. He was a 20-year-old waiter who had been the slave of lawyer John W. Tyler. His story is shared in the Executive Committee Report of the Eastern New York Anti-Slavery Society in 1843.

Henry Terry escaped from Madisonville, near New Orleans around 1843, and wandered through Mississippi, North Carolina, Virginia, and eventually north to Albany. He had many injuries including having had the toes on his right foot cut off by a cotton gin and his nose broken by the butt of a driver's whip. His story is shared in the Executive Committee Report of the Eastern New York Anti-Slavery Society in 1843.

Miss Sarah Smith escaped violent and cruel enslavement in New Orleans and came to Albany with her husband, four-year-old daughter, and unborn child. This story is mentioned in the *Memoir of Rev. Abel Brown*. It originally appeared in *The Tocsin of Liberty*.

Elizabeth Castle was a dressmaker from Baltimore, who escaped along with three other slaves, Polly, Marianna, Marianna's daughter, and an unborn child, also fugitives from Baltimore. They sought relief and assistance in Albany, but being pursued by slave-catchers they were forced to go to Canada. This story is mentioned in the *Memoir of Rev. Abel Brown*. It originally appeared in *The Tocsin of Liberty*.

Elizabeth, 24, fled from David Judah, a ship merchant from Baltimore, leaving behind her sister. Her journey to Albany took two weeks. Her story is shared in the Executive Committee Report of the Eastern New York Anti-Slavery Society in 1843.

Jeremiah Boggs was a slave from Richmond, Virginia. He traveled three weeks before reaching Albany. He had been sold six different times as a slave and badly treated. Among the indignities he endured as a slave were stabbings and beatings. His story is shared in the Executive Committee Report of the Eastern New York Anti-Slavery Society in 1843.

William Johnson fled from Richard White of St. Louis. He escaped in New Orleans and traveled nine weeks before reaching Albany. His story is shared in the Executive Committee Report of the Eastern New York Anti-Slavery Society in 1843.

Eliza Wilson endured great suffering as a slave. She had been beaten with sticks, stripped and beaten with a cat-o'-nine-tails repeatedly and washed with salt brine to make the pain worse. She was badly scarred. She was kept illiterate and was made to work as a field hand. She finally escaped and passed through Albany on her way to Canada. This story is mentioned in the *Memoir of Rev. Abel Brown*. It originally appeared in *The Tocsin of Liberty*.

John Henry Hill passed through Albany in 1853 on his way to Canada from Virginia. His journey also took him through Philadelphia and New York City. He continued on through Rochester before reaching Canada. This story is mentioned in a National Park Service guide to researching the Underground Railroad entitled *Exploring a Common Past*.

William "Box Peel" Jones got a job, making $16 a month, and stayed in Albany at 125 Lydius Street before going to Canada; his story is told in William Still's *The Underground Railroad*.

Appendix IV

Leadership of the Orthodox Congregational Church, Union Village

Pastors

Rev. R.A. Avery, 1837
Rev. John Smith, 1838–1841
E.C. Pritchett, 1841–1845
Rev. Sabin McKinney, 1845–1846
Rev. Josiah Grinnell, 1847–1850
Rev. C.S. Shattuck, 1850–1860

Trustees

Horace Bigelow	Cortland Cook
Hiram Corliss	John Masters
Daniel Frost	Leonard Gibbs
W.H. Mowry	H.V. Horton
Luke Prentiss	Edwin Wilmarth
James Watson	Ira Wales
Gilbert Bailey	Wm. M. Holmes, son of Henry Holmes
Henry Holmes	Deodatus D. Haskell
Charles Gunn	Abel Wilder, blacksmith

Deacon

John Clark
Rufus A. Lamb

(Manual of the Orthodox Congregational Church)

Appendix V

STATISTICS ON THE BLACK POPULATION IN THE TOWN OF GREENWICH, 1840 TO 1860

The 1840 federal census lists ten blacks in the town of Greenwich; the 1850 federal census, 28; the 1855 state census, 55; and the 1860 federal census, 58. Out of 28 blacks in the 1850 census, 18 were living with white families; out of 55 in the 1855 census, only five remained from 1850; out of 58 in the 1860 census, only four remained from the 1850 census and ten from the 1855 census. Out of 13 black families listed as heads of households during the 1850 and 1860 censuses, four were originally from the state of Maryland, including the Maynard family with 12 members. Of six black members of the Free Church in the 1850 census, two lived in Greenwich; of six members in the 1860 census, two lived in Greenwich. However, none of those blacks who were members during the 1850 census were still members during the 1860 census. These facts indicate the transient nature of the black population in the county and the town. This could be because some of these individuals were fugitive slaves or relatives of fugitive slaves. The censuses also show a movement that centralized the county's black population in the town of Greenwich. Their movement there supports the likelihood of the presence of the Underground Railroad.

Black Population Shift in the County to Town of Greenwich 1840 to 1860

1840	10 black residents out of 263 county total	= 4.6 %
1845	33 out of 297	= 11.1 %
1850	31 out of 307*	= 10.1 %
1855	55 out of 220	= 25.0 %
1860	58 out of 250*	= 23.2 %

Blacks Living with Members of the Free Church

1850

Priscilla Weeks, 30, laborer living with Henry Holmes family
Samuel Jones, 21, with John T. Masters family
Robert Jones, 30, with William H. Mowry family
Cornelia Wanton, 23—she married John Maynard—with Abel Wilder
Crusoe Freeman, 71, John Epps, 23, Henry Epps, 26, Eliza Livingston, 30, with LeRoy Mowry
Lavinia Epps, Free Church member, 20, living with Pardon Bassett, whose wife Mary Bailey Bassett
   is listed as a member

1855

Harriet Barker with Cortland Cook, son-in-law of Hiram Corliss

1860

Gilbert Van Buren, 19, (no POB listed), John T. Masters
Harriet Barker with Hiram Corliss

Blacks Who Were Members of the Free Church and Dates of Membership

Priscilla Weeks (Salter), Apr 22, 1837 to July 26, 1851
Avery and Margaret Ann Hazzard, Jan 8, 1842—apparently living in the town of Jackson
Edward and Hannah Weeks, July 25, 1846 to Aug. 23, 1856—apparently living in Jackson
Cornelia Wanton (Manyard/Maynard), May 7, 1848
Harriet Barker, Dec. 29, 1855
Catharine Schuyler, April 26, 1856
Henry Epps, Jan 3, 1858
Lavinia Hazzard Epps, Mar. 20, 1858
Leonard Hazzard, Sept. 4, 1858
Matilda Irick, Sept. 4, 1858

*Actual census figures show 350 and 259 blacks in the county for 1850 and 1860 respectively. However, the author was able to identify only 307 and 250 through personal inspection of the census records, probably due to the illegibility of the microfilm.

Other Blacks Living in the Town
of Greenwich with White Families*

1850

Ellen Eletheniarder, 16, (Maryland) with Joseph R. Naylor family
Sarah Maynard, 17, (MD) with Seneca McNeil
Susan Maynard, 20, (MD) with Reuben Stone
Henry Jones, 28, at John Tucker farm
Judeth Johnson, 26, at Willard White farm
Thomas DeRidder, 41, at William Christie farm
Harry DeRidder, 24, at John Whittaker farm

1860

Charlotte Hose, 15, with Amanda Curtis
William Jackson, 25, (VA) at Casper place
Sylvia DeRidder, 18, at Alexander Cherry farm

Blacks Who Maintained a Residence in
the Town of Greenwich 1850 to 1860

James Schuyler, 1850, 1855, 1860
Bridget DeRidder, 1850, 1855, 1860
Henry Jones, 1850, 1855, 1860
Charles Fields, 1850, 1860
Lavinia Epps, 1850, 1855
Henry Epps, 1850, 1855
Dian Tobias, 1850, 1855
Harriet Barker, 1855, 1860
Solomon Johnson, 1855, 1860
Eli Hazard, 1855, 1860
Catherine Hazard, 1855, 1860
John Maynard, 1855, 1860
Sarah Maynard, 1855, 1860
Augustus Deridder, 1855, 1860

*Place of birth in parentheses.

Appendix VI

HOMES WITH PROBABLE ABOLITIONIST SYMPATHIZERS DESCRIBED IN EVEREST'S PIONEER HOMES

Everest Number

29. **Marsh-Stafford Farm**, Route 22, Plattsburgh; S.H. Marsh was a member of the Beekmantown Anti-Slavery Society.

45. **Baker-Bidwell House**, Route 3; Dr. L.F. Bidwell, who purchased it in 1846, was a subscriber to the *Herald of Freedom*.

58. **Allen-Beckwith House**, Beekmantown; Dr. Baruch Beckwith, who lived here from 1836 to 1849, was a vice-president of the county society and a member of the Beekmantown society.

59. **Douglass Farm**, E. Beekmantown; S. Douglass was a member of the Beekmantown society and subscriber to the *Herald of Freedom*.

60. **John Howe, Jr., Farm**, E. Beekmantown; Howe owned the farm until 1854, and was a member of the Beekmantown society and subscriber to the *Herald of Freedom*.

62. **Beckwith Home**, Beekmantown Corners; George Beckwith, son of Baruch, moved here in 1836. He was among those who met with Gerrit Smith during his 1845 visit.

63. **Barber Homestead**, Barber Road in Beekmantown; four members of the Beekmantown Society were named Barber.

68. **Jonathan Douglass Mansion**, Chazy Village; a J. Douglass belonged to the Beekmantown Society.

74. **Solomon Fisk Home**, Chazy Village; Fisk was a member of the county society.

80. **Ira Fisk Home**, Route 9, Chazy; his son founded abolitionist Wesleyan Methodist Church in West Chazy.

83. **Ransom's Tavern**, Chazy Landing, a center of social activities; G. Ransom of Chazy belonged to the county society.

91. **Smith Homestead**, Lake Street, Rouses Point; purchased by Ezra Thurber in 1825 and rented to Baptist preacher, Holland Turner.

103. **Moore Homestead**, Champlain; owned by Noadiah Moore family.

104. **Moore Farmhouse**, Champlain; early home of Pliny Moore, father of Noadiah; it remained in the Moore family for many years.

106. **Perry-Kaufman House**, Champlain; in the Perry family from 1819–1880; P. Perry was a member of the Champlain society.

110. **Kellogg House**, Route 9, Champlain, original owner, allegedly Daniel Kellogg; also owned by Charles A. Moore, whose relationship to Noadiah is unknown; Moore sold it to another abolitionist, Lewis Kellogg, who stood by Noadiah Moore during the public stand against slavery at the First Presbyterian Church; could possibly have been used by Noadiah Moore as an Underground Railroad station.

117. **Shedden House**, Mooers; James S. Shedden was a vice-president of the county society and a member of the Mooers Society.

119. **Turner-Roberts Home**, Salmon-River Road, Schuyler Falls; Owen T. Roberts was a member of the Beekmantown Society, and Peter J. Roberts, who lived here from 1832 to 1865, may have been the same person as P.B. Roberts who was the Chairman of the March 16, 1846, County Liberty Party convention and a distributor of the *Herald of Freedom*.

122. **Weston-Vaughn House**, Mason St., Schuyler Falls; owned by family of Elijah Weston; three Westons were officers in the West Peru society; an E. Weston was a subscriber of the *Herald of Freedom*.

132. **Weaver House**, Schuyler Falls; Peter Weaver was a vice-president of the county society, the Liberty Party candidate for state assembly in 1846, and a subscriber to the *Herald of Freedom*, for which his son, Stephen, was a distributor.

137. **Allen Farm**, Bedell Road, Peru; a Z. Allen was a subscriber to the *Herald of Freedom*.

148. **Arnold Home**, Route 22B, Peru; owned by Elisha Arnold, prominent early settler; at least four Arnolds were members of the Peru and W. Peru societies.

178. **John Henry Signor House**, AuSable; Philip Signor was president of the West Peru Society.

Appendix VII

POSSIBLE PARTICIPANTS IN EASTERN NEW YORK'S UNDERGROUND RAILROAD

Abbreviations

AMEZ	African Methodist Episcopal Zion
AVC	Albany Vigilance Committee
ENYASS	Eastern New York Anti-Slavery Society
FSL	Fugitive Slave Law
NSFA	Northern Star and Freeman's Advocate
NYC	New York City
NYCV	New York Committee of Vigilance
NYS	New York State
OSDASS	Old Saratoga District Anti-Slavery Society
TVC	Troy Vigilance Committee
UGRR	Underground Railroad
UNASSNY	United Anti-Slavery Society of New York
WUBA	Washington Union Baptist Association

Names of blacks are in **bold italics**.

New York City

New York City directories between 1839 and 1853 were consulted. Multiple addresses were found for a number of individuals, and in most cases, the address listed is the most stable; in some, two addresses are listed. Addresses also were found in the *Colored American* and *Emancipator*.

Barker, George R.: Founding member of the NYCV, who also was a member of the Eastern New York Anti-Slavery Society executive committee and who for a time had an Albany address.

Beecher, Henry Ward: Brooklyn. According to Charles Ray, he used Beecher's Plymouth Church as a safe house (Ray 25).

Bell, Phillip A.: 15 St. John's Lane / 99 Leonard (after 1850). NYCV. Publisher of *The Colored American*.

Brown, Robert, Esq.: Chairman of the 1835 NYCV organizational meeting.

Cornish, Samuel: NYCV; UASSNY. Editor of *Freedom's Journal* and first editor of *The Colored American*; close associate of Charles Ray.

Culver, Erastus: Brooklyn. Washington County abolitionist and former Congressman, he moved to Brooklyn in 1851 and established a law firm that represented blacks accused of being fugitive slaves in several high profile cases. Around 1854, he became a judge, and during the next years he freed several fugitive slaves whose cases were brought before him by slave-catchers. A leader in the formation of the Republican Party, he campaigned extensively for Lincoln, who rewarded him with an ambassadorship to Venezuela.

Downing, George T.: Originally from New York, he moved to Providence in 1855 where he aided fugitive slaves and became a black leader of national prominence.

Downing, Thomas: 5 Broad; h. 245 Broadway / 4 Temple (after 1850). UNASSNY. Owner of popular Oyster House, he is said to have aided fugitive slaves.

Dresser, Horace: Ofc 89 / 82 Nassau; h. 268 W. 18th St. Attorney who worked with the NYCV to aid free blacks and fugitive slaves apprehended by slavecatchers.

Elston, Alexander: 8 Downing. UNASSNY. Boot maker.

Gibbs, Leonard: Ofc: 18 Wall St.; h. 22 Second St. Attorney from Washington County, who lived in NYC from 1840 to 1845 and who was an Underground Railroad conductor while living there.

Harned, William: NYCV.

Harris, Dennis: His sugar refinery on 108 Duane Street is believed to have harbored fugitive slaves (Johnson 289).

Higgins, J.W.: NYCV. Grocer.

Hodges, Willis Augustus: Williamsburgh Editor of the *Ram's Horn*, he moved to Franklin County for a time where he headed a colony of black farmers called Blacksville from 1848 to 1856.

Hopper, Isaac T.: Bookstore, 143 Nassau; h. 110 Eldridge. Quaker who openly harbored fugitive slaves and as a result was disowned. He was the president of the NYCV when it integrated and reorganized in 1847.

Jocelyn, the Rev. Samuel: A white pastor of a black congregation in Connecticut, whose attempt to start a school for blacks there was prevented. He later settled in New York City, where he became a leading member of the American Anti-Slavery and close friend of Arthur Tappan.

Johnson, Oliver: 63 Pike Vermont native and associate of William Lloyd Garrison, he moved to NYC to work for Horace Greeley. While in NYC, he is known to have assisted VT conductor R.T. Robinson. He later became editor of the *Pennsylvania Freeman*.

Johnson, William P.: 31 N. Pearl St.; h. 153 Orange St. NYCV; UASSNY. Bakery goods; close associate of Charles Ray.

Johnston, William: 198 Hudson St. Grain merchant. Secretary of the NYCV.

Leavitt, Joshua: Editor of the *Emancipator* and leading member of the American Anti-Slavery Society who assisted the mutineers of the *Amistad*.

Legre, Joseph: 47 Watts. UASSNY. Tailor.

Lester, Andrew: 80 Pine/19 William (after 1850); h. 89 Varick/143 W. 25th St. (after 1850). ENYASS; NYCV. Dry goods merchant.

Miter, the Rev. John J.: NYCV. Spent time in Troy.

Noble, Linnaeus: 78 Cedar. ENYASS; Liberty Party Candidate. Owner of a towboat line between New York and Oswego; he lived at various times in Albany, NYC, and later moved to Fayetteville, near Syracuse, where he participated in the Jerry Rescue.

Paton, Isaac

Pennington, J.W.C.: 23 Lispenard St. Fugitive slave and pastor of the First Colored Presbyterian Church (the Shiloh Church), 1848–1855, taking over at the death of Theodore Wright. He was the pastor at Frederick Douglass's wedding. His church moved from William to Prince Street in 1851, and came to be referred to as the Prince Street Church. In 1854, he became embroiled in a widely-publicized affair involving Judge Erastus Culver, when Pennington's brother and two nephews escaped from slavery in Maryland and came to him for assistance but then were apprehended by slavecatchers.

Powell, William P.: 330 Pearl St.; h. 61 Cherry St. Chaired FSL meeting of 1850 at the Zion Church; proprietor of Colored Sailors' Home.

Ray, Charles: 153 Orange St. Editor of the *Colored American*; pastor of the Bethesda Colored Congregational Church; longtime NYCV member; admitted Underground Railroad conductor; and advocate for Gerrit Smith's land offer. He married Abel Brown and second wife, Catherine.

Raymond, the Rev. John T.: Pastor of the Zion Baptist Church (1832–1839) at 486 Pearl Street and Abyssinian Baptist Church (1848–1854); in between those appointments, he served for eight years as pastor of a church in Boston.

Ruggles, David: 36 / 65–67 Lispenard / 62 Leonard St. UASSNY. Ruggles was the leader of the NYCV in its formative years. It is claimed that he aided more than 600 fugitive slaves, among them Frederick Douglass. He became involved in a dispute over the use of NYCV funds with Samuel Cornish in 1840 that caused him to leave NYC and settle in Northampton, MA, where he established a water cure treatment spa.

Smith, Dr. James McCune: ofc. 93 / 55 W. Broadway (after 1850); h. 153 Reade / 15 N. Moore (after 1842). NYCV. Advocate for black rights and for the Gerrit Smith land offer, he was the attending physician at the NY Colored Orphan Asylum.

Tappan, Arthur: store at 122 Pearl St.; h. Brooklyn. ENYASS. Wealthy merchant; president of the American Anti-Slavery Society and American and Foreign Anti-Slavery Society; he attended NYCV meetings during its formative years; said it was the model for succeeding Underground Railroad operations.

Tappan, Lewis: Brooklyn. NYCV; ENYASS. Collaborated with brother Arthur in the Underground Railroad. Nationally prominent figure in abolitionist circles.

Van Rensselaer, Thomas: 122 Water St. NYCV; UASSNY. Fugitive slave who settled in NYC and opened a restaurant. He strongly supported William Lloyd Garrison and was co-editor with W.A. Hodges of the *Ram's Horn*, supplying the financial support.

Wilson, Thomas. UASSNY.

Woods, Aaron. UASSNY.

Wright, Elizur: Leading member of the American Anti-Slavery and prolific abolitionist speaker and writer.

Wright, Richard P.G: Schenectady. NYCV. Barber.

Wright, Theodore S.: 28 John St. / 2 White St. ENYASS. Longtime pastor of the Shiloh Church, mentor of Henry Garnet, president of the NYCV, Wright collaborated with Charles Ray and William Johnston in arranging the transport of fugitive slaves from NYC. He was active in the National Negro Conventions and in the American Anti-Slavery Society and American Foreign and Anti-Slavery Society. His father, the barber R.P.G. Wright of Schenectady, was a member of the NYCV and widely active in the Negro convention movement.

Zuille, John T. Active in the Negro convention and suffrage movements.

Mid-Hudson Region

Names of abolitionists are also drawn from the following reports not otherwise cited in the text: "Greene County Anti-Slavery Society," *Friend of Man* 19 December 1838, and "Unionville, Orange County," *Friend of Man* 17 April 1839: 3.

Alsdorfs: Newburgh, Orange County. Family of dance teachers who aided runaways.

Armstrong, Ira: Poughkeepsie, Dutchess. Officer of an anti-slavery society.

Armstrong, Martin: Poughkeepsie. Officer of an anti-slavery society.

Austin, Thomas: Poughkeepsie. Officer of an anti-slavery society.

Baldwin, Anson: Cairo, Greene. Officer of an anti-slavery society.

Barber, the Rev.: Amenia, Dutchess. Officer of an anti-slavery society.

Beach, John: Hunter, Greene. Officer of an anti-slavery society.

Blake, Tunis: Hudson, Columbia County. Attended 1840 Black State Convention.

Blount, the Rev. Nathan: Poughkeepsie. Pastor of the AMEZ Church during the 1830s; agent of the *Colored American* and *Emancipator*; member of the American Anti-Slavery Society.

Boston, Uriah: Poughkeepsie. Barber. One of Poughkeepsie's most prominent black citizens; attended NYS Black Convention of 1840; agent for the *Northern Star and Freeman's Advocate*.

Bramer, Nathaniel: Port Jervis, Orange.

Bull, John Milton: Walton Lake, Orange. Transported runaways to and from the Rev. Wood's Barn.

Carman, Joseph: Cairo, Greene. Officer of an anti-slavery society.

Carpenter, John: Scarsdale, Westchester.

Chandler, Joseph: Unionville, Orange.

Colter, James: Unionville, Orange.

Conklin, Isaac "Hike": McGuinnesburg, Orange.

Cross, Martin: Catskill, Greene. Agent for the NSFA.

DeVinne, the Rev. D.: Cairo, Greene.

Dorland, Edward: Washington, Dutchess. Officer of an anti-slavery society.

Droyer, Mathias: Chester, Orange. Worked with Vail and Graham in aiding runaways.

Dubois, Peter F.: Pleasant Valley, Dutchess.

Dusinbury, John: Poughkeepsie.

Edwards, Col. William: Hunter, Greene. Officer of an anti-slavery society.

Fairchild, Henry: Poughkeepsie.

Fellows, the Rev. L.H.: Durham, Greene. Officer of an anti-slavery society.

Gannon, Don and Dim: Southfields, Orange.

Graham, Dr.: Chester, Orange. Assisted R.M. Vail in aiding fugitive slaves.

Green, Hawley: Peekskill, Westchester. Barber alleged to have aided runaway slaves.

Green, P.: Hudson, Columbia. Attended 1840 Black State Convention.

Green, William: Hudson, Columbia. Agent, NSFA.

Groomer, Solomon: Hudson, Columbia. Attended 1840 Black State Convention.

Hall, James: Southfields, Orange.

Hammond, Thomas: Dover, Dutchess. Officer of an anti-slavery society.

Hawley, Major Ezra: Catskill, Greene. Officer of an anti-slavery society.

Hazard, B.W.: Cairo, Greene.

Hesdra, Edward: Nyack, Rockland.

Hubbard, Jabez: Greene County. Officer of an anti-slavery society.

Jackson, Robert: Catskill, Greene.

Jenney, William: Poughkeepsie.

Johnson, David: Cairo, Greene.

Kanous, Peter: Unionville, Orange.

Jay, William, Judge: Bedford, Westchester. Son of Chief Justice of the Supreme Court John Jay, whose Bedford home is alleged to have been an UGRR stop.

Leet, Henry: Cairo, Greene.

LeRow, George: Poughkeepsie.

Lewis, Abraham: McGuinnesburg, Orange.

Low, John: Poughkeepsie.

Mars, the Rev. James N.: Poughkeepsie. Pastor of AMEZ Church; attended NYS Black Convention of 1840; agent for the *Colored American*; sent to Canada by the Wesleyan-Methodist Church to minister to fugitive slaves in 1846.

McGeorge, William: Poughkeepsie.

Mead, Walter: Cairo, Greene.

Moffat, Benjamin: Unionville, Orange.

Mott James: Purchase, Westchester.

Murray, O.S.: Goshen, Orange. Director of Erie Railroad, who gave passes to fugitive slaves and collaborated with R.M. Vail.

Noble, Walker: Cairo, Greene.

Orsban, Henry: Orsbanville, Greene.

Osterhout, C.: Hudson, Columbia. Attended 1840 Black State Convention.

Parker, William H.: Hudson, Columbia. Attended 1840 Black State Convention.

Parkman, James: Hudson, Columbia. Attended 1840 Black State Convention.

Pell, Joseph: Hudson, Columbia. Agent, NSFA.

Payne, C.: Newburgh, Orange. Agent for the *Colored American*.

Peck, Alfred: Big Hollow, Greene. Agent for *Albany Patriot*.

Pope, Lyman: Durham, Greene. Officer of an anti-slavery society.

Powell, Aaron: Chatham, Columbia. Quaker abolitionist and anti-slavery lecturer from 1855 on. Leader of the Personal Liberty Law movement just prior to the Civil War. He later became Editor of the *National Anti-Slavery Standard*.

Roberts, the Rev. Philetus: Pleasant Valley, Dutchess. President of Dutchess County anti-slavery society; pastor of the First Baptist Church, Pleasant Valley.

Roe, Peter: Cornwall, Orange County. A vice-president representing Dutchess County in the state anti-slavery society; was host to Abel Brown in 1844.

Roney, the Rev.: Newburgh, Orange County.

Safford, James M.: Cairo, Greene.

Sands, John: Peekskill, Westchester. Quaker whose house on 1112 Main Street is alleged to have been a stop.

Sanford, Joseph M.: Cairo, Greene.

Sayre, the Rev. William N.: Pine Plains, Dutchess. Officer of an anti-slavery society.

Sherwood, Rev.: New Windsor, Orange.

Sleight, Solomon: LaGrange, Dutchess. Officer of an anti-slavery society.

Smith, Richard: Catskill, Greene.

Starr, David L.: Poughkeepsie. Officer of an anti-slavery society.

Stone, Abijah: Windham, Greene. Officer of an anti-slavery society.

Thompson, Samuel: Poughkeepsie. A Quaker, who was a vice-president of the state anti-slavery society and the Eastern New York Anti-Slavery Society, representing Dutchess County.

Thompson, William: Athens, Greene. Agent, NSFA.

Ticknor, Norman: Lexington, Greene. Officer of an anti-slavery society.

Tillman, Lloyd: Hudson, Columbia. Attended 1840 Black State Convention.

Towot, John: Nyack, Rockland. Worked with the Tappans.

Tuckerman, the Rev. Frederic: Poughkeepsie.

Turner, Peter: Harriman, Orange.

Underwood, the Rev. A.: Poughkeepsie.

Vail, R.M.: Chester, Orange. Retailer who aided fugitive slaves in collaboration with the Erie Railroad.

Van Alstyne, William: Hudson, Columbia. Attended 1840 Black State Convention.

Van Fleet, Benjamin: Unionville, Orange.

Van Fleet, Samuel: Unionville, Orange.

Van Loon, the Rev. Charles: Poughkeepsie. Albany native, who was pastor of the First Baptist Church of Poughkeepsie (1843–1847); friend of Abel Brown; vice-president of the Eastern New York Anti-Slavery Society.

Van Wagner, James: Poughkeepsie.

West, William M.: Poughkeepsie.

Willet, Mr.: Orange County. Erie Railroad conductor who let fugitive slaves ride free.

Wood, the Rev. James Washington: Chester, Orange. Pastor of the First Presbyterian Church.

Albany County

Barker, George R.: Eagle Tavern New York City broker, member of executive committee of the New York Committee of Vigilance, and the executive committee of the ENYASS; member of the New York Young Men's Anti-Slavery Society.

Belden, Selah: 30 Patroon (Clinton Ave.).

Bradt, Peter: S. Pearl Street. Boatman.

Brooks, C.: 83 State Street. AVC 1856.

Brown, the Rev. Abel: 209 Green Street. Brown was a Baptist minister who first came to this area 1841 to be the pastor of the Sand Lake Baptist Church. A ceaseless conductor of fugitive slaves, he was an agent and publisher of the *Albany Patriot*, and the secretary of the Eastern New York Anti-Slavery Society's executive committee. He died in 1844 from illness brought on by overwork at the age of 34. It is said he aided more than 1,000 fugitive slaves in his short life.

Burton, Charles C.: 3–5 Green Street; h. 9 Swan Street. Looking glass dealer.

Chambers, John: 12 Van Tromp. Barber. Thompson Society.

Chaplin, William L.: Liberty Party Candidate. Former secretary of the NYS Anti-Slavery Society, he was a prolific lecturer who traveled throughout the state on numerous occasions and was instrumental in abolitionizing the North Country. He later became Washington correspondent and editor of the *Albany Patriot*. While in Washington, he became involved in aiding fugitive slaves, and in 1850 after the demise of the *Patriot*, he was apprehended while aiding the escape of fugitive slaves, and imprisoned. He eventually was

bailed out of prison and thereafter retired from the abolitionist wars.

Colburn, Nathan, Jr.: 15 Van Tromp. Lumber business.

Crocker, George L.: 4 Union. His coffee and spice store was at the same address as the office of the ENYASS.

Christian, David: 1252 Broadway.

Crapo, William: N. State Street; h. 2 William Street. Grocer, fruit dealer. Executive committee of ENYASS.

Cutler, Benjamin: 78 Cherry. AVC 1845. Identified by William Henry Johnson as Underground Railroad agent.

Dale, William A. Tweed: 173 Lydius. Teacher and principal, who also was president of the Sailors' Bethel Church in Troy, whose pastor for a time was Fayette Shipherd. Officer of an anti-slavery organization.

Dennison, Mrs. Dilzey: 7 Cross Street (now Sheridan Place).

Douge, Michael: 91 Williams St. Barber. Officer of an anti-slavery organization and member of the Thompson society.

Elkins, Thomas: 188 Lumber St. AVC 1856.

Fanning, Hiram: Market & Lumber St. Officer of an anti-slavery organization.

Fassett, Timothy: 48 Steuben St.

Freeman, E.P.: 39 Columbia. Officer of an anti-slavery organization.

Gardner, William: 49 Second Street. Barber. AVC 1856.

Gladding, Timothy: 23 Park St. AVC 1845.

Goodwin, Edwin W.: 57 DeWitt. Executive committee of ENYASS. Portrait artist and editor of the *Tocsin of Liberty* and *Albany Patriot*; worked with Abel Brown and Charles Torrey in forwarding fugitive slaves.

Gorsline, Esek. Liberty Party candidate.

Graham, James. Liberty Party candidate.

Hammond, Samuel: 28 Spring St. Attorney who was the editor of the *State Register*.

Hepinstall, Christopher: 59 Liberty St.; h. 24 State St. Executive committee of ENYASS.

Hepinstall, George: 30 Hudson.

Hill, George T.: Lydius. Proprietor of Delevan House, a Temperance hotel.

Jackson, James C.: Editor of the *Albany Patriot*.

Johnson, Capt. John: 198 Lumber St. Boatman. AVC 1856.

Johnson, William Henry: Noted Albany resident, whose autobiography published in 1900 claims his participation in some of the extraordinary events of antebellum history and which identifies many Albany blacks who participated in the Underground Railroad.

Kelley, the Rev. J.J.: AVC, 1856. Pastor of St. John's Church, 36 Ferry Street.

Lane, James D.: Sailor who was sentenced to 12 years in prison for aiding fugitive slaves while his boat was docked in Norfolk, VA in 1843; as of 1849, he was still in prison.

Lattimore, Benjamin: 9 Plain St. Grocer and son of president of African Temperance Society. Member of Thompson Society and executive committee of ENYASS.

Lester, Andrew: Executive committee of ENYASS. Lester was also a member of the New York Committee of Vigilance and probably a New York City native; it is not known whether he was black or white.

Martin, Homer: Hamilton St. Officer of an anti-slavery organization. Liberty Party candidate.

Martin, Hiram. AVC 1845.

Marvin, Uriah: 14 Lumber Street. Lumber business.

Matthews, William: Franklin & Hamilton St. Barber. AVC 1856.

Mayell, William: 102 Herkimer. Executive committee of ENYASS.

Mayell, Jefferson. Liberty Party candidate.

McClure, James: 198 State & 12 Van Schaick.

McGowan, Minos: 184 N. Pearl St. Lumber business. Officer of an anti-slavery organization. AVC 1856.

McIntyre, William P.

Moore, William R.: 80 Broad St.

Morgan, George

Morton, Charles: S. Pearl & Maiden Lane. Publisher of the *Northern Star & Freeman's Advocate*. Member of the Thompson Society.

Myers, Stephen: 198 Lumber St. & others. Myers was born as a slave in Rensselaer County and freed in 1818. In his earlier years, he worked as a grocer and a boatman. After joining the Thompson Society of black Temperance men, he became a lecturer and newspaper editor and publisher. Foremost among his newspapers was the *Northern Star and Freeman's Advocate*, which was published from 1842 to 1849 and which prior to Frederick Douglass's *Northern Star* was the nation's foremost black newspaper. During this time, he continued to work as a steward on at least two different steamboats, the *Diamond* and the *Armenia*, and was known for his culinary expertise. A member of the AVC in 1856, he eventually became Albany's UGRR superintendent, as well as an influential lobbyist for the rights of blacks. It is not known how many fugitive slaves he aided, but 1,000 would be a conservative estimate.

Osborn, William. Liberty Party candidate.

Paul, Nathaniel: Born in Exeter, NH, 1795; an important clergyman, he was pastor of the Albany African Church Association from 1822–1830, located on the northern section of Hamilton St. between Grand and Fulton, and pastor of the African Baptist Church on William and Van Zandt St. from 1830–33 (he was in England from 1832–33). A member of the Thompson Society, he became an agent for the Wilberforce Colony, the first major black colony in Canada, which consisted of both freemen and fugitive slaves. He also was a leading advocate for black rights in New York State. He spent several years in England promoting the emancipation cause; however, he spent all the money he raised for the Wilberforce Colony; by the accounts of colony leader Austin Stewart, he lived extravagantly. He died penniless in 1839 in Albany.

Pepper, Calvin: High Street. Officer of an anti-slavery organization.

Pladwell, Joseph: 18 Canal St.

Platto, Frederick. Liberty Party candidate.

Pugsley, Cornelius: Delevan House.

Richardson, William. AVC 1845.

Richardson, Thomas R.: 75 Washington Ave. AVC 1845.

Robinson, Primus: 83 State St. Grocer, identified as collaborator with Stephen Myers by William Henry Johnson.

Rogers, John: 116 Water St. AVC 1845.

Royce, James: 2 Van Tromp.

Safford, Nathaniel: 227 Broadway. This lumber dealer, who was president of the Albany Anti-Slavery Society, was active at the state and national levels in anti-slavery and Liberty Party operations and served on the executive committee of the ENYASS. He was in the lumber business and also was the proprietor of a Temperance House at 280 N. Market St. from 1832–1840.

Sands, the Rev. John: 269 Lumber St. AVC 1846. Pastor of the Wesleyan African Church, Third Street, Arbor Hill.

Sherwood, William: 136 Green St. AVC 1845.

Smith, Israel: President of Albany Temperance Society, 1840, and an officer in the Albany Anti-Slavery Society during the 1840s.

Stewart, John G.: Barber; publisher of the *Northern Star & Freeman's Advocate*. Member of the Thompson Society.

Strain, Joseph: 59 Church Street; h. 63 Church & 196 Lydius. Soap, candle manufacturer.

Taylor, James: 85 Van Woert.

Teall, E.M.: 40 Quay St.; h. 160 Broadway. Canal boat operator.

Thompson, Richard: 142 S. Pearl; also lists business locations at 96 State St. and 12 Exchange Street; h. 92 State St. Founder of the Thompson Society for black men of Temperance. He operated the Colored American Temperance House at 142 S. Pearl St.

Tillinghast, William: 13 Hudson St.; h. 57 Union St. Sperm whale oil and candles dealer.

Topp, William H.: 98 & 143 Green St. AVC 1846. This prosperous tailor was personally acquainted with William Lloyd Garrison and was connected to the black community in New York City, his wife serving in benevolent organizations there. After Stephen Myers, he is the most influential black Albany resident in the cause for emancipation and was Myers' coworker in the Underground Railroad.

Torrey, Charles T.: The notorious Torrey lived in Albany for only about a year; however, during that time, he was very active in the business of forwarding fugitive slaves. No address is listed for him in any of the Albany City directories. He died in 1846 in a Maryland prison, where in 1844 he had been given a six-year sentence for aiding fugitive slaves.

Townsend, Tappen: 138 Hamilton. AVC 1845; Liberty Party candidate.

Twichell, Winslow. Liberty Party candidate.

Van Vranken, Francis: 67 Second St. Barber. Member of the Thompson Society.

Wilcox, A.O.: Market & Ferry. Innkeeper. Executive committee of ENYASS.

Wilson, the Rev. John: 12 Union St.

Williams, Chauncey P.: 81 Columbia. Executive committee of ENYASS and a Liberty Party candidate. A forwarding merchant for the lumber industry; Williams later was president of the National Albany Exchange Bank.

Williams, Josiah B.: Temperance House. Forwarding merchant, lumber industry; may have been related to Chancey Williams (above), although it could be merely coincidental that both were forwarding merchants for the lumber industry.

Wood, James S.: 129 Lumber St. AVC 1846.

Wright, Richard: 367 State St. AVC 1846.

Rensselaer County

Aikens, Isaac: Greenbush. Executive committee of ENYASS.

Aikens, Jesse. Liberty Party candidate.

Arnold, Oliver: Arnold moved to Troy from Chestertown sometime after 1853; he was an alderman in 1856.

Baltimore, George B.

Baker, Ezekial: Schaghticoke. Liberty Party candidate.

Barnes, S.D.: Liberty Party candidate.

Bates, the Rev. Merrit B.: Liberty Party lecturer and associate of Abel Brown; founder of True Wesleyan Methodist Church in 1844 on Federal St. between River and North Second Sts., which lasted only a few years.

Bigelow, Thaddeus B.: 29 River St. President, Troy A-S Society, 1838; assisted incorporation of Liberty Street Presbyterian Colored Church in 1840; custom house officer during 1840s; left Troy, 1849.

Bingham, Southy: 146 Third. TVC 1857.

Birdsall, Z.P.: 58 & 345 Congress St. Officer of an anti-slavery society.

Bishop, William E.: Church near Ferry. Whitewasher. TVC 1857.

Brown, the Rev. Abel: Brown, who was pastor of the Sand Lake Baptist Church from April 1841 to April 1842, moved from Albany to Troy in the spring of 1844. He was a member of the executive committee of ENYASS.

Burton, Platt: West Sand Lake.

Conklin, Henry: West Sand Lake. Liberty Party candidate.

Dorr, William. Officer of an anti-slavery organization. Liberty Party candidate.

Dox, the Rev. H.L.: Sand Lake. Franckean Synod.

Fox, Isaac: Sand Lake. Owner of glass factory that local historian Judith Rowe claims hid fugitive slaves in barrels during transport of sand.

Fubbard, James: 73 ? Congress & Church near Ferry. Tailor and waiter. Officer of an anti-slavery society.

Garnet, Henry: 68 Fifth & 137 Fourth. Officer of an anti-slavery society and pastor of Liberty Street Presbyterian (Colored) Church 1841–48. His mentor was the Rev. Theodore Wright, president of the New York Committee of Vigilance. The second most important U.S. black leader after Douglass, he was known to be a brilliant orator and gave a famous speech at National Negro Convention in Buffalo in 1843 calling on slaves to resist. He was chosen by Lincoln to be the first black American to give a speech in Congress shortly after the passage of the 13th amendment that freed the slaves. He died in Liberia.

Gibbs, the Rev. Jonathan C.: TVC 1857. Pastor, Liberty Street Church during 1850s.

Gilbert, Uri: Employer of Charles Nalle and one of wealthiest men in Troy, he purchased Nalle's freedom after Nalle's rescue; Troy mayor after the Civil War.

Grant, Gurdon: 106 Fourth St. Officer of an anti-slavery society, founder and trustee of Bethel Free Congregation and member of Troy Board of Trade.

Gregory, Dr. C.H.: Sand Lake. Executive committee of ENYASS.

Giffith, Smith: Nassau. Executive committee of ENYASS. Liberty Party candidate.

Hagerman, Charles. TVC 1857.

Hawkins, Captain: 37 Green (Zebedee). TVC 1857.

Henry, William: 26 Division. TVC 1857. He supplied board to the fugitive slave Charles Nalle at time of his arrest and was one of the leaders of Nalle's rescue.

Hooper, John H.: 153 Second St. Whitewasher, identified by Siebert as UGRR conductor.

Howe, James H.: 168 Second St. Troy businessman and officer of an anti-slavery organization.

Hyde, Hiram L.: Liberty Party candidate.

Jones, Elijah: Lansingburgh. Liberty Party candidate.

Lawyer, the Rev. John D.: Sand Lake. Franckean Synod.

Marsh, Prentiss. Liberty Party candidate. Executive committee of ENYASS.

Miter, the Rev. J.J.: Participated at the annual meeting of the New York Committee of Vigilance in 1837; later that year went to Alton, IL, in 1837 after death of Lovejoy to form an anti-slavery society.

Moore, Pliny A.: 128 First St. & 139–152 River St. Railroad agent and merchant like his brother, William, in Albany, who also was a participant in abolitionist meetings. Officer of an anti-slavery society.

Owens, Philips Owens: 320 Congress St. Whitewasher. TVC 1857.

Parks, James, Jr.: West Sand Lake.

Payne, the Rev. Daniel: Payne was the pastor of the Troy AMEZ Church in 1837 and president of the Troy Mental and Moral Improvement Association; he later moved to Rochester, and then Ohio, and became a national leader of the American Methodist Episcopal Zion church.

Payne, Robert: Member of Albany's Thompson Society.

Rand, Ezekial Rand: Fourth near Main St. Officer of an anti-slavery society.

Rich, William: 29 Elbow (Fulton). Barber; chairman of the publishing committee of the Union Meeting of Colored People of Albany, Troy, and vicinity in 1837; trustee of Liberty Street Presbyterian Church; president at the Prigg Meeting; he was reported to be the stationmaster in the 1857 report of the Troy Vigilance Committee.

Schoonmaker, R.: 129 William St. Whitewasher. TVC 1857.

Seldon, Clarence: 53 Franklin St. Barber. Officer of an anti-slavery society.

Sheldon, Charles: 76 River. Officer of an anti-slavery society.

Sheldon, Preston. Liberty Party candidate.

Shipherd, the Rev. Fayette: 28 Fourth & 44 Seventh St. Documented UGRR conductor; associate of Abel Brown and Henry Garnet; pastor of Bethel Free Congregation 1832–34 & 1839–1842, organized for the spiritual benefit of the boatmen in 1832 on the corner of Fifth and Fulton; pastor of the Free Church on east side of Seventh Street between Albany and State Sts., organized in 1843, and the site of abolitionist and Liberty Party conventions. Executive committee of ENYASS.

Thuey, Alexander: 66 Fifth St. Trustee of Liberty Street Church. Officer of an anti-slavery society.

Van Alstyne, the Rev. Nicholas: Sand Lake. Franckean Synod.

Van Hoosen, Garret: Hoosick Falls. President of county Liberty Party and documented UGRR conductor; middleman in association with Fayette Shipherd and Charles Hicks of Bennington, VT.

Washington, Lewis: 172 & 153 Second St. Fugitive slave lecturer and close companion of Abel Brown, he was appointed as a Liberty Party agent after Brown's death.

Way, Fresly / Frisby: Lansingburgh. Chairman of the FSL Meeting of 1850 in Lansingburgh during which a strong commitment was made to aid fugitive slaves.

Willard, George: West Sand Lake.

Washington County

Allen, the Rev. B.: Vermont. WUBA.

Andrews, Edwin: Union Village. Officer of an anti-slavery society.

Anthony, Dwight: Union Village. Barber.

Avery, the Rev. R.A.: Union Village. Free Church.

Bailey, Gilbert: Union Village. Free Church.

Baker, Albert L.: Fort Ann.

Barber, the Rev. Philander.

Barbour, William. Officer of an anti-slavery society.

Barnard, John: Union Village. Officer of an anti-slavery society.

Bartlett, Lyman: Jackson. Liberty Party candidate.

Bigelow, Erastus: Union Village. Free church.

Bigelow, Dr. I.S. Officer of an anti-slavery society.

Bigelow, Horace: Union Village. Free Church. Liberty Party candidate.

Bigelow, Thomas: Hartford. Officer of an anti-slavery society. Liberty Party candidate.

Boyd, John H.: Whitehall.

Bullions, the Rev. Alexander: Cambridge.

Carlisle, John: Adamsville. WUBA.

Church, Leonard: Salem. Officer of an anti-slavery society. Liberty Party candidate.

Clark, John: Union Village. Free Church. Officer of an anti-slavery society.

Clarke, Jeremiah: Whitehall. Liberty Party candidate.

Cleaver, Hervey: Union Village. Officer of an anti-slavery society.

Coffin, Charles.

Colver, the Rev. N.: Union Village. WUBA. Nathaniel Colver assumed the pastorate at the Bottskill Baptist Church in 1834 after several years as an associate while the pastor in Fort Ann. That year he also took up the cause of abolition in earnest and from that time devoted most of his energies to anti-slavery. While at Bottskill, he lectured in the Adirondacks and Vermont and Massachusetts as an agent for the New York State and American Anti-Slavery societies. In 1839, he left Union Village and shepherded the Tremont Tabernacle in Boston to national prominence in the cause for emancipation.

Cook, Cortland: Union Village. Free Church.

Corliss, Almy: Union Village. Free Church. OSDASS.

Corliss, Dr. Hiram: Union Village. Corliss was probably the most important abolitionist north of Albany. He was founding president of the Washington County Anti-Slavery Society and the Eastern New York Anti-Slavery Society, the latter which had members as far south as New York City. Active in the leadership of Temperance and Medical societies, and the founder of the Orthodox Congregational Church, a comeouter church formed solely because of its devotion to emancipation, he was a Liberty Party candidate and president of the OSDASS.

Cormack, the Rev. William: Kingsbury. WUBA.

Crary, John: Salem.

Culver, Erastus: Union Village. Culver was the founding secretary of the Washington County Anti-Slavery Society. A Baptist (member of WUBA) and a Whig, he went on to great success as a politician and was elected to the New York State Assembly in 1838 and to Congress in 1844. In 1851, he moved to Brooklyn and opened a law office, which handled several high profile cases involving fugitive slaves. In 1854, he became a judge and made a reputation by protecting the rights of fugitive slaves. He also was among the founders of the Republican Party and campaigned heavily both for Fremont and Lincoln. The latter awarded him with an ambassadorship to Venezuela in 1862. Following his ambassadorship, he returned home to Union Village in semi-retirement where he took over as president of the Greenwich National Bank.

Estee, Clark. Officer of an anti-slavery society.

Frost, Daniel: Union Village. Free Church.

Gibbs, Leonard: Union Village. Gibbs was born in Granville in 1800 and became active in abolition during the early years of the movement. He was elected to the state assembly in 1838. In 1840, he moved to New York City, where he was a member of the American Anti-Slavery Society and, it is believed, was involved in the Underground Railroad. He moved back to Washington County in 1846, settling in Union Village, where he became a trustee of the Free Church and joined Hiram Corliss as the county's leader in abolition. In 1851, he served as Jerry Henry's lawyer during the famous Jerry Rescue in Syracuse. At his home in Union Village, he hosted both George Thompson and William Lloyd Garrison and, it is believed, many a fugitive slave. He was a Liberty Party candidate and a member of the OSDASS.

Gillette, the Rev. George: Granville. WUBA.

Gillis, George: Argyle. Officer of an anti-slavery society.

Green, Jonathan: Union Village. Officer of an anti-slavery society.

Griffin, Isaac: Quaker Springs. OSDASS.

Grinnel, Josiah: Union Village. Pastor of the Free Church, 1847–1850.

Gunn, Charles: Union Village. Free Church. Liberty Party candidate.

Haskell, Deodatus: Union Village. Free Church.

Hatch, Ira: Union Village.

Holmes, Henry: Union Village. Officer of an anti-slavery society.

Holmes, William A.: Union Village. Free Church.

Horton, H.V.: Union Village. Free Church.

Jackson, Irwin: Whitehall. Shoemaker.

Jackson, John: Fort Ann. Laborer; two different listings in 1860 census, one for head of household, the other living in the house of lumberman Franklin Thompson.

Johns, William: Town of Greenwich. Farm laborer born in Maryland.

Johnson, John: Jackson. Two listed, one could be the son based on age difference, and the latter lists birth in Virginia.

Joseph, Thomas: Whitehall. Barber.

Kellogg, the Rev. Lewis: Whitehall.

Kneeland, George: Whitehall. Boatman.

Lamb, Rufus A.: Union Village. Free Church.

Lansing, Wendell: Union Village. Founding member of the Washington County Anti-Slavery Society and editor of the *Union Village Banner*, he moved to Essex County in 1839, where he continued his activity in anti-slavery and edited the *Essex County Republican* and *Northern Standard*. His farm in Wilmington, Essex County, is believed to have been a stop on the Underground Railroad.

Lewis, Green R.: Galesville. Officer of an anti-slavery society.

Manyard, John: Town of Greenwich. Farmer who moved to Greenwich from Maryland in 1853.

Manyard, John, Jr.: Town of Greenwich.

Manyard, Samuel: Town of Greenwich.

Marsh, Martin. Officer of an anti-slavery society.

Martin, Andrew: Salem. Liberty Party candidate.

Martin, Mason: Argyle. Liberty Party candidate.

Mason, the Rev. J.O.: Union Village.

McKallor, Anthony: Argyle. Deacon in the abolitionist Presbyterian Church of Argyle. Liberty Party candidate and officer of an anti-slavery society.

McKinney, the Rev. Sabin: Union Village. Pastor of the Free Church for two years and son-in-law of Hiram Corliss, he moved to Fredonia in 1847.

Miller, the Rev. James P.: Argyle. Pastor of the South Argyle Presbyterian Church, he was one of the county's most active abolitionists and a vice-president of the Eastern NY Anti-Slavery Society. He moved to Oregon in 1851.

Morris, David: Jackson. Farm laborer, born in Delaware; his wife was born in Maryland.

Mosher, Henry: Easton. OSDASS officer.

Mowry, W.H.: Union Village. Son of the wealthy cotton manufacturer William Mowry, he devoted his life to the cause of abolition. Executive committee of the ENYASS. Along with Hiram Corliss, he founded the Free Church, and his wife, Angelina, also was active in the cause. Their house on Church Street is believed to have been a stop on the Underground Railroad. He died in 1850.

Parker, C.L.: Hartford. Officer of an anti-slavery society.

Peckham, Joseph: Easton. OSDASS officer.

Pettibone, George: Whitehall. Relatively prosperous black who was employed with the waterworks.

Prentiss, Luke: Union Village. Free Church.

Pritchett, the Rev. E.C.: Union Village. A native of Utica, Pritchett was for a time the secretary of the NYS Anti-Slavery Society and served on the executive committee of the ENYASS. During the 1830s, he traveled widely as an abolitionist lecturer in northern New York. In 1841, he came to Union Village where he was pastor of the Free Church until 1845.

Randall, Orlando: Union Village. Builder of the Free Church. Officer of an anti-slavery society.

Reid, James: Hebron. Liberty Party candidate.

Richards, Ralph: Whitehall & Hampton. Personal friend of John Brown, he was a leader in the county's Republican Party and served the party in the state's assembly and senate. Officer of an anti-slavery society. Liberty Party candidate.

Sarle, John: Granville. Liberty Party candidate.

Schuyler, Felix: Whitehall. Barber.

Schuyler, Thomas: Easton. Farmer.

Shattuck, the Rev. C.S.: Union Village. Western New York native, he was pastor of the Free Church, 1850–1860.

Shaw, the Rev. J.B.: Granville. Methodist minister whose house legend claims to have been an Underground Railroad stop.

Shipman, Hiram: Fort Ann. Officer of an anti-slavery society. Liberty Party candidate.

Shipman, Orrin B.: Fort Ann. Lecturer for the Liberty Party and follower of William Miller, his house in Fort Ann, now the Old Stone Library, is believed to have been a stop on the Underground Railroad.

Skinner, C.G.: Cambridge.

Skinner, Nathan

Smith, the Rev. John: Union Village. Pastor of the Free Church, 1838–1841.

Steele, James: Salem. Liberty Party candidate.

Stiles, Ransom: Argyle. Civic leader in Argyle during the 1840s and 1850s, excavation of his house during the 1950s revealed a long tunnel leading from the basement of his house.

Straight, John: Granville. Officer of an anti-slavery society.

Tobey, Francis: Easton. Neighbor of Esther and Job Wilbur, he was among the leaders of the vigilance committee protecting the Salter brothers during the 1858 incident involving slavecatchers.

Tuttle, the Rev. A.C.: Hartford.

Van Buren, John: Jackson. Laborer.

Van Vrankin, P.: Kingsbury. Barber.

Wait, the Rev. A.: Fort Edward & Pawlet, VT. WUBA.

Wales, Ira: Union Village. Free Church.

Watson, James: Union Village. Free Church.

Weeks, John: Jackson. Prosperous black farmer and former slave whose daughters married the fugitive slave Salter brothers.

Weeks, Edward: Jackson. A member of the Free Church, his sisters married the Salter brothers.

Weldon, Francis: Union Village. Officer of an anti-slavery society.

Wells, Elijah: Cambridge. Officer of an anti-slavery society.

Whipple, Marmaduke: Union Village. Officer of an anti-slavery society.

Wilbur, Esther: Easton. OSDASS. Leader in the abolition movement in Easton during the 1850s. Her house was a well-known stop on the Underground Railroad.

Wilbur, Job: Easton. Husband of Esther. OSDASS officer.

Wilbur, John: Easton. OSDASS officer.

Wilbur, Phebe: Easton. OSDASS.

Wilbur, Samuel: Easton. Secretary of the Old Saratoga District Anti-Slavery Society, he escorted both George Thompson and William Lloyd Garrison during their visits to Union Village.

Wilder, Abel: Union Village. Free Church.

Wilmarth, Edwin: Union Village. Free Church.

Wilson, Isaac: Hebron. Officer of an anti-slavery organization.

Witherspoon, the Rev. Andrew: Union Village.

Clinton County

The following list is taken from participants in anti-slavery meetings, members of the Liberty Party, subscribers to the *Herald of Freedom*, and those identified by Gerrit Smith as abolitionists following his 1845 visit to Clinton County. The list covers the period from 1835 to 1846. This does not mean that they were Underground Railroad agents, but it does mean that they were sympathetic.

Adams, William Y.: Plattsburgh.

Addoms, the Rev. John Townsend: Plattsburgh.

Allen, H.: Beekmantown.

Allen, Z.: AuSable Forks.

Anderson, George: Point Au Roche.

Arnold, Ashley: Peru. Officer of an anti-slavery society.

Arnold, E.J.: Peru.

Ashmun, Samuel: Champlain. Father of colonizationist Jehudi Ashmun.

Ashmun, Orson B.: Champlain. Editor of the *Herald of Freedom* and younger brother of Jehudi Ashmun. Liberty Party candidate. Officer of an anti-slavery society. (*Source: Gerrit Smith Tour*).

Bailey, the Rev. Phineas: Beekmantown.

Barber, A.D.: Beekmantown.

Barber, Alonzo: Beekmantown.

Barber, B.N.: Beekmantown.

Barber, J.W.: Beekmantown.

Barker, John H.: Peru. Officer of an anti-slavery society.

Barnes, H.

Barnes, Rollin: Chesterfield.

Beckwith, Beruck: Beekmantown. Officer of an anti-slavery society.

Beckwith, George: Plattsburgh.

Bedel, Levi: Birmingham.

Bidwell, Dr.: Plattsburgh.

Bigelow, A.: Keeseville.

Blackman, A.J.C.: Mooers.

Blanchard: Plattsburgh.

Boardman, Horace: Plattsburgh. Officer of an anti-slavery society. (*Source: Gerrit Smith Tour*).

Boardman, Lucius

Bowron, H.: Peru.

Brace, James

Brighard, James

Brigham, William H.: Keeseville.

Brisbin, E.: Champlain.

Brown, William G.: Plattsburgh. (*Source: Gerrit Smith Tour*).

Burdick, L.J.: Plattsburgh.
Buxton, Gilbert C.: Plattsburgh.
Chamberlain, Ira P.: Chazy. Officer of an anti-slavery society.
Chellis, Theran: Point Au Roche.
Cook, Calvin: Clintonville.
Cromwell, Charles: Peru.
Daily, John: Mooers.
Dilematter, J.: Peru.
Doolittle, L.
Douglass, James: Beekmantown.
Douglass, S.: Beekmantown.
Drury, Ebenezer: Peru.
Dunn, the Rev. H.: Mooers.
Elkins, the Rev. David: Point Au Roche.
Ferris, Charles: Peru.
Fink, Newell: Point Au Roche.
Fisk, S.: Chazy.
Fisk, William C.: Chazy.
Flack, James W.: AuSable Forks. Officer of an anti-slavery society.
Forge, Travers: Peru.
Garrett, R.S.: Beekmantown.
Haff, the Rev. Abraham: Peru. Officer of an anti-slavery society.
Havens, S.V.R.: Plattsburgh.
Hays, Daniel: Plattsburgh.
Hays, Simeon: Plattsburgh.
Hewitt, Henry: Plattsburgh.
Hoag, Daniel S.: Keeseville.
Hoag, E.: Peru.
Hoag, Elijah: Keeseville.
Hoag, Embree: Keeseville. Officer of an anti-slavery society.
Hoag, Nathaniel: Keeseville.
Hood, A.J.C.: Mooers.
Howar, Ira: Peru.
Howe, John S., Jr.: Beekmantown.
Hubbell, Silas: Champlain. Officer of an anti-slavery society.
Huff, E.D.: Peru.
Innsley, Henry G.: Plattsburgh.
Irvin, J.: Champlain.
Jackson, Orman: Plattsburgh.
Jackson, Stephen A.: Plattsburgh.
Jacobs, Leonard: Peru.
Keese, A.: Peru.
Keese, Anderson: Keeseville.
Keese, Hannah E.: Peru. Peru Female Anti-Slavery Society.
Keese, John H.: Peru.
Keese, Oliver: Peru.
Keese, Ruth H.: Peru. Peru Female Anti-Slavery Society.
Keese, S., II: Peru.
Keese, Samuel: Peru.
Keese, Willetts: Peru.

Keese, William: AuSable.
Kellogg, L.: Champlain.
Ketchum, Benjamin: Plattsburgh.
Kitchell, the Rev. Jonathan: Peru.
Knapp, Abel: Mooers.
Ladd, A.R.: Beekmantown.
Lansing, Wendell: Wilmington & Keeseville. Founding member of the Washington County Anti-Slavery Society and editor of the *Union Village Banner*, he moved to Essex County in 1839, where he continued his activity in anti-slavery and edited the *Essex County Republican* and *Northern Standard*. His farm is believed to have been a stop on the Underground Railroad.
Lapham, Nathan: Peru.
Lapham, Richard: Peru.
Linsley, Henry G.: Plattsburgh.
Lockwood, J.H.: Champlain.
Lockwood, R.S.: Saranac. Officer of an anti-slavery society.
Loomis, Gamaliel: Plattsburgh.
Loomis, Dr. E.S.: Champlain.
Loomis, Thomas: Plattsburgh.
Marsh, S.H.: Beekmantown.
Marshall, L.: Beekmantown.
Martin, Dorus: Ellenburgh. Officer of an anti-slavery society.
Moore, Edward: Champlain. (*Source: Gerrit Smith Tour*).
Moore, Noadiah: Champlain. Officer of an anti-slavery society. Liberty Party candidate.
Moore, William: Beekmantown.
Nays, Robers: Mooers.
Nichols, Eleazer: Peru.
Osgood, D.: Peru.
Perry, P.: Champlain.
Pope, Dr. Martin (Essex County)
Ransom, G.: Chazy.
Rice, Nathan: Peru.
Richard, Ira: Mooers.
Richardson, Asa: Beekmantown.
Rickison, George: Peru.
Roberts, O.T.: Beekmantown.
Roberts, P.B. Officer of an anti-slavery society.
Savage, H.D.: Champlain.
Seaton, the Rev. C.M.: Mooers.
Severance, George: Chazy.
Shedden, James S.: Mooers. Officer of an anti-slavery society.
Signor, Phillip: Peru. Officer of an anti-slavery society.
Simonds, B.J.: Beekmantown.
Skinner, Erastus: Plattsburgh.
Slason, C.S.: Beekmantown.
Smith, Eliza T.: Peru. Peru Female Anti-Slavery Society.

Smith, Mary: Peru. Peru Female Anti-Slavery Society.

Smith, R.: Beekmantown.

Smith, Stephen K.: Peru. Officer of an anti-slavery society.

Stafford, J.G.: Peru.

Stafford, R.: Plattsburgh.

Stearns, Hamilton J.: Beekmantown. Officer of an anti-slavery society.

Stearns, Thomas: AuSable Forks.

Thurber, "Gen." Ezra: Rouses Point.

Trombly, A.: Beekmantown.

Waters, Levi: Chazy.

Walpole, Joseph: Peru.

Wardner, Nathan: Port Douglas.

Watson, Thomas B.: Peru. Attorney, who early in his career helped abolitionize the Adirondack region, traveling anti-slavery lecture circuit. Officer of an anti-slavery society.

Weaver, Peter: Schuyler Falls. Officer of an anti-slavery society. Liberty Party candidate.

Weaver, Stephen: Schuyler Falls.

Wells, H.C.: Beekmantown.

Weston, Abner: Peru. Officer of an anti-slavery society.

Weston, E.

Weston, Lorenzo Milt: Peru. Officer of an anti-slavery society.

Weston, Nucum: Peru. Officer of an anti-slavery society.

Witherall: Beekmantown.

Witherspoon, the Rev. A.: Peru.

Wing, Stephen: Plattsburgh.

Saratoga County

Allen, Daniel: Greenfield. Liberty Party candidate.

Allen, Smith: Greenfield. Officer of an anti-slavery society.

Anthony, John: Greenfield.

Anthony, Mason: Greenfield. Several accounts refer to Mason as the county's leading conductor. Officer of an anti-slavery society. Liberty Party candidate.

Armstrong, James: Edinburgh. Liberty Party candidate.

Barker, John: Edinburgh. House has secret room that may have hidden fugitive slaves.

Benton, George: Greenfield. Officer of an anti-slavery society.

Benton, Samuel. Officer of an anti-slavery society.

Billings, Elias: Schuylerville.

Blodgett, Samuel. Officer of an anti-slavery society.

Briggs, J.C. Officer of an anti-slavery society.

Chester, the Rev. A.T.: Ballston Spa.

Corey, David. Officer of an anti-slavery society.

Davis, Dr. Sam: Ballston. Former slave owner whose house had hidden area that may have been used for fugitive slaves.

Delevan, E.C.: Ballston. Temperance leader and friend of Gerrit Smith.

Dubois, Cornelius: Hadley. Officer of an anti-slavery society.

Fitch, Mr. Henry: Efnor Lake. Local legend identifies his wilderness cabin as a stop on the UGRR.

Gansevoort, Gen. Peter: Gansevoort. Former slave owner whose house, local legends claims, became a stop on the UGRR.

Green, Thomas C.: Ballston Spa & Stillwater. Abolitionist, active statewide, who contributed money to Hiram Wilson to aid fugitive slaves in Canada. Officer of an anti-slavery society. Liberty Party candidate.

Greene, William P.: Ballston.

Griffen, Isaac: Quaker Springs. Quaker lore identifies his house as a stop on the UGRR. OSDASS.

Grey, John. Officer of an anti-slavery society.

Hall, H.H. Officer of an anti-slavery society.

Hill, Orrin: Quaker Springs.

Houghton, Nathaniel: Corinth.

Hoyt, Caleb E.

Kellett, the Rev.

Lamb, Rufus: Quaker Springs. OSDASS.

Lockwood, Clark: Maltaville.

McOmber, P.H.: Ballston Spa & Stillwater. Officer of an anti-slavery society.

Morey: Milton. Local legend claims house was a stop on the UGRR.

Mott, Jesse: Quaker Springs. Officer of an anti-slavery society.

Noyes, Henry: Edinburgh. Liberty Party candidate.

Scofield, Minor: Corinth.

Shepherd, William R.: Quaker Springs. OSDASS.

Sherman, Edmund J.: Hadley. Daughter's diary reveals his participation in the UGRR. Liberty Party candidate.

Sherman, Elijah: Quaker Springs. OSDASS. Officer of an anti-slavery society.

Shove, Eliza: Quaker Springs. OSDASS.

Smith, Horace E.: Locust Grove. Liberty Party candidate.

Smith, W.C. Officer of an anti-slavery society.

Thatcher, Dr.

Thomas, Moses.

Walworth, Reuben, Judge: Saratoga Springs. State's highest judicial official and Temperance leader; he was a friend of Gerrit Smith and entertained William Lloyd Garrison; legend claims a former slave who was a servant in his household hid fugitive slaves in the Judge's cellar.

Wilbur, Henry: Quaker Springs. OSDASS.

Wilde, Deborah: Quaker Springs. OSDASS.

Wilde, Jonathan: Quaker Springs. OSDASS. Officer of an anti-slavery society.

Wilde, Sarah: Quaker Springs. OSDASS.

Wilkins, Elder J.B.: Milton.

Wright, Cornelius: Quaker Springs. Quaker lore identifies his house as a stop on the UGRR.

Yeomans, Vincent: Milton. Liberty Party candidate.

Warren County

Arnold, Oliver: Chestertown. The owner of the Temperance Tavern in Chestertown from 1832–1853, he was listed as a vice-president in the NYS Anti-Slavery society in 1840. Liberty Party candidate.

Baker, the Rev. Thomas: Darrowsville. Pastor of the Wesleyan-Methodist Church, legend claims he hid fugitive slaves at his parsonage.

Beach, Henry: Luzerne.

Boyd, Rufus: Glens Falls. (*Source: Samuel Boyd account*).

Burnham, Cyrus: Glens Falls. Purchased Eagles Nest camp from Gerrit Smith in 1848. (*Source: Gerrit Smith tour*).

Cameron, James I.: Caldwell.

Dayton, the Rev. James: Stony Creek.

Fowler, Mr.: Chestertown.

Hawley, George: Glens Falls. Officer of an anti-slavery society.

Leggett, Joseph: Chestertown. President of the county Liberty Party, his son's description of fugitive slaves being hidden at his house is part of family legend. Officer of an anti-slavery society.

Hotchkiss, David: Chestertown.

McNutt, Dr. Hiram: Glens Falls/Warrensburg. Local legend claims his houses were stops on the UGRR.

Milne, the Rev. A.D.: Chestertown. Pastor of Chestertown Baptist Church; editor of

The Star of Destiny, a Baptist monthly, and the *Glens Falls Messenger* (1856–58). Officer of an anti-slavery society.

Paddock, Ira A.: Glens Falls.

Putnam, the Rev. Enos: Johnsburg. Wesleyan-Methodist minister, whose daughter's diary describes his participation in the Underground Railroad.

Rice, Julius H.: Glens Falls. Legend says his house along the south shore of the Hudson River was a stop on the UGRR.

Satterlee, Leroy: Queensbury. Officer of an anti-slavery society.

Somerville, Wesley: Johnsburg.

Stoddard, Dr. Joseph: Glens Falls. (*Source: Samuel Boyd account*).

Tripp, Myron: Chestertown. Founder of the Darrowsville Wesleyan-Methodist Church; legend says he collaborated with the Rev. Baker.

Tyrell, Judge: Rt. 9, near Igerna. Hidden room found in his house. (*Source: Gerrit Smith tour*).

Van Pelt, John: Glens Falls. Barber whose fugitive slave wife was forced to flee to Canada when slavecatchers came to town. (*Source: Samuel Boyd account*).

Wells, the Rev. Amos: Glens Falls. Officer of an anti-slavery society.

Wilcox, Mr.: Luzerne. (*Source: Sherman diary*).

Williams, the Rev. Charles: Queensbury. Pastor of West Mountain Baptist Church, which legend claims may have been a UGRR stop. Officer of an anti-slavery society.

Willson, Allen T.: Queensbury. Officer of an anti-slavery society.

Essex County

Alexander, John F.: Westport.

Allen, G.W.: Moriah. Officer of an anti-slavery society.

Ames, Alfred: Elizabethtown. Officer of an anti-slavery society.

Blake, Joseph: Elizabethtown.

Blish, Daniel: Jay.

Boynton, J.C.: Jay. Officer of an anti-slavery society.

Bullard, Stephen: Ticonderoga.

Bullen, L.: Moriah.

Butler, L.: Moriah.

Calhoun, Joel A.: Westport.

Chandler, John: Westport. Officer of an anti-slavery society.

Chase, R.C.R.

Clarke, C.M.: Elizabethtown.

Clinton, the Rev. O.P.: Lewis.

Cole, Albert P.: Westport.

Cole, Caleb: Westport.

Cook, the Rev. Stephen: Willsboro.

Cutting, William J.: Westport. Officer of an anti-slavery society.

Edgerton, James B.: Moriah. Liberty Party candidate.

Estee, the Rev. Sidney A.: Westport & Ticonderoga.

Finch, Isaac: Jay. Officer of an anti-slavery society.

Finch, William W.

Firril, O.: Elizabethtown.

Frisbie, L.: Westport.

Garner, William: Elizabethtown.

Gaves, H.B.: Crown Point. Officer of an anti-slavery society.

Gay, Jesse: Elizabethtown. Many of the reports of anti-slavery society meetings in the county were written by Gay, who often served as the organization's secretary.

Gilman, Fay P.: Keene.

Goodrich, Andrew: Elizabethtown.

Goodrich, Erastus: Elizabethtown.

Grant, the Rev. William: Moriah.

Grant, Stillman: Moriah.

Hall, Henry: Jay.

Hall, Monroe: Jay.

Hammond, Calvin: Westport.

Hammond, Gideon: Westport. Officer of an anti-slavery society.

Hammond, Luther B.: Westport.

Harris, Isaac: Westport.

Havens, George: Moriah.

Hikok, Rogers: Wilmington.

Hillman, Joseph: Keene.

Hodges, the Rev. C.W.: Westport & Essex.

Hoffnagle, John: Willsboro. Officer of an anti-slavery society.

Jones, Pierpont: Jay. Liberty Party candidate.

Kent, D.H. Westport.

Kimball, James: Chairman of the 1850 FSL Meeting held in Jay. Officer of an anti-slavery society.

Kingsley, the Rev. W.

Lansing, Wendell: Wilmington. Founding member of the region's first anti-slavery society in Washington County in 1834; legend says his farm in Wilmington was a frequent haven for fugitive slaves.

Law, Shelden: Moriah.

Livingston, Deacon: Lewis.

MacDougall family: Elizabethtown. According to Emily McMasters, the MacDougall family who lived in the "old Bradford House" worked with the Rev. Thomas Baker and John Brown in transporting fugitive slaves.

Merriam, William B.: Westport.

Mihills, U.D.: Keene.

Newell, E.P.: Jay. Officer of an anti-slavery society.

Newell, Hiram: Jay.

Newell, Peter C.: Jay.

Nichols, Dan: Westport.

Nichols, Ezra: Elizabethtown.

Nichols, Jonathan: Westport.

Osgood, Iddo: North Elba.

Person, N.N.: Elizabethtown.

Pope, Martin: Chesterfield. Officer of an anti-slavery society.

Porter, James P.: Moriah.

Post, Asa: Elizabethtown.

Potter, the Rev. Lewis: Westport.

Potter, Warren: Westport.

Prindle, the Rev. Cyrus: Jay. Prindle was a well-traveled Wesleyan-Methodist minister, who did a great deal of outreach. He openly admitted he was involved in the Underground Railroad and spent time in Canada assisting fugitive slaves.

Purmont, George E.: Jay.

Purmont, John: Jay.

Purmont, John, Jr.: Jay.

Ramney, H.D.: Westport.

Reed, the Rev. L.: Moriah.

Rome, L.: Elizabethtown.

Sampson, I.J.: Elizabethtown.

Shaw, Enos: Keene.

Shepherd, Samuel: Moriah.

Skiff, David C.: St. Armand.

Slaughter, Oliver: Westport.

Smith, Elias: Moriah.

Smith, John G.: Westport.

Smith, the Rev. Lyman: Moriah.

Spooner, Alfred S.: Elizabethtown.

Stow, John G.: Westport.

Thompson, Roswell: North Elba. Thompson's son, Henry, and daughter, Isabella, married a son and daughter of John Brown; two of his other sons, William and Dauphin, died at Harpers Ferry.

Tinney, Joel: Westport.

Titus, E.G.: St. Armand.

Tobey, Jesse, Jr.: Jay.

Warren, Samuel. Officer of an anti-slavery society.

Wheeler, Elder Lloyd: Lewis. Officer of an anti-slavery society.

Whitney, Lemuel: Westport.

Wilkins, Samuel A.: Westport.

Williams, A.: Westport.

Wise, Enos: Elizabethtown.
Woodruff, the Rev. S.: Westport.

Franklin County

(Most of those listed were identified in *Historical Sketches of Franklin County* by Frederick Seaver.)

Beaman, Timothy: Malone.
Bell, Truman: Malone.
Berry Jehiel: Malone.
Bicknell, Simeon: Malone.
Bigelow, Rensselaer: Malone.
Bowles, the Rev. Charles: Malone. Son of black minister the Rev. Charles Bowles.
Burnap, the Rev. Bliss: Malone & Bangor.
Canfield, Thomas H. Organizer of first societies in the county.
Case, the Rev. Anthony: Malone.
Cheney, George A.: Fort Covington.
Conant, Dr. Ophir: Malone. Conant was a vice-president in the Eastern NY Anti-Slavery Society.
Dickinson, Horace: Malone.
Dimick, Major: Malone.
Drew, Samuel C.: Malone.
Harwood, Simeon C.: Malone.
Hawley, Milo: Malone.
Hitchcock, Albon H.: Malone.
Holland, James H.: Malone.
Hutton, George H.: Malone.
Johnson, the Rev. Charles: Malone.
Langdon, Sylvester: Malone.
Longley, Henry: Malone.
Mason, William: Malone.
Merill family: Merillville.
Millar, the Rev. A.: Malone.
Noble, Daniel: Fort Covington.
Orcutt, Alva: Malone.
Paddock, the Rev. Stephen: Malone.
Paddock, Thomas S.: Malone.
Parkhurst, Jabez: Fort Covington. Seaver singles him out as the county's foremost conductor of fugitive slaves. He was also the most active abolitionist, traveling at least as far as Albany to attend meetings, the leader of the county's Liberty Party, and a vice-president in the state anti-slavery society.
Parmalee, the Rev. Ashbel: Malone. Long-time pastor of the Congregational Church in Malone, which legend claims was an UGRR stop, he also was a supporter of colonization, which was opposed by most abolitionists.
Peck, Phineas: Malone.

Perrin, Solon: Malone.
Powell, Thomas R.: Malone.
Quaw, the Rev. J.E.: Malone.
Schoolcraft, Philip: Malone.
Spencer, Ira: Malone.
Tobery, George: Malone.
Townsend, Amasa: Malone.
Wallace, Jonathan: Malone.
Westcott, Oliver: Malone.
Woodruff, the Rev. Silas: Malone. Succeeded Parmalee as pastor of the Congregational Church.

St. Lawrence County

Aiken, David: Lisbon. Wesleyan-Methodist Church.
Allen, Hugh: East Stockholm. Wesleyan-Methodist Church.
Allen, John: Morley. Wesleyan-Methodist Church.
Allen, William: Morley. Wesleyan-Methodist Church.
Babcock, Jesse: Dexter.
Beach, Ira: East Stockholm. Wesleyan-Methodist Church.
Bese, Stephen: exec. officer of an anti-slavery society.
Bloodget, Samuel: Russell.
Bloss, Walter W.,: Parishville.
Bowles, the Rev. Charles, Jr.: Hopkinton. Son of black minister, the Rev. Charles Bowles, who for many years ministered to congregations in Vermont and Washington County, NY.
Buffam, Thomas Buffam: Morley. Wesleyan-Methodist Church.
Byington, the Rev. John: Bucks Bridge.
Calhoun, J.A.: Parishville.
Calhoun, Joel A.: Parishville. Officer of an anti-slavery society.
Chamberlain, Anson: Chamberlain Corners.
Chamberlain, Ralph Chamberlain: Chamberlain Corners.
Chapman, Augustus: Morristown.
Clemens, D.: Morley. Wesleyan-Methodist Church.
Collester, Arba: Russell. Officer of an anti-slavery society.
Crary, Nathan, Jr.: Officer of an anti-slavery society.
Cushman, Myron: S. Hammond.
Dayton, Norman: Canton.
Golding, W.W.
Goodale, Francis: Parishville.

Green, Nathan. President of Parishville Anti-Slavery Society.

Greene, the Rev. Henry. Officer of an anti-slavery society.

Hawes, Cassim. Officer of an anti-slavery society.

Hubbard, Claudius.

Hudson, Stephen, Jr.: Parishville.

Hulburd, Calvin T.: Brasher Falls.

Jenkins, Elias: East Stockholm. Wesleyan-Methodist Church.

Johnson, John: Gouverneur.

Kelsey, James: East Stockholm. Wesleyan-Methodist Church.

King, James T.: Russell

Knowles, Esq., Liberty. First president of St. Lawrence Anti-Slavery.

Martin, John: Lisbon. Wesleyan-Methodist Church.

Martin, Thomas: Lisbon. Wesleyan-Methodist Church.

Meyers: Point Rockaway, Waddington.

Miles, Harvey: Russell. Officer of an anti-slavery society.

Morgan, Elihu: Russell.

Ogden, David: Ogden Island, Waddington.

Ogden, the Rev. George.

Pegler, the Rev. George: Parishville.

Perkins, John: Parishville. Officer of an anti-slavery society.

Perkins, Leonard: Parishville.

Plat, Joseph: Lisbon. Wesleyan-Methodist Church.

Reddington, William L.,: Parishville.

Seger, Joel: Morley. Wesleyan-Methodist Church.

Smith, Truman. Officer of an anti-slavery society.

Stillman, Austin: East Stockholm. Wesleyan-Methodist Church.

Storrs, Isaac: Lisbon. Wesleyan-Methodist Church.

Taylor, Fisk: Parishville. Officer of an anti-slavery society.

Warren, Arastus: Russell. Officer of an anti-slavery society.

Webster: South Hammond.

Whitney, Zelotus: Morley. Wesleyan-Methodist Church.

Williams, James, Esq.: President of Russell Anti-Slavery Society.

Yale, Barnabus

Yale, Lord C. Officer of an anti-slavery society.

WORKS CITED

"AAS Annual Business Meeting." *National Anti-Slavery Standard*, 16 May 1844: 199.

"The Abolition Convention." *Washington County Journal*, 26 Feb. 1852: 2.

"Abolitionism in Kentucky." *Pennsylvania Freeman*, 27 Nov. 1851: 1.

Adams, Alice Dana. *The Neglected Period of Anti-Slavery in America (1808–1831)*. Cambridge: Radcliffe College, 1908.

African Americans in Albany, Ruth Roberts Collection, Box I, Folder 25, Albany Institute of History and Art, Albany, NY.

Africans in America: Judgment Day. PBS Online. www.pbs.org/wgbh/aia/part3/3p1518.html.

Africans in America: Judgment Day. PBS Online. www.pbs.org/wgbh/aia/part4/4p2930.html.

"Aid the Fugitive." *Emancipator*, 8 June 1843: 23.

"Albany Anti-Slavery Convention." *Friend of Man*, 14 March 1838.

Albany Directory and City Register. Albany, NY: Edmund B. Child, 1829–1837.

Albany Directory and City Register. Albany, NY: L.G. Hoffman, 1837–1852.

Albany Directory and City Register. Albany, NY: J. Munsell, 1853–1860.

"Albany Liberty Party Convention." *Albany Patriot*, 2 April 1845.

Albany Patriot, 2 April 1845.

Allen, Everett. *Children of the Light: The Rise and Fall of New Bedford Whaling and the Death of the Arctic Fleet*. Orleans, MA: Parnassus Imprints, 1983.

Allen, William G. *The American Prejudice Against Color*. London: W. & F.G. Cash, 1853.

Alsdorf, Dorothy. "History of our area." *Ballston Journal*, 27 Sept 1978.

"Annual Meeting of the New York State Anti-Slavery Society." *Friend of Man*, 21 September 1841: 186.

"Annual Report of the Albany Female A.S. Society." *Albany Patriot*, 10 May 1848.

Annual Report of the Committee. Albany: Eastern NY A.S. Society & Fugitive Slaves, 1843.

"Another Fugitive Slave Case." *Glens Falls Free Press*, 17 September 1851.

"Another Martyr to Liberty." *The Liberator*, 16 Aug. 1850.

"Anti-Nebraska, County Mass Meeting." *People's Journal*, 3 August 1854.

"Anti-Slavery Convention at Peru." *National Anti-Slavery Standard*, 27 Dec. 1856: 3.

"Anti-Slavery Convention." *Friend of Man*, 26 Sept. 1838.

"Anti-Slavery in Action in 1838: A Letter from Vermont's Secretary of State." *Vermont History*. Vol. 41, 1973: 7–8.

"Anti-Slavery Indifference." *National Anti-Slavery Standard*, 6 Dec. 1856: 3.

"Anti-Slavery Movements." *Friend of Man*, 21 July 1836: 18.

"Anti-Slavery Societies." *The Liberator*, 4 August 1837: 137.

"Anti-Slavery Society." *Albany Patriot*, 21 May 1845: 110.

Aptheker, Herbert. *Abolitionism: A Revolutionary Movement*. Boston: Twayne Publishers, 1989.

_____. "Militant Abolitionism." *Journal of Negro History*, Oct. 1942: 438–484.

"Arrest and Imprisonment of William L. Chaplin." *The Liberator*, 23 August 1850.

"The Arrest—The Rescue—The Flight." *The Liberator*, 21 Feb. 1851: 30.

"The Assault Upon Rev. John G. Fee."

"Attempt to Kidnap a Colored Woman." *The Liberator*, 6 Sept. 1850.

"Attempted Suicide of a Fugitive." *Syracuse Daily Standard*, 26 Oct. 1850.

Bacon, Charles L. *The Gibbses of Granville, New York*. Milford, NH: Cabinet Press, 1984.

Bailey, William S. "The Underground Railroad in Southern Chautauqua County." *New York History*, Vol. XVI, No. 1, January 1935.

Barbour, Hugh *et al.*, editors. *Quaker Crosscurrents: Three Hundred Years of Friends in the New York Yearly Meetings*. Syracuse: Syracuse University Press, 1995.

"A Bell Tolled." *Sandy Hill Herald*, 13 Dec. 1859: 2.

Bell, Howard Holman. *Minutes of the Proceedings of National Negro Conventions, 1830–1864*. 1969.

"Berkshire's Old Underground Railroads." *Berkshire Hills*, 1 Jan. 1901: 7.

Blankman, Edward. "Under the North Star." *Adirondack Life*, March-April 1983: 34–38.

Blockson, Charles L. *The Underground Railroad: First Person Narratives of Escapes from Slavery*. New York: Prentice Hall, 1987.

Boller, Jr., Paul. "Washington, the Quakers, and Slavery." *Journal of Negro History*, April 1961: 83–88.

Bolster, Jeffrey. *Black Jacks: African American Seamen in the Age of Sail*. Cambridge: Harvard University Press, 1997.

Boyd, Samuel. "In Days of Old Glens Falls—As I Remember It." Glens Falls, 1927.

Bradford, Sarah Hopkins. *Harriet Tubman: The Moses of Her People*. New York: Corinth Books, 1961.

Briaddy, Katherine Q. *Ye Olde Days: A History of Burnt-Hills-Ballston Lake*. Ballston Spa: Journal Press, 1974.

Britten, Evelyn. *Chronicles of Saratoga*. Saratoga Springs: Bradshaw, 1947.

Broadwell, Andrew. "The Thurber Family of Rouses Point." Unpublished, No date.

Brooks, Elaine. "The Massachusetts Anti-Slavery Society." *Journal of Negro History*, July 1945: 311–330.

Brothers, Waymand. Personal Interview. May 2002.

Brown, C.S. *Memoir of Rev. Abel Brown*. Worcester, 1849.

Brown, George S. *Brown's Abridged Journal, Containing a Brief Account of the Life, Trials and Travels of George S. Brown, Six Years a Missionary in Liberia*. Troy, NY: Prescott and Wilson, 1849.

Brown, Henry. *Narrative of the Life of Henry Box Brown*. Manchester: Lee and Glynn, 1851. (This book is available electronically through the University of North Carolina at Chapel Hill Library).

"Brutal Outrage." *The Liberator*, 14 July 1848: 110.

Burr, David H. "State of New York." New York: J. H. Colton & Co., 1836.

Burrows, Edwin G., and Mike Wallace. *Gotham: A History of New York City to 1898*. New York: Oxford University Press, 1999.

Calarco, Tom. "Did Sign at Vaughn Corners in Kingsbury Show Slaves the Way?" *The Chronicle*, 3 Dec. 1998.

_____. "Underground Railroad." *Homestyle Magazine*, March 1999.

_____, and Hope Ferguson. "Riding the Underground Railroad." *Glens Falls Post-Star*, 10 March 1991: 1.

Campbell, Stanley W. *The Slave Catchers 1850–1860*, Chapel Hill: University of North Carolina Press, 1970.

Caro, Edythe Quinn. *The Hills in the Mid-Nineteenth Century: The History of a Rural African-American Community in Westchester County, N.Y.* Valhalla, NY: Westchester County Historical Society, 1988.

"The Case of William L. Chapman." Boston: The Chaplin Committee, 1851.

"Catskill, N.Y." *Friend of Man*, 18 August 1836.

"Cazenovia Convention." *The Liberator*, 30 August 1850.

"Champlain, NY." *Friend of Man*, 3 Nov. 1836: 78.

"The Chaplin Meeting." *The Liberator*, 24 Jan. 1851.

"Chester to Canton Road." *Tahawus Cloudsplitter*, Vol. XXI, No. 5, Sept-Oct. 1969.

Christianson, Scott. "The Battle for Charles Nalle." *American Legacy*, Winter 1997: 30–35.

"Circular from the Chaplin Fund Committee." Cazenovia, NY. 22 August 1850.

"Clinton County Convention." *Friend of Man*, 26 July 1837: 23.

Coleman, Edward M. "William Wells Brown as an Historian." *Journal of Negro History*, January 1946: 47–59.

Collison, Gary L. *Shadrach Minckins: From Fugitive Slave to Citizen*. Boston: Harvard University Press, 1997.

The Colored American, 14 March 1840: 3.

"Coloured Gentlemen at Saratoga." *National Anti-Slavery Standard*, 18 Aug. 1855.

"Comfort and Economy for the Traveller." *Albany Patriot*, 10 May 1848.

"Communications." *Friend of Man*, 9 Sept. 1840: 189.

"Convention at Albany." *Friend of Man*, 23 Feb. 1841: 67.

"Convention at Troy." *Albany Patriot*, 29 Jan. 1845.

"Convention of Christians and Christian Ministers." *Albany Patriot*, 30 Sept. 1846.

Cook, Flavius. *Sketches of Essex County*. W. Lansing & Sons, 1858, 93.

Corbin, Jay S., compiler. *Centennial Souvenir History of Gouverneur, Rossie, Fowler, Hammond, Edwards, DeKalb*. Watertown, NY: The Hungerford-Holbrook Co, 1905.

Corey, Allen. *Gazetteer of the County of Washington, New York, 1849–50*. Schuylerville, NY, 1850.

Corliss-Sheldon Families Genealogical Biographic. Hartford: States Historical Society, Inc., Publishers and Engravers.

"Correspondence of the Albany Patriot." *Albany Patriot*, 1 Jan. 1845; 15 April 1846; 28 Oct. 1846: 203.

Country Properties Real Estate. Description of Forbes House. 1999.

Cramer, Clayton E. *Black Demographic Data, 1790–1860*. Westport, CT: Greenwood Publishing Group, Inc., 1997.

Crannell, Linda. Telephone interview with researcher of history of Argyle Poorhouse. 16 Oct. 1999.

Cross, Whitney R. *The Burned Over District*. Ithaca: Cornell University Press, 1950.

Curtis, Gates, ed. *Our County and Its People: A Memorial Record of St. Lawrence County, N.Y.*, 1894.

"Death of Abel Brown." *Albany Patriot*, 27 Nov. 1844.

"Death of William H. Topp." *National Anti-Slavery Standard*, 19 December 1857.

"Deaths." *Plattsburgh Republican*, 28 May 1842.

"Decision of the Supreme Court." *National Anti-Slavery Standard*, 15 May 1842: 189.

"Decision of the Supreme Court." *Northern Star and Freeman's Advocate*, 17 March 1842.

"The 'Delevan House.'" *Albany Patriot*, 27 January 1847: 47.

Doolittle, Will. "Argyle Black Man Among Area's Civil War Veterans." *Glens Falls Post-Star*, 3 Aug 1997: B1.

Dougan, Arthur. Personal Letter. 4 April 1998.

Douglass, Frederick. *Life and Times of Frederick Douglass*. Hartford, CT: Park Publishing Co., 1881.

_____. *My Bondage and My Freedom*. New York: Miller, Orton, & Mulligan, 1855.

Downs, Robert B. *Books That Changed the World*. New York: New American Library, 1956.

Drew, Benjamin. *A North-Side View of Slavery*. Reading, MA: Addison-Wesley Pub. Co., 1969.

Durant, Samuel W. *History of St. Lawrence County*. Philadelphia: L. H. Everts & Co., 1878.

"Duty of the People of the North to Incite and Assist the Slaves of the South to Escape from Slavery." *The Liberator*, 10 Jan. 1851.

"Eastern New York Anti-Slavery Society Organizational Meeting." *The Emancipator*, 12 May 1842: 7.

Editorial. *Northern Star and Freeman's Advocate*, 3 January 1843.

Emancipator, 30 June 1836: 34; 18 August 1836; 2 Nov. 1837: 104; 22 Nov. 1838; 29 June 1843: 34.

"Essex County Anti-Slavery Convention." *Friend of Man*, 23 August 1837.

Everest, Allan Seymour. *Pioneer Homes of Clinton County, 1790–1820*. Plattsburgh, NY: Clinton County Historical Association, 1966.

_____. *Pliny Moore, North Carolina Pioneer of Champlain, N.Y.* Plattsburgh: Clinton County Historical Association, 1990.

_____, ed. *Recollection of Clinton County and the Battle of Plattsburgh, 1800–1840; memoirs of early residents from the notebooks of D.S. Kellogg*. Plattsburgh, NY, 1964.

_____, ed. *Recollections*. Plattsburgh: Clinton County Historical Association, 1964.

"An Exciting Slave Case." *The Liberator*, 16 August 1850.

Field, Phyllis. *The Politics of Race in New York*. Ithaca: Cornell University Press, 1982.

Finney, Charles G. *Systematic Theology*.

"First Annual Report of the New York Committee of Vigilance for the Year 1837." New York: Piercy & Reed, 1837.

Fish, Martin. Personal Interview. May 1999.

Fleming, Thomas J. "The Trial of John Brown." *American Heritage*, August 1967: 28–33; 92–100.

Foner, Eric. "Politics and Prejudice: The Free Soil Party and the Negro, 1849–1852." *Journal of Negro History*, Vol. 50, 1965: 239–256.

Foner, Philip S. and George E. Walker, eds. *Proceedings of the Black State Conventions, 1840–1865.* Philadelphia: Temple University Press, 1979.

"For several years..." *Northern Star and Freeman's Advocate*, 3 March 1842.

"For the Patriot." *Albany Patriot*, 29 Jan. 1845

"Forte letter to Cuffe." Africans in America, Part 3, cited at http://www.pbs.org/wgbh/aiaold/part3/3h484.html

"Franckean Lutheran Synod." *Friend of Man*, 14 June 1837.

"Franklin County." *Friend of Man*, 25 January 1838.

"Frederick Douglass." *The Liberator*, 27 Sept. 1850: 156.

"Freedom and Slavery for Afric-Americans." *National Anti-Slavery Standard*, 1 Feb. 1844: 139

"Freedom of Discussion." *Salem County Post and North Star*, 11 November 1835: 1.

"Friday Evening, May 26, 1854..." *Albany Evening Journal*, 26 May 1854: 2.

Friedman, S. Morgan. "The Inflation Calculator." http://www.westegg.com/inflation/.

Friend of Man, 18 July 1838; 21 Sept. 1841:186; 11 Jan. 1842.

"A Friendly Tribute." *The Liberator*, July 8, 1853:106.

"From Peru." *Friend of Man*, 26 April 1837.

"From the Boston Traveller of Saturday morning." *Albany Evening Journal*, 29 May 1854.

"From the Plains of Saratoga." *Friend of Man*, 26 April 1837.

Frothingham, Octavius Brooks. *Gerrit Smith: A Biography*. New York: G.P. Putnam's Sons, 1878.

"The Fugitive Slave Law." *Sandy Hill Herald*, 3 Dec 1850.

"A Fugitive Slave." *Emancipator*, 12 October 1837: 94.

"Fugitive Slaves in Canada." *Essex County Republican*, 26 Oct. 1850.

"Fugitives in Canada." *The Liberator*, 19 May 1854: 80.

Gara, Larry. *The Liberty Line: The Legend of the Underground Railroad.* Lexington: Univ. of Kentucky Press, 1967.

"George Corliss Papers." Brown University, Box 13 / Folder 9.

"George Thompson in Union Village." *The Liberator*, 28 Feb. 1851: 35.

"George Thompson, M.P." *Albany Patriot*, 5 Jan. 1848: 32.

"Gerrit Smith Anti-Slavery Tour." *Albany Patriot*, 25 June 1844: 130–131.

"Gerrit Smith's Land." *Albany Patriot*, 26 April 1848.

"Glens Falls." *Albany Patriot*, 12 Nov. 1845: 2.

Goodell, William. *Slavery and Anti-Slavery: A History of the Great Struggle in Both Hemispheres; with a View of the Slavery Question in the United States.* New York: William Harned Publishers, 1852.

Goodman, Paul. *Of One Blood: Abolition and the Origin of Racial Equality.* Berkeley: University of California, 1998.

Graham, Kathryn. "A Negro from the North." Unpublished paper.

Granville Sentinel, 11 Dec. 1991.

"Great Meeting of Colored People in Troy." *Albany Patriot*, 28 Oct. 1846.

"Greene County Anti-Slavery Society." *Friend of Man*, 26 June 1839: 7.

Griffen, Harry Wygant. *Ancestry and Descendants of Jonathan Griffen, 1757–1837.* Ballston Lake, NY: Meader Family Association, 1983.

Gross, Bella. *Clarion Call.* New York, 1947.

_____. "Life and Times of Theodore S. Wright, 1797–1847." *The Negro History Bulletin*, June 1940.

Groth, Michael E. "Forging Freedom in the Mid-Hudson Valley: The End of Slavery and the Formation of a Free African-American Community in Dutchess County." Ph. D. Thesis. SUNY Binghamton, 1994.

Gurnet, Kate. "Land of the free." *Times-Union*, 24 Feb. 2002: G1, G4.

"H.B. Northup, Esq..." *Sandy Hill Herald*, 25 Jan. 1853: 2.

Hall, Terri "A Conductor on the Freedom Train." *Gannett Westchester Newspapers*, 23 Feb. 1986: E1.

Hanna, Mrs. Howard. Personal Letter. 10 Feb. 1992.

Harlow, Ralph Volney. *Gerrit Smith, Philanthropist and Reformer.* New York: Henry Holt and Company, 1938.

"The Harper's Ferry Outrage." *Sandy Hill Herald*, 1 Nov. 1859: 2.

Hart, Larry. *Tales of Old Schenectady*. Scotia, NY: Old Dorp Books, 1975.

Hayner, Rutherford. *Troy and Rensselaer County, NY*. New York: Lewis Historical Publishing, Co., 1925.

Hearn, Chester G. *Companions in Conspiracy*. Gettysburg: Thomas Publications, 1996.

"Hearsay and History." *Greenwich Journal*, 30 March 1949.

Henderson, Alice H. "The History of the New York State Anti-Slavery Society," Ph.D. Thesis. University of Michigan, 1963.

Hendricks, John R. "The Liberty Party in New York State, 1838–1848." Ph.D. Thesis. Fordham University, 1959.

Hibbard, George S. *Rupert, Vermont, Historical and Descriptive*. 1899.

Hill, Daniel G. "Black History in Early Toronto" *Polyphony Summer 1984*, 28–30.

Himes, Joshua V. *View of the Prophecies and Prophetic Chronology, Selected from the Manuscripts of William Miller with a Memoir of His life*. Boston: Moses A. Dow, 1841.

"Hiram Corliss Obituary." *Troy Times*, 8 Sept 1877; as quoted in Corliss-Sheldon Families Genealogical Biographic. States Historical Society, Inc. Hartford, CT: Publishers & Engravers.

Hirsch, Leo H. "The Negro and New York, 1783 to 1865." *Journal of Negro History*, October 1931: 382–473.

"History of Bethel Free Church, Troy, N.Y." Pamphlet. Undated.

"History of the Chestertown Leggett Homestead." Unpublished flyer. Leggett Family.

Hochschild, Harold. *Township 34: A History with Digressions of an Adirondack Township in Hamilton County in the State of New York*. New York, 1952.

Hodges, Graham. "David Ruggles: The Hazards of Anti-Slavery Journalism." *Media Studies Journal*, Spring/Summer 2000.

Hodges, Willis Augustus. *Free Man of Color: The Autobiography of Willis Augustus Hodges*. Knoxville: University of Tennessee Press, 1982.

Holden, A.W. *A History of the Town of Queensbury, in the State of New York: With Biographical Sketches of Many of Its Distinguished Men, and Some Account of the Aborigines of Northern New York*. Albany: J. Munsell, 1874.

"The Hostile Camps." *Plattsburgh Republican*, 12 Nov. 1859: 3.

Hough, Franklin. *History of St. Lawrence and Franklin Counties*. Albany: Little and Co., 1853.

Howe, Samuel G. "The Refugees from Slavery in Canada West: Report to the Freedmen's Inquiry Commission." Boston: Wright & Potter, 1864.

Howell, George Rogers, and Jonathan Tenney, eds. *History of Albany County*. Albany, 1886.

Hulslander, Laura Penny. *Washington County Poorhouse Records*. El Paso, TX: Sleeper Press, 1997.

Hurd, Duane Hamilton. *History of Clinton and Franklin Counties*. 1880. Plattsburgh, NY: Clinton County Bicentennial American Revolution Commission, 1978.

"In Pursuance of the Previous Notice ..." *Plattsburgh Republican*, 12 September 1835.

"Inauguration of the Republican Party in the State of New York." *National Anti-Slavery Standard*, 6 October 1855.

"The Inflation Calculator." http://www.westegg.com/inflation.

"Interesting Correspondence." *Glens Falls Republican*, 22 April 1846.

"Interesting Slave Case." *National Anti-Slavery Standard*, 12 Dec. 1857: 3.

Item. *Friend of Man*, 19 Jan. 1837: 123.

"J.B. Watson Reports on Success of Abolitionist Lecture in Jay, NY." *Friend of Man*, 10 May 1837: 186.

Jacobs, Harriet. *Incidents in the Life of a Slave Girl*. Minneola, NY: Dover Publication, 2001 (originally published 1861).

Jeanne Roberts Foster to Philip Sullivan, Schenectady, NY, 19 Nov. 1963.

"Jesse Williams, Argyle, Wins Historical Society's Contest" *Glens Falls Post-Star*, 6 July 1959.

Johnson, Crisfield. *History of Washington Co., New York, with Illustrations and Biographical Sketches of Some of Its Prominent Men and Pioneers*. Philadelphia: Everts & Ensign, 1878.

Johnson, William Henry. *Autobiography of Dr. William Henry Johnson*. Albany: Argus Company Printers, 1900.

Johnson, Willis Fletcher. *History of the State of New York: Political and Governmental*. Syracuse: Syracuse Press, Inc., 1922.

Jones, Kathryn Butler. "They Called It Timbucto." *Orion*. Winter 1998: 17, 27–33.

_____. Personal Interview. February 1999.

_____. Telephone conversation with author, February 1999.

Journal of the Life of Joseph Hoag. London: A.W. Bennett, 1862.

"Judge Conklin's Decision," *Union Village Journal*, 18 Sept. 1851:2.

Keese, Willis T. *Keese Family History and Genealogy, from 1690-1911.* Keese family, 1911.

Kerber, Linda K. "Abolitionists and Amalgamators: The New York City Riots of 1834." *New York History*, 1967.

King, Roger A. *The Underground Railroad in Orange County: The Silent Rebellion.* Monroe, NY: Library Research Associates, Inc., 1999.

"Labor Abroad." *Albany Patriot*, 7 Apr. 1847.

LaGrasse, Carol *et. al. An Enduring Heritage.* Stony Creek, NY: Stony Creek Community Association, 1989.

Landon, Fred. "Documents: Records Illustrating the Condition of Refugees from Slavery in Upper Canada before 1860." *Journal of Negro History*, April 1928: 199–205.

_____. "Henry Bibb, Colonizer." *Journal of Negro History*, October 1920: 437–447.

_____. "The Negro Migration to Canada after the Passing of the Fugitive Slave Act." *Journal of Negro History*, Jan. 1920: 22–37.

Laponsee, Lorna. "North Country Residents Played Key Roles in Underground Railroad." *Watertown Daily Times*, 26 Aug. 1968.

"The Late E.W. Goodwin." *Albany Patriot*, 30 December 1846.

"The Late Insurrection at Harper's Ferry." *Troy Daily Whig*, 22 Oct. 1859: 2.

"The Late Wendell Lansing." *Plattsburgh Sentinel*, 29 May 1887: 8.

"The Latest Kentucky Mob." *The Liberator*, 14 August 1857.

"Lectures by A.M. Powell." *The Liberator*, 4 May 1855: 72.

Lee, Luther. *Autobiography of Luther Lee.* New York: Phillips & Hunt, 1882.

"Letter from A.M. Powell." *National Anti-Slavery Standard*, 13 Dec. 1856: 3; 27 Dec. 1856: 3; 10 Jan. 1857: 3.

Letter from Abel Brown to Charles Hicks. Albany, NY. 9 June 1842 (Courtesy Vermont Historical Society).

Letter from Chauncy Knapp to Mason Anthony. Montpelier, VT, 20 Aug. 1838 (Courtesy of Vermont History Society).

"Letter from Colver." *The Emancipator*, 14 Dec. 1837: 129.

"Letter from Dr. Corliss." *The Liberator*, 7 Apr. 1854: 55.

Letter from Fayette Shipherd to Charles Hicks. Rensselaer County, NY, 24 Nov. 1840 (Courtesy of Vermont Historical Society).

"Letter from Henry C. Wright." *The Liberator*, 2 September 1853: 137.

"Letter from J.G. Whittier." *Pennsylvania Freeman*, 15 Aug. 1839.

Letter from John G. Fee, Madison County, Kentucky, to Simon Jocelyn and Arthur Tappan, American Missionary Association, New York, NY, January 14, 1857.

Letter from John Jay Shipherd to Fayette Shipherd. Oberlin, OH. 5 September 1840.

Letter from Leonard Gibbs to Gerrit Smith, Greenwich, 27 Oct. 1859.

Letter from Martin Townsend to Wilbur Siebert. Troy, NY, Sept. 7, 1896.

"Letter from Mr. Stanton." *Pennsylvania Freeman*, 11 July 1839: 4.

Letter from Rachel Clothier. Corinth, NY. 8 January 2001.

Letter from Valera Bickelhaupt. Hammond, NY. 14 January 2002.

Letter from Wilbur Siebert to Martin Townsend. Cambridge, MA, Sept. 14, 1896; April 1, 1897.

Letter of Diantha Gunn. 29 July 1856.

Letter of Diantha Gunn. Union Village, NY. 19 August 1856.

"Letter to the Liberty Party." Peterboro, NY 7 May 1846.

Letter. Boston, 17 June 1854.

"Letters from Hiram Wilson." *Journal of Negro History*, July 1929: 344–349.

"Liberty Party Convention." *Glens Falls Free Press*, 1 Oct. 1851.

"Liberty Party National Convention." *Albany Patriot*, 11 December 1844.

"List of the Colored Temperance Societies addressed to the Northern Star office." *Northern Star and Freemen's Advocate*, 2 Jan. 1843.

"List of the Officers of the New York State Anti-Slavery Society." *Friend of Man*, 23 Sept. 1840: 200.

Loding, Paul. Personal Interview. Fall 1998.

Loguen, J.W. *The Rev. J.W. Loguen as a Slave and as a Freeman*. New York: Negro Universities Press, 1968.

Lovejoy, J.C. *Memoir of Rev. Charles T. Torrey*. Boston: John P. Jewett & Co., 1847.

MacMorris, Mary MacDougall. *Argyle, Then—Now & Forever*. Argyle: Bullard-Glencraft, Inc., 1964.

Macy, Jesse. *The Anti-Slavery Crusade*. New Haven: Yale University Press, 1919.

"Man-Hunting in New York." *The National Anti-Slavery Standard*, June 3, 1854: 7.

Manual of the Congregational Church in Union Village, Washington County, NY. Albany: Munsell & Rowland, 1860.

Mason, Howard C. *Backward Glances*. Glens Falls, NY: Webster Mimeoprint Services, 1963–1965.

Matlack, Lucius C. *The History of American Slavery and Methodism, from 1780 to 1849: and History of the Wesleyan Methodist Connection of America; in Two Parts, with an Appendix*. New York, 1849.

"Matters and Things." *Friend of Man*, 11 Jan. 1842.

May, Samuel. *The Fugitive Slave Law and Its Victims*. New York: American Anti-Slavery Society, 1861.
_____. *Some Recollections of Our Anti-Slavery Conflict*. Boston: Fields, Osgood & Co., 1869.

McCracken, Henry Noble. *Blithe Dutchess: The Flowering of an American County from 1812*. New York: Hastings House, 1958.

McGowan, J. A. *Station Master on the Underground Railroad: The life and letters of Thomas Garrett*. Moylan, PA: Whimsie Press, 1977.

McIlvaine, Florence. "Stone Walls Form Enduring Monuments to One of Area's Founders of Methodism." *Glens Falls Post-Star*, 18 Aug. 1960: B1.

McKivigan, John R. *The War Against Pro-Slavery Religion*. Ithaca: Cornell University Press, 1974.

Meader Nye, Jane. *The Meader Family Association Newsletter*. Ballston Lake, NY, 2001.

Meader, Granville, compiler. *John Meader of Piscataqua: His Ancestors and Descendants*. Baltimore: Gateway Press, Inc., 1975.

"Meeting in Jay." *Essex County Republican*, 26 Oct. 1850.

"Meeting of Colored Citizens." *National Anti-Slavery Standard*, 10 Oct. 1850: 78.

"Meeting of the Executive Committee of the Anti-Slavery Society of Eastern NY." *Albany Patriot*, 13 November 1844: 11.

"Meetings of Colored Citizens." *National Anti-Slavery Standard*, 10 Oct. 1850: 78.

"Memorial to Henry Wilbur." New York Yearly Meeting of the Religious Society of Friends, 1915.

Minutes of the Fourth Annual Meeting of the Washington Union Baptist Association. Union Village: Lansing, 1838.

The Mirror of Liberty, July, 1838: 7; August 1838: 4.

Mitchell, Robert W. "Biracial Activity in Vermont as Old as State Itself." *Rutland Daily Herald*, July 1976: B41.

"Mob Violence Still Prevailing in Kentucky." *The Liberator*, 18 Sept. 1857: 152.

"Monument to Asa S. Wing." *National Anti-Slavery Standard*, 22 September 1855.

Morhous, Henry C. *History of the Village of Greenwich, NY*. Scrapbook with miscellaneous clippings, 1878.

Mowry, William A. *The Descendants of John Mowry of Rhode Island*. Providence: Preston & Rounds Co., 1909.

"Mr. Thompson at Springfield." *The Liberator*, 25 Feb. 1851: 35.

"Mrs. Ellsword's Scrapbook." Unpublished copy of notes found in archive at Saratoga County Historian's Office.

Munsell, Joel, ed. *Collections on the History of Albany: From Its Discovery to the Present Time. With Notices of Its Public Institutions, and Biographical Sketches of Citizens Deceased*. Albany: J. Munsell, 1865–71.

"My Friends Please Notice." *Emancipator*, 17 Aug. 1837: 63

"N. M.'s Slaves." *Herald of Freedom*. Champlain, NY: Executive Committee of the Clinton County Liberty Party, Vol. 1, No. 8, May 1844.

"N. York—Franklin Co.—Rev. Mr. Colver" *Friend of Man*, 17 November 1836.

"National Anti-Slavery Nominating Convention." *Pennsylvania Freeman*, 23 April 1840: 1.

"The Nebraska Bill Passed—Another Triumph of the Slave Power" *The Liberator*, 26 May 1854: 82.

"A New Saint." *Plattsburgh Republican*, 19 Nov. 1859: 2.

The New York City Directory (various years). New York: John R. Doggett, Jr., Publisher.

The New York City Directory for 1842 and 1843. New York: John R. Doggett, Jr., Publisher, 1843.

New York State Census, Washington County, NY, 1855.

"New York, had her Representatives been faithful ..." *Albany Evening Journal*, 23 May 1854: 2.

"New York." *The Emancipator*. 22 February 1838.

"No Go." *People's Journal*, 3 Nov. 1859: 2.

"Nominations." *Albany Patriot*, 21 Apr. 1847.

Northup, Solomon. *Twelve Years a Slave*, edited by Sue Eakin and Joseph Logsdon. Baton Rouge: Louisiana State University Press, 1968 reissue of 1853.

"Noted Men and Women of the Champlain Valley and the Adirondacks." *Plattsburgh Sentinel*, 23 Jan. 1891.

"Notice. Execution of John Brown." *People's Journal*, 1 Dec. 1859.

"Notice." *Glens Falls Republican*, 8 April 1846.

Nye, Charles Freeman. "An Address of Charles Freeman Nye, July 14, 1902 ..." Champlain, NY: Moorsfield Press, 1928.

Oates, Stephen B. *To Purge This Land with Blood: A Biography of John Brown*. New York: Harper & Row, 1970.

"Obituary." *Albany Patriot*, 30 June 1847.

"Obituary." *National Anti-Slavery Standard*, 11 June 1859.

"Old Canton and the Underground Railway." *St. Lawrence Plain Dealer*, 18 Nov. 1941.

Rural News. Ogdensburg, 1975.

Savage, Thom. "Brasher Falls House: Whispers of the Past." 1981.

Tedford, Pauline, and Tom Fife. *Waddington, St. Lawrence County, NY: A Look at Our Past*. Town of Waddington, 1976.

"One Hundred and Twenty-Five Years for Christ 1843–1968." Wesleyan-Methodist Church, 1968.

Parker, William. "The Freedman's Story." *Atlantic Monthly*, Vol. XVII, February, March 1866.

Parrott, Jane. Former town of Chester historian. Unpublished notes.

Pasternak, Martin B. *Rise Now and Fly to Arms: The Life of Henry Highland Garnet*. New York: Garland Publishers, 1995.

Patrick, David. "The Pliny Moore Children and their Descendents." Unpublished document.

Paul, Nathaniel. "An Address Delivered on the Celebration of the Abolition of Slavery in the State of New York." Albany: Trustees for the Benefit of the First African Baptist Society, 1827.

Pendleton, Leila A. *A Narrative of the Negro*. Washington: Press of R.L. Pendleton, 1912.

People's Journal, 22 April 1858; 8 Dec. 1859.

"Personal Effort a Good Beginning." *Vermont Freeman*, 15 April 1843: 1.

"Peru, N.Y." *St. Louis Observer*, 17 Sept. 1835: 1.

Pettit, Eber M. *Sketches in the History of the Underground Railroad* ... Fredonia, NY: W. McKinstry & Son, 1879.

Phillips, Marjorie Hoag. *Quaker Street, a village founded by Quakers*. Quaker Street, NY, 1965.

Pillsbury, The Rev. Parker. *Acts of the Anti-Slavery Apostles*. Concord, NH, 1883.

"Plattsburgh, Jan. 20, 1838." *Plattsburgh Republican*, 20 Jan. 1838: 2.

Porter, Dorothy B. "The Organized Educational Activities of Negro Literary Societies, 1828–1846." *The Journal of Negro Education*, Oct. 1936: 555–576.

Powell, Aaron M. *Personal Reminiscences of the Anti-Slavery and Other Reforms and Reformers*. Plainfield, NY: Caulon Press, 1899.

"A Pre-Revolutionary House." *Greenwich Journal*, 8 Oct. 1913.

"Proceedings of the Colored Citizens of Lansingburgh in relation to the FSL." *Lansingburgh Democrat*, Oct. 1850.

"Proceedings of the New York State Anti-Slavery Convention held at Utica, Oct. 21, and New York State Anti-Slavery Society held at Peterboro, Oct. 22, 1835." Utica: *Standard and Democrat*, Oct. 1835.

"Proceedings of the Washington County Anti-Nebraska Mass Meeting." *People's Journal*, 17 August 1854: 2.

"The Progress of the Anti-Slavery Cause." *Friend of Man*, 9 Sept. 1840: 190.

"Public Meeting." *Troy Daily Times*, 6 Oct. 1857.

Quarles, Benjamin. *Black Abolitionists*. New York: Oxford University Press, 1969.

"Radical Political Convention." *National Anti-Slavery Standard*, 17 July 1855.

Ray, Florence T. *Sketch of the Life of Rev. Charles B. Ray*. New York: Press of J. J. Little & Co., 1887.

Renehan, Edward J. *The Secret Six: The True Tale of the Men Who Conspired with John Brown*. New York: Crown Publishers, 1995.

"Report of the Ladies' A.S. Society of Albany." *Albany Patriot*, 2 July 1845.

"Rev. Enos Putnam Sleeps in Churchyard at Johnsburg," *WarrensburgLake George News*, 2 August 1962

"Rev. N. Colver." *Emancipator*, 16 Mar. 1837: 182.

"Rev. Nathaniel Colver." *Emancipator*, 2 Mar. 1837: 174.

"Right and Wrong in Boston." *National Anti-Slavery Standard*, 3 June 1854.

Ripley, C. Peter, ed. *The Black Abolitionist Papers*. The United States, vol. 4, 1847–1859. Chapel Hill: University of North Carolina Press, 1991.

Rist, Leslie. "Chester to Canton Road." *Tahawus Cloudsplitter*, Vol. XXI, No. 5, Sept-Oct. 1969: 9–10.

Robinson, Dona. Personal Interview. March 2002.

Rowe, Judith. Sand Lake, NY, town historian. Personal Interview. January 1999.

Royce, Caroline Halstead. *A History of Westport, Essex County, NY*. Elizabethtown, NY, 1904.

Russell, Ray. "Underground Room Found by Workers at Junior High." *Plattsburgh Press-Republican*, 27 April 1974.

Salem Press, 8 Nov. 1859.

Sandy Hill Herald, 25 April 1854: 2.

"Saratoga Anti-Slavery Meeting." *Friend of Man*, 7 Nov. 1838.

"Saratoga County." *Friend of Man*, 28 Oct. 1840: 10.

"Saratoga Liberty Nominating Convention." *Albany Patriot* 14 Oct. 1846.

Savage, W. Sherman. "Abolitionist Literature in the Mails, 1835–36" *Journal of Negro History*, April 1928: 150–184.

"A Scandalous Proceeding." *Plattsburgh Republican*, 10 Dec. 1859: 2.

Schenectady Directory and City Register, for the Year 1841-42. John H. Riggs: Schenectady, NY, 1842.

Scouller, James Brown. *History of the Presbytery of Argyle of the United Presbyterian Church of North America*. Harrisburg, PA: Patriot Publishing Co., 1880.

Seaver, Frederick. *Historical Sketches of Franklin County*. Albany: Lyon, 1918.

"The Second Anniversary of the Dutchess County Anti-Slavery Society," *National Anti-Slavery Standard*, 6 Aug. 1840: 35.

Sherman, Lydia Frances. "My Year in Washington (1848–1849)." Typed copy of diary located at Brookside Museum, Ballston Spa, NY.

Shields, Addie L. *The John Townsend Addoms Homestead: Including a study of slavery and the Underground Railroad As It pertains to Clinton County, NY*. Plattsburgh, 1981.

Shipherd, Fayette. "A Legacy for My Beloved Wife, Catherine Shipherd." Unpublished memoir. Troy, 1846.

_____. "My Legacy to My Beloved Wife and Children." Unpublished memoir. 1870.

Siebert, Wilbur H. *The Underground Railroad: From Slavery to Freedom*. New York: Macmillan, 1898.

_____. *Vermont's Anti-Slavery and Underground Railroad Record*. 1937. New York: Negro Universities Press, 1969.

"Silver Greys Obeying the Golden Rule." *National Anti-Slavery Standard*, 13 Oct. 1855.

"Sixth Annual Report of the Peru Female Anti-Slavery Society." *Clinton County Whig*, 23 Jan. 1841: 2–3.

"Slave Catching in New York—First Case Under the Law." *The Liberator*, 4 Oct. 1850: 159.

"The Slave Catching Law." *The Liberator*, 4 October 1850: 159.

"Slave Emigration." *Glens Falls Clarion*, 8 October 1850.

"Slave Insurrection in Virginia." *National Anti-Slavery Standard*, 22 Oct. 1859.

Smith, Rev. J.A. *Memoir of Nathaniel Colver, D.D.* Boston: Durkee and Foxcroft, Publishers, 1873.

"Spirit of the Times—More Mobbing." *The Liberator*, 2 Jan. 1836: 3.

"Spirit of the Washington County Press." *Salem Press*, 15, 22 Oct. 1850.

"St. Lawrence Anti-Slavery Convention." *Friend of Man*, 4 Oct. 1837: 63.

Stanton, Henry B. *Random Recollections*. Macgown & Slipper, 1886.

"State Anti-Slavery Meeting." *Friend of Man*, 30 Sept. 1840: 201.

Stavis, Barrie. *The Sword and the Stone*. New York: A.S. Barnes & Co., 1970.

Steward, Austin. *Twenty-Two Years a Slave, and Forty Years a Freeman; Embracing a Correspondence of Several Years, While President of Wilberforce Colony, London, Canada West*. Rochester: William Alling, 1857.

Still, William. *The Underground Railroad*. Philadelphia: Porter & Coates, 1872 (rev. 1886), reprinted, Arno Press, 1968.

"Story of a Slave Whose Journey ..." *National Enquirer, and Constitutional Advocate of Universal Liberty*, 21 September 1837: 8.

Strong, Douglas M. "The Application of Perfectionism to Politics." *Wesleyan Theological Journal*,

Spring 1990. (Edited by Michael Mattei for the Wesley Center for Applied Theology at Northwest Nazarene University © Copyright 2000 by the Wesley Center for Applied Theology).

Sullivan, Sean. "A History of Dunham's Basin." Unpublished paper. 1963: 11.

Sylvester, Nathaniel Bartlett. *History of Saratoga County*. Philadelphia: Everts & Ensign, 1878.

Tappan, Lewis. *Life of Arthur Tappan*. New York: Hurd & Houghton, 1870.

Tefft, Grant J. *The Story of Union Village*. Greenwich, NY: *Greenwich Journal*, 1942.

Terpin, Michael. "Charting the Stops on the Way to Liberty." *Watertown Daily Times*, 26 July 1979: 18A.

"Third Annual Report of the Albany Female A.S. Society, Oct. 9, 1846." *Albany Patriot*, 30 Dec. 1846.

Thompson, Harold. *Body, Boots, and Britches: Folktales, Ballads and Speech from North Country New York*. New York: Dover Publications, 1939.

"Three Fugitive Slaves, Arrested in NY and Given Up to their Owners." *The Liberator*, 2 June 1854: 87.

Thurston, Elisha P. *History of Greenwich*. H.D. Morris, 1876

"To the Friends of the Fugitives from Slavery." *National Anti-Slavery Standard*, 3 October 1857.

"To the Public." *Northern Star and Freemen's Advocate*, 8 Dec. 1842.

"To Vigilance Committees." *National Anti-Slavery Standard*, 29 June 1843: 15.

"The Tocsin of Liberty and Rev. C.T. Torrey." *Northern Star and Freeman's Advocate*, 8 Dec. 1842.

"Too Good to Be Lost." *People's Journal*, 10 Dec. 1857.

The Tribune Almanac for the Year 1838-to-1868. New York: New York Tribune, 1868.

"Trip to Northern New York." *The Liberator*, 19 March 1852: 46.

"The Trouble at Harpers Ferry." *People's Journal*, 27 Oct. 1859: 2.

"Troy Anti-Slavery Society." *Friend of Man*, 14 March 1838.

Troy City Directory. Troy, NY, 1835–1857; 1838–1843.

Turner, Lorenzo Dow. *Anti-Slavery Sentiment in American Literature Prior to 1865*. Port Washington, NY: Kennikat Press, 1966.

"Turner's Confession." http://www.melanet.com/nat/nat.html.

U.S. Census, 1790–1820.

U.S. Census, Washington County, NY, 1850; 1860.

U.S. Federal Census. Washington: Bureau of the Census, 1790–1820.

U.S. Federal Census. Washington, DC: Bureau of the Census, 1840–1860.

"Uncle Tom's Cabin." *Sandy Hill Herald*, 1 Feb. 1853: 2.

"Underground Railroad." *National Anti-Slavery Standard*, 17 June 1854: 15.

"The Underlying Factors of the Civil War" cited at http://pages.prodigy.net/jtell/Civilwar.html.

"Union Meeting of the Colored People of Albany, Troy, and Vicinity." *Friend of Man*, 12 April 1837.

"Upper Canada." *Friend of Man*, 19 Jan. 1841: 46.

Van Vranken, Thomas. Personal Interview. Fall 1998.

Vermont Freeman, 1 July 1843: 3; 2 August 1844: 3.

"Victims of the Fugitive Slave Law of 1850 and Reaction." *Green Mountain Freeman*, 24 Oct. 1850.

Vigilance Committee Office. Broadside. Albany, NY, July 1856.

"Vigilance Committees." *Emancipator*, 25 Oct. 1838.

"Vigilance Committees." *Friend of Man*, 18 Apr 1838.

Walker, David. "Walker's Appeal in Four Articles; Together with a Preamble, to the Coloured Citizens of the World, but in Particular, and Very Expressly, to Those of the United States of America Written in Boston, State of Massachusetts, September 28, 1829," Boston, 1830.

Walker, George E. *The Afro-American in New York City 1827–1860*. New York: Garland Publishing, Inc., 1993.

Ward, Samuel Ringgold. *Autobiography of a Fugitive Negro: His Anti-Slavery Labours in the United States, Canada, and England*. London: John Snow, 1855.

Warren County Book of Deeds. No. 27: 192.

"Washington County Anti-Slavery Society." *The Friend of Man*, 7 July 1836.

"Washington County." *Friend of Man*, 21 Oct. 1840: 7.

"We have been much amused ..." *Northern Star and Freeman's Advocate*, 10 March 1842: 30.

Weisberger, Bernard A. *They Gathered at the River*. Boston: Little, Brown & Co., 1958.

Weise, Arthur J. *History of the City of Troy*. Troy, NY: William H. Young, 1876.

Weise, Arthur J. *Troy's One Hundred Years*. Troy, NY: William H. Young, 1891.

Wellman, Judith. National Register for Historic Places Documentation: Asa and Caroline Wing House, Section 8, 2001.

Wesley, Charles. "The Negroes of New York in the Emancipation Movement." *Journal of Negro History*, Oct. 1942: 65–103.

"West India Emancipation." *National Anti-Slavery Standard*, 11 August 1855.

"What the South Has Had." *People's Journal*, 27 October 1859: 2.

"When Greenwich Was a Hot-Bed of Anti-Slavery Sentiment." *Greenwich Journal*, 21 December 1938.

Whitaker, Robert. "Time Shrouds Malone's Underground Railroad." *Plattsburgh Press-Republican*, 22 November 1987.

White, Dorothy Gray, *Let My People Go—African Americans 1804–1860*, as cited in "Chronology on the History of Slavery, 1790–1829," http://www.innercity.org/holt/slavechron.html.

Wiese, Arthur J. *Troy's One Hundred Years*. Troy, NY: William H. Young, 1891.

Wilbur, Oren B. Unpublished memoir, sections of which have been extracted in *History of Washington County. Chapters in the History of the Town of Easton, NY*. Washington County Historical Society, 1959: 108–112.

Wilbur, Oren B. Unpublished papers. Easton, NY: Wilbur Family.

Wilson, Carol. *Freedom at Risk: The Kidnapping of Free Blacks in America—1780–1865*. Lexington: University of Kentucky Press, 1994.

Windley, Lathan A. *Runaway Slave Advertisements: A Documentary History from the 1730s to 1790*. Westport, CT: Greenwood Press, 1983.

Winks, Robin W. *The Blacks In Canada*. Montreal: McGill-Queen's University Press, 1971.

Woodson, Carter G., ed. *Negro Orators and their Orations*. "The Progress of the Anti-Slavery Cause." Speech by Theodore S. Wright. Washington: The Associated Publishers, Inc., 1925.

"The Work Goes Bravely On." *The Emancipator*, 20 October 1835.

Zimm, Louise Hasbrouck, ed. *Southeastern New York: A History of the Counties of Ulster, Dutchess, Orange, Rockland, and Putnam*. New York: Lewis Historical Publishing Co., Inc., 1946.

Zirblis, Raymond Paul. *Friends of Freedom*. Montpelier: Vermont Division of Historic Preservation, 1996.

INDEX

Numbers in *italics* indicate photographs and illustrations. Numbers with symbols (*†‡) indicate footnotes.